THE LEAGUERS

THE MAKING OF PROFESSIONAL FOOTBALL IN ENGLAND, 1900–1939

THE LEAGUERS
THE MAKING OF PROFESSIONAL FOOTBALL IN ENGLAND, 1900–1939

Matthew Taylor

LIVERPOOL UNIVERSITY PRESS

First published in 2005 by
LIVERPOOL UNIVERSITY PRESS
4 Cambridge Street, Liverpool L69 7ZU

British Library Cataloguing-in-Publication data
A British Library CIP record is available

ISBN 0-85323-639-9 cased
ISBN 0-85323-649-6 limp

Typeset in Minion with Chianti by
Northern Phototypesetting Co. Ltd, Bolton, Lancs.
Printed and bound in the European Union by
Bell and Bain Ltd, Glasgow

Contents

Acknowledgements

Various individuals and institutions have assisted in the course of the research and writing of this book. My greatest debt is to Pierre Lanfranchi, the supervisor of the PhD out of which this book developed. He has provided encouragement and inspiration in equal measures and remains a continual source of advice and criticism both in my own work and in the collaborative projects we have since pursued. My second supervisor, Wray Vamplew, helped to guide me through the early setbacks and provided pertinent and useful comments throughout. Tony Arnold, Neil Carter, Neal Garnham, Roy Hay, Richard Holt, Martin Johnes, Tony Mason, Bert Moorhouse, William Morgan, Stephen Wagg and James Walvin also assisted at different stages with interesting ideas and valuable insights. At De Montfort University, I was lucky enough to receive the support and encouragement of friends and colleagues in the International Centre for Sports History and Culture and the History department more generally. In addition to Pierre, Wray, Dick and Tony M, I would like to thank Daryl Adair, Nick Carter, Tony Collins, Mike Cronin, John Martin, Jason McDonald, Panikos Panayi, David Ryan, David Sadler, Mark Sandle and David Thoms. My new colleagues at Portsmouth, meanwhile, provided a supportive environment to discuss ideas and the necessary space to complete the manuscript.

A number of football clubs and bodies proved remarkably open and friendly to my inquiries. I am especially grateful to David Barber at the Football Association, Lorna Parnell at the Football League and Gordon Taylor at the Professional Footballers' Association, who allowed me to study private archives and documents. The administrators, archivists and club historians at Arsenal, Aston Villa, Huddersfield Town, Oldham Athletic, Sheffield United, West Bromwich Albion and Wolverhampton Wanderers were inviting and helpful, as were the staff at the various libraries and public record offices I visited across the country. Jeff Walden kindly gave permission for me to study files relating to football broadcasting at the BBC's Written Archives. Terry Frost, Garth Dykes and Andy Porter similarly provided useful leads on the biographies of certain Football League officials.

Finally, I would like to thank my family, especially my parents, whose constant patience, encouragement and emotional (and sometimes material) support over the past decade or so have been invaluable. This book is dedicated to them.

List of Tables and Figures

Tables

Figures

Introduction

> All the town knew of the success long before they returned home by train. Thousands of the club supporters besieged the railway station, swept aside the police and surrounded Captain Cobbold's compartment. Cheering figures swayed on the lampposts and roofs.
>
> A horse-shoe garland, in the club's colours, blue and white, was placed round Captain Cobbold's neck as he was carried shoulder-high to an open motor-coach.
>
> The crowd swelled as the triumphant procession toured the town's main streets. Traffic was held up for 90 minutes and special police reinforcements were called out to deal with the disorganisation.[1]

Such scenes as those witnessed in Ipswich on the evening of 31 May 1938 had long been commonplace in English football. The role of clubs as focal points for community, town or regional pride was nowhere more clearly demonstrated than in the triumphal return of cup- and championship-winning teams. Occasions of this kind represented the most intense example of the 'periodic affirmation of collective identity' that was apparent in the mainly working-class support of the local club. By the twentieth century they had become both 'a ritualized festivity and a vibrant form of street theatre'.[2] Yet on this occasion no matches or trophies had been won. Success had been secured not on the Wembley turf in front of thousands of spectators, but at London's King's Hall Holborn Restaurant. The prize that the 15,000 or so Ipswich Town supporters had gathered to celebrate was the club's election to the Football League.

This book seeks to explain why the simple fact of a club's admittance to a sporting competition should have been infused with such significance. As such, it is a history of the formative years of professional football in England and a study of the Football League.[3] The two, it is argued here, are inextricable; by the 1920s at least, English professional football was, to all intents and purposes, the Football League. This is not to deny that professional teams existed outside its ambit. In 1914 there were 158 clubs engaging professional players, only 40 of which were League members.[4] Most of these, however, would have employed no more than a handful of professionals. Many either joined the League or attempted to do so in the course of the period under study, and those that did not played in competitions which strove in a variety of ways to emulate their senior rival. Most importantly, the Football League was symbolically representative of the professional game. It ran the most prestigious sporting competition with the best-known players in the largest and best-equipped stadia in the country. All the features of the game in England at the highest level – from the transfer system and the maximum wage to the offside law and 'third back' game – were established directly or indirectly by the League and its member clubs. More than just an important actor in the story, the Football League was the context in which the professional game developed.

The foundation of the League in 1888 provoked mixed reactions. For many sports enthusiasts, its creation was fundamental to the long-term survival of professional football. A fixed programme of matches between the leading clubs appeared to solve the insecurities, financial and otherwise, inherent in the 'lax and loose system' prevalent before 1888.[5] The system was immediately popular among spectators and much of the local and national press. Within five months of the inaugural season, *Athletic News* declared that from a 'financial point of view, the competition has been a distinct success' while others agreed that 'inclusion in the League means an almost safe exchequer for the season for a club … and a very great addition to the interest in its matches'.[6] By 1906, the League's founder William McGregor could describe the 'principle' of league football as 'the dominating influence in the game', replicated in competitive sports across the globe and even by the colleges of Oxford and Cambridge, those bastions of amateur ideals.[7]

For others, the Football League was synonymous with the ascendancy of commerce and money over true sport. Critics, such as the Football Association (FA) Vice-President N. L. Jackson, maintained a vigorous attack on the principles and structure of the League: it was decried as a purely commercial and selfish venture conducted without consideration of the needs of the smaller clubs and provincial associations.[8] As the former amateur international G. O. Smith noted in 1899: 'Opponents of the League describe it as a combination founded on self-interest, the members of which are only kept together by motives of selfishness and hopes of mutual profit'.[9] According to this view, the Football League augmented professional football's negative features. A contemporary account described the system as 'bad for the players, worse for the spectators. The former learn improvident habits, become vastly conceited, whilst failing to see that they are treated like chattels, and cannot help but be brutalised. The latter are injured physically and morally'.[10] Even the term 'league' took on a pejorative meaning in certain circles. McGregor himself acknowledged the opposition that the League attracted as 'an all-powerful combination of clubs to which £.s.d. is admittedly the most vital consideration'.[11] In less than two decades, the Football League had become unquestionably the most controversial and possibly the most influential sporting competition in England.

If the League was important within football, did it have any significance beyond this relatively closed world? Questions of this kind have been critical for historians of sport, providing a justification for what might otherwise be seen as a trivial study of a marginal subculture. One could certainly make a case for the Football League's evolution into a major social and recreational institution, with its own bureaucracy and administrative structure, its own rules, regulations and policy imperatives. At the League's Jubilee Banquet in 1938, FA President William Pickford summed up the broader role of the League as follows:

> If one thinks of the vast assets of the League clubs in property alone … of the huge sums they raise and distribute among players and staffs, the Exchequer, the Postmaster General, the railway and transport companies, and a hundred and one others, and endeavour to visualise the interest, excitement and pleasure that its competitors bring into the lives of millions of people, one can begin to form an idea of its importance in the life of the nation.[12]

While this view of the League may be hyperbolic, the basic impression it gives is nevertheless of some importance. The economic dimensions of its activities are perhaps the easiest to quantify. The investigative body Political and Economic Planning's 1951 report on football suggested that, in the 1937–38 season, 31.43 million spectators paying £1.57 million in admission charges had watched matches in the four divisions of the League. *The Economist* concurred, estimating annual takings in 1937 for the whole of the League at about £1.5 million.[13] In addition, the League was related to a number of ancillary industries, most significantly the pools and the sporting press. As *The Times* commented in 1937, 'The pools, the transfer system and the amount of money involved in the gates have turned football into something like a national industry.'[14] 'Football' in this sense was synonymous with the Football League.

The League could also be seen as the conveyor of a significant cultural phenomenon. Whether or not one accepts the view that football in this period represented the working man's religion or was organically linked to the working-class community, it clearly mattered to many people and formed an important part of English social life.[15] Successful clubs such as Aston Villa and Arsenal, and players like Billy Meredith, 'Dixie' Dean and Alex James represented, especially in the period of a proliferating sports-related media and the cult of the cigarette card, cultural reference points that went beyond the local community. Moreover, the Saturday afternoon League programme had become a characteristic ritual of professional sport in this country. According to Richard Holt, this 'world of clanking turnstiles and vast stadia [represented] the most popular and highly organised programme of spectator sport in existence'.[16] And, from the early 1930s onwards, millions more were symbolically attached to the League through the emergence of the football pools and its subculture.

Aside from the wider economic and cultural implications of its activities, the League was a major social institution in its own right. This period saw the development of a network of links with sporting, social and governmental bodies and the emergence of a distinctive public image. As Pickford's quotation indicates, the League made personal and formal contacts with several government departments, lobbied for concessions in travel costs and even publicly pronounced its position on the outbreak of war in 1914. Indeed, its decision to continue League football up to July 1915 resulted in what its President, John McKenna, referred to as a 'tirade of abuse' from the middle and upper classes, and even some pressure on the government to ban professional football. In its attempts to rehabilitate its public image, the League, along with the FA, donated significant amounts of money to charities and the war effort, a practice that was extended after the war to include donations to disaster appeals.[17]

Unlike other sporting bodies like cricket's MCC, therefore, the Football League was more than a private club. By 1900, at least, it was a self-consciously public body, whose decisions and actions had a resonance in the wider social and political arena. Having said this, the League retained in many respects a distinctly private and insular perspective. Committee members were often highly suspicious of outsiders, whether from within the football world or not, and of extraneous attempts to interfere with League affairs. Hence, in 1912, the Management Committee banned people not officially associated with League clubs from attending the annual meeting and, throughout the period, prevented press access to those meetings considered to be of a private and confidential nature.[18] Correspondence and inquiries from external bodies such as the Players' Union, the BBC and the Pools Promoters' Association were ignored or, at best, merely acknowledged. Furthermore, for much of the period up to 1920, and arguably for some time thereafter, the League as a collective eschewed any pretensions to act as a governing body of professional football, preferring instead to behave in an aloof, self-concerned and parochial manner. It is not insignificant that from 1902 onwards the League was based at Preston, or that all four presidents in this period, as well as the secretaries and other office staff, were drawn exclusively from Lancashire. It could be, at different times, both proud of its regional roots and conscious of its wider responsibilities on a national scale. The League thus exhibited a complex set of identities: a curious blend of the public and the private, the national and the parochial.

Yet for all the Football League's significance as a popular institution within English society, this book is not intended as a conventional social history of sport. Most academic studies of sporting activity have been premised on the assumption that they offer particular perspectives on broader historical issues. Studying sport, it is often argued, can contribute to our understanding of larger historical debates concerning such matters as modernisation, class and gender relations, local, regional and national identities and so on. It can be seen as a 'window' or 'lens' with which to shed light on the society under investigation. For Jeff Hill, this 'reflectivist' tendency has reinforced 'the idea of sport as a cultural by-product of other (implicitly more important?) economic and social forces' rather than as an autonomous sphere of human activity.[19] Although doubtless essential in establishing sport as a legitimate area of historical inquiry, this should not be seen as the only way of 'doing' sports history. In contrast to the justifications of what might be called the '*and* society' approach to the history of sport, this book starts from the assumption that professional football was important in and of itself. More particularly, it is an attempt to examine what the US historian Stephen Hardy has termed the development of sport 'from the inside out'. Its focus is on the structure and organisation of professional football, its internal politics, and the choices faced by its legislators. As much institutional, business and labour history as social history, this book is concerned more with the production than the consumption of football, reflecting a switch in perspective from 'the broad sweep of social forces to the minute elements of decision-making'.[20] It is concerned with the making of what could be called the institution or the industry of professional football, from the struggles over the finances of the game and the treatment of players to campaigns to popularise it on a national and international basis. There is no suggestion here that football ought to be wrenched from its social, cultural and economic context and studied in isolation from the world of which it was a part. Rather, what is proposed is an alternative way of approaching the history of the game, with the initial focus placed on the Football League itself – and what Hardy terms 'the central issues as the sports organizations defined them'[21] – before moving on to consider the way in which it interacted with, or insulated itself from, the wider environment. Above all, this book is unapologetically *about* football, its development as a profession and an industry; it is not (primarily at least) about the relationships *between* football and other things.

Considering professional football from the inside out rather than the outside in represents less a radical break with the existing literature than a slight shift in emphasis. Indeed, many of the themes central to *The Leaguers* build upon the work of the pioneers of the field. The monographs of Tony Mason, Steven Tischler, Charles Korr and Nicholas Fishwick have taken us a long way in understanding the objectives, composition and management of professional clubs, while Stephen Jones has placed the club and the industry firmly in its wider economic and commercial context.[22] Many of the questions Mason posed in his ground-breaking *Association Football and English Society*, particularly relating to the organisation and management of clubs and the role of the professional as a worker, remain crucial for any student of the game and are fundamental to this study.[23] What is different here is an insistence on the central role of the Football League as an active institutional agent in the development of football and the crucible in which the modern game was forged. Given the quality of much of this historiography, it is somewhat surprising that little attention has been paid to what was effectively professional football's controlling body. Indeed, there is an implicit strand of thinking in some of these studies that treats football's 'ruling class' – club-owners, directors, the FA and the League administration – as a monolithic group. Tischler, in particular, uses the terms 'football establishment', 'football hierarchy' and 'football authorities' as interchangeable labels to describe any elite owners or officials.[24] Although it is true that to some extent those groups were interchangeable – club directors were League Committee members and Committee members were often FA Councillors – it is nonetheless an oversimplification that fails to recognise the League as an autonomous institution.

If the Football League has been left largely untouched by academic studies, the popular history of the game provides similarly uneven coverage. This might seem perplexing at first glance, given Mason's comments that the early history of football has been written largely 'in terms of the institutions, players and matches'.[25] There are indeed a number of articles, including those by the League's founder William McGregor in the 1906 *Book of Football* and by journalist and ex-player Ivan Sharpe, which discuss the structure and development of the League. Percy Young's 1968 book, *A History of British Football*, dedicates some space to a narrative of League affairs.[26] Perhaps this material has led professional historians to steer clear of the subject? Whatever the case, another of Mason's comments, that football history before the 1970s 'was largely in the hands of administrators and journalists', seems particularly pertinent in the case of the League.[27]

Essentially, the history of the Football League has been written uncritically and with no analytical perspective. There have been two general histories of the League. The first, titled *The Story of the Football League*, was written in 1938, the League's Jubilee Year, by the-then President Charles Sutcliffe, Secretary Fred Howarth and a Preston journalist, J. A. Brierley. As might be expected, it is an uncritical celebration of the organisation's development which, informative though it is, tells us more about the League's self-image in 1938 and the preoccupations of its authors than anything else. A more recent work is Simon Inglis's *League Football and the Men Who Made It*, published in 1988 as the 'Official History of the Football League'. Inglis, a journalist and architect best known for his writing about football grounds, does inform his narrative with an element of social history and understands that the League did not develop in isolation but within a wider social, economic and political framework. Nevertheless, although it is rich in detail and relatively objective for an 'official' history, it ultimately presents a picture of the League as the League would want to be seen. As with the Jubilee history, sources are assessed uncritically and there is no real attempt to examine the changing institutional role of the League over the course of the twentieth century.[28]

The application of economic theory to sports history has helped clarify the distinctive role of organisations like the Football League. Wray Vamplew's study of British professional sport up to 1914 is the essential work in this respect. Drawing on the work of North American sports economists, Vamplew sought to analyse the theories relating to sporting leagues in an historical context, perceiving the Football League as a commercial cartel 'with a central controlling body setting the economic rules, operating quality control via promotion and relegation and other restrictions on entry, and … circumscribing the economic freedom of sports labourers in an effort to maintain equality of competition'.[29] Yet, as his study centred on cricket, horse racing and rugby league as well as football and stretched only as far as 1914, Vamplew was unable to fully analyse the problematic development of the League cartel, including conflicting interests and changing objectives and policies. Tony Arnold's business history of professional football in Bradford has also proved instructive by approaching the issues from a regional perspective. For Arnold, the business activity of the Bradford clubs, City and Park Avenue, was linked to local trade and economic fluctuations but was, at the same time, contingent upon the regulations imposed upon them as members of the Football League. League clubs thus displayed dual personalities, as both semi-autonomous local sporting institutions and national cartel members.[30]

Yet while a recognition of the often peculiar economic arrangement of professional football generally, and the Football League in particular, will inform much of this study, its importance should not be overstated. Although economic considerations may have been central to League and club officials, the pursuit of profit clearly was not. Mason, Fishwick and Vamplew have persuasively argued that club directors and shareholders were rarely influenced primarily by the profit motive. Not only did the FA restrict the dividend payable to shareholders to 5 per cent before 1914, and 7.5 per cent thereafter, but they also expressly forbade the payment of directors. Consequently, *Athletic News* could assert that 'No one who is out for a business return will look at football shares.'[31] More fundamentally, concentration on the economic side of the League tends to obscure the social, political and purely sporting factors that might have led the League to operate as it did. The principles of equality of competition and fair competition that became so central to League officials in this period were influenced as much by sporting values and conceptions of fair play as by the desire to increase gate receipts. Profit maximisation was certainly not a major aim of those who ran the League; instead, they were motivated by a range of objectives centred around the need to secure the survival of the League and enhance its status as a competition and an institution. Clearly, professional football was a business and the Football League acted as a cartel, but never in a conventional sense.

There are, of course, other ways of conceptualising the Football League. Confusingly, contemporaries used the term in at least three different senses: as a description of the competition itself; a collective expression for the clubs that comprised its membership; and a reference to the executive body that ran it. For *Athletic News*, it was 'the great organiser and controller' of the professional game; FA President Charles Clegg perceived it more narrowly as 'a body of entertainers' whose primary aim was to distract the public.[32] Such perspectives are not mutually exclusive: the League was all these things at the same time. Further to this, it is argued here that the League should also be recognised by historians as an employers' association. In certain crucial respects, its role within its own industry was comparable to that of organisations such as the Engineering Employers' Federation and the National Federation of Building Trade Employers, which sought to combine industrial relations functions with trade regulation and political activities in order to represent 'as best they could, the collective interests of capital'.[33] Historians of football have hitherto barely acknowledged this, neglecting the League's regulation of so many aspects of the industry – from the setting of wage levels, conditions and standards of work to the organisation of fixtures and financial arrangements between clubs – and the significant powers delegated to it by its constituent clubs. This is not to ignore, of course, the distinctive features of employer combination in sport. Unlike in most other industries, it is essential for employers to combine in order to create a product, and thus collective action was intrinsic to the industry rather than the product of a defensive reaction to state intervention, external competition and the rise of trade union power. However, even if it differed from many employers' associations in its genesis and in some of its methods, the Football League nonetheless exhibited a host of features characteristic of these bodies.

The central sources for this book are the archives and records of the Football League, the FA, the Professional Footballers' Association (the Players' Union or PFA) and the professional football clubs that were full or associate members of the League. The League, the FA and the Players' Union formed what Geoffrey Green called the 'three corners of the triangle' in the administration of English football, and their interaction determined the development of the game. The minute books of executive, committee and sub-committee meetings have been consulted, along with files of correspondence or other records. The Football League, however, did not allow access to its private minutes, correspondence and other records, and so it was necessary to make use of both the printed version of the minutes kept by the FA and the member clubs, and the reports of meetings in the press. The clubs whose archives have been consulted are intended to reflect a representative sample of League membership, both in terms of geography and playing success. Aston Villa, Walsall, West Bromwich Albion and Wolverhampton Wanderers from the Midlands, Darlington from the North-east, Oldham Athletic from Lancashire, Huddersfield Town and Sheffield United from Yorkshire, Arsenal and West Ham United from London and Ipswich Town from East Anglia provided a geographical cross-section. In playing terms, they represent a mixture of consistent First Division clubs, teams who spent time in both the top two divisions and, in Darlington, Ipswich Town and Walsall, clubs from the Third Division sections. The material available at the clubs varied significantly, although there were extensive and complete minute books of board meetings, along with correspondence, wage books and the like at Aston Villa, Sheffield United and West Ham United. For this reason, the evidence used is to some extent weighted towards the experience of these three clubs.

Newspaper sources are also central to this study. Local and national as well as sporting and non-sporting newspapers have been consulted. Most important, perhaps, is *Athletic News*, a sporting newspaper published in Manchester from 1875 to 1931. Its relevance to students of professional football is explained not merely by its circulation figures and popularity, significant though these were. Its quoted readership leapt from some 20,000 in 1888, the year in which the League was founded, to 180,000 by 1896, and Mason has claimed that 'it was without doubt the country's leading football weekly in the last decade of the nineteenth century and the first 15 years of the twentieth'; by 1919 weekly sales were at 170,000. These declined thereafter until it was taken over by the *Sporting Chronicle* in 1931.[34] What is more important is the reputation it developed throughout most of this period as a mouthpiece for particular sections of the football establishment, especially the Football League. The national scope of its reporting and its serious and sober approach to the game gave it the label, before the First World War at least, as '*The Times* of football'.[35] More than this, its close links with League administrators and club directors made it almost the official voice of the League: Inglis has described it as 'the League's very own in-house publication'.[36] It has thus been used extensively throughout the following chapters, alongside other newspapers and journals such as *Thomson's Weekly News* and the *Topical Times*, and sections of the national popular press, all of which covered football politics comprehensively but offered a more critical commentary on the activities of the League and its clubs.

Although the autobiographies or memoirs of some players and administrators whose careers coincided with the 1900–39 period have been used, it is necessary to emphasise the limitations of such sources. In general, though players do make references to their relationships with their clubs and sometimes to contract disputes or negotiations, there is rarely any mention of the Football League itself. This can certainly be interpreted as evidence of the distance between the players and the League, but it also reflects the fact that there is very little behind-the-scenes discussion in football players' autobiographies: not surprisingly, the game itself is invariably given the bulk of the attention. For administrators, the main problem is the paucity of published memoirs. Not one of the Management Committee members or club directors of the period wrote autobiographies, and only William Pickford, Frederick Wall and Stanley Rous did so at the FA. Such references as there are to the lives and careers of League representatives have had to be pieced together through newspaper accounts, obituaries and one or two collective biographies which appeared in Gibson and Pickford's *Association Football and the Men Who Made It* and Sutcliffe and Hargreaves' *History of the Lancashire FA*.[37]

The chronological boundaries of this book also need to be explained, as they do not conform to what might be considered the natural time-span for a study of the Football League. Although the League was founded in 1888, the start of the twentieth century has been taken as the starting point because it coincided with a number of significant changes in its organisation and policy. First, the introduction of the maximum wage in 1901 marked a watershed not only in the management and control of football employees, but also in the broader approach of the League executive towards the idea of equality of competition. The introduction of the system of automatic promotion and relegation between the two divisions in 1898 had similar implications, while other developments – such as the creation of the Inter-League Board with Scotland a year earlier – led Sutcliffe to regard this period 'as marking a definite turn in the League's history'.[38] Secondly, the ostensibly trivial change in secretaries from Harry Lockett to Tom Charnley in 1902 actually heralded a significant development in that the Football League was established in its first permanent offices in Preston. This gave the organisation a central headquarters for member clubs and outside parties to contact, but also gave the impression that this was a stable, secure and *permanent* body. Previously, one can argue, the League was essentially little more than a mailing or telegraphic address, and not a physical entity in its own right. While 1900 is the starting-point, however, discussion of the League's development in the preceding 12 years is nonetheless crucial as a background to the events of the twentieth century. The beginning of the Second World War acts as an obvious chronological end for the study as, in contrast with the 1914–18 war, the League competition was abandoned immediately and clubs pledged themselves unanimously to devote facilities and manpower to the war effort. Regional League and cup competitions did slowly reappear, but these were recognised as fundamentally different in every respect from peacetime football.[39] Moreover, the basic continuity that marked the management of the Football League in the First World War was not repeated in the Second: the officials and executive that emerged in 1945 were very different from those which had taken the decision to suspend the League programme in September 1939.

The book is divided into thematic chapters focusing on different aspects of the development of the professional game, the Football League's internal structure and politics, and its relations with other bodies in the football world as well as with its audience and the broader public. While the chapters have not been arranged chronologically, it is nonetheless recognised that the period can be separated into distinct phases. The most obvious division would be first, 1900–14, then the period of the First World War, 1914–18, and finally the inter-war period, with the depression years of the late 1920s and early 1930s perhaps representing a further chronological departure. There are certainly aspects of the League's activities that can be easily separated into these time-frames, but there is also evidence of considerable continuity across them, and so it was decided to use thematic chapters, which either explicitly or implicitly incorporate this chronology. Certain chapters are broadly based on these chronological periods. Chapter 1, in particular, concentrates on the pre-1914 period, while Chapters 6 and 7 cover mainly the inter-war years.

Chapter 1 provides an initial overview of the origins and aims of the Football League. The bulk of the chapter focuses on the contested process of League expansion and the debate around its transformation into a national league. It also looks at the process of electing clubs in the context of the wider economic and geographical development of the League. Chapter 2 looks at how professional football was governed, setting out the institutional framework and ideological environment within which the League developed and its policies were constructed. Individual sections explore the internal structure and composition of the League, and examine the League's relationships with its member clubs and with the governing body of English football, the FA.

Chapters 3 and 4 are concerned with the Football League's performers and labour force: the players. As well as establishing empirical data on various aspects of the employment of players – such as wages, transfer conditions, contracts and insurance – these chapters analyse the development of labour relations in both their institutionalised, formalised version and their more spontaneous forms. What is more, they seek to determine how players were treated by their employers and to relate this to working conditions in industry, as well as in parallel sporting and recreational sectors. Chapter 5 looks specifically at the organisation of the League as a sporting cartel in the context of economic theory and practice. It assesses the importance of the pervasive ideology of equality, and traces its influences on policy making at executive and club level. The last two chapters focus on the broader issues of the Football League's connection with, first, international football and, second, the 'football' and 'general' public. Chapter 6 is divided into two sections, which consider in turn the League's relations with the more immediate Scottish, Welsh and Irish games, and with football beyond Britain and Ireland, especially in continental Europe. The League's role in the promotion of the game both inside and outside football grounds is discussed in Chapter 7, and the Conclusion briefly draws together the main themes and arguments of the book.

A final word is needed to explain the use of certain terms in the text. For the sake of convenience and to avoid too much repetition, certain common terms have been shortened or used interchangeably with others. The Football League Management Committee is abbreviated in most cases to the 'Management Committee', but the terms 'Committee' and 'executive' have also been used. The Football League is similarly referred to at times as the 'League' and occasionally, in line with the practice of diplomatic historians, is identified by the centre of its government (or its headquarters) as 'Preston'. The Association Football Players' (and Trainers') Union[40] is referred to throughout the text by its popular title, the Players' Union.

Notes

1 *Daily Herald*, 31 May 1938.

2 R. Holt, 'Football and the Urban Way of Life in Nineteenth-Century Britain' in *Pleasure, Profit and Proselytism: British Culture and Sport at Home and Abroad, 1700–1914*, ed. J. A. Mangan, London, Frank Cass, 1988, p. 77; J. Williams, '"One Could Literally Have Walked on the Heads of the People Congregated There": Sport, the Town and Identity' in *Social Conditions, Status and Community, 1860–c.1920*, ed. K. Laybourn, Stroud, Sutton, 1997, p. 128.

3 The Football League was not an entirely English institution. A number of leading Welsh clubs joined from the inter-war years onwards but the competition continued (outside the principality at least) to be popularly associated with England. On the history of football in Wales, and the relations between the Welsh and English game, see M. Johnes, *Soccer and Society: South Wales, 1900–1939*, Cardiff, University of Wales Press, 2002, and M. Johnes, *A History of Sport in Wales*, Cardiff, University of Wales Press, 2005.

4 *Football Players' Magazine*, April 1914.

5 W. McGregor, 'The Origin and Future of the Football League' in *Association Football and the Men Who Made It*, ed. A. Gibson and W. Pickford, London, Caxton, vol. 2, 1906, p. 2.
6 S. Tischler, *Footballers and Businessmen: The Origins of Professional Soccer in England*, New York, Holmes and Meier, 1981, p. 59.
7 McGregor, 'The Origin and Future', p. 1.
8 Tischler, *Footballers*, p. 58; W. Vamplew, *Pay Up and Play the Game: Professional Sport in Britain, 1875–1914*, Cambridge, Cambridge University Press, 1989, p. 125; B. Dobbs, *Edwardians at Play: Sport, 1890–1914*, London, Pelham, 1973, pp. 45–46. Also see D. Birley, *Land of Sport and Glory: Sport and British Society, 1887–1910*, Manchester, Manchester University Press, 1995, p. 36.
9 G. O. Smith, 'Origin and Benefits of the League and the Effects of Professionalism on the Game' in *Football*, ed. M. Shearman, London, Longmans, 1899, p. 171.
10 E. Ensor, 'The Football Madness', *Contemporary Review*, Vol. 74, 1898.
11 McGregor, 'The Origin and Future', p. 1.
12 Quoted in S. Inglis, *League Football and the Men Who Made It*, London, Collins Willow, 1988, p. 162.
13 S. Jones, 'The Economic Aspects of Association Football in England, 1918–39', *British Journal of Sports History*, Vol. 1, 1984, pp. 288–89; *The Economist*, 17 April 1937.
14 Quoted in J. Walvin, *The People's Game: The History of Football Revisited*, Edinburgh, Mainstream, 1994, p. 128.
15 See N. Fishwick, *English Football and Society, 1910–50*, Manchester, Manchester University Press, 1989, Chapter 7; S. Jones, *Sport, Politics and the Working Class*, Manchester, Manchester University Press, 1988, pp. 54–58. Also T. Mason, *Association Football and English Society, 1863–1915*, Brighton, Harvester, 1980, Chapter 8.
16 R. Holt, *Sport and the British: A Modern History*, Oxford, Clarendon, 1989, p. 2.
17 A. J. Arnold, '"Not Playing the Game"?: Leeds City in the Great War', *International Journal of the History of Sport*, Vol. 7, 1990, pp. 112–13.
18 Football League Minutes, Management Committee, 10 May 1912.
19 J. Hill, 'British Sports History: A Post-Modern Future?', *Journal of Sport History*, Vol. 23, 1996, p. 16.
20 S. Hardy, 'Entrepreneurs, Organizations and the Sport Marketplace: Subjects in Search of Historians', *Journal of Sport History*, Vol. 13, 1986, pp. 15, 16. North American sports history has been more at ease with this type of approach. See, for example, Robert Burk's two-volume study of the labour relations of professional baseball: *Never Just a Game: Players, Owners and American Baseball to 1920*, Chapel Hill, University of North Carolina Press, 1994; and *Much More Than a Game: Players, Owners and American Baseball since 1921*, Chapel Hill, University of North Carolina Press, 2001.
21 Hardy, 'Entrepreneurs', p. 16.
22 Mason, *Association Football*; Tischler, *Footballers*; C. Korr, *West Ham United: The Making of a Football Club*, London, Duckworth, 1986; Fishwick, *English Football*; Jones, 'Economic Aspects'.
23 On the significance and impact of Mason's work, see R. Holt, '"No Ideas But in Things": Tony Mason's *Association Football and English Society*', *The Sports Historian*, Vol. 22, 2002, pp. 1–15.
24 Tischler, *Footballers*, *passim*.

25 T. Mason, 'Football and the Historians', *International Journal of the History of Sport*, Vol. 5, 1988, p. 136.
26 W. McGregor, 'The League and the League System' and 'The £.s.d. of football' in *Book of Football*, ed. Anon, London, The Amalgamated Press, 1906; I. Sharpe, 'The Men who Made League Football' in *Association Football*, ed. A. H. Fabian and G. Green, London, Caxton, 1960, pp. 283–309; P. M. Young, *A History of British Football*, London, Stanley Paul, 1968, Chapters 11–13.
27 Mason, 'Football and the Historians', p. 136.
28 C. E. Sutcliffe, J. A. Brierley and F. Howarth, *The Story of the Football League, 1888–1938*, Preston, The Football League, 1938; Inglis, *League Football*. There have been other works relating to the League that focus mainly on statistics and the achievements of famous players and clubs. See, for example, R. C. Churchill, *English League Football*, London, Nicholas Kaye, 1961; M. Golesworthy, *We Are the Champions: A History of the Football League Champions, 1888–1972*, London, Pelham, 1972; and, more recently, B. Butler, *The Football League: The First 100 Years*, Guildford, Colour Library, 1988.
29 Vamplew, *Pay Up*, p. 17.
30 A. J. Arnold, *A Game That Would Pay: A Business History of Professional Football in Bradford*, London, Duckworth, 1988.
31 Quoted in Mason, *Association Football*, p. 48. Also see Vamplew, *Pay Up*, Chapter 10; Fishwick, *English Football*, pp. 27–32.
32 *Athletic News*, 24 May 1920; comment by FA President Charles Clegg at the Football League 'Coming of Age' Banquet, reported in *Athletic News*, 14 June 1909.
33 A. J. McIvor, *Organised Capital: Employers' Associations and Industrial Relations in Northern England, 1880–1939*, Cambridge, Cambridge University Press, 1996, p. 15.
34 Mason, *Association Football*, p. 191; Fishwick, *English Football*, p. 102.
35 Fishwick, *English Football*, p. 102.
36 Inglis, *League Football*, p. vi.
37 A. Gibson and W. Pickford, *Association Football and the Men Who Made It*, London, Caxton, vol. 3, 1906; C. E. Sutcliffe and F. Hargreaves, *History of the Lancashire FA, 1878–1928*, Blackburn, Toulmin, 1928.
38 Sutcliffe, Brierley and Howarth, *Story of the Football League*, p. 13.
39 P. Lanfranchi and M. Taylor, 'Professional Football in Second World War Britain' in *War Culture: Social Change and Changing Experience in World War Two*, ed. P. Kirkham and D. Thoms, London, Lawrence and Wishart, 1995, pp. 187–97.
40 In 1919, the name was altered to the Association Football Players' and Trainers' Union, and in 1958 it became the Professional Footballers' Association.

CHAPTER ONE

Making a National League

Football in England has not always been a national game, in the sense of an all-embracing competitive structure incorporating every part of the country. The story of the sport's journey from codification and bureaucratisation in the public schools of the south to commercial and professional penetration in the north, and then back again, is much too familiar to repeat here.[1] That professional football was essentially a northern creation is without dispute, but historians are less sure about how long it remained the preserve of a particular part of the country: when exactly did the 'sport of the north', in its professional guise at least, become a national game?[2] Certainly, by the mid-1920s England's principal cup and league competitions were unequivocally national in scope, even if regionalism still remained vital to the administration of the sport. Above all else, it was the development of the Football League that was the key to the nationalisation of the association game. Founded in 1888 by 12 of the leading professional clubs in the North-west and the Midlands as a means of ensuring regular competitive fixtures, the League was initially a rather unorganised and marginal body. By the Second World War, however, it controlled the largest sporting competition in the world and was possibly even more powerful than the game's governing body.

The growth of the League during its first 35 years was in many respects a remarkable phenomenon. From a modest numerical and regional base, by 1923 it could claim a membership of 88 clubs and had grown from a single division in 1888 to comprise three divisions (the Third having Northern and Southern Sections) by 1921. Geographically, too, the League had expanded to a point at which it could truly be called national, with members in places as diverse as Newcastle and Plymouth, Bristol and Norwich, Hartlepool and Exeter. Such a transformation was symptomatic of more general trends in English society. The late nineteenth century witnessed what Jose Harris has called 'a subterranean shift in the balance of social life away from the locality to the metropolis and the nation'.[3] The pivotal change came in the economic sphere, where from about 1870 the influence of metropolitan-based finance replaced that of northern manufacture. Accompanying this were discernable trends in education, technology, cultural life and even language which, taken together, began to restructure society on a more uniform, centralised and national basis. By the 1890s, for example, the retail, advertising and newspaper trades had all assumed a predominantly national character beyond the scope of local social and market forces.[4] The early part of the century, and more specifically the inter-war period, also witnessed a profound increase in industrial concentration through both amalgamation and the disproportionate growth of certain firms. Such trends were clearly evident in manufacturing, banking and retailing. In industries such as the railways, where regrouping in 1923 converted 120 small and medium-sized companies into just four large-scale enterprises, some firms were able to occupy semi-monopolistic positions.[5]

It is true that the formation of the Football League itself provided a framework for a greater rationalisation and centralisation of professional football, and broke down to some extent the provincial focus of competition. Furthermore, as the senior and most prestigious league in England and unrestricted by nominal ties to specific regions, the League was widely regarded as the most appropriate agency for the development of a national championship. Yet, despite all this, the making of a 'national' Football League was not the coherent and logical process one might assume. There was no blueprint or strategic plan to absorb the most prominent non-League clubs in order to increase the status and power of the League. Rather, it grew in a haphazard manner, increasing its size in fits and starts and only attaining a truly national constituency after nearly 20 years of discord and a series of failed schemes. The aim of this chapter is to trace the basic development of the Football League in this period, examining the conflicting interest groups that sought to quicken or retard this process. The first section will look at the debate around the idea of a 'national' League and the related attitude of League clubs towards the Southern League and its membership. This will be followed by a detailed examination of the changing composition of the League, focusing in particular on the election process for clubs. However, first it is necessary to briefly examine the initial objectives of the League's founders.

The origins of the League and the objectives of its founders

In view of the expansion and influence of both the Football League and the league system during the twentieth century, it has been tempting for writers to overemphasise the scope of the original scheme. The suggestion, popularised by the founder William McGregor, that the League was initially advocated as a governing body of professional football is therefore rather misleading.[6] Although certain club directors may have privately envisaged the League as the basis of a professional football empire in competition with the FA, its creation was essentially a practical response to a number of difficulties in the management of clubs which had arisen following the legalisation of professionalism in 1885. The most obvious problem was the lack of a pre-arranged and permanent schedule of matches. For clubs with large wage bills to meet in addition to other expenses, gate receipts provided no guarantee of a sufficient regular income. As McGregor commented, 'fixtures were kept and cancelled in a capricious way'.[7] The common arrangement of home and away matches, with the host retaining the gate money, was frequently disrupted by unexpected cup engagements, incomplete teams and bad weather. Without contractual commitments, a club either suffered considerable losses or its secretary was forced at the last minute 'to have to rush about, wire, and write all over the country in order to get a match'.[8] At best this rendered fixture lists useless; at worst it could lead to bankruptcy.

Those matches that were played were often uncompetitive affairs which drew small crowds. The leading clubs generally entered as many as four or five cup competitions, mainly local or county-based, which could produce unattractive one-sided matches in the early rounds or, worse still, blank dates if they were knocked out.[9] Potentially profitable were the periodic friendly fixtures with local rivals and, increasingly from the mid-1880s, major sides from outside the area. Yet even prestigious opponents could not guarantee large attendances. Aston Villa and Bolton Wanderers, both founder members of the League, reportedly drew only 4,000–5,000 spectators for their matches in pre-League days, compared with attendances of 7,000–8,000 less than five years later.[10] With the onset of economic depression in 1886 and 1887, the financial problems of clubs became even more acute. Attendances fell in manufacturing areas, and clubs struggled to maintain programmes of regular competitive football.[11] As McGregor asserted in his famous letter of

2 March 1888: 'Every year it is becoming more and more difficult for clubs of any standing to meet their friendly engagements and even arrange friendly matches. The consequence is that at the last moment … clubs are compelled to take on teams who will not attract the public'.[12] For McGregor's Aston Villa and other clubs, this situation had become administratively and financially intolerable.

The solution to these problems – the system of a fixed programme of home and away matches – was certainly not a new one in 1888. It was widely believed that the idea was taken from US baseball, although McGregor himself claimed that the inspiration had come from cricket's County Championship. Even so, cricket provided the inspiration rather than the model, as home and away fixtures were not compulsory and McGregor wanted 'a more definite plan of all playing against one another'.[13] Moreover, the journalist and editor of *Athletic News*, James Catton, asserted at a later date that the League had more modest antecedents in local football competitions such as the Scarborough Wednesday League (1881) and the Glossop and District Amateur League (1887). It certainly appears that leading sporting newspapers, like *Athletic News* and the *Sunday Chronicle*, were advocating the use of the system in professional football some time before March 1888.[14] It is likely therefore that most of the clubs that McGregor circularised in March, and which subsequently attended meetings throughout the spring and summer, were already familiar with the broad outlines and principles of the league system.

An examination of the League's first set of rules indicates the fairly limited objectives of McGregor and the original 12 clubs.[15] Above all, the League's significance rested on the structure of its programme, or the concept of 'fixity of fixtures'. This, as the *Birmingham Post* acknowledged in retrospect, was 'the ruling idea of the scheme'.[16] Member clubs agreed to 'support each other, and bind themselves to carry out in the strictest sense the arrangement for matches between them, and not allow them to be cancelled on account of any cup competition or other matches'.[17] In addition, each club was expected to 'play its full strength in all matches' and to ensure punctual kick-off times, the latter to avoid circumstances common before 1888 when 'games started 30, 40 and even 60 minutes late, often after intending spectators had returned home'.[18] Writing in 1901, John Lewis, a director of Blackburn Rovers at the time of the League's creation and now a Vice-President, reasserted these three aims as the foundation of the League system.[19] League rules also provided details of administrative structure and procedure, including the system of club representation, and the duties and responsibilities of the

General Committee and Management Committee. However, apart from the acknowledgement that matches 'shall be played under the rules of the Football Association', no reference was made to the League's position vis-à-vis the FA or any other body.[20] For those involved in its establishment, it would seem that the League was primarily perceived as a system of competition rather than an administrative or governing body, although the latter was a necessary corollary of the former. According to Charles Sutcliffe, a former Burnley director and prominent Management Committee member: 'The League at its inception was merely a system. It produced arrangement, reliability, and competition, out of chaos, unreliability, and mere exhibition'.[21]

A further implicit aim of the League, of course, was to stimulate gate revenue. As well as being the most prominent clubs, the original 12 members were also among the best supported. It has been suggested that Everton, for example, a relatively modest club in terms of cup success, was selected entirely because of its large home attendances.[22] However, this point should not be taken too far. Although good gates were clearly an important factor in the selection of clubs, it was assumed that the system, rather than the clubs themselves, would assure these. The initial selection procedure was certainly more ad hoc than might be supposed, based on existing networks of contact between clubs and club officials rather than a systematic analysis of gate receipts. Furthermore, it was not altogether clear beforehand that the proposed league would be a financial success. Both Sheffield clubs, for example, opposed the scheme because they believed it would be too costly for those involved.[23] Only with hindsight did both the press and aspiring clubs generally acknowledge the financial benefits League membership conferred.[24] For the founder members, the impact of the League on gate receipts was certainly dramatic. Wolverhampton Wanderers took just £821 at the gate in its last non-League season, but by 1893–94 this had increased to £3,356; Blackburn Rovers' receipts similarly rose from £1,424 in 1887–88 to £5,190 by 1901–02. As Catton noted, the establishment of the Football League 'galvanised the dry bones of club football into life and endowed the game'.[25]

Building an empire?
The early growth of the League, 1888–1905

Table 1.1 shows the various stages of expansion from 1888 to 1939, in terms both of the number of divisions and the total number of clubs. As can be seen, the League experienced fairly rapid growth in its first decade, with a three-fold increase from 12 to 36 clubs by 1898. Much of this growth was built into the League's original rules, which stated that there should be 'two classes of League clubs – First and Second – each to consist of twelve clubs'.[26] There is also some evidence that, had it been possible to arrange the extra fixtures, the original League would have incorporated three additional clubs: Nottingham Forest, Sheffield Wednesday and the Lancashire side Halliwell.[27] Expansion was therefore on the agenda for many directors and officials from the very start.

Table 1.1: The growth of the Football League by clubs, 1888–1939

	Division 1	*Division 2*	*Division 3 (South)*	*Division 3 (North)*	*Total clubs*
1888–91	12				12
1891–92	14				14
1892–93	16	12			28
1893–94	16	15			31
1894–98	16	16			32
1898–1905	18	18			36
1905–15	20	20			40
1919–20	22	22			44
1920–21	22	22	22*		66
1921–23	22	22	22	20	86
1923–39	22	22	22	22	88

*Simply called Division Three.
Source: Based on Butler, *The Football League*, p. 33.

The precise mode of expansion, however, remained undecided. At the 1891 annual meeting, a scheme to extend the League to 36 clubs divided into three sections was rejected in favour of a modest increase from 12 clubs to 14.[28] A year later, the Second Division was finally established by the partial annexation of the Football Alliance. Three of the leading Alliance clubs – Sheffield Wednesday, Newton Heath (later to become Manchester United) and Nottingham Forest – joined the extended First Division, while the remainder, together with Sheffield United, Burslem Port Vale and Northwich Victoria, formed the new Second Division. Of the Alliance clubs, only Birmingham St George's was denied League membership. The formation of a Second Division had a number of benefits. As well as absorbing and thus eliminating a rival competition, the move safeguarded the developing retain-and-transfer laws by subjecting the most active poachers of players to the League's authority. In addition, the League gained a number of successful and attractive playing sides. Most of the leading clubs and players outside the League were associated with the Football Alliance. Wednesday had been beaten finalists in the 1890 FA Cup, and in 1892 Forest reached the semi-finals, taking the eventual winners West Bromwich Albion to three replays. Bolton's secretary Harry Downs recalled in 1901 that the inclusion of the Alliance was considered extremely advantageous – 'a stroke of business' even – to the League by many contemporaries.[29]

From its inception, however, both the principle of the Second Division itself and the status attached to it were heavily questioned in some circles. Although its clubs had equal representation and voting rights, there was a distinct feeling that the Second Division was merely an appendage to the League proper, and lacked the glamour and prestige of the First Division. John Lewis maintained a persistent opposition to the idea of the Second Division as an inherent part of the League structure, insisting even towards the end of 1901 that it was just 'a means to an end' and its only function was as a waiting room for the First Division.[30] The attitude of certain other clubs served to confirm the division's inferior position. Even before the official inauguration of the Second Division at the 1892 meeting, Liverpool was rejected for refusing to consider joining any competition other than the First Division. After failing in their applications to the First Division, Newcastle East End and an amalgamated Middlesbrough club also rejected assured places in the newly-formed Second Division, ostensibly on account of increased travelling costs but, more specifically, due to doubts over the standard and appeal of the other applicants.[31] There was still much uncertainty the following year when the two defeated First Division clubs in the initial series of test matches, Notts County and Accrington, were reportedly unable to give 'a definite reply as to joining the Second Division', although they both eventually decided to stay.[32] For a number of the League's founder members, the Second Division appeared to be a threat to their elite status and exclusivity as well as their bank balances. Fear of dropping to the Second Division was so acute that relegated clubs habitually proposed an enlargement of the First Division at annual meetings as a means of securing their own rank. Even as late as 1906, William McGregor could bemoan the marked inferiority of the Second Division and the weakness, both in financial and playing terms, of a number of its clubs.[33]

The creation of the Second Division also marked the arrival of the principle of merit promotion, albeit initially in the form of the flawed test-match system.[34] Prior to 1892, the constitution of the First Division was determined by vote, with the bottom four clubs each season applying for re-election. This procedure continued for the bottom clubs in the Second Division (with only three clubs seeking re-election from 1896), but movement between divisions was now determined by the result of sudden-death matches played on neutral grounds between the lowest three First Division and the highest three Second Division clubs. The first series of matches in May 1893 highlighted the potential inequities of the system. While the second- and third-placed clubs in the lower division both won their matches and thus progressed to the First Division, champions Small Heath (later renamed Birmingham) were defeated by the higher division's bottom club Newton Heath, and remained in the Second. The experience of refereeing test matches over the two previous seasons had convinced Lewis by 1895 that the system should be abolished. At that year's annual meeting, he argued that clubs who had worked their way to the top of the divisional table over the course of the season 'deserved promotion without any such ordeal'. Moreover, he was concerned that test matches were not true tests of playing strength, as temporary transfers of players were often made to strengthen weak teams.[35] Though the latter point was dealt with by the instigation of a short-term residential qualification, the clubs chose to modify rather than abolish the system. Instead of meeting in a one-off match, the two bottom clubs in the First Division and the champions and runners-up in the Second competed in a play-off group, in which each played the two clubs from the other division twice while the pair from the same division did not meet at all. The difficulties of this arrangement were clearly shown at the end of the 1897–98 season, when an allegedly arranged goalless draw between Stoke and Burnley assured both of a First Division place. According to Charles Sutcliffe, a Director of one of the guilty clubs, this match 'put a stop to a system which had always been clumsy and often had brought about a perversion of the football values of the season's play'.[36] From 1898–99 onwards, test matches were discarded in favour of an automatic two-up, two-down system of promotion and relegation.

It was also decided at the 1898 annual meeting to further enlarge the League, though again differences existed over the exact details. The representatives of Woolwich Arsenal and Aston Villa both favoured a regionalised Second Division, the former proposing a 16-club First Division and a 32-club Second divided equally between Northern and Southern Sections, and the latter requiring similarly organised divisions of 18 and 24 clubs respectively. These fairly radical suggestions were, however, easily defeated by Burnley's proposal of a simple increase of each division by two.[37] Certainly this enlargement was passed partly to compensate the two sides, Newcastle United and Blackburn Rovers, which had suffered because of the arranged test match, but there was also an underlying financial motive. Sutcliffe, Burnley's representative, supported his proposal with reference to the increased revenue from additional 'League matches [which] always paid' as opposed to 'friendlies [which] never paid'.[38]

At this time, the question of whether the League should be expanded remained quite separate from the more general idea of a national league. We have seen that in many cases, expansion was advocated as a form of self-preservation for lowly clubs. This was the case in both 1901 and 1902, when Preston North End led unsuccessful campaigns for a 40-club League, a development that on either occasion might have given the club a place in the First Division. More importantly, supporters of expansion began to argue that it offered two fundamental advantages: greater financial security for clubs, and increased status and authority for the League as a whole. On the first point, it was asserted that a few extra League matches per season, played midweek if necessary, would increase the annual income of the majority of clubs who were unable to make extra money from successful FA Cup runs. As many clubs already filled blank fixture dates with friendlies or minor cup competitions, why not play more League matches, which always guaranteed more satisfactory gates? Second, many shared the view of Lincoln City's John Strawson, who believed that in future disputes with the FA or any other organisation, a larger and wider-reaching League would be more influential: 'the more strength and importance that could be bestowed upon the Football League, the less danger there would be when trouble arose'.[39]

In general, it was the wealthier clubs who blocked moves to expand. The attitude of Aston Villa was typical. Villa's directors consistently opposed the enlargement of the First Division, although they had no objection to a larger second group 'providing some provision be made whereby their voting power should not predominate over that of the First Division'.[40] The main fear, according to the club's representative Fred Rinder, was of 'too much football … there was only a certain amount of money to be spent on football, which was essentially a Saturday afternoon game'.[41] Yet critics revealed that Villa itself often fitted in more than one match per week: in fact, the club had played 16 games in just three weeks in April 1902. It seems, once again, that the real motives were financial. More League matches would mean increased compensation to other clubs for loss of League gates when fixture dates had to be switched, a situation that successful cup sides like Villa and Sheffield United particularly resented.[42] By 1905, however, opinion had shifted to the point where Sucliffe's proposal of 20 clubs in each division received support from leading clubs like Liverpool and Newcastle United. It was passed by 31 votes to six without any counter-argument, although Sheffield United (among others) remained unmoved in its opposition.[43]

The Leaguers and the South, 1905–20

Writers concerned with the development of the Football League have often adopted a Whiggish approach, characterising the organisation's rise from a regional to a national body as inevitable and unproblematic. From this viewpoint, the League was always envisaged as a national competition, even if its founder members came from just five counties and the process of expansion was slow and faltering.[44] Yet only in retrospect is it possible to detect straight paths and simple processes of this kind. Although the idea of expansion *seems* to have had an inevitable logic, in reality the issue was highly contentious. Not only did it raise economic and logistical difficulties, it was also shot through with fundamental questions regarding the ownership and identification of the League. Should it be a self-absorbed organisation concerned only with the interests of its members, or did it have a broader responsibility for the welfare and development of the game in general? Were its officials guardians of the Football League or missionaries of football? Such questions were bound up in an ongoing debate concerning the future of the Football League as a national or a parochial body and, more specifically, its relationship with rival competitions like the Southern League.

From early on, the idea of the League becoming a national competition was regularly discussed. McGregor, founder, Chairman and then life member, was its most influential proponent. The 'nationalisation' of the League was in his view an inevitable evolutionary process. By 1906, he foresaw the 'gradual bringing in of influential clubs at present outside the organisation, with the object of sooner or later making the League a truly national body. While it does not include Southampton, Portsmouth and Tottenham Hotspur, it cannot be said to be truly representative'.[45] Sutcliffe was similarly convinced of the League's national pretensions. Though a Lancashire patriot and a fierce opponent of the gentlemen amateurs of the South who dominated the FA, Sutcliffe nevertheless retained a vision of the Football League as a national competition in waiting. Writing at the same time as McGregor, he saw the League developing into 'a great National League, comprising within its borders the best, and all the best, clubs in the country'.[46] Sutcliffe had been instrumental in the expansion of membership from 32 to 36 clubs in 1898 and then from 36 to 40 in 1905, and from late 1906 onwards he publicised (in his weekly *Athletic News* column) schemes for the creation of a national league through the incorporation of the Southern League. Many influential commentators agreed with McGregor and Sutcliffe. In 1905, one observer could argue that recent developments pointed towards a national League in the future although, significantly, he thought that 'this is more likely to come by evolution than revolution'.[47]

The piecemeal absorption of clubs from outside the League's original geographical base had indeed been a feature of this evolution from the early 1890s onwards. As we will see in the next section, the annual election system gave member clubs the opportunity not only to replace weak or unsuccessful clubs, but also to expand the League's boundaries by bringing in new members from hitherto unrepresented parts of the country. This could, of course, also be achieved by actually increasing the size of the League and thus making more places available to outsiders. However, neither the executive nor the clubs were empire-builders: in fact, the spatial growth of the League in its first decade was rather cautious. Expansion was initially into the North-east, with the inclusion in 1890 of Sunderland, while in 1892, as we have seen, the League brought in clubs from South Yorkshire, Cheshire, Lincolnshire and Manchester when it absorbed the Football Alliance. Nevertheless, this locational spread made little impact on the general pattern of membership, which continued to be dominated by the original areas. As John Coyle has noted, the League's growth in its first decade was marked by gradual territorial expansion, with the voting members opting for clubs from towns and cities 'on the fringes of [its] existing strongholds' such as Crewe, Northwich and Burton.[48] In fact, of the 32 member clubs in the 1899–1900 season, nine were from Lancashire and 16 from the Midlands. John Bale is thus right to observe that the League at this time 'had scarcely spread beyond a triangular belt between the Mersey and the Humber'.[49]

The most striking omissions, in view of the emerging 'national league' debate, were clubs from London and the South. Only Woolwich Arsenal (in 1893) and Luton (in 1897) had been elected by the turn of the century. To a certain extent, this reflected the continued dominance of amateurism in the South and the relatively slow adoption of professionalism, which, although not a stated prerequisite for applicants, was closely associated with the origins and ethos of League football. However, it can also be explained by the establishment of the rival Southern League in 1894, a competition that quickly acquired as members many of the leading professional clubs in the South.[50] By the late 1890s, Southern League clubs were beginning to seriously rival their Football League compatriots on the field. Southampton was particularly successful in the FA Cup, reaching the semi-final in 1898 and the final in 1900 and 1902, while Tottenham Hotspur actually won the 1901 competition. It is therefore hardly surprising that sections of the press, along with representatives of both leagues, began publicly (and, one suspects, privately) to debate the possibility of amalgamation and the creation of a genuinely national league.

Arsenal, the Football League's first London club, played a major role in this debate. Coyle has suggested that the election of the club by the Management Committee in 1893 was 'a key component in their strategy of becoming recognised as a national league'.[51] While it is doubtful that a distinct strategy of this type really existed, particularly at this early stage, it is clear that the inclusion of Arsenal was symbolic of the League's intention to be something more than a regional or 'Northern' body. It was also recognition of the London club's bold decision to turn professional in opposition to the dominant amateur ideology of the London FA. Henceforth, Arsenal became the League's 'flagship franchise in London' and the focal point for further discussions of expansion into the south.[52] The appointment of an Arsenal director, George Leavey, in 1901 as the first representative of a Southern club on the Management Committee was another important step in this direction, particularly because Leavey had shown an active commitment to amalgamation with the Southern League. In May 1900 he had organised an informal meeting between representatives of the two leagues, and the following February he proposed an enlargement of the First Division to 20 clubs and a second, Southern-based section for the lower division.[53] Although both attempts failed, *Athletic News* still considered his appointment to be 'a very significant step, for Mr Leavey will work might and main for the end he has in view – the union of the parent body with its Southern contemporary'.[54]

Between 1901 and 1908, Bristol City, Chelsea, Clapton Orient, Fulham and Tottenham Hotspur were elected to the Football League, generally against the wishes of, and with protest from, the Southern League. Yet despite continual hostility between the two bodies over the poaching of clubs and players, the idea of an amalgamated national league would not disappear. In March 1909 the Southern League Management Committee approached Preston with a proposal to fuse the leagues into a 60-club competition, consisting of a First Division of 20 clubs and two second divisions, north and south; the latter with equal status, voting rights and chances of promotion. Hence the First Division of the Southern League would be on a par with the Second Division of the Football League. Representatives and supporters of the League dismissed the scheme emphatically. *Athletic News* argued that the Southern League clubs wanted 'power and the prospects of promotion … and they offer NOTHING in return', while Fulham Chairman Henry Norris admitted in his *Football Chat* column that in seeking fusion on more or less equal terms, 'the

Southern League is asking too much'.[55] Even Sutcliffe, who like Norris supported the principle of amalgamation, warned League clubs that they would 'be making a tremendous concession to a weaker organisation if they enter into the suggested agreement'.[56] The clubs, therefore, rejected the proposal unanimously, but the idea of an additional division under the League's auspices remained on the table. Weakened by the almost annual secession of its clubs to the senior body, the Southern League could hardly argue with this, and so in April 1909 entered into negotiations for the inclusion of its 18 leading clubs as the basis of a new Football League Third Division.[57]

The debate surrounding this proposed Third Division tapped into wider disagreements over the role, obligations and identification of the Football League in the early twentieth century. Opponents of national expansion were to be found on the Management Committee as well as in club boardrooms, and drew on arguments that remained essentially unchanged from the early 1890s. First, the Football League was regarded as a self-concerned organisation whose interests were bound up solely with those of the clubs comprising its membership: anything beyond this, including the development of a national league, was considered marginal or even irrelevant. Lewis, one of the most vociferous opponents of change, employed arguments of this type frequently in his newspaper columns. In April 1905, he informed *Athletic News* readers that:

> The League has never set itself up to be a 'national competition', and although it embraces clubs as far apart as Newcastle and London, Sunderland and Bristol, it has never encouraged the idea which has sprung up of late, especially in the South, that it should represent the whole country … In the beginning it regarded itself as an association of 12 good clubs banded together for mutual advantage, and although it now numbers 36 clubs it neither claims to be a 'representative national body' nor do anything except regulate its own competition.[58]

During the 1909 debate, he reasserted his view that 'the Football League does not aspire to be a National League', but expressed concern that it was in danger of opening its doors too widely to ambitious clubs across the country and hence being 'forced into the position of a national body'.[59]

Secondly, opposition was often expressed in terms of the broader north–south rivalries or anti-metropolitanism of the period. In contrast to McGregor and Sutcliffe's conception of the Football League as an embryonic national body, others regarded it as a small, selective and geographically restricted competition in which the provinces, and Lancashire especially, should be free from metropolitan control. The entry of four London clubs after 1905, and subsequent proposals of amalgamation with the South, thus appeared to threaten not only the existing power structure but also the identity of the League. 'For some time I have held and expressed the opinion that the Football League was in danger of assuming too much of a London complexion', Lewis noted in May 1909, going on to suggest that 'if a Third Division is brought into existence under the suggested scheme it can only be a matter of a very few seasons before … a competition which was provincial in inception, and provincial in spirit, will have all its safeguards broken down'.[60] Tom Houghton, chairman of Preston North End, thought that as the Southern League 'had always been their [the League's] enemies … in a football sense' rather than compatriots, they should be left to organise their own competition. Other club directors at the decisive general meeting of 30 April 1909 agreed that, while they favoured the formation of a Third Division in principle, certain clubs in the North and the Midlands had stronger claims than the 18 Southern clubs, whom 'they knew nothing about'.[61]

Those who supported amalgamation with the South regarded it as a way of solving financial difficulties as well as a means of strengthening the competition. It was thought that the continual traffic in players between the two leagues would be ended by the creation of a single professional authority, and that clubs would henceforth have tighter control over their employees. In support of the proposal, John Bentley agreed that the new Third Division would solve financial difficulties by making 'clubs more secure and players more settled'.[62] As such, it would not only be 'an advantage in the control of professional football' but 'make the League far more powerful'.[63] For leading administrators like Bentley and Sutcliffe, of course, the concept of a national league also offered the possibility of self-aggrandisement. After all, it should not be forgotten that these were ambitious men who were by this point more concerned with the progress of the League as a whole than with the wellbeing of their individual clubs. They were self-styled 'League men' whose public profiles were bound up in the status of the organisation they had created and developed. For all this, the anti-national league lobby was ultimately successful at the 1909 meeting, where the proposed Third Division was rejected by three votes. However, negotiations between the two leagues eventually paid dividends the following February, when agreement was reached to recognise each other's registration and transfer rights.

While there were further proposals for an extension of the Football League's geographical constituency in the following five years, it was the effect of the First World War which amplified demands for a genuinely national league under its aegis. The League continued to operate during the war years, albeit in a modified regional form, but its Southern counterpart was unable to continue, even rejecting the idea of district competitions 'owing to geographical difficulties'.[64] These difficulties were partly the result of the Southern League's own policy of expansion, which had not only brought in a number of clubs from Wales, the South-west and East Anglia, but also some from the Midlands and the North, like Northampton Town, Walsall, Stoke, Coventry City and Stalybridge Celtic. Indeed, by the 1914–15 season Brentford was the only Second Division club located within 100 miles of London.[65] The Football League benefited from the Southern League's wartime inactivity, admitting Stoke in 1915 and co-opting Coventry City in 1918 before electing them as full members, along with West Ham United, a year later. These acts led to a crucial breach in relations between the two bodies, with the Southern body claiming ownership of the players of its former clubs and, in July 1919, withdrawing from the 1910 transfer agreement. This decision seems to have weakened the Southern League's bargaining position and its claims to be treated as an equal partner in the League combine. *Athletic News* felt that the Southern League had now reduced itself 'to quite a parochial organisation', while the Football League was increasingly coming to be perceived, and to perceive itself, as a national competition.[66]

The immediate post-war years witnessed the final victory for the Football League's 'nationalists'. There were two main stages to this. First of all, the loyalty of the London contingent needed to be re-established, and this was achieved through a mixture of negotiation and concession. The wartime London Combination, consisting of both Football and Southern League clubs, had been successful enough to prompt calls for a post-war London League. The possibility of a split was increased by the prospect of the absence of metropolitan clubs from the top division due to the relegation of Chelsea and Tottenham Hotspur in the 1914–15 season. However, the Football League's decision to expand the First Division by two offered a lifeline to these clubs, who according to precedent would be awarded the additional places. Chelsea, who had been demoted partly as the result of a match-fixing scandal, were duly elevated, but controversy was caused by the decision to elect Arsenal, only fifth in the Second Division before the war, in place of its north London rival.[67] While many commentators at the time and since have been baffled and outraged by the decision – two Arsenal historians even calling it 'the single most outrageous enterprise … in the history of English football'[68] – it was in fact quite compatible with the wishes of those for whom a national league required strong representation in the capital. Some months before the decision was made, *Athletic News* commented that 'for the sake of the game, London, unlike any other city, ought to have the opportunity of seeing the best teams … does anyone think that New York or Boston would ever be deprived of class baseball?'[69] Arsenal, with its new stadium, crowd potential and long service, much more than Tottenham, which was but 'young in League life', seemed to offer the greater opportunities. Moreover, it was felt that the League owed Arsenal a particular debt. The club had entered the Football League in its formative years – 'when we were building' – and had 'never wavered in loyalty'. It was Arsenal that was 'the pioneer of the League system in the metropolis' and which 'had a vision of the ultimate strength and national character of The League'.[70] The elevation of Arsenal in 1919 was evidence of a new national self-image and a commitment on the part of the Football League to complete its national expansion.

Secondly, the League's status as a national league was confirmed with the creation of a Third Division in 1920. This was essentially the work of Sutcliffe, the leading advocate of expansion, who used his position as a columnist on *Athletic News* to provoke discussion on the matter and lay down a plan which allowed expansion without compromising the power of the existing League members. His scheme was for a Third Division separated into Northern and Southern sections, the latter consisting of the Southern League First Division, admitted as associate rather than full members, with no voting or transfer rights, and controlled by the Management Committee. Within two weeks a group of Northern clubs had committed themselves to Sutcliffe's scheme, and a few days later the Southern Leaguers agreed to apply to the Football League for their election en bloc. The idea soon received approval from the Management Committee, although the formation of a Northern section was postponed for at least a year as a consequence of widespread doubts over the financial and playing strengths of the proposed clubs. Despite some opposition at the annual meeting, mainly from Everton, whose representative thought the clubs needed more time to consider such a 'huge revolution' in the League's composition, the Third Division was finally to become a reality.[71]

In making the case for expansion, Sutcliffe drew on a Whiggish notion of progression to the Football League's 'natural' status as a national body. The League's history up to that point was framed by what was presumed to be its ultimate objective: to become a 'truly' or 'genuinely' national league. He told the meeting that as a League 'they had always been making progress. They have never gone backwards and he hoped they would continue to go higher and higher, until they had reached that perfect organisation which should be the ambition of every national body.' The anti-expansionist and anti-nationalist sentiments of Lewis, Houghton and others were dismissed: for Sutcliffe there was no question that theirs was 'a great national League' which 'should comprise all the great clubs in the country'.[72] Moreover, in contrast with the expressions of regionalism and self-protection that won the day in 1909, Sutcliffe emphasised the League's duty to popularise the game of football. The consensus, he told his readers, was that 'the League cannot stand still, that it is the competition to which all eyes are turned… The Football League is pre-eminent and owes a duty to the public'.[73] According to this view, there was little need for debate. The Football League could hardly ignore its destiny as *the* English league, responsible for the development of the professional game in the South as well as the North.

Making Leaguers: the election of clubs

The development of the Football League was not simply a matter of expansion. As sports economists have demonstrated, changes in the composition of an agreed number of clubs can act as a means of controlling league quality and maintaining financial viability. In contrast to some US sports, the League had no equivalent to the franchise system that allows league executives to move club franchises to areas of greater crowd potential.[74] Rather, changes could be effected through the annual election system. The clubs with the poorest playing records during the season were compelled to apply for re-election, and they were joined in the election ballot by aspirants from outside the League. Member clubs were then able to vote by secret ballot on the applicants most suitable for admission. This section will look at the whole election process, concentrating particularly on the motives of those voting and the implications this had on the changing composition of the Football League. Stephen Tischler has argued that population size and the ability to draw crowds were the exclusive factors determining which clubs were chosen. In other words, economic criteria alone influenced the voting clubs.[75] On the other hand, Tony Arnold has suggested that a broad range of influences, including 'references to geographical and traditional factors as well as economic or playing attributes of the various applicants' came to bear upon the clubs at election time.[76] While an analysis of individual cases would make it difficult to support Tischler's view, it would nevertheless appear that economic factors weighed most heavily with the clubs when deciding on which teams should be members of the Football League.

Initially, the League's bottom four clubs had to apply for re-election each season, but this was reduced to three in 1898 and then two in 1908. From 1921, the bottom two clubs in each section of the Third Division were forced to apply for re-election to their sections, and this continued up to, and after, 1939. Applications for membership had to be sent in writing to the League offices well in advance of the annual meeting (by 10 May each year after 1915), and until 1924 a representative of each applicant club was allowed to address the voting members for up to three minutes. If two applicants received the same number of votes the unsuccessful applicants withdrew and a second ballot was taken, each member voting just once, and if this proved inconclusive the League executive – the Management Committee – made the decision.

It appears that initially, many applicants relied upon receiving support on the day of the AGM, either through informal canvassing or via the formal address to voters. *Athletic News* observed in 1903 the role played by the directors at the meeting: 'Hither and thither the representatives of the applying clubs flick about to secure votes, until those who are safe and sound themselves become bored and readily promise to vote for all and sundry'.[77] The same newspaper noted two years earlier how 'personality and a pleasing voice primed with confidence go a long way when a club is applying for membership'. Some speakers, like Middlesbrough's Henry Walker and J. H. Cook of Doncaster Rovers, were regarded as expert orators who could elicit support successfully.[78] Other applicants hoped to bolster their claims by enlisting local dignitaries, such as mayors or MPs, to address the meeting on their behalf. Yet although oratorical skills were an advantage, it is unlikely that a good speech ever got a poor applicant elected. In the matter of elections, a 'good knowledge of soccer politics' helped rather more than speeches.[79] By 1924 it was felt that the speeches were irrelevant, the Management Committee deciding to discontinue them 'as clubs had presumably made up their minds for whom they would vote'.[80]

Formal canvassing methods soon followed, as the minute books of several clubs reveal. This canvassing was done through the distribution of a circular letter 'setting out the advantages and claims' of the club in financial, sporting and geographic terms.[81] Oldham Athletic issued 250 copies of such a circular in 1906, and supplemented this with the personal efforts of club representatives. Both Charles Sutcliffe, who was acting as solicitor to the club and was soon to join the directorate, and the team manager were requested to use their influence at forthcoming meetings of the governing bodies in support of Oldham's application.[82] This attempt failed, but in March 1907 the Oldham board appointed a special sub-committee to make arrangements for the club's next application. These included the distribution, throughout the North and Midlands, of an advertisement in the shape of a football with the inscription 'Oldham wants League Football', as well as a personal deputation to every voting club.[83] Similarly, West Ham United sent three directors and a secretary on separate visits to Birmingham, Grimsby, Hull, Lincoln, Nottingham and Coventry in support of its 1919 application.[84] The South Shields manager Jack Tinn went further the same year by personally canvassing every League club, while the board circulated an election prospectus. Folkestone and Bath City officials reportedly 'travelled thousands of miles' in support of their unsuccessful applications in 1935.[85]

The example of Ipswich Town indicates how sophisticated and expensive applications to join the Football League had become by the 1930s. In November 1936, almost six months before the next annual meeting, a director was appointed to begin 'propaganda work on behalf of this club with the Football League' and an initial sum of £200 was allocated specifically for this purpose.[86] In April 1937, the Secretary-Manager was instructed to apply formally for admission to the Third Division Southern Section and to proceed with a brochure to be circulated to all League clubs. Although the application proved unsuccessful, the club's Finance Committee reported that £340 in total had been laid out in support of the application.[87] Six years earlier, Mansfield Town had reportedly spent £1,000 in the 'propaganda work' that resulted in the club's election to the Southern Section.[88]

To have any chance of being elected, then, it was clearly becoming essential to do more than simply state one's case: the facts could not be left to speak for themselves. Prior to the 1920 annual meeting, *Athletic News* observed that of the seven candidates for inclusion in the Second Division, only the four who had 'prosecuted an active canvass' had any real hope of success.[89] The press could be a useful ally in such a situation. From 1900 onwards, sporting and general papers began to discuss seriously the merits of various candidates and to print extracts from, or the whole of, their circular appeals. By 1911, *Athletic News* was devoting a considerable amount of front page space to these appeals, and it was generally accepted that newspapers were important in publicising a club's case. In 1909, the Sheffield weekly *Football and Sports Special* lauded one candidate for its close contact with the press throughout its campaign, and contrasted this with the complacency of a rival club: 'we heard practically nothing of what they were doing, or whether they desired any sort of help'.[90]

Many applicants also actively sought the support of influential clubs and directors. Friends within the League circle could offer practical assistance and give greater weight to arguments for admission. Middlesbrough's election to Division Two at the first attempt in 1899 was thought to have been 'thanks to the influence of the Northern delegates'.[91] Ipswich Town's successful application in 1938 probably owed much to the personal canvassing of the Arsenal chairman, Sir Samuel Hill-Wood, on the club's behalf. Hill-Wood was an acquaintance of his Ipswich counterpart, Captain Cobbold, and had helped the Suffolk club's preparations the previous season by offering practical assistance, including a set of tip-up seats for their stadium. Following Ipswich's election, the secretary was instructed to write to Hill-Wood 'and thank him for all he had done for this club'.[92] Some clubs approached members of the Management Committee directly, even though it was customary for the Committee to remain neutral in the election of clubs. Charles Sutcliffe thus reported in 1920 that certain clubs had contacted him and other Committee members to test the likelihood of being elected if an application were made. This type of activity was common among clubs that risked being fined by or expelled from their respective leagues if they applied to join the Football League.[93]

More seriously, there was a problem of candidates offering baits and incentives, usually of a financial nature, to voting clubs. Chelsea and Clapton Orient began this trend in 1905 by agreeing to pay Northern clubs £20 and Midlands clubs £15 for each visit to London over a period of three years.[94] Following similar promises by Fulham two years later, several clubs began to feel such payments constituted bribes, or at least gave the payer unfair advantages, and in 1908 it was resolved that 'no club applying for admission to the League should be allowed to hold out any inducement whatever in the shape of travelling expenses to clubs already holding membership'.[95] It seems unlikely that this edict prevented applicants from offering surreptitious inducements in order to facilitate their election, though there is a lack of solid evidence. The Sheffield United directors were certainly aware of improper conduct on the part of certain candidates during the 1920 elections, and called on the Management Committee to take action. It would appear that nothing was done, as by 1931 the President had to warn non-League clubs that the practices of 'touting for votes' or 'keeping open house' would be punished in future by disqualification.[96]

More sinister still were allegations that League clubs were offered inducements to resign their membership. Although the contemporary press and the clubs vociferously denied that such dishonourable conduct ever occurred, it is evident that some clubs were so anxious to join the League that they were prepared to pay for the opportunity. An example comes from Oldham Athletic's admission to the League in 1907. The club's minutes reveal that on 10 June 1907, the directors were informed of Burslem Port Vale's financial difficulties. They agreed to offer Vale £1,000, including the transfer of two players, 'on their resigning membership of the Football League Ltd, [and] providing this Club is elected to said League in their place'.[97] Four days later Vale notified the League of its resignation, and on 15 June Oldham was elected on the basis that it had headed the voting list of unsuccessful candidates at the AGM.[98] There were rumours of a similar arrangement between Tottenham and Stoke the following year, even though Stoke announced that its resignation 'had not been influenced in any way by financial inducements from any club desirous of obtaining a position in the League'.[99]

Although it appears that in the majority of cases there was no hint of any direct financial benefit from supporting one candidate over another, indirect financial benefit was another matter. Contemporary observers believed that financial strength and crowd potential were increasingly becoming deciding factors in the election of clubs. Big city clubs offered the potential of large attendances. Estimated crowds at matches in Sheffield, Birmingham and Liverpool in 1893–94 and 1894–95 ranged from 22,000 to 44,000, while Northwich averaged only 1,325 during 1893–94.[100] However, it is difficult to prove conclusively that big city clubs were automatically favoured. Voting took place by secret ballot, and the votes of individual clubs, and perhaps more importantly the reasons behind them, are hard to ascertain. Club minute books are unfortunately taciturn on this subject, not least because decisions were often not taken at board level, but instead were discussed informally and left to the club representative's discretion.

Some indication of clubs' thinking might be provided by studying the arguments made by prospective members, both at the annual meeting and in canvassing material. It is firstly important to distinguish between existing members applying for re-election and those outside the League seeking to gain entry, as they tended to employ distinct lines of argument. The main tactic of the first group was to stress their long connection with, and loyalty to, the League. For major clubs that seldom finished in the re-election places, this was a fairly straightforward matter. In 1903, Burnley's representative promised that his club 'would not offend again', while Nottingham Forest's appeal for re-admission in 1914 was based entirely on its 'long and honourable career' and past contribution to the League.[101] For a club like Lincoln City, which was regularly required to justify its League status, the need to evoke a sense of tradition and loyalty was crucial. A typical example was the club's circular appeal of 1911, which stated that 'Our connection with the League has extended over 18 years and during that period all the duties and obligations of League Membership have been honourably fulfilled.' It was also mentioned that 'we are … one of the oldest clubs in the country'.[102] Third Division clubs were not averse to making similar appeals between the wars. Facing re-election in 1938, Walsall could draw on its history as a founder member of the Second Division and its 'famous Cup victory over Arsenal' in 1933, but it was perhaps just as important that the club had no significant record of re-election, as opposed to defeated Gillingham who 'had applied half-a-dozen times'.[103]

The approach of non-League clubs was different. They felt they had more to prove and tended to adopt more substantial and wide-ranging arguments. Oldham Athletic's circular appeal of 1907 was characteristic of the type of document sent to the electorate. It began by stating that the intention of the document was 'to lay before you the reasons why we consider our admittance will be beneficial not only to the League but to Association Football, its followers and supporters generally; with the object of gaining your assistance and support at the Annual Meeting of the League'. It then covered a number of areas in which the club was presented as reaching the necessary standards or offering something extra to the League. First, the population within the town, the parliamentary borough and a five- and ten-mile radius were stated, along with details of geographical accessibility and transport facilities. Secondly, emphasis was placed on the pedigree and record of the team in their present league competition and the FA Cup. Thirdly, the club's ability to attract good crowds – 'we have been able to obtain 8,000 spectators regularly' – and its ground capacity and facilities were all noted. Fourthly, the financial basis and security of the club were outlined, and finally the document stressed the role of the club in popularising the association code in the area, the implication being that their election would strengthen this process.[104] By the end of the 1900s, Oldham's format had almost become a blueprint for non-League candidates. Of course, clubs placed emphasis on what they considered their strong points to be – playing records, facilities or finances – but few chose to deviate from the general pattern. Some circulars, like that supporting Huddersfield Town's application in 1910, were especially meticulous. In addition to the standard contents, the club directors included a report by the renowned architect and engineer Archibald Leitch on the proposed development of the Leeds Road ground, and even a list of railway tariffs for travelling teams and spectators.[105] Others chose to emphasise population, with mixed results. In 1915, *Athletic News* reported Darlington's claim to be 'the centre of a population of 250,000' while 'the county borough (of Walsall) has a population of 100,000' and Coventry 'has a population approaching 150,000'. In 1919 Rochdale claimed to be at 'the centre of a population of over 400,000 residing within a six-mile radius', and Cardiff City, elected in 1920, claimed a more realistic population of 250,000.[106]

The importance of adequate railway facilities deserves special attention here. While it would be too deterministic to suggest that the growth of the League retraced that of the national railway system, there was undoubtedly a close link between the two. As James Catton remarked in 1919:

> What has been the first point urged in any membership for application to The Football League? The ease with which visiting clubs could get to the new centre and away from it. If the proposed new centre was served by several railway companies and linked with various lines, the facts weighed with those who had cast their votes.[107]

For all clubs, then, a good railway link became an essential prerequisite for admission: for some it was the main selling point. Those located at the extremities of the country were especially anxious to overcome the concerns of existing members over possible transport difficulties. Darlington based each of its annual applications to the League between 1910 and 1914 on the town's position at 'the centre of the North-Eastern Railway system'. It was also emphasised that the 'North-Eastern Railway Company are making [Darlington] their headquarters, and are transferring their works from Gateshead and York'.[108] Though not a 'railway town' in the sense of Darlington, Carlisle United's successful 1928 circular noted that the town was 'one of the best served railway centres in the British Isles'. York City's address in the same year stated that the city was 'situated on a main line between Edinburgh and London and served by a railway service second to none'.[109] Furthermore, as the rail network expanded in the first two decades of the century, and competition between companies increased, so most club grounds became served by two or more stations or lines. For example, teams or supporters destined for either Bradford club in 1910 could travel on the Midland,

North-Eastern, Lancashire and Yorkshire, Great Northern or Great Central railways. Ten years later, a connection had been added by the London and North-Western Railway.[110]

The impression given in these circular appeals is that the financial strength and potential of clubs underpinned the whole election system. As early as the 1905 annual meeting, *Athletic News* noted that 'the tone was of big populations and money'. At the same time, John Lewis stressed his objection 'to the elbowing out of old clubs to make room for new ones with no recommendations but money, and the fact that they are in bigger centres of population'.[111] In November 1911, *Athletic News* again reported the opinion of an ex-club director that 'no town of less than a population of 250,000 could run a first-class professional team', although the paper then went on to list seven First Division clubs situated in towns of less than 200,000 and a further two in less than 100,000.[112] Yet by the First World War, a number of small towns such as Glossop, Burton and Gainsborough, all with populations below 50,000, had lost their League representatives to larger centres. In the five years between 1903 and 1908 alone, four clubs from the capital were elected, together with two from Bradford, England's eighth largest city, and one from the fifth largest, Leeds. All the canvassing in the world could not disguise the fact that, between the early 1900s and 1920, Football League members favoured the cause of big cities over that of small towns.[113]

Tottenham Hotspur's election in 1908 can be viewed as evidence of the League showing favour to 'big city' clubs. As Stoke's H. D. Austerberry told his fellow representatives: 'the face of football politics has vastly changed during the past few years, and whether they wished it or not, they knew very well that a little struggling club that came to the annual meeting and applied for admission would not stand the slightest chance'.[114] Tischler cited the Tottenham/Lincoln case as an example of the way in which poorer clubs from smaller cities were discarded in favour of wealthier and better situated outfits.[115] This was undoubtedly a factor in the Management Committee's decision, but there were other considerations too. Tottenham had an impressive playing record, both in the Southern League and the FA Cup, whereas Lincoln had finished in the bottom three on a number of occasions, including the two previous seasons. *Athletic News* believed that Lincoln had received sufficient warning and had appealed for help too often: 'The members of the League can grow tired of re-electing a club in an age where the tendency is to concentrate the best professional football in the largest centres'. Also, the widespread feeling that Lincoln acted as a nursery club for Chelsea may have lost it support.[116] In contrast, the press generally agreed that Tottenham was an attractive side that drew large crowds and could survive in better company. One writer felt sympathy for Lincoln, but could not 'help thinking that the presence of a powerful club like Tottenham will be for the general advantage of the competition'.[117] The *Yorkshire Post* agreed that 'Tottenham always play good football and they will be an attraction wherever they play.'[118]

Although the issuing of circulars provided some clues as to the informal criteria applied to potential applicants, such as population, ground capacity and access to transport nodes, no formal minimum standards were in fact laid down until the 1920s. The catalyst for change was the formation of the Third Division's Northern Section, which was thought to include little-known clubs with unproven track records. As we have already noted, the Management Committee recommended at the 1920 AGM that the Northern Section be delayed for 12 months, since proposed members were 'not strong enough financially or in playing strength'.[119] The Committee put into place a vetting process for all applicants, through a system of ground inspections and questionnaires. Prospective members were required to have dressing rooms, accommodation for match officials and other facilities on their grounds. In addition, the Management Committee sent each candidate a list of questions 'which are so searching as to obtain complete information with reference to applying clubs'. It inquired into the condition and status of the club, its financial position and future prospects, gate money received, and the nature and holding capacity of the ground, enclosures and stands. *Athletic News* advised candidates to add details of the size of the local population and catchment area.[120] Again, in 1924 the Committee examined the credentials of outside applicants and only recommended those it felt reached the necessary standards, but it was not until 1927 that entry qualifications were formalised. Thereafter, applicants were required to supply the Committee with balance sheets for the previous two seasons, details of members and shareholders, average attendances for both first and reserve team fixtures, and particulars of ground capacity, location and dressing-room facilities.[121]

The creation of the Third Division was followed by a period of consolidation, during which the League became the subject of accusations from those outside that their entry was effectively barred. After 1922, the Management Committee agreed to allow each Third Division section to recommend the clubs to be elected, a recommendation which would then 'carry weight with the League in any decisions arrived at'.[122] Invariably, self-protection and group loyalty led to support for retiring members at the expense of outside applicants. In the Northern Section, for example, Barrow finished bottom on four occasions between 1924 and 1930, but were re-elected each time. Sometimes the full members chose to ignore the recommendations, as when Aberdare Athletic was voted out in 1927, but in the main the First and Second Division clubs favoured the status quo. This approach was heavily criticised, notably in *Athletic News*, which accused the League of making itself a 'close corporation' to which 'no outsiders need apply'. In one particularly scathing attack, it condemned the League's 'narrow, unprogressive policy' of re-electing the bottom clubs, thus ruling out 'ambitious centres and possibly stronger centres'.[123] The Management Committee denied any intention of closing the door to aspiring clubs: they 'wanted the strongest competitions, but the clubs of the Third Division should know what was best for themselves'.[124] In 1929, the Third Division's collusive, self-perpetuating policy was exposed by revelations that representatives of the two retiring clubs had been present throughout the Southern Section's private meeting and that the recommendation to the full members was decided not by secret ballot but by a show of hands. Under the circumstances, one non-League club official thought the whole affair 'a waste of time', while *Athletic News* branded such action conservative, selfish and 'all too sentimental'.[125] The so-called 'old pals' act' continued to operate throughout the 1930s, despite *Sporting Chronicle*'s condemnation of the election process as 'a farce'. As a result, only four clubs in the Southern Section and three in the Northern Section lost their places between 1921 and 1939.[126]

The election system assisted the Football League in expanding into hitherto-untouched areas of England and Wales, and while crowds and finance were of great significance, some attention should be given to strategic factors. There is some suggestion that in the 1900s the League, either at Management Committee level or through the collective wishes of the clubs, made a conscious effort to expand into areas previously dominated by professional rugby. Graham Williams has referred to the 'aggressive recruitment' of clubs from rugby strongholds, while Simon Inglis suggested that by 1903 the League had begun plotting 'the colonisation of England at the expense of every rival organisation in both football and rugby'.[127] These comments appear to be supported by the bare facts: Bradford City in 1903, Leeds City and Hull City in 1905, Oldham Athletic and Bradford Park Avenue in 1907 and Huddersfield Town in 1910 all came into the Football League from towns with deep rugby traditions. The two Bradford clubs, and Leeds City, were formed from previous members of the Northern Union, while the others had strong rival Northern Union clubs. Moreover, in each club's application to join the League, much was made of the local competition between the codes. Bradford Park Avenue's representative, for example, supported his claim by declaring that his club's decision to take up soccer 'meant the extinction of Northern Unionism ... in Yorkshire'.[128]

Whether the League had a strategy for extending its sphere of influence into these areas is unclear. In the case of Bradford City, there were suggestions that 'undue influence' had been put on voting clubs by the Management Committee, and the local press was convinced that assurances had been made by the League's rulers to admit City well before the club had been formally constituted.[129] However, it is worth emphasising that the election ballot was the province of the clubs, and that League places were not normally in the Committee's gift. That is not to say that Committee members did not actively canvass on City's behalf. Catton, close to informed opinion in the League, expressed 'a hope in favour of Bradford', a new club which 'seems to have many friends, and I trust their professions will be backed by votes'.[130] The clubs were unlikely to go against such canvassing, since Bradford City was a 'big city' club offering the potential of attractive fixtures and big crowds. Once again, the electorate 'had an eye on the potential offered by rival candidates' when casting their ballots.[131] The fact that clubs controlled the election process was evident in the failed application of the amateur, London-based Argonauts club in 1928. Some five months before the League annual meeting, the club's founder, R. W. Sloley, met the FA secretary Frederick Wall and the League executive to discuss the possible admission of the club. Wall informed Sloley of his belief that the League 'would regard the application favourably', and the Committee itself told him that while 'the matter was one which the Clubs would have to decide ... they would welcome such a club'.[132] In addition, *Athletic News* noted in May that 'an emphatic impression, decidedly favourable to the amateur club, has been created in Football League circles' by Argonauts' decision to play at Wembley Stadium rather than White City.[133] Yet despite this apparent support, Argonauts were defeated by 17 votes in the election ballot.

Similarly, it is doubtful whether the election of clubs from London and Southern England was linked to any broad strategic initiative. Some Management Committee members, and certain club directors, may indeed have wished to establish a broader base for the Football League in the South, but individual enmities and jealousies tended to preclude the achievement of this long-term goal. The pattern of Welsh membership is also better explained by reference to changing economic fortunes than to strategic policy. In 1920, when Cardiff City applied to become the League's first Welsh member, *Athletic News* asked 'why should South

Wales, now a hot-bed of soccer, be outside the pale?'[134] It also noted, more significantly, that Cardiff was a large centre of population, so now – as so often before – geographical expansion chimed in with economic factors. By the early 1920s there were six Welsh clubs in the League drawing relatively good gates, but by the early 1930s severe economic depression and unemployment in the South Wales coalfields had necessitated the replacement of Aberdare Athletic and Merthyr Town and the temporary exclusion of Newport County.[135] Expansion could be assisted by the election process, but only so long as the clubs who held the votes could see economic benefits in choosing a club from a hitherto-untapped area.

* * *

In the course of no more than two decades, the Football League transformed itself from an organisation of professional clubs based mainly in the North-west and Midlands into a national body encompassing an entire Southern division, ten clubs in London and others in Wales. The road to a national league did not consist of a series of ordered steps taken with a clear end in sight. Because there was never a consensus within the Management Committee or among the clubs for expansion, growth was largely piecemeal and ad hoc. Certain periods, particularly the 1890s and early 1900s, and then after the First World War, were marked by expansion that was both quantitative (in terms of increased membership) and qualitative (with members coming in from parts of the country that had not previously boasted a Football League club). Other times were of consolidation, usually marked by allegations from outsiders of a 'closed shop'.

The election system allowed the League to review and modify its membership on an annual basis. The preceding discussion has shown that while guarantees of large crowds and financial stability were the most important criteria for the election of new members (or the retention of existing ones), they were in fact part of a broader collage of interlocking motives and interests that vied for prominence in the minds of club representatives. Above all, it is important to recognise that the League executive did not have the power that North American sports bodies hold, namely to transfer a club to another city when that club had ceased to be a financial benefit to the competition. That said, some of the transfers of membership, particularly during the 1900s, where small town clubs were voted out to make way for those representing big cities, do hint at an informal franchising system, with League membership effectively transferred to clubs with greater economic potential. The fact that the election system remained within the control of the member clubs meant that factors such as local connections and loyalty could, and did, influence voting patterns. However, clubs perceived as being weak in playing or financial terms could only depend on such factors for a short period of time. Clubs understood that their economic interests would only be served by ensuring that their fellow members were able to compete effectively. As in most industries, performance was ultimately what mattered most.

Notes

1 On this, see Mason, *Association Football*; Walvin, *The People's Game*; D. Russell, *Football and the English: A Social History of Association Football in England, 1863–1995*, Preston, Carnegie, 1997, pp. 8–29.

2 T. Mason, 'Football, Sport of the North?' in *Sport and Identity in the North of England*, ed. J. Hill and J. Williams, Keele, Keele University Press, 1996, pp. 41–52.

3 J. Harris, *Private Lives, Public Spirit: A Social History of Britain, 1870–1914*, Oxford, Oxford University Press, 1993, p. 19.

4 See Harris, *Private Lives*, pp. 17–23; D. Read, *The English Provinces, c. 1760–1960: A Study in Influence*, London, Edward Arnold, 1964, Part 5; A. Briggs, *Victorian Cities*, London, Penguin, 1968, p. 48; G. Shaw, 'The Evolution and Impact of Large-Scale Retailing in Britain' in *The Evolution of Retail Systems, c.1800–1914*, ed. J. Benson and G. Shaw, Leicester, Leicester University Press, 1992, pp. 135–65; T. R. Nevett, *Advertising in Britain: A History*, London, Heinemann, 1982, Chapter 5.

5 L. Hannah, *The Rise of the Corporate Economy*, second edition, London, Methuen, 1983, Chapter 1; S. V. Ward, *The Geography of Interwar Britain: The State and Uneven Development*, London, Routledge, 1988, p. 14; B. W. E. Alford, 'New Industries for Old?: British Industry Between the Wars' in *The Economic History of Britain Since 1700, Volume 2: 1860 to the 1970s*, ed. R. Floud and D. McCloskey, Cambridge, Cambridge University Press, 1981, pp. 323–28.

6 McGregor, 'The League and the League System', p. 174; Vamplew, *Pay Up*, p. 125; B. Murray, *Football: A History of the World Game*, Aldershot, Scholar, 1994, p. 38.

7 McGregor, 'The Origin and Future', p. 5.

8 McGregor, 'The League and the League System', p. 171. Tischler, *Footballers*, p. 57, gives examples of the disputes that arose between clubs as a result of fixture problems.

9 McGregor, 'The Origin and Future', p. 2; R. C. Churchill, *English League Football*, p. 15.

10 Tischler, *Footballers*, p. 58; *Athletic News*, 6 January 1908.

11 Tischler, *Footballers*, pp. 57–58.

12 Quoted in Sutcliffe, Brierley and Howarth, *Story of the Football League*, p. 2.

13 See McGregor's comments at the League's 'Coming of Age' Banquet, reported in *Athletic News*, 14 June 1909.

14 *Athletic News*, 12 February 1906. This information comes from James Catton's review of McGregor's 'The Origin and Future'.

15 The original 12 clubs were Accrington, Aston Villa, Blackburn Rovers, Bolton Wanderers, Burnley, Derby County, Everton, Notts County, Preston North End, Stoke,

West Bromwich Albion and Wolverhampton Wanderers.
16 McGregor's obituary in *Birmingham Post*, 21 December 1911.
17 Quoted in Tischler, *Footballers*, p. 59.
18 Sutcliffe, Brierley and Howarth, *Story of the Football League*, pp. 1, 3, 5.
19 *Athletic News*, 23 December 1901.
20 Sutcliffe, Brierley and Howarth, *Story of the Football League*, pp. 4–5.
21 *Athletic News*, 11 January 1909.
22 McGregor, 'The League and the League System', p. 173; P. M. Young, *Football on Merseyside*, London, Stanley Paul, 1963, p. 29. Only three of the founder members – Aston Villa, Blackburn Rovers and West Bromwich Albion – had won the FA Cup prior to 1888.
23 Sutcliffe, Brierley and Howarth, *Story of the Football League*, p. 2; P. M. Young, *Football in Sheffield*, London, Stanley Paul, 1964, p. 57; Churchill, *English League Football*, p. 16.
24 For press reactions to the League's inaugural season, see Tischler, *Footballers*, p. 59.
25 McGregor, 'The *£. s. d.* of Football', p. 62; Arsenal FC (AFC), Catton Folders, E–F, notes for a speech on 'The Football League', n.d., p. 500c.
26 Sutcliffe, Brierley and Howarth, *Story of the Football League*, p. 5.
27 Sutcliffe, Brierley and Howarth, *Story of the Football League*, p. 3.
28 J. A. H. Catton, *The Real Football: A Sketch of the Development of the Association Game*, London, Sands, 1900, p. 85.
29 'Harricus' (A. H. Downs), 'The Football League, 1888–1901', *Athletic News*, 4 February 1901.
30 *Athletic News*, 23 December 1901. As late as 1909, Lewis still distinguished the First Division from the Second by referring to the former as 'the real League'. *Football and Sports Special*, 16 January 1909. Also see the comments of James Catton ('Tityrus') in *Athletic News*, 1 June 1908.
31 Catton, *The Real Football*, p. 88; A. Appleton, *Hotbed of Soccer: The Story of Football in the North East*, London, Rupert Hart-Davis, 1963, pp. 83, 122.
32 Quoted in Sutcliffe, Brierley and Howarth, *Story of the Football League*, p. 77.
33 McGregor, 'The Origin and Future', p. 6.
34 Much of the following is based on Sutcliffe, Brierley and Howarth, *Story of the Football League*, pp. 77–78, and 'Harricus' (A. H. Downs), 'The Football League, 1888–1901', *Athletic News*, 4 February 1901.
35 Catton, *The Real Football*, p. 93.
36 Sutcliffe, Brierley and Howarth, *Story of the Football League*, p. 77.
37 Sutcliffe, Brierley and Howarth, *Story of the Football League*, p. 78.
38 Quoted in Vamplew, *Pay Up*, p. 126.
39 Reports of Football League AGMs in *Athletic News*, 20 May 1901, 2 June 1902.
40 Aston Villa FC (AVFC), Board Minutes, 28 February 1901.
41 Report of Football League AGM in *Athletic News*, 20 May 1901.
42 Clubs were required to compensate their opponents for switching fixture dates (often from Saturdays to Mondays) due to FA Cup ties, which took precedence. Until 1912 there were no fixed regulations for compensation, and so claims were made but generally opposed, leaving the Management Committee to reach a decision. See, for example, AVFC, Board Minutes, 29 March, 19 April 1900.
43 *Athletic News*, 5 June 1905; Sheffield United FC (SUFC), Football Committee Minutes, 11 May 1905.
44 For an example of this view, see Churchill, *English League Football*, pp. 16–17.

45 McGregor, 'The Origin and Future', p. 6.
46 *Athletic News*, 10 December 1906.
47 Quoted in K. Robbins, *Nineteenth-Century Britain: Integration and Diversity*, Oxford, Clarendon, 1988, p. 163.
48 J. Coyle, 'English sports leagues, franchising and the management of expansion: the Football League and the Northern Union up to 1923', unpublished MA dissertation, De Montfort University, 1997, p. 42.
49 J. Bale, *Sport and Place: A Geography of Sport in England, Scotland and Wales*, London, C. Hurst, 1982, p. 28.
50 On the origins and growth of the Southern League, see L. Francis, *Seventy Years of Southern League Football*, London, Pelham, 1969; P. Harrison, *Southern League Football: The First Fifty Years*, Gravesend, self-published, 1989.
51 Coyle, 'English sports leagues', p. 95.
52 See Coyle, 'English sports leagues', pp. 95–101.
53 *Athletic and Sporting Chat*, 9 May 1900; AVFC, Board Minutes, 28 February 1901.
54 *Athletic News*, 20 May 1901.
55 *Athletic News*, 15 March 1909; *Football Chat*, 10 March 1909.
56 *Athletic News*, 22 February 1909.
57 Football League Circular to Clubs, 30 April 1909; *Football Chat*, 21 April 1909.
58 *Athletic News*, 24 April 1905. For similar comments, see *Football Chat*, 12 March 1907.
59 *Football and Sports Special*, 16 January 1909; *Birmingham Sporting Mail*, 17 April 1909.
60 *Football and Sports Special*, 17 April 1909.
61 Report of Football League SGM in *Athletic News*, 3 May 1909.
62 Report of Football League SGM in *Athletic News*, 3 May 1909. See also Henry Norris's comments in *Football Chat*, 7 April 1909.
63 *Football Chat*, 7 April 1909.
64 *Athletic News*, 24 July 1916.
65 Harrison, *Southern League Football*, p. 24.
66 *Athletic News*, 28 July 1919.
67 See Inglis, *League Football*, pp. 113–17.
68 M. Tyler and P. Soar, *Arsenal, 1886–1986: The Official Centenary History of Arsenal Football Club*, London, Hamlyn, 1986, p. 42.
69 Quoted in Coyle, 'English sports leagues', p. 100.
70 *Athletic News*, 17 March 1919.
71 Inglis, *League Football*, p. 121.
72 Report of Football League AGM in *Athletic News*, 7 June 1920.
73 *Athletic News*, 3 May 1920.
74 P. J. Sloane, 'Restriction of Competition in Professional Team Sports', *Bulletin of Economic Research*, Vol. 18, 1976, p. 112; Vamplew, *Pay Up*, p. 112.
75 Tischler, *Footballers*, pp. 81–82.
76 A. J. Arnold, 'Rich Man, Poor Man: Economic Arrangements in the Football League' in *British Football and Social Change: Getting into Europe*, ed. J. Williams and S. Wagg, Leicester, Leicester University Press, 1991, p. 52.
77 Report of Football League AGM in *Athletic News*, 1 June 1903.
78 Reports of Football League AGMs in *Athletic News*, 20 May 1901 and 6 June 1904; G. F. Allison, 'The Rise of Middlesbrough FC' in *Book of Football*, ed. anon, London, Amalgamated Press, 1906.

79 G. Williams, *The Code War: English Football Under the Historical Spotlight*, Harefield, Yore, 1994, p. 176.
80 Football League Minutes, 2 June 1924 (AGM).
81 Oldham Athletic FC (OAFC), Board Minutes, 19 April 1906.
82 OAFC, Board Minutes, 19 April 1906.
83 OAFC, Board Minutes, 11 March 1907; G. Dykes, *Oldham Athletic: A Complete Record, 1899–1988*, Derby, Breedon, 1988; *Athletic News*, 13 May 1907.
84 West Ham United FC (WHUFC), Board Minutes, 25 February 1919.
85 D. Twydell, *Denied FC: The Football League Election Struggles*, Harefield, Yore, 2001, p. 172; *Sporting Chronicle*, 3 June 1935.
86 Suffolk Record Office (SRO), Ipswich Town FC (ITFC), Board Minutes, 2 November 1936.
87 SRO, ITFC, Board Minutes, 5 April 1937; Finance Committee Minutes, 12 June 1937.
88 *Topical Times*, 18 July 1931.
89 *Athletic News*, 31 May 1920.
90 *Football and Sports Special*, 12 June 1909.
91 Allison, 'Rise of Middlesbrough FC', p. 203.
92 SRO, ITFC, Board Minutes, 3 May 1937, 7 June 1938.
93 *Athletic News*, 3 May 1920. The Southern League took a particularly hard line against member clubs that applied to join the Football League. Queen's Park Rangers and Tottenham Hotspur were initially expelled from the former body in 1908 when their applications to the latter failed. Aldershot's 1932 election to the League was tempered by a £500 fine for leaving the Southern League and the London Combination. See Francis, *Seventy Years*, p. 43; *Sporting Chronicle*, 11 April 1932.
94 Report of Football League AGM in *Athletic News*, 5 June 1905; Sutcliffe, Brierley and Howarth, *Story of the Football League*, p. 79.
95 Report of Football League AGM in *Athletic News*, 1 June 1908.
96 SUFC, Football Committee Minutes, 1 June 1920; Football League Minutes, 1 June 1931 (AGM).
97 OAFC, Board Minutes, 10 June 1907. The club paid Burslem Port Vale £1,150 in total, and actually had to take out an overdraft of £400 to do so. Minutes, 12, 13 June 1907.
98 *Manchester Evening News*, 14 June 1907.
99 *Birmingham Sporting Mail*, 20 June 1908. See also the account in J. Holland, *Spurs: A History of Tottenham Hotspur Football Club*, London, Sportsman's Book Club, 1957, pp. 74–75.
100 Williams, *The Code War*, p. 125; D. Twydell, *Rejected FC: Volume 3*, Harefield, Yore, 1992.
101 Report of Football League AGMs in *Athletic News*, 1 June 1903, 1 June 1914.
102 Lincoln City FC Election Circular, quoted in *Athletic News*, 22 May 1911.
103 *The People*, 29 May 1938; Report of Football League AGM in *Sporting Chronicle*, 31 May 1938.
104 Oldham Athletic FC, 'Circular to Clubs in support of Application for Admission to the Football League', April 1907. I would like to thank Garth Dykes for this reference.
105 Huddersfield Town FC election circular, quoted in *Huddersfield Daily Examiner*, 18 April 1910.

106 *Athletic News*, 24 May 1915; 3 March 1919; 1 March 1920.
107 *Athletic News*, 13 October 1919.
108 Darlington FC election circular, quoted in *Athletic News*, 8 May 1911. Darlington was not admitted into the League until 1921 as part of the newly formed Third Division Northern Section.
109 Carlisle United FC and York City FC election circulars, quoted in *Athletic News*, 4 June 1928. York was elected to the Third Division the following season.
110 See P. J. Cain, 'Railways 1870–1914: The Maturity of the Private System' in *Transport in Victorian England*, ed. M. J. Freeman and D. H. Aldcroft, Manchester, Manchester University Press, 1988, pp. 115–18; Football League Handbooks, 1909–10, 1919–20.
111 Report of Football League AGM in *Athletic News*, 5 June 1905; *Athletic News*, 24 April 1905.
112 *Athletic News*, 6 November 1911.
113 See A. J. Arnold, 'The Belated Entry of Professional Soccer into the West Riding of Northern England', *International Journal of the History of Sport*, Vol. 6, 1989, pp. 326–27.
114 Report of Football League AGM in *Athletic News*, 1 June 1908.
115 Tischler, *Footballers*, p. 82.
116 *Athletic News*, 8 July 1908.
117 *Birmingham Sporting Mail*, 4 July 1908.
118 Quoted in G. W. Simmons, *Tottenham Hotspur Football Club: Its Birth and Progress, 1882–1946*, London, Tottenham Hotspur FC, 1947, p. 75.
119 Football League Minutes, 29 May 1920.
120 Football League Minutes, 10 January 1921; *Athletic News*, 17 January 1921.
121 Football League Minutes, 12 May 1924; 8 April 1927 (SGM); Sutcliffe, Brierley and Howarth, *The Story of The Football League*, p. 99.
122 Football League Minutes (Third Division Southern Section SGM), 6 March 1922.
123 *Athletic News*, 4 June 1928; 12 March 1928.
124 Football League Minutes, 30 May 1927 (AGM).
125 *Athletic News*, 20 May 1929.
126 *Sporting Chronicle*, 3, 4 June 1935; 6 June 1939. The clubs were Aberdare (1927), Merthyr (1930), Newport (1931) and Gillingham (1938), and Durham (1928), Ashington (1929) and Nelson (1931).
127 Williams, *The Code War*, p. 125; Inglis, *League Football*, p. 56.
128 *Manchester Evening News*, 31 May 1907.
129 *Athletic News*, 1 June 1903; Arnold, *A Game That Would Pay*, p. 25.
130 'Tityrus' in *Athletic News*, 1 June 1903.
131 Vamplew, *Pay Up*, p. 126.
132 *Athletic News*, 2 January 1928; Football League Minutes, 16 January 1928. Sutcliffe's interpretation of the meeting was slightly different. The Committee, in his view, had informed Sloley that it 'would show no prejudice' against the Argonauts but 'could make no guarantees'. *Topical Times*, 28 January 1928.
133 *Athletic News*, 21 May 1928.
134 *Athletic News*, 1 March 1920.
135 Johnes, *Soccer and Society*; G. Williams, 'From Grand Slam to Great Slump: Economy, Society and Rugby Football in Wales During the Depression', *Welsh History Review*, Vol. 11, 1983, pp. 346–48.

CHAPTER TWO

Governing Football

Many contemporaries were unimpressed by the manner in which professional football in England was governed. An anonymous club director commented in May 1938 that the administration of the elite game was 'not a bit clever', and joked that the Football League's executive body should in future be known as 'the *mis*-management committee'.[1] S. J. de Lotbiniere, meanwhile, the BBC's Director of Outside Broadcasts, was left mystified by his dealings with football officialdom: 'it is difficult to fathom all the complications of League and/or Association permissions' he admitted to League Secretary Fred Howarth in January of the same year.[2] The tendency to confuse one organisation with another or to conflate the game's various power blocs into a single ruling group was a common feature of contemporary accounts. References to football's 'leaders', 'ruling class' and 'establishment' were typical. Similarly, the FA and the Football League were often referred to interchangeably as the game's 'governing body'. Historians, however, need to be more precise. In the rush to contextualise the development of professional sport by relating it to wider trends in society, insufficient attention has been paid to the internal politics which have always existed within and between ruling bodies. Although they may not be particularly glamorous subjects, institutions are undeniably important. Football's power struggles and internal tensions had a crucial bearing on the way both the game itself and its associated culture developed. To understand the emergence of the transfer system, the maximum wage, the offside rule and so forth, we have to be aware of the contrasting functions, interests and ideologies of the FA, the League and the professional clubs. We also need to know something of the individuals who wielded power within these organisations.

This chapter will examine the governance of professional football in England. It starts from the premise that the game was controlled not by a single unified body, but rather by three distinct groups: the FA, the Football League and the professional clubs affiliated to these bodies. As might be expected, relations between these groups were marked by both cooperation and conflict. They were not static, but subject to considerable change over time. In particular, this period witnessed the rise of the Football League's authority in relation to both the FA and the League clubs. By 1939, there was little doubt that the League, through its Management Committee and its officers, had established considerable, if incomplete, control over the professional game.

The FA and the Football League

From a strictly theoretical standpoint, the functions and responsibilities of the Football League and the FA were easy to differentiate. Founded in 1863 – a quarter of a century before the League – the FA was instrumental in codifying and standardising the laws of the game. From its early years it also concerned itself with the development of the national FA Cup competition, established in 1871, and the organisation of the national team. In addition, the FA was responsible for the administration of the game as a whole, from the grassroots of junior, district and county associations through to professional football. Acting as an umbrella body, it authorised competitions and leagues throughout the country, including the Football League. Thus, in theory, the League acted only in accordance with, and under the licence of, the FA, annually applying to the FA Leagues Sanction Committee for permission simply to continue or to alter its constitution. From the start, the FA's position as the supreme football authority in the country was therefore widely recognised: Geoffrey Green has, at different times, called it 'the monarchy' and 'the highest parliament in English football'.[3]

League officials publicly acknowledged the position from the beginning, even if some club directors no doubt harboured private ambitions to wrest control of the professional game from the FA. William McGregor soon realised that 'when the League meet, they are actuated by the interests of the League clubs. The general good of the game is not their chief concern', and hence 'it is best for the whole government of the game to be in the hands of the Football Association'.[4] Another future League president, Charles Sutcliffe, made the point more succinctly: 'In football the FA is omnipotent. It is a dominating, while the League is a subservient, body.' In a separate article he compared the governing powers of the FA to those of the MCC in cricket and the Jockey Club in horse racing.[5] In practice, however, relations were considerably more complex. The respective functions of the two bodies were never delineated at birth nor enshrined in any joint agreement, but remained contingent upon their changing power relations.

Hence, as the League grew in size, prestige and power it became increasingly difficult to avoid conflicts of authority and jurisdiction. Moreover, although the League saw its role as limited to 'look[ing] after its own affairs', this desire for self-government created inevitable contention with the FA, as the bodies shared the membership of clubs and the registration of players.[6] The League's interests also extended beyond its own competition to the FA Cup and the national team, to which it contributed the premier clubs and the majority of players: in fact, after 1920 almost every full England international was employed by a Football League club. By the Second World War, as we can see from Figure 2.1, the League was hardly a subordinate body: it had emerged 'much more in the position of a central control over the business and financial side of football than … the Association'.[7]

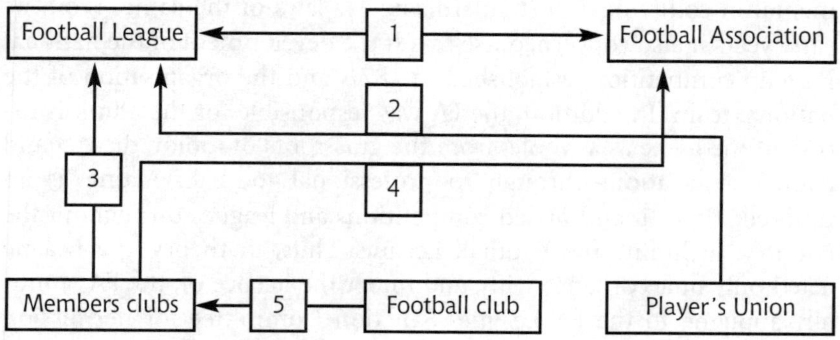

KEY:
1: Contact via the FA Council and joint commissions.
2: No joint consultation body. Contact occurred when disputes arose.
3: Represented through nomination and voting of the Management Committee and direct representation at AGM.
4: Represented through membership of county football associations.
5: Selected through the Football League election system. First and Second Division clubs were full members while Third Division clubs were associate members, with limited rights of voting and representation.

Figure 2.1: Organisational structure of professional football in England, c. 1932

Source: Based on Political and Economic Planning, 'English Professional Football', *Political and Economic Planning*, vol. 32, Appendix 4: Professional Football Organisation Chart, 1966.

Relations between the Football League and the FA in the early twentieth century were fundamentally shaped by the debate over amateur and professional football. Historians have established that the legalisation of professionalism in 1885 was less an attempt by the FA to embrace the phenomenon than to restrain and control it.[8] Stringent birth and residential qualifications were initially imposed on professional players, although these were soon relaxed and by 1889 had been abolished entirely.[9] Yet the FA still intended to 'keep professionalism at arm's length' through the barring of professionals from club or association committees and the inauguration of a separate amateur cup tournament (in 1893).[10] In these circumstances, it is hardly surprising that the Football League was effectively marginalised at first by the governing body. When Charles Alcock, an old Harrovian and Secretary of Surrey County Cricket Club as well as the FA, published his *Football Annual* for 1890, the League merited only a paragraph of copy along with the final championship table. In contrast, the activities of the provincial associations occupied 27 pages, while results and descriptions of public school football and rugby took a full 30 pages. Although he recognised that the league system was 'not without its advantages', Alcock warned that 'if carried to excess, as it undoubtedly is in many parts, [it] is calculated to do harm to, rather than benefit the game'.[11]

The struggle over professionalism, and the establishment of the Football League as its monument, created deep divisions within the amateur elite that ran the FA, leading in 1890 to the resignation of the Old Etonian President Major Marindin and five vice-presidents from Southern amateur clubs in reaction to the aforementioned abolition of the 'stringent conditions' on professionals. Equally, representatives of the League clubs were more numerous and prominent on the FA Council by the mid-1890s.[12] Despite this, the amateur–professional tensions did not disappear with the arrival of Northern administrators like Chairman Charles Clegg, a Sheffield solicitor, and Birmingham's Charles Crump at the higher echelons of the FA. In fact, Clegg and Crump differed from those they replaced in terms of tactics rather than sentiment. They were still amateurs first and foremost, but were prepared to tolerate the Football League providing that it recognised its inferior status and subordinated itself to the FA's absolute rule.

A perfect illustration of the contrasting League and FA conceptions of the professional side of football can be derived from the crisis precipitated by Queen Victoria's death in January 1901. On hearing of the monarch's passing, the FA Emergency Committee, consisting of Clegg, Crump and Alcock, unilaterally postponed the following Saturday's FA Cup first-round ties. This action was greeted with almost unanimous criticism from the League Management Committee and club directors, partly because it meant that two sets of gate receipts would be lost as the Queen's funeral was to take place the following Saturday, but more significantly because the decision had been taken without consulting the League. President John Bentley felt that a decision that affected thousands of spectators, hundreds of players and the finances of scores of professional clubs 'ought to have been left to … a more representative body than the Emergency Committee, who have little or no connection with club management and consequently hardly realise what it means'.[13] In a letter to *Athletic News*, Committeeman Charles Sutcliffe objected to the fact that the Football League, 'consisting of 26 of the 32 clubs in the ties, were not consulted upon the most important and far-reaching resolution passed for many years'. While he was 'not jealous of the FA', Sutcliffe believed that the League was 'sufficiently important … to entitle them to some respect, consideration, and even deference'.[14] What is more, it appears that dissatisfaction among League clubs over their treatment at the hands of the FA was spilling over into serious consideration of mass secession. For 'Grasshopper', the cup-tie debacle showed 'more plainly than ever the necessity of a separate government being acquired for the professional branch of the game'.[15] There was talk in League circles of a clique within the FA Council intent on 'being antagonistic to the professional clubs'. The journalist and former Bolton Secretary Harry Downs was in no doubt that the two bodies were 'slowly and gradually drifting apart' and that a split in the near future was likely.[16]

Sutcliffe's retrospective account of his early years as a member of the Management Committee is particularly revealing of the mutual distrust between the League and FA around the turn of the century. He remembered that a prominent FA councillor had encouraged him to reform the League's executive body, because 'The FA has no love for the Management Committee of the League. It is no credit to the game.' He went on to describe the League's attitude towards the FA:

> I found a bitter feeling not merely amongst many members of the … Management Committee but among many clubs against the FA… The League was face to face with a supercilious autocratic bearing on the part of some members of the Council of the FA that was obnoxious. The League was regarded as of no moment in football. As the mainstay of the system of professionalism in football it was looked upon as corrupt and degrading. The professional element of the FA was too easily outvoted and overridden by the amateur element. The vote and influence of minor county associations who knew nothing of the then requirements of spectacular and popular football governed the game. These things rankled in the minds of the League clubs and the League Committeemen.[17]

Before 1910, the main conflict between League and FA centred on the financial arrangements between clubs and players. The retain-and-transfer system had been a particular bone of contention since the early 1890s. In 1894 the FA attempted to abolish transfer payments altogether, while five years later Clegg was behind another unsuccessful attempt to prohibit the 'objectionable system' of buying and selling players. The Management Committee opposed both recommendations on the grounds that richer clubs would be able to acquire the best talent without the necessity of compensating the clubs losing the players' services.[18] Yet the issue was really one of power and control. The League was anxious to ensure autonomy in what it considered to be its own affairs. The questions of transfers, wages, bonuses and all matters of finance should 'be the concern solely of the League'.[19] As Bentley noted, 'The serious battle will be fought on what the League considers a principle, and that is being allowed to work out its own particular competition in its own particular way whilst at the same time observing the rules of the parent body'.[20] The FA also took steps to regulate the payment of players. The League had attempted to impose its own wage limit in 1893, but it was left to the FA in 1900 to introduce a maximum wage of £4 per week (£208 per annum) and to ban the payment of bonuses for wins and draws. The measure did receive significant support from some League officials and club directors, but opponents of the rule argued that it gave the amateurs of the FA unwarranted control over the private affairs of League clubs. Aston Villa's Fred Rinder believed that 'the Association should not interfere with the internal finances of the clubs, but simply devote itself to making laws and seeing that … contracts entered into between clubs and players were loyally complied with'.[21]

The accounts of both Geoffrey Green and Charles Sutcliffe place considerable emphasis on the so-called breakthrough of 1904, when the FA finally agreed that the responsibility for financial dealings between clubs should rest with the Football League. Henceforth, the FA was to restrict itself to the role of arbiter between the club and player and to detect sharp practice by clubs. It is difficult, however, to identify any obvious shift in relations between the two bodies after 1904. The decision seems to have been informal and un-minuted, and whether it really represented a 'vital change' in FA policy, as Green has claimed, is a matter for conjecture.[22] Although it may have been more cautious and conciliatory than before, the FA continued in its attempts to intervene in the operation of the transfer system and the remuneration of players. E. L. Holland made two unsuccessful proposals to the Council in 1904 aimed at amending what he regarded as the unsatisfactory 'regulations and conditions affecting the employment of professional players'.[23] The following year, recommendations by Alcock and G. S. Sherrington of the Suffolk FA to wipe the wage and bonus regulations from the rule book, and then by the Rules Revision Committee to introduce a sliding scale of wages based on service and seniority, were similarly rejected. Sherrington's idea for a £350 ceiling on transfer fees was passed, but when the rule came into effect three years later it was easily evaded and lasted only three months.[24]

The FA made one final effort during the summer of 1908 to bring the League clubs into line when it offered an amnesty for previous breaches on the condition that they observed the rules and reported suspected misdemeanours in the future. It was not until the following February that the offer was collectively accepted by the clubs, although the League assured the governing body that it knew nothing of alleged abuses of transfer allegations.[25] Yet despite the formal declarations of solidarity and cooperation, relations had almost reached breaking point. A meeting of League clubs in September 1908 actually considered the possibility of seceding from the governing body if their proposals to allow player bonuses for wins and draws were not met. Fulham's Chairman Henry Norris similarly suggested that as many as 20 League members were prepared to break away from the FA if their attempts to remove wage restrictions proved unsuccessful at the 1909 annual meeting.[26] Indeed, by this stage the FA faced League hostility on at least two fronts: from the richer and more successful clubs who wanted to wipe away all laws relating to the financial nexus between employers and employees, and from the weaker members and League officials who considered the FA to be applying its rules half-heartedly and allowing offenders to break regulations almost at will.

The weight of these criticisms, buttressed by a particularly bitter annual meeting in 1909, finally persuaded the FA to formalise its 1904 decision by passing over the responsibility for club finances to the League in early 1910. The influence of Clegg was undoubtedly central to this decision. It is significant that at the 1908 annual meeting it was the FA Council itself, with Clegg as its spokesman, which proposed the deletion of the maximum wage rule. The proposal failed, but the following year the FA chairman tried again. Clegg's principal argument touched upon the previous assertions of Rinder and others that the FA was not the appropriate body to deal with issues of this kind:

> The majority of clubs and players throughout the country were not personally concerned in those [wage and bonus] regulations. Why should members of the Council be troubled over

> them?… Those who were involved in the financial matters were surely the best persons to make the necessary arrangements for protecting their own interests… The Council wished to leave each section free to control money matters in accordance with their own desires.[27]

The opposition of the pro-wage-limit members was sufficient to bring about a narrow defeat of the FA's motion, but by the end of the year definite steps had been taken to settle the question. On 10 January 1910, the FA issued a circular signalling its intention to delete all its rules relating to the financial arrangements between clubs and players, with the exception of the maximum wage, on the grounds that such concerns were 'incompatible with the position of the Football Association as the governing body of a national sport'.[28] This was finally achieved at an extraordinary general meeting in April. As commentators were quick to recognise, administrative power in the professional game had now shifted significantly from the FA to the League.[29]

1910 represented a crucial turning point in relations between the two bodies. At the Football League's 'Coming of Age' banquet in June 1909, FA Vice-President Charles Crump had differentiated between the FA as a magisterial body and the League as a body of entertainers: 'The duty of the Association was legislative and administrative, and the duty of the League was to provide attractive football for the country.'[30] Such a distinction could hardly be justified after 1910. The Management Committee's newly-defined authority over the financial dealings of its clubs heralded a burst of activity aimed at detecting breaches of rule.[31] Yet there still remained a certain amount of confusion over the respective duties of the League and FA in relation to misconduct and breaches of rule by clubs, officials and players. As many cases affected both League and FA rules, the matter of jurisdiction was a complex one. Writing in January 1911, Sutcliffe attempted to clarify the situation by distinguishing between complaints against League clubs which pertained only to the League competition and rules, and those which affected 'the game in general, its character and good name'. He suggested that the latter should be investigated either by the FA alone, or by a joint commission. This was not just because the FA had wider powers of inquiry, but also because it could call upon a

> more complete machinery for these investigations. The League has no Emergency Committee, and the Management Committee only meets monthly. The President has no special executive powers… The FA has long been the great judicial power in foot-

> ball, and its rules have been gradually built up to answer all the requirements suggested by long experience.[32]

The common practice before this time had been for an FA commission to pass sentence and for the League subsequently to consider any breaches of its own rules. There are some examples of joint FA–League commissions, such as that established to consider the reconstruction of Newton Heath as Manchester United in 1902, but these were comparatively rare and were always established on the initiative of the governing body so as to facilitate its investigation.[33] However, in 1905, following Alf Common's sensational £1,000 transfer from Sunderland to Middlesbrough, the League Management Committee decided to instigate its own inquiry independently of the FA and, a year later, another League commission investigating irregular transfers to the Middlesbrough club effectively reversed the situation by uncovering and reporting a number of breaches of FA rules.[34] It appears that even club officials were unsure where one body's jurisdiction ended and the other's began: Manchester City in 1906 and Sheffield United in 1911 were both censured by the League for reporting complaints over transfers to the FA Secretary instead of the Management Committee.[35]

A formal decision was obviously necessary, and this was reached in December 1911. Firstly, the distinction advocated by Sutcliffe months earlier was formalised by allowing the FA 'full authority' to inquire into suspected breaches of its rules relating to all affiliated clubs and registered players, but giving the junior body power whenever possible to deal independently with 'Money claims between Clubs belonging to the Football League in League matters'. Secondly, the agreement established 'a general principle in the problem of joint discipline': henceforth, any FA commission investigating a League club was to include members of the Management Committee who were also FA Councillors.[36] Indeed, from this point onwards the concept of joint investigations and administrative cooperation became established practice over a range of issues. In 1912 the Management Committee accepted that joint FA–League commissions 'should have full power to act on behalf of the Football League' and, over the next ten years or so, such commissions dealt with questions involving the Players' Union, the illegal approaching of players, match-fixing, bribery and even regulations affecting club shareholders.[37] Even in cases where the League was not officially involved, the FA would forward its report to Preston, and the Management Committee would decide whether to punish offenders on the basis of the FA's conclusions.[38] Green is right to suggest that after 1911, the League tended not to undertake independent full-scale inquiries, even if it continued to look into matters of a financial nature within its membership.[39] In this area, as perhaps in no other, relations between the two bodies were necessarily close.

The inter-war period witnessed a considerable strengthening of the position of the Football League within the FA's own administrative structure. From the League's inception, many of its officials and committeemen were also FA Councillors, although significantly they were elected via their local football associations or regional divisions rather than through any connection with the League. As it grew in size and significance, the League argued that it should have a more permanent influence on the decision making of the FA and, for this reason, League president John Bentley was nominated in 1902 as an FA Vice-President. At the annual meeting, Tom Sidney, the Staffordshire delegate and League Vice-President, suggested that 'as the Football League, directly and indirectly, had really been the means of the Association occupying its present commanding position, the League should be honoured by their President becoming an officer of the Association'. Bentley lost the vote narrowly, mainly as a result of opposition from the amateur clubs and county associations: in fact, one reporter commented that the contest was not 'one of League v. Association, but rather of professionalism v. amateurism'.[40] Nevertheless, three years later the articles of association were changed specifically so as to allow his admittance as an additional Vice-President.[41] Equally, the influence of League committeemen on the standing committees of the FA increased steadily. By the 1920s, Preston could call on at least one representative on the most important committees. As an officer of the FA, the League President was in a particularly good position to influence policy and decision making. From the 1919–20 season onwards, for instance, John McKenna was appointed to the Consultative, Finance, International Selection, Leagues Sanction and Appeals Committees, and additionally took the vacant place on the International Football Association Board, which was responsible for coordinating the actions of each FA in the UK, as well as proposing changes in the laws of the game.[42] By the mid-1920s, McKenna had also become a member of perhaps the most exclusive and powerful FA subgroup: the Emergency Committee, which controlled the Association's business (in conjunction with the Secretary) between meetings of the Council.

Yet what the League really wanted was direct representation on the Council similar to that enjoyed by distinct interest groups like the army, the public schools and Oxford and Cambridge universities. While it could be claimed that those Management Committee members on the legislative body of the FA were League representatives first and foremost, technically they remained attached to their particular club or association. Even as a Vice-President, McKenna was linked officially with Liverpool FC, while Sutcliffe and John Lewis nominally represented Rawtenstall and the Lancashire FA respectively. Yet it was not until April 1929 that the Management Committee resolved to tackle the issue. It circularised its clubs to elicit opinion on the degree of representation it should agitate for, and organised a conference with the FA Council to discuss the whole question.[43] The request was supported by the now-familiar argument that 'the income of the Football Association depended largely upon the Cup ties in which the League clubs took part' and that 'the League contributed all the players in the international matches not only for England, but practically all for Wales and many for Scotland and Ireland'.[44] As it happened, the FA took little persuading, allowing the League four seats on the Council by right and a free choice of its own representatives. A year later, League representation was increased to eight, which meant that the entire Management Committee automatically became members of the Council.[45] Although there is some dispute over its precise implications, this was unquestionably a significant step for the Football League. A later League Secretary, Alan Hardaker, has argued that the move was a clever ploy by the FA to divide the loyalties of committeemen, but Simon Inglis is more convincing in his view that this rule change 'made the League the single most powerful group in the FA' and tied the administration of the two bodies closer together than ever before.[46] The evidence points strongly to the enhancement rather than the diminishment of League power as a result of its new status, and there is certainly little doubt that the policy process and internal functioning of the FA was increasingly subject to League input from this point onwards.

The Football League: structure and organisation

So far, we have noted the central position established by the Football League in the organisation of professional football in England, symbolised above all by its significant representation on the FA Council. By the 1930s at least, and possibly as early as 1910, the Football League had established its hegemony over the management of the elite professional game. Most commentators perceived the administrative relationship between the two bodies as one based on parity rather than hierarchy. In this respect, the structure of English football was markedly different from other sports and other countries, where the functions of governing body and national league organiser were usually combined. As far as the professional side of the sport was concerned, the League stood alongside the FA at the peak of the football hierarchy (see Figure 2.1).

In its organisation, structure and internal dynamics, the Football League resembled many voluntary clubs and associations of this and earlier periods. If not strictly a private members' club like cricket's MCC, it nonetheless retained an exclusivity in its membership and a secrecy in its operations which had much in common with the nascent societies of the seventeenth and eighteenth centuries and the middle-class sporting clubs of the late Victorian years.[47] The League was one of those national associations which came to develop what Jeffrey Hill has called 'a club ethos' due to its 'lengthy existence and the limited circulation of personnel among [its] leading officials'.[48] Yet its founders and officers also promoted it as a fundamentally meritocratic and democratic body. Any club or club official could become a member so long as the required standard was reached; excellence rather than status was the criteria for entry. Unlike the FA, which was perceived as representing various power blocs within the English ruling class, the League liked to see itself as above privilege and open to all. As Charles Sutcliffe observed in 1934, the members of the governing body 'were the aristocrats of the game, we the democrats'.[49] In this respect, the Football League exhibited the same 'peculiar mixture of oligarchy with apparent democracy' characteristic of both late Victorian urban political societies and bourgeois sporting associations.[50]

The two main actors within the decision-making environment were the member clubs (under the collective guise of the General Committee) and the Management Committee. The first official set of rules from 1888–89 defined the system of control clearly. The central legislative body, the General Committee, consisted of a representative of each club who, in turn, elected the Chairman, Treasurer, Secretary and Management Committee. The latter was given the task of appointing match officials, dealing with infringements of League rules and, more generally, conducting 'the business of the League'.[51] So the Management Committee acted as executive and judiciary to the General Committee's legislature. Yet, initially at least, the activities of the Management Committee were rather haphazard and its relationship with the clubs confused. In particular, clubs seemed reluctant to distance themselves from direct control over the management of the League, regularly calling general meetings to discuss minor issues and individual breaches of rules. For example, during the League's second season the question of fog-affected matches was believed to be 'of too important a character to be considered by the Management Committee' and was left over for the clubs to decide upon. The conduct of players on the pitch was also initially dealt with by an unwieldy conference of all member clubs.[52]

Nevertheless, by the start of the twentieth century the fundamental division of authority within the League structure was widely acknowledged: while the clubs made the rules, the Management Committee administered them. Any suggestion that the latter should take the initiative in framing and altering rules was strongly rebuffed.[53] In practice, however, as the status of the Management Committee improved and the clubs grew confident enough to delegate certain powers, so the Committee became more influential in rule making. By about 1910 it had become the leading figure in this area, with any revision of rules requiring either its support or sanction. At the 1912 annual meeting, for instance, the Committee's recommendations for the payment of compensation for postponed matches were carried ahead of counter-proposals from Hull City and Middlesbrough. Proposals brought forward independently by clubs – such as Derby County's regular attempts to increase the number of relegated and promoted clubs from two to four, and Arsenal's proposals for a limit on transfer fees in the 1920s – were invariably defeated, as they were perceived as lacking official approval.[54] Until the 1930s, the Management Committee's legislative role was legitimised by convention rather than any constitutional right. Only retrospectively was it formally given the discretion 'to submit any alteration of Rule thought desirable'.[55]

The most important event in the legislative calendar was the annual general meeting, held in May or June each year in London, generally during the same week as the FA annual meeting. As with any limited company, it involved the presentation of the balance sheet and the annual report to the member clubs (the shareholders).[56] More importantly, it was also the occasion for the election of clubs and officials, and the alteration or addition of rules. As with the election process for clubs discussed in Chapter 1, the system tended towards conservatism. This was not least because changes in the League's constitution or rules required a three-quarters majority. Committeeman John Lewis complained in 1902 that this precluded experimentation, as 'at most annual meetings of the League the majority of proposals fall to the ground'.[57] Representation and voting were initially based on broadly egalitarian principles. Until 1920, clubs in all divisions were entitled to attend and vote at any League meeting, but the newly formed Third Division Northern and Southern Sections were only granted the status of associate members, without voting rights or automatic representation at meetings. Not until 1929 were they given even minimal representation, and then only two votes per section.

As we have established, the Management Committee was effectively the executive body of the League. The original Committee was made up of just five members, including a Chairman, Secretary and Treasurer, but by 1893 it had been reorganised to consist of a President, two Vice-Presidents and a general committee of four. At this point, each division was represented by two committee members, and separate meetings of the divisional bodies were held, but in 1909 the divisional distinction was abolished and club representation as a whole extended to six. In addition, the League's founder, William McGregor, had become a Life Member of the League in 1902, with the power to attend and vote at Management Committee meetings. Following McGregor's death in 1911, former President John Bentley took a similar position until he too died in 1918, after which the Committee reverted to nine permanent members. Until 1917 the Committee was elected annually, but thereafter half the members and the Senior Vice-President were elected together with the President one year, and the other half with the Junior Vice-President the next. This certainly ensured a great deal of continuity in the Committee's personnel, a situation aided by the fact that there were no restrictions on the time a member could spend on the Committee, despite a proposal by West Bromwich Albion that a committeeman should hold office for only two years. Clubs rarely voted individuals off the Committee: only six suffered this fate between 1900 and 1939, and two of these regained their places within a year. Indeed, some committeemen kept their places for over 30 years, long after they had ceased to be actively connected with their clubs.[58] Only death, or possibly retirement, it seems, could change the complexion of the League executive. For much of the period, and especially between the wars, the League was dominated by elderly officials with long voluntary careers in local and national football administration behind them. One newspaper's jibe in 1933 at the conservatism of these 'football septuagenarians' was not far from the truth: two of the Committee were in their seventies at the time, while the vast majority were over sixty.[59] In this sense, the administration of the elite game was not dissimilar from the 'middle-class gerontocracy' that controlled junior football at the same time.[60] It was therefore considered particularly apt that Arthur Dickinson should die only half an hour before a Management Committee meeting after 20 years on the executive. As the League's own memorial noted, 'Mr Dickinson could be said to have grown up with the League; he had spent a lifetime in the game and grown old in its service'.[61]

Press criticism often focused on the conservatism of the Football League in terms of both structure and personnel. Following the rejection of a raft of new proposals at the 1933 annual meeting, a *Sporting Chronicle* correspondent called for 'an infusion of strong young blood' to replace the 'grand old men' of the Committee. He went on: 'Election to high places seems a "lifetime job", as closely guarded as the closest corporation. To oppose a retiring member smacks of disloyalty in official eyes and minds.'[62] Loyalty and service to the League were certainly highly valued and, in common with other such organisations, recognised through a formal 'honours' system of long-service medals, life membership caskets and other titles and related insignia that helped to create an integrative understanding of 'tradition' within the League.[63] The founders of the League, particularly the 'father', William McGregor, were central to how the organisation portrayed and defined itself. Portraits of past Presidents hung in its committee rooms along with photographs of Management Committees over the years, emphasising not only the League's solidarity 'but also its institutional heritage and permanence'.[64] Tradition and heritage were naturally equated here with experience and stability. In an environment where seniority and service to the League were the main criteria for holding office, there was limited opportunity to challenge the control of 'grand old men' such as John Lewis, John McKenna and Charles Sutcliffe.

Committee members were also expected to be loyal to the League in preference to the wishes of their clubs or other associations. When this position was compromised, or a member became involved in a potential scandal, it was assumed that he would resign immediately. It was surely no coincidence, for instance, that in 1910 John Bentley offered his resignation as President (as well as FA Vice-President) shortly after his position at Manchester United, and the club's general finances, had been subjected to an investigation by the governing body.[65] At that year's annual meeting, he noted that there was 'considerably more opposition than usual' to his presidency, and cited the influence of medical problems 'and other things' for his decision to retire.[66] Likewise, in 1927 when Arsenal was fined for breaches of League and FA rules, and Chairman Sir Henry Norris suspended for financial irregularities, William Hall, Norris's right-hand man and the club's representative on the Management Committee, resigned his place immediately.[67] It was crucial to the executive that it should be seen as an independent and respectable body of administrators whose hands had not been sullied by any serious involvement in rule breaking.

Under the League's written rules and by convention, the Management Committee enjoyed a fairly broad scope of control and a wide range of functions. Its prescribed duties remained remarkably consistent throughout the period: to govern and conduct the business of the League, and deal 'as they may think fit' with offences or any matters not specified in the rules.[68] In practice, these functions fell into five main categories. Firstly, the Committee penalised clubs and players for breaching League rules. Clubs could be fined for anything from minor infringements, like the failure to return forms or late payment of the League levy, to more serious matters, such as late kick-offs, fielding weak teams or illegal payments to players. Likewise, players were suspended for breaking their agreements through insubordination, betting, breaching training rules and the like.[69] Secondly, it arbitrated in disputes betwen member clubs and between clubs and players. Certain meetings were set aside specifically to deal with these problems, prompting Bentley to observe that in such cases the Committee was transformed into something akin to a County Court.[70] Dissatisfied parties could also appeal against the Committee's decision to the Board of Appeal, an independent body consisting of three FA councillors. Thirdly, as previously mentioned, the Committee gradually became involved in drafting new rules, altering existing ones and, through circulars to its members, obtaining a collective League opinion on important legislative matters without calling a general meeting. Linked to this, the Committee also had an important advisory role. As well as providing guidance on fundamental issues of policy, it was expected to advise clubs privately on individual matters relating, for example, to players' agreements, the insurance of players or the use of grounds for non-football-related activities.[71] Finally, the Committee acted for its member clubs in negotiations at a wider level. This included not only a mandate to reach agreement with other football associations and leagues, but also to lobby railway companies, tax officials and even government departments in order to secure the best possible terms and conditions for its members.[72]

The highest and most prestigious office in the Football League was that of President. Initially the position carried little formal authority. Only in 1893 was the President, previously known as the Chairman, given the right to vote at all meetings and ex officio membership of all committees. As in many organisations, however, authority derived as much from force of personality and length of tenure as from any prescribed duties. As Table 2.1 indicates, the presidents during this period remained in office for a considerable time: Bentley completed 16 years, McKenna a remarkable 26. What is more, his election was generally unopposed and his authority rarely challenged at annual meetings. When George Leavey of Arsenal was nominated to challenge Bentley in

1904, it was viewed by League representatives and the press as an act of disloyalty. He was convincingly beaten by 34 votes to four, and lost his place on the Management Committee.[73] In contrast with the MCC, whose President could hold office for only one year, the League presidency was conceived as a long-term, even permanent, position. In 1931 McKenna was persuaded by a 'strong appeal' from the member clubs to continue as President following his decision to stand down after 21 years in the post; in the event, he remained as President until his death five years later.[74] Stability and continuity were clearly prized here above any aspirations to open democracy.

Table 2.1: Presidents and Secretaries of the Football League, 1888–1939

	President	*Club*		*Secretary*
1892–94	William McGregor	Aston Villa	1888–1902	Harry Lockett
1894–1910	John Bentley	Bolton Wanderers and Manchester United	1902–33	Tom Charnley
1910–36	John McKenna	Liverpool	1933–56	Fred Howarth
1936–39	Charles Sutcliffe	(Burnley)		
1939–49	William Cuff	Everton		

Note: Club in brackets indicates that the President had ceased formal administrative links.

The President was expected to be active in the formulation of policy and the general running of the League. McKenna, for instance, was a member of all but one of the League's permanent sub-committees, as well as being honorary treasurer from 1912 onwards. During the war he also chaired the sub-committee of the Lancashire Section, and was instrumental in organising the Relief Fund for clubs in addition to his regular duties.[75] This is not to say that the President was necessarily an autocratic or even a dominant figure. By contrast with the control allegedly exercised by Charles Clegg over the FA Council, the League President's powers appear relatively limited.[76] Just as important was the latter's role as spokesman and figurehead of the League. At official dinners, banquets and luncheons, the President represented and effectively spoke for the League as a whole. On behalf of the League he attended the celebrations of championship and cup winners, and the funerals of leading figures and associates in the football world. Indeed, ceremonial duties were perhaps the most time-consuming part of the President's job. The opening of new stands was one such duty, and a regular occurrence. For example, McKenna was asked by West Ham United to formally open its new stand on 29 August 1925, but had to decline as he was engaged at Portsmouth on the same day. Two weeks later he opened a new stand at Wolverhampton Wanderers.[77] The visit to Wolverhampton indicates the symbolic importance attached to the presidency. McKenna and two Management Committee colleagues were invited to the official luncheon, and greeted with a scoreboard display announcing 'A Hearty Welcome to the President and all the League officials'. The club programme joined the celebrations by declaring that 'the opening of the stand has been associated with a ceremony such as most Clubs crave but few are privileged to cater for'.[78] In some respects these sentiments were akin to those normally reserved for royal visits, and the presence of League dignitaries may have served a similar function. Ceremonial occasions of this type could be as important in the comparatively private world of football as in the public life of the industrial city, where processions, banquets and 'centipedic funerals' simultaneously provided opportunities for the expression of civic identities and the 'symbolic display of leadership and authority'.[79]

The Secretary was at the administrative core of the League's operations. In common with those of the Management Committee and the President, the Secretary's powers widened as the League grew. Initially he was required only to 'conduct the correspondence of the League', but by 1892 the office had been amalgamated with that of Treasurer and the Secretary became a paid official of the League.[80] He thus became formally responsible for the League's finances and the general supervision of administrative operations at its headquarters. In addition, regulations precluded him from voting at meetings or retaining any official or unofficial connections with member clubs. It was not until Tom Charnley took over as Secretary in 1902, however, that the position became full-time and the League acquired a permanent office, rather than being run from the Secretary's private address. Charnley's predecessor Harry Lockett had attempted to run his own printing company at the same time as being League Secretary. As Inglis has revealed, this proved impossible, and Lockett was forced to resign after admitting embezzling League funds to aid the expansion of his business.[81] Despite a suggestion that the League's headquarters should be in Manchester, the first office was situated at Winckley Street in Charnley's native Preston. It remained here throughout the period, moving to Tithebarn Street in 1905, to Castle Chambers in 1913 and then to an address in Winckley Square in November 1926.[82]

As the amount of work involved in running the day-to-day affairs of the League increased, so it became necessary to enlarge the administrative staff. With Charnley's appointment the League took on an office worker, Harry Downs, who had been Bentley's assistant and then

Secretary at Bolton Wanderers. By 1920 it had become necessary to take on an Assistant Secretary, and rather than advertising the post, Charnley appointed his son-in-law Fred Howarth. Indeed, the League office remained almost entirely the preserve of the Charnley–Howarth family. Tom Charnley junior, a director of Preston North End and Charnley's nephew, joined the staff in 1930 and became Assistant Secretary on his uncle's retirement, while Fred Howarth's nephew Eric was employed as a clerk from 1934.[83] In this context, it is hardly surprising that the fourth Secretary, Alan Hardaker, considered on his arrival in 1951 that the League 'had been a family business for half a century'.[84]

Although the Secretary had no formal power to direct League policy, he could have some influence in the decision-making process. The position entailed much more than simply drafting the minutes and balancing the books. Howarth, in particular, was fairly outspoken on certain matters of policy, particularly the maximum wage, which he defended vehemently against its critics. He was also instrumental in the League's ill-fated attempt to destroy the pools companies in 1936, and in the establishment and administration of the Jubilee Fund from 1938.[85] Moreover, as the only official involved with the League's business on a daily basis, the Secretary effectively controlled the flow of information to and from the League office. All inquiries from clubs, players, the FA and the press were dealt with initially by him. On significant matters of policy he was instructed by the Management Committee, but he was still allowed a certain amount of discretion and flexibility in issuing circulars, replying to correspondence and dealing with other matters arising between Committee meetings. In fact, as Hardaker's autobiography indicates, it was even possible for the Secretary to manipulate the agenda and records of Management Committee meetings. Howarth allegedly removed from the official minutes any business, even resolutions, with which he disagreed, and would also collect the members' private notes at the end of each meeting. According to this account, Howarth was able to dominate the Management Committee: 'If Fred Howarth did not like an idea it was never implemented – or even recorded'.[86]

Football men: the collective culture of the Management Committee

In most respects, those who ran the Football League were not extraordinary men. Drawn mainly from the ranks of the provincial professional and managerial classes, they enjoyed neither great wealth nor particular notoriety. For the most part their achievements were made in the closed worlds of committee and annual general meetings, but their decisions determined the way in which the League specifically, and professional football generally, developed in England and beyond. While it is hardly surprising that these men are less well known than the great players, managers or even directors of the period, the neglect of the administrators and legislators is undoubtedly a major omission in the historiography of the English professional game. Football history may not have had an equivalent figure to the great baseball commissioner Judge Kenesaw Mountain Landis, but in this period, at least, Charles Sutcliffe arguably carved out for himself a similarly central governing role. This section will look in more detail at the men who controlled the League through a social and cultural profile of the Management Committee and its leading figures.

A natural starting-point is to consider the occupations of the committeemen. From 1900 to 1939 inclusive, 31 men served on the Committee, and there were four Presidents. As the Appendix shows, membership was confined exclusively to the broad categories of higher professionals, employers and managers.[87] More specifically, the Committee was dominated by small businessmen, local government officials and, most numerous of all, solicitors. Taken together, these groups made up over two-thirds of the total membership during this period. Manual workers and clerks, both of whom were fairly influential in the early development of professional clubs and on club directorships in general, were not represented at all on the Management Committee.[88] Large manufacturers and employers were similarly less prepared to become League committeemen on top of being club directors, and even if they did, they rarely sought higher office as Vice-President or President. Indeed, it is noticeable that none of the most prominent and wealthy club owners made any attempt to gain election to the Committee. For men like building contractor Harry Mears at Chelsea, the brewer J. H. Davies at Manchester United, the politicians Samuel Hill at Glossop and Henry Norris at Fulham and Arsenal, and the mill-owning Crowthers at Huddersfield Town, it would seem that the community prestige or psychic income to be gained from patronage of the local club could hardly be replicated by a place on the Management Committee.[89]

The work of historians on the occupational composition of club directorates provides a useful comparison. On the period before 1914, Mason, Tischler and Vamplew have all emphasised the predominance, both numerically and financially, of manufacturers, traders and those involved in commerce.[90] There seems to have been little change between the wars, although no comprehensive studies of this period have been made. Ross McKibbin has argued that football directors were 'characteristic of the inter-war provincial middle classes, often Freemasons, usually smallish successful businessmen'.[91] Local industrialists controlled the boards of the Sheffield clubs, making up as much as 55 per cent of the total, while at West Ham United and the two Bradford clubs employers and proprietors similarly represented almost half the directorates.[92] As League committeemen were drawn from this pool of club directors, we can hardly be surprised at the similarities in composition. Yet joining the executive of a national league was not the same as becoming a director of a local club. The distinction becomes clearer if we consider the relatively high proportion of managers and administrators on the Management Committee. Clearly, management positions in local government or business demanded the same type of organisational skills and experience of committee work as was required for the League. It is also likely that such occupations allowed greater flexibility to travel long distances to committee or sub-committee meetings, often at short notice.

Interesting comparisons can also be made between the occupational composition of the Management Committee and other executive bodies. The FA Council, traditionally recruited from public schools, universities and members of the aristocracy and the upper-middle class, maintained a fairly elite presence well into the twentieth century. Nevertheless, in common with the League, solicitors and other professionals gained an increasing influence in the higher echelons of the governing body. By 1903, the professional classes accounted for approximately 50 per cent of the Council, while managers and administrators and clerical workers followed with 26.1 per cent and 8.7 per cent respectively. Despite the increasing influence of professional, and especially Football League, clubs on the decision-making process, the Council still included just three representatives from the employer and proprietorial bracket.[93] The Committee of cricket's MCC, by contrast, reflected the elite profile of the membership and its 'strong personal links with the political and social establishment'. During the inter-war years, it could boast 20 peers (inherited and created), 16 colonels, senior figures in the worlds of industry, banking and insurance, a Prime Minister, a Home Secretary and a sprinkling of MPs. Almost all had attended public schools and the vast majority were 'men of wealth'.[94] It should be no surprise that the Northern Rugby Football Union, a body with similar geographical and social roots, bore closest comparison to the League. Its general committee was also run principally by local employers, merchants and professionals, although managers and administrators were less involved than in the League. Between 1895 and 1910 only one leading member of the Union, a works manager, came from this category.[95]

There is, of course, a limit to what we can say about the men who ran the League on the basis of occupation alone. Solicitors on the Committee, for example, were not a monolithic group and may have become involved for any number of reasons quite unconnected with their occupation. The political and religious affiliations of committeemen, their beliefs and, more broadly, their lifestyles, are all therefore essential guides to the status, identity and culture of the Management Committee. It is to these elements that we now turn.

Perhaps the most important defining characteristic of the Committee was its regional concentration in the North-west of England. Almost a third of Committee members were directors or secretaries of Lancashire clubs, as were all four presidents in this period, although McKenna was an Irishman rather than a native Lancastrian (see Appendix). In addition, as we have seen, after 1902 the League was based at Preston and its secretarial staff were drawn exclusively from within Lancashire. Whether this regional bias was reflected in the way the League was run is a matter for conjecture. It is certainly possible to present a picture of the Committee's Lancashire leaders as an insular, tight-knit group with similar backgrounds and personalities. Bentley, Lewis, Sutcliffe and McKenna, in particular, served together for many years on the Lancashire FA, the FA Council and various other bodies in addition to the Management Committee, and seem to have become friends as well as associates. Contemporary descriptions also indicate a common thread of personal characteristics – bluntness, honesty, respectability and sobriety – although it is difficult to know how far these were based on stereotypical images of middle-class Lancastrians, or northerners in general.[96]

Although the evidence concerning the religious beliefs of members is patchy, it is possible to detect a dominant strand of Nonconformity, again principally among the Lancashire leadership. Lewis was the son of a preacher and, in common with Sutcliffe, McGregor and the secretaries Charnley and Howarth, was an active and devout Methodist all his life.[97] William Cuff and his family were prominent members of St Domingo's Methodist Chapel, from which Everton originated. Cuff's father had been a trustee, and Cuff continued the association by becoming the chapel's choirmaster.[98] Other fragmentary evidence suggests that Amos Brook Hirst, who attended the largely Nonconformist Huddersfield College, and William Bellamy were also Methodists.[99] The only Catholics on the Committee in our period, McKenna and Dr James

Baxter, were (not surprisingly) both from Liverpool, which accounted for approximately one fifth of England's Catholic population. Tom Houghton, who was briefly a member of the Committee before his death in 1912, appears to have been the only prominent Anglican.[100]

The overwhelming tone of Nonconformity on the Committee seems to have been reflected in attitudes towards drink and gambling. McGregor and Sutcliffe were both teetotallers and active members of the temperance movement, as was Lewis, whose sister Elizabeth Ann set up the renowned Lees Hall Teetotal Mission in Blackburn. Lewis, in fact, was a regular speaker at the Mission, while Sutcliffe, too, spoke publicly on the temperance question and even gave evidence to a Royal Commission on the dangers of alcoholism.[101] Elsewhere, Walter Hart followed his father and uncle by supporting the movement and becoming a leading member, and eventually President, of the Birmingham Temperance Society.[102] On the other hand, the Committee included a number of members directly or indirectly associated with the drink trade. John Cameron and Phil Bach, for example, both became publicans after retiring from their respective careers. Houghton was for many years licensee at the Volunteer Inn in Preston and an agent for William Younger brewers, while John Peel Oliver operated as a wine and spirit merchant and ran Newcastle's Crown Hotel.[103] Moreover, many committeemen were directors of clubs with close and long-standing connections with the drink trade. The most striking example was Bentley's second club, Manchester United, which was owned by the chairman of Manchester Breweries and controlled almost exclusively by directors and employees of the company.[104] West Bromwich Albion, represented on the Committee by Henry Keys and William Bassett, was heavily dependent on loans from local breweries, particularly during a number of financial crises between 1905 and 1909. Other clubs, such as Tom Sidney and Arthur Oakley's Wolverhampton Wanderers and Morton Cadman's Tottenham Hotspur, leased their grounds from brewery companies.[105] Even the abstaining Sutcliffe was for a little over a year a director of Oldham Athletic, whose Boundary Park ground was owned by the local J. W. Lees Brewery. The Lees Brewery and Manchester Breweries were also major shareholders in the club.[106] In reality, then, temperance remained a personal issue. The attitudes of certain influential members could have little impact on the mutual dependence that characterised the relationship between many League clubs and the drink trade.[107]

The Committee was more unified in its opposition to gambling, mainly due to its potentially damaging effects on the game. Primarily, of course, betting on football was opposed on moral grounds but, in addition, there was a fear that it would lead to widespread corruption, with players bribed and matches fixed. Significantly, this fear was perhaps most apparent in the League heartland of Lancashire. As well as having some of the highest conviction rates for street betting, the county boasted a large sporting and gambling press and, in Liverpool, the headquarters of the pools industry.[108] Hence, League Committee members were instrumental in lobbying the FA (and Parliament) to legislate against football betting. Lewis and Sutcliffe were both involved in the FA's 1913 inquiry into coupon betting on football, which, though exonerating players, asserted that such betting remained 'a serious menace to the game'. Lewis himself warned the FA Council in 1914 that if bookmakers were allowed to increase their influence, 'not a single member of that Council will remain in control of the game of football'.[109] The League as a body also publicly supported the Ready Money Football Betting Act, presented in 1920 to Parliament by the Arsenal chairman and MP Sir Henry Norris.[110]

The Management Committee's collective opposition to all forms of betting was displayed most clearly in its own measures. Throughout the 1920s, the executive took action in individual cases to prevent clubs being associated with coupon betting, sweepstakes or other forms of gambling.[111] In the following decade, opposition was directed more towards the pools. In theory, the pools represented less of a threat to the game, as there were fewer incentives to rig matches. However, this did not stop the Committee enacting measures to distance the League and its clubs from any contact with the pools companies. In June 1934, the Committee rejected a scheme developed by a Liverpool accountant, Watson Hartley, to charge pool companies for copyright on League fixtures, by declaring that 'there can be no connection, however vague, between the League and betting'.[112] A year later it banned advertisements in club programmes or on grounds and, as we shall see below, in 1936 initiated the so-called 'Pools War' by withholding the publication of fixtures until the last moment in an attempt to destroy the pools companies. Even after this had failed, the Committee rejected an offer in 1938 by the Pools Promoters Association to contribute £5,000 per year to the Jubilee Fund.[113] Yet although these actions were determined above all by ethical and moral motives – all members of the Committee, and most club representatives, agreed that pool betting was a menace, or, as William Cuff put it, 'a social canker'[114] – this did not insulate the League from attack by more radical anti-gambling elements. The Anglican Bishop Welldon, in particular, Dean of Manchester and then Durham and a prominent leader of the National Anti-Gambling League (NAGL), was a consistent critic of the ruling bodies and their failure to rid professional football of all associations with gambling. The NAGL was also instrumental in prosecuting a number of newspaper publishers – including in 1901 the Hulton Press, which produced *Athletic News* – for running football coupon competitions.[115]

Many Committee members were actively involved in local public life as town councillors, magistrates, school or hospital governors and the like. Houghton, for example, was a councillor for 14 years and Vice-Chairman of the Preston Conservative Association. Walter Tempest was also a Tory councillor (although he had originally been a Liberal), and later became Lord Mayor of Blackburn.[116] In keeping with its Nonconformist complexion, however, the Committee was predominantly Liberal. McGregor, Leavey, Baxter and Oakley were all card-carrying Liberals, the latter pair representing the party on their respective town councils. Sutcliffe, too, was particularly active in local civic life, at different times as President of the Rossendale Liberal Party, a town councillor, an alderman and, for one year, Deputy Mayor.[117] Nor were such activities restricted to the politically active. Bassett, famous above all as an England international and an FA Cup winner with his local West Bromwich Albion club, was appointed a borough magistrate in 1935. He was also on the Board of Management of the West Bromwich and District General Hospital. According to his obituary in 1937, Bassett 'was not content simply with being a football hero; he rendered great service in the social and political life of the borough'.[118] Freemasonry, recognised as an important element in the creation of a unitary civic culture, was also a common characteristic of the committeemen. Between 1910 and 1939, the Committee included a coterie of freemasons, notably two of the Presidents, McKenna and Cuff, and one Vice-President, Fred Rinder.[119]

It is tempting, in view of this evidence, to regard the Management Committee members as leading civic figures and to see their involvement in football merely as an extension of their activities in other areas of local political and social life. Such an interpretation fits neatly with what Richard Trainor has termed the 'duplicate membership' of local institutions among the Victorian Black Country elites, or what Alice Russell has referred to as 'the overlapping character of leadership' in many industrial towns, whereby individuals 'often played several decision-making roles concurrently, so that their authority was manifestly multi-dimensional'.[120] At the club level, there is every indication that prominent figures regarded a place on the board of the local club directorate as but one aspect of their wider civic interests and duties. Whether such involvement was linked to paternalism and a selfless benevolence, or an attempt to control workers in their recreations as well as their work, the implication is that it was certainly not just about football itself.[121] The collective culture of the Management Committee seems to offer a different perspective. As we have shown, Committee members could be Nonconformists, teetotallers, councillors or magistrates, but above all they were football administrators, or in popular parlance, football legislators. For many committeemen, football had ceased to be merely a hobby or an interest long ago: it had become a way of life, almost a surrogate occupation.

With few exceptions, football took up most of the spare time of members. As well as Management Committee meetings, there were subcommittees, inquiries and impromptu conferences on top of the weekly board meetings of one's own club and the work involved in organising transfers and other team matters. In addition, most members sat on the council of their respective divisional or county FA, and on the committees of other local leagues and competitions. Sutcliffe, described by contemporary accounts as the 'brains of football', is the most striking example. Apart from his League and club responsibilities, he was a leading member of the Lancashire FA, becoming its President in 1926, and one of its representatives on the FA Council, where he also served on the International Selection, Rules Revision and Referees' Committees. He was also President of the Northern Counties Amateur Championship, founder of the Referees' Union, Chairman, then Vice-President, of his local Rossendale United club, and a representative on the Appeals Committees of approximately 20 other leagues.[122] Accordingly, he spent much of his time 'rushing [at] midnight or early morning to London, Birmingham or Scotland by rail' to attend meetings and other football-related activities.[123] Nor, it seems, was he the exception. During the last season before his death, Rinder allegedly travelled over 1,000 miles a week on football matters, and Lewis, a frequent visitor to the continent and colonies on football trips, was said to have once covered 2,200 miles in 15 days in England.[124] In this context, it is hardly surprising that the Committee increasingly attracted men who had retired from their careers, or were nearing retirement, and could hence devote more time and energy to football.[125]

In some cases, members were able to make a living or at least subsidise their regular earnings as a result of their connections with the game. Certain members were part-time (in Bentley's case, full-time) sporting journalists. McGregor, for instance, wrote regularly for the *Birmingham Daily Mail*, *Sporting Mail*, *Sports Argus* and *Birmingham Daily Post* after the turn of the century. He also gave his name to advertise some of William Shillcock's products, like the 'McGregor football' and the 'McGregor lace-to-toe football boot'.[126] After leaving *Athletic News*, Bentley was engaged by J. H. Davies 'to manage day-to-day football affairs' at Manchester United for £300 per year.[127] Sutcliffe's work as a solicitor also appears to have been augmented through football contacts. As well as acting for Aston Villa in the famous Kingaby case of 1912, which established the legality of the transfer system, he represented the League during the West Trials of 1917–18, which arose out of an allegedly 'arranged' match between Liverpool and Manchester United two years earlier. All this was in addition to his role as solicitor for the League's Mutual Insurance Federation (see Chapter 4). It is not clear how much money Sutcliffe earned from his football-related work, although no doubt it could be profitable. Indeed, he was paid at least £50 for a few months assisting the floatation of Oldham Athletic in 1906.[128] However, this should not be taken to mean that all Committee members were profiteers. Only the leading figures were able to gain financially in this way and, even then, it is unlikely that this was sufficient to compensate for the time and money spent on League business. Sutcliffe, after all, was said to have neglected his private practice and 'sacrificed his career as a lawyer for the sake of the Football League'.[129]

Furthermore, most members had been actively involved in other levels of the game, as players or match officials. Lewis, for example, proclaimed as the 'Prince of Referees', was probably the best-known official of his day. He refereed three FA Cup Finals between 1895 and 1900, and numerous internationals before retiring in 1905. Brought out of retirement to officiate at the 1908 Olympic Games in London, he was still refereeing at the age of 64, when he was persuaded to take control of the 1920 Olympic Final.[130] Sutcliffe was also an established international referee, while Bentley, the Secretary Lockett, Bellamy and Oakley were all at some point on the League list of referees or linesmen.[131] Most Committeemen played football at some stage in their youth, and a number reached fairly high standards. Apart from Bassett and Bach, both of whom were ex-professionals, Bentley and Lewis were successful county players. Bentley was a regular for one of the leading Lancashire clubs, Turton, and the Bolton Association, and Lewis appeared for the club he helped to form, Blackburn Rovers, and Darwen in its amateur days. Among many other examples, Vice-President Harry Radford and Morton Cadman also made impressions initially as leading amateur players with their respective clubs.[132] At this point, it is worth noting the consistent presence, even as late as the 1930s, of Committee members who had been instrumental in the formation and development of clubs prior to the adoption of professionalism in 1885. Far from being hostile towards amateurism, many of those who ran the League retained strong sympathies with elements of the amateur ethos. Bentley was unlikely to have been alone in holding 'Pure amateurism in every sport ... to be the highest state'.[133] Like many others, his experiences of football were rooted in the take-off era of the 1870s to the 1890s, and he remained in many ways a product of this late Victorian age.

If most members of the Management Committee were recognised principally for their involvement with football, the leading figures were unquestionably 'League men'. In fact, some were only nominally associated with their clubs, and acted in practice as neutral League officials. Lewis severed official connections with Blackburn Rovers in the early 1920s, although he attended some games and remained vocal at annual meetings, while Sutcliffe restricted his association with Burnley to that of spectator for much of this period. Similarly, the pressure of McKenna's duties as League President was instrumental in his leaving the Liverpool board in 1922.[134] On becoming a Life Member in 1912, Bentley acknowledged that although he was 'connected with many other organisations, the Football League would always be his pet'. Writing in 1906, Sutcliffe expressed similar sentiments: 'The League's interests are mine. I am a League man, a League lover, and a League servant above all'.[135] It would be a mistake to underestimate the importance of these statements. For all their occupational, social and political similarities, members of the Management Committee were bound together mainly by their collective passion for football in general, and the League in particular.

In its essential features, the Football League Management Committee resembled countless middle-class organisations, sporting and otherwise, established in the late Victorian era. While entry was theoretically open to any club director, administrator or (before 1917) paid official, in practice the League was ruled by members of a small elite group with similar backgrounds, interests and affiliations and, most importantly, with long associations as football politicians and administrators dating back to the first decade of the professional game. There was no formal 'blackballing' clause, but selection nevertheless involved a lengthy system of nomination, canvassing and voting, which ensured that only the favoured or the acceptable would be admitted.[136] As former professional footballers it might be thought that Bassett and Bach were exceptions to the rule, but both had been established for some time as club directors with respectable professional careers. Their elections were to some extent recognition of the social distance travelled since their playing days. Notwithstanding the appearance of democracy, therefore, the League executive was a closed oligarchy, dominated throughout the first four decades of the twentieth century by no more than half a dozen key individuals.

The League and its clubs

At the heart of the governance of English professional football was the relationship between the Football League and its member clubs. That this relationship, and its implications for the development of the game, has received little attention in the existing literature might be explained by the tendency to place football employers into a monolithic group and to assume that a collective body such as the Football League represented a simple aggregation of the interests of its constituent clubs. Possibly because sporting clubs were necessarily more inclined to combination and cooperation than most other employers, it might be assumed that their interests naturally converged and consensus was easily reached. In League football at least, however, a collective approach could not be taken for granted; it had to be argued for, legitimised and forged over time in the face of divisions, conflict and individualistic tendencies. We have seen that in its first decade, the Management Committee struggled to establish a central position in the decision-making process, with clubs resisting central control and continuing to assert their independence of League rulings and Committee decisions. Most clubs regarded themselves as autonomous organisations rather than League clubs first and foremost. Arguably, the onset of war in 1914 and the development of mutual support schemes to ensure the economic survival of all member clubs in the absence of a comprehensive league competition were fundamental in imbuing clubs with a sense of commitment to the League itself. During the inter-war period, the scope of the League executive's powers was extended further as it developed tighter regulatory control over its member clubs. Certainly, by 1939 the Football League could no longer be seen as a suzerain but was increasingly perceived by the press, and sometimes even by member clubs, as an almost autocratic ruler.

The developing relationship between the League and its clubs over this period could usefully be seen in a similar context as the growth and influence of employers' organisations in a host of other industries.[137] Notwithstanding the peculiarities of employer combination in sport, the Football League clearly shared many of the characteristics of conventional employers' associations. Operating as an employers' trade union, the League combined intervention in the industrial relations sphere and the labour market with the regulation of trade and a range of broader advisory and pressure group functions. As Political and Economic Planning's 1951 report noted, the League

> regulates its member clubs in such matters as wages, bonuses, transfers and percentages of gates to be paid to visiting clubs, lays down conditions under which matches take place, and determines many other club activities. This is a wide authority, covering many points of procedure from international transfers … and disciplinary action against clubs and players, down to the colour of linesmen's flags.[138]

By the Second World War, there had not only been a transformation in the relationship between the executive and the clubs, but a fundamental shift in the function and purpose of the Football League. In the 1890s and the first few years of the twentieth century, the League could be understood as little more than a rudimentary voluntary association, with 'a set of rules, a declared purpose and a membership defined by some formal act of joining'.[139] It had little meaning as a body independent of the clubs forming its membership: it was a competition organiser and an arbiter in the event of disputes, but played no role in determining the decision making of the clubs. Gradually, however, the League was able to make a similar transition to that of other employers' associations, from 'transient, ad hoc, localised and relatively weak bodies to permanent, representative, centralised and, in many cases, relatively powerful institutions'.[140] The Management Committee came to wield increasingly centralised and bureaucratic control over its membership in all issues affecting the running of the competition, from players to referees and grounds to ticket prices, in an effort to ensure the maintenance of its primary ethos: the notion that the League should be, as far as possible, a fair competition between equals. By 1939, the Committee had developed into much more than a regulatory power: it was initiating policy and setting the parameters for decisions made in the boardrooms of every Football League club.

The role of member clubs in financing the League provides a good example of this transformation. Clubs were initially reluctant to make significant contributions to the League's general administrative funds. Subscriptions and entrance fees were low, and constituted a minor source of income relative to the receipts from Inter-League and other representative matches. In 1900, annual subscriptions were pegged at just £10 10s for First Division members, and half that amount in the lower division. Re-elected clubs and those joining the League paid an entrance fee of £5 5s, as did clubs promoted from the Second Division to the First. League rules did entitle the Committee to organise special fund-raising matches or make additional levies on members, as it did at the beginning of the 1901–02 season, but this did not affect the general belief that the funding of the League was, in President John Bentley's words, 'unbusinesslike and unsound'.[141] The fickle nature of representative match receipts and the need to place its finances in 'a sure and satisfactory state' convinced the Management Committee in 1908 to raise the entrance fee for joining clubs to £300, out of which £200 was granted to the club losing its membership. Yet proposals for a more comprehensive scheme of 'taxing' club income were consistently rejected before the First World War. Advocates of taxation insisted that it was a club's duty to contribute to the working expenses of the League. *Athletic News*, for one, noted that 'The League has made the clubs into wealthy organisations, and the clubs should see that the League does not suffer financial embarrassment'.[142] Critics objected not so much to the amount of taxation as the principle underlying it. Revenue, especially gate money, tended to be regarded by most clubs as the product of individual endeavour, even though visiting teams provided the necessary competition and the League itself gave the fixture context and meaning (see Chapter 5).

The onset of war and the obvious difficulties this generated for League finances were crucial factors in the eventual introduction of the taxation principle. At the 1916 annual meeting, the Management Committee introduced a 1 per cent 'tax' on the net gate and stand receipts of member clubs in order to pay for management expenses.[143] Initially justified as an extraordinary measure to save the League from bankruptcy, taxation increasingly became accepted as a basic duty of membership during the inter-war years. The system continued immediately after the war, with each member club now contributing 0.5 rather than 1 per cent, and remained for 1920–21 with the proviso that the Management Committee could suspend contributions during the season if sufficient funds became available. In fact, the League's finances were stable enough to allow the Committee to discontinue taxation midway through both the 1921–22 and 1922–23 seasons, although it is notable that clubs were still required to send the League secretary details of their match takings and payments.[144] In 1924, the Committee introduced a new taxation scheme covering both the League's working expenses and the mutual insurance of players. Henceforth, First and Second Division clubs were to contribute 1 per cent of their takings from League matches, while those in the Third Division Southern and Northern Sections gave 1.5 and 2 per cent respectively (see Chapter 4). No additional subscriptions or levies were demanded, and the following year the scheme was extended to include a similar tax on cup-tie gate receipts. Of this income, the Committee proposed to direct a little under one-half – an estimated £5,000 per annum – to run and administer the League.[145] During the inter-war period, club funding via taxation represented the League's primary source of revenue, accounting for somewhere between 65 and 80 per cent of annual income.[146] At both a practical and symbolic level, taxation tied the clubs and the League closer together, acknowledging the collective nature of the football 'product'.

The creation of the Football League naturally represented a crucial step towards the weakening of club autonomy, irrespective of the clear financial and organisational benefits it brought. As League members, clubs had less freedom to choose which teams they played, where and when, and under what circumstances. The Club Secretary's role of arranging the season's fixtures was superseded by the process of annual fixture meetings, and any subsequent disputes that arose were settled by the League Secretary and ultimately the Management Committee. Friendly matches were still occasionally arranged when a club had no prior League and cup commitments, but this became increasingly uncommon with the gradual enlargement of the divisions to 16, 18, 20 and then 22 members by the end of the First World War. Moreover, from the early 1890s onwards regulations were developed precluding clubs from arranging friendly fixtures that might affect the gates of fellow members.[147] Kick-off times were also brought more closely into the executive's sphere of influence when it was agreed in 1921 that Saturday matches should begin no later than 3.15 p.m. Previously, kick-off times had ranged from 1 p.m. to 5 p.m., and some clubs had given themselves greater flexibility by not even advertising a scheduled time of kick-off. From the following year, clubs could apply to begin matches later than the standard 3.15 p.m., but this was to be decided in advance and at the discretion of the Committee.[148]

In other areas, the transfer of power and responsibility from club to League was a much more gradual and complicated process. The location and standard of club grounds provides a case in point. Although the League agreed in 1891 not to allow entry to any club with a ground closer than three miles to that of an existing member, clubs were otherwise able to move grounds as and when they wished without receiving prior Committee approval.[149] As most changes of this kind involved switching to a location within one or two miles of the previous ground – and always in the same town or city – there was rarely opposition from any party. However, when in 1913 Arsenal proposed to move from Woolwich to a stadium 14 miles away in north London, immediate objections were raised by Tottenham Hotspur and Clapton Orient, whose grounds were situated within two and a half miles of the proposed site. These clubs pressed the Committee to stop the move, but it was decided to take no action as 'there is ample opportunity for three League clubs within the area' and, more importantly, 'under the rules and practice of the League there is no right to interfere'.[150] This clearly enraged the opponents of the move, who remained convinced that even without a precedent for its action, it would have been within the Committee's power to intervene. At the next annual meeting, Orient's Captain Wells-Holland successfully proposed a rule change ensuring that 'each club shall register its ground with the Secretary, and no club shall remove to another ground without first obtaining the consent of the Management Committee'.[151] In a similar case in 1919, the Management Committee appeared to endorse the requested transfer of the struggling Huddersfield Town club to nearby Leeds.[152] Convinced by poor attendances and gate receipts that 'Huddersfield people ... do not want Soccer football' and that as a Football League town 'Huddersfield has failed', the Committee ordered the club to repay a £25,000 debt to director J. Hilton Crowther, or face the whole operation – players, liabilities and league position included – moving to Leeds.[153] Although the financial assistance of three local benefactors and a profitable FA Cup run and promotion campaign eventually proved sufficient to clear the debt and keep the club at Huddersfield, the episode proved that the executive was prepared to intervene in the affairs of its member clubs when the viability of the competition was threatened. As the non-Huddersfield press was keen to point out, gate money was no longer a purely domestic issue after the wartime introduction of pooling policies, but affected the finances of visiting clubs and the health of the League as a whole (see Chapter 5). In this way, the Committee's preference for the Leeds scheme can be seen as a logical attempt to maintain the quality of the membership.

During the first 20 or so years of the League, clubs were generally left to build and develop their grounds as they wished. Only where issues of crowd control were concerned did the Committee seek to intervene, and even then it was reluctant to order clubs to make alterations. Significantly, clubs were only *advised* to erect fences or railings around the pitch to prevent crowd encroachment, and to provide dressing-room accommodation for officials and visiting teams, enabling them to leave the field without fear of assault.[154] The number of members who actually followed the Committee's advice in cases of this kind is hard to determine. It was reported in 1913 that both Bolton Wanderers and Oldham Athletic were building new dressing-room accommodation 'to be completed to the satisfaction of the League', but these were isolated instances and certainly did not prevent the continued issuing of recommendations rather than commands relating particularly to inadequate provision for visiting teams and match officials.[155] The influx of the new associate members in the early 1920s, however, led the Committee to develop tighter controls over the standards of ground facilities. Prospective candidates for the Third Division Northern Section were expected to replace inadequate accommodation for spectators and provide comfortable dressing-room facilities that were attached to the ground. Regular visits and reports by Committee members ensured that Wigan Borough, Accrington Stanley, Halifax Town and Walsall, amongst others, undertook rebuilding projects to bring their grounds up to the required standard by the start of their first League seasons. From 1927 onwards, each club applying for membership was instructed to send the details of its ground's holding capacity, stand and covered accommodation and dressing-room facilities. Any candidate failing to meet the Committee's recognised standards – uncodified but established by convention over previous years – was unlikely to be recommended at the annual elections.[156] The executive was also known to step in to ensure that the standard of the playing field itself was maintained. Poor pitch conditions on a number of grounds at the end of the 1928–29 season led the Committee to issue a resolution prohibiting clubs from sub-letting the pitch during the close season, or otherwise interfering with the playing surface.[157]

The bureaucratic tendencies at the centre of the League extended as far as the supply of information from the clubs to the public. On a number of occasions, the Management Committee was accused of attempting to censor the opinions of the nominally independent editors of club programmes. In 1905, for example, the Stoke programme editor and Club Secretary H. D. Austerberry was forced to withdraw charges he had made of bias in the appointment of League referees. The Committee's action did not escape criticism. Austerberry felt he had 'as much right as members of the … Committee to write generally on a system to which he objected', and even *Athletic News* expressed its amusement at 'the extremely autocratic attitude' of the executive towards a small, private football publication. Similar retractions and apologies were demanded when Hull City in 1912, and then West Ham in 1921, used the club programme to criticise the playing methods of opponents.[158] The Committee was again denounced by critics for its autocratic action following a series of incidents in 1920. First, Chelsea was brought to book for printing 'an offensive paragraph' in the club programme relating to the workings of a League Commission.[159] Second, clubs were instructed not to disclose their gate money to the public and, finally, two clubs were fined for breaching League rules by providing meals for match officials. For *Football Field*, the Committee's behaviour was unnecessary and tactically ill-judged: 'It is possible to rule with too hard a hand'.[160]

While *Football Field*'s perception of the Management Committee as an increasingly autocratic body may not have been universally shared, there can be little doubt that League clubs between the wars were more tightly regulated than ever before. In addition to laying down conditions relating to the fundamentals of club management – players' transfers, grounds, commercial activities and so on – the executive also sought to control and monitor the minutiae of club life. From the beginning of the period, club colours had to be registered with the League Secretary. From 1909 onwards, goalkeepers were required to wear jerseys in one of three (later four) colours, distinct from the shirts of both competing teams. Initially, these regulations were either ignored or not taken seriously by clubs and match officials, but the Committee began to issue small fines, and warned in 1913 that 'in future all clubs not complying with the rule will be severely dealt with'.[161] Clubs could apply to change their official colours at the start of each season, but playing in unauthorised colours without permission became a disciplinary offence in the same bracket (though not with the same penalty) as more serious misdemeanours such as unauthorised payments to players.[162] Perhaps the most important aspect of any member club's identity, its name, was also subject to registration by the Committee, with alterations needing executive approval. Although the Committee rarely did more than rubber-stamp name changes, this itself could be a convoluted affair, as when the newly-elected Boscombe club applied to alter its name to Bournemouth United but within a month requested another name change to Bournemouth and Boscombe Athletic.[163] By the 1930s, then, substantial and crucial areas of club activity were subject to central regulation, and many decisions taken by a club's board of directors had first to be registered and sanctioned by Preston before being put into motion.

The most visible strand of the Committee's power over clubs was its disciplinary function. Here, again, the executive became less hesitant and more severe in its treatment of clubs after the First World War. While fines imposed for simple administrative slackness, such as the late arrival of result slips or transfer documents, remained fairly constant, penalties for more serious breaches of rules rose sharply. For example, FA Cup finalists Everton and Newcastle United were both fined £50 for fielding 'unrepresentative' teams for League matches towards the end of the 1905–06 season; by 1912, £100 and £150 were more common penalties.[164] Before 1924 League rules prohibited the Committee issuing fines exceeding £150, but when Newcastle was found guilty of playing weak teams in no fewer than seven League fixtures during its victorious FA Cup run, a massive £750 fine was imposed and the Committee was henceforth given the freedom to exact 'such fine as they shall think fit'. This incident reflected a distinct tightening of club discipline, a policy that had been explicitly revealed by McKenna at the previous annual meeting.[165]

In theory, the expulsion of a club from the League was a matter for the members collectively. A simple majority at the annual meeting could vote to exclude any club whose conduct was deemed 'objectionable'. Yet, as in many other areas, in practice such matters were left for the Committee to investigate and ultimately decide upon. There is little doubt that expelling a club was considered a drastic measure and a last resort: just one club suffered this fate before 1939, and then in peculiar circumstances. Following a series of fines and suspensions in 1911, Middlesbrough was formally warned by the Committee that further offences would mean immediate expulsion, but despite some newspaper pressure it was always likely that the club would be given a reprieve.[166] When the executive did actually expel a member – Leeds City in 1919 – it was not so much for breaking League rules as for challenging its authority.[167] A tip-off from a former Leeds player led the League and the FA to organise a joint commission to investigate alleged illegal payments to players during the war. Such investigations were certainly not uncommon and, if the allegations had been proved, it is likely that certain directors and players would have found themselves heavily fined and temporarily suspended. There would have been no precedent, however, for expelling the club itself. The reason for the expulsion was the refusal of club directors to hand over a set of documents, including the accounts from 1916–18, as required by both League and FA rules. As *Athletic News* noted in its editorial, by refusing to obey the commission's orders Leeds City had 'automatically suspended themselves'.[168] Some critics of the expulsion, notably the Lord Mayor of Leeds, Joseph Henry, believed that the League representatives on the commission were instrumental in persuading the FA members to expel rather than fine the club, partly as a result of pressure from the aspiring Port Vale club, which hoped to fill Leeds's place.[169] In his examination of the affair, Tony Arnold explained the commission's action as 'a dramatic gesture by men who knew they had badly misjudged the political symbolism of professional soccer in the early years of the Great War'.[170] While both explanations probably contain elements of truth, the decision on the League's part, at least, was entirely in keeping with the Management Committee's emerging self-confidence and disciplinary zeal. When the Committee was increasingly intent on asserting its authority and stamping out irregularities, member clubs could hardly be allowed to ignore established procedures or, more importantly, defy official commands.

It is hardly surprising that division and disunity emerged as perennial problems for an amalgamation of sporting clubs as large and diverse as the Football League. The Management Committee's role in bolstering solidarity and smoothing over discontent was crucial, but it could not conceal the persistence of internal divisions and fragmentation among its membership. The First World War, in particular, was a crucial period in the development of relations between the League and its clubs, although Simon Inglis's view that the League emerged in 1918 as a more tightly bound and unified organisation than ever before is highly debatable.[171] The evidence for this seems to be based largely on the proclamations of the Committee itself, and especially the habitual references in circulars, annual reports and meetings to the 'loyalty' of members towards the League. Yet, in many ways, the language of loyalty disguised fundamental conflicts and differences of opinion that persisted throughout the war years. Above all, it needs to be remembered that a small but significant group of leading clubs took no part whatsoever in the League's modified system of regional competitions from 1915–16 onwards. The West Midlands triumvirate of Aston Villa, West Bromwich Albion and Wolverhampton Wanderers, in particular, felt from the beginning that the Committee's pleas for loyalty ought not to distract clubs from more pressing concerns: 'There came a time when there were greater interests either than The League or football. In their opinion such a time had now arrived.'[172] At the 1915 annual meeting, Villa's chairman unsuccessfully moved 'That no matches be played under the auspices of The Football League during the war, and that the League clubs be allowed to play what matches they desired'.[173] So, along with Sunderland and Middlesbrough, these clubs effectively closed down for the duration of the war. If we add the five London clubs that achieved a kind of semi-autonomy as members of the London Combination, it is hard to see how the League could be regarded at this point as 'a strong, confident organisation with almost complete mastery over its members'.[174]

What is more, there was only limited support for the wartime organisation of the League among those clubs which continued to participate in its competitions. While the majority of clubs at the critical 1915 annual meeting agreed 'that some kind of football should be played', many also expressed their preference for organising their own fixtures with local opponents rather than participating in competitions run by the League. Everton's representative W. R. Clayton thought that the League 'should close their doors until the war is over, but clubs should have the liberty to make their own arrangements irrespective of the League or any other organisation'.[175] While subsequently accepting League control over the regionalised wartime tournaments in principle, some clubs were more reluctant than before the war to acquiesce to the central authority of the Management Committee. Certainly, if Sutcliffe and others expected their schemes for the financial relief of necessitous clubs and the pooling of gates to automatically bind the members more tightly to the League structure, they were to be disappointed. At the 1916 annual meeting, a group of the richer clubs, led by Everton, effectively held the League to ransom by threatening to withdraw and form a separate section if the pooling system introduced the previous season was not abandoned. This was no idle threat as Everton, Liverpool, Manchester City and Blackburn Rovers from the Lancashire section, along with Sheffields United and Wednesday, Bradford City, Park Avenue and Birmingham from the Midlands, had all apparently intimated willingness in private correspondence to form an independent competition that would allow them to retain all their own gate receipts.[176] Further conflict was avoided when the richer clubs agreed to gate pooling as a temporary wartime measure, but even then Everton and other Lancastrian clubs refused to pool gate receipts across both sections. Clayton, for one, was 'not prepared to finance the Midlands clubs; they must look after themselves'.[177] Even in wartime, then, loyalty to the League was never unconditional, and the Committee's control over its membership was often fragile.

The threat of breakaways or secession was a common feature of the League's formative years, but had largely dissipated by the turn of the century. Less conspicuous expressions of independence such as unofficial meetings of clubs remained, however, a continuous thorn in the side of the executive and a challenge to its rhetoric of unity and loyalty. Even though it was customary for clubs to meet to discuss rule changes and forge collective policy, the Management Committee often objected when League matters were debated outside its jurisdiction. A notable example came in 1909, when two unauthorised conclaves of Midlands and Yorkshire clubs were arranged prior to that season's annual meeting. The main purpose of the gatherings, it would appear, was to agree on a collective approach towards the Management Committee elections and to remedy the perceived dominance of the Lancastrian representatives.[178] In response, the Lancashire clubs arranged their own regional meeting, and the London contingent were reported to have done likewise. This separatist activity was strongly condemned by the executive. Bentley had no objection to clubs discussing League matters that directly affected them, 'but when it came to a section of clubs convening a meeting … to settle certain matters in connection with the management of the League … it was a grave affair… As a matter of principle, such proceedings are entirely wrong'.[179] This warning did nothing to prevent a clique of Midlands and Yorkshire clubs meeting in 1913 under similar circumstances at Leeds 'to consider the question of better representation on the Management Committee'.[180] The machinery of official League meetings seems to have successfully contained even the more dissident directors and club officials for most of the 1920s, but by 1930 the dilatory nature of decision making had sparked another wave of independently organised club gatherings. This time, the meetings were neither secret nor restricted along regional lines. Arsenal and Huddersfield Town, for example, initiated a series of conferences attended by First and Second Division representatives to consider issues ranging from the release of players for international matches through to the reform of the throw-in law.[181] The Management Committee considered their resolutions, but when the stance of the clubs on international fixtures was rejected, a further independent conference was arranged. In the opinion of the Committee this was a serious offence that threatened disorder and questioned its overall authority within the League. In a letter to the Huddersfield Chairman, Preston expressed its view that the meeting 'may be regarded as lacking in courtesy to the President and the Committee and … be thought suggestive of disloyalty'. If the clubs had wanted such a meeting, the letter went on, it was surely the responsibility of the Committee itself to arrange it.[182] Yet despite the executive's unease, a precedent for independent club meetings had been set, and by 1935 unofficial assemblies of clubs were taking place annually before the FA Cup final and the FA and League annual meetings.[183]

The events surrounding the so-called 'Pools War' of 1936 provide the most revealing example of open conflict between the League executive and the member clubs. It is not necessary here to detail the precise chronology of events or to examine the attitudes of those involved towards the football pools in particular and betting in general.[184] What is of interest, however, is the virtual breakdown of relations within the League for a little over a fortnight as a result of the Management Committee's attempts to destroy the pools companies. In purely constitutional terms, the Committee did seem initially to have a mandate for its action. At a private meeting of clubs on 20 February 1936, the Committee was formally empowered 'to take such steps as it deems expedient to bring about the suppression of betting'.[185] At the same time, Sutcliffe outlined the plan to change the original fixture lists and withhold the alterations for long enough each week to prevent the pools companies from printing and distributing coupons. Yet although the large majority of clubs – 64 of the 85 present – had voted to allow the Committee to proceed with this plan, voices of dissension were raised almost immediately. The Leeds United board, led by the most vocal of the malcontents, Alderman Alf Masser, issued a public statement decrying the Committee's action of cancelling fixtures as futile; Manchester City resolved to oppose the proposals at future meetings 'in every shape and form'. Sunderland, Derby County and a number of anonymous club directors all joined the criticism, and there was talk of collective action to reverse the original decision.[186]

More serious perhaps than this straightforward condemnation of the Committee's plans was the suggestion by Masser and others that the decisions reached at the 20 February meeting contravened a number of the League's own rules. At a conference of those Northern clubs that had already expressed their opposition to the Committee – Manchester City, Stoke, Blackburn Rovers and Newcastle United as well as Leeds and Sunderland – Sutcliffe was accused of breaching three separate rules. First, the intention to rearrange fixtures that had already been confirmed at the annual fixtures meeting would be a breach of Rule 23. Second, despite the fact that associate members could only vote collectively under Rule 3, the Committee had allowed individual votes to each Third Division club representative. Finally, by calling the meeting at less than the required seven days' notice, and without a full agenda available to clubs in advance, Rule 80 had also been broken. Some clubs argued that they had therefore not been fully prepared to consider such an important question. The fact that the Committee had also rejected the request of those representatives 'who desired the opportunity of conferring with their co-directors on proposals of such a revolutionary character' particularly vexed certain members.[187]

As a direct challenge to the Committee's policy, then, these clubs called a rebel meeting of all full members for the following Monday, 2 March, at Leeds Town Hall, scheduled purposely for the same day as a Committee gathering in London. Opposition to the League gathered pace, with no fewer than 36 of the 44 full member clubs sending representatives to Leeds, ironically including seven clubs associated with Committee members. The experience of the first Saturday of rearranged fixtures had further embittered a number of clubs whose attendances were either well down or who – in the case of five clubs whose new opponents were due to play in FA Cup ties – had no fixture at all. While maintaining the rhetoric of 'loyalty' to the League and the Management Committee and showing appreciation of 'the great services rendered by them', the clubs showed determination and virtual unanimity in their objective to reverse League policy.[188] With no votes against and just ten abstentions, the meeting resolved 'that while they accepted that the Management Committee had been given a mandate to scrap the fixtures, the clubs now urged the restoration of the fixtures and a return to the status quo'.[189] In these circumstances there was little the Committee could do but bow to the collective will of its membership. At an official League meeting a week later, the Leeds resolution was unanimously passed and it was agreed that the original fixtures be immediately resumed.

Although this was the only major confrontation between the Committee and the clubs in the period, the events surrounding the 'Pools War' can nevertheless be seen as clear evidence of the usually latent collective power of the clubs. More than any other factor, including the widespread press and public opposition, it was the orchestrated protest campaign of Masser and others that forced the Committee to back down. Without the active support of the majority of its members – and regardless of the apparent backing of its policy given at the 20 February meeting – it became impractical for the executive to successfully take on the pools industry. Writing in 1926, the journalist James Catton outlined the 'harmonious and … co-operative' relationship that resulted from a situation where the Management Committee was trusted in most cases to make an accurate assessment of the position of its member clubs and take the lead in initiating policy developments.[190] Yet the events of February and March 1936 show that League clubs were far from taciturn and impotent when they felt their views were not being represented. Certainly, the assertion that the Management Committee effectively 'led' the Football League and its clubs needs to be qualified by a recognition of the checks and balances available to clubs through both the formal mechanisms of annual meetings and rule changes, and the less formal, independent and impromptu action such as the anti-Committee movement of Masser and others.

Notes

1 *Topical Times*, 21 May 1938.
2 BBC Written Archives Centre (WAC), Football League Ltd File 1a, 1936–46, S. J. de Lotbiniere to Fred Howarth, 10 January 1938.
3 G. Green, *The History of the Football Association*, London, Naldrett, 1953, p. 391; 'The Football Association' in *Association Football*, ed. A. H. Fabian and G. Green, London, Caxton, vol. 1, 1960, p. 47. For a contemporary view, see W. Pickford, 'How Soccer is Controlled', *The Listener*, 29 September 1937, pp. 656–57.
4 W. McGregor, 'The League and the League System', p. 174.
5 *Athletic News*, 30 January, 9 October 1911.
6 W. McGregor, 'The Origin and Future', p. 5.
7 Political and Economic Planning, 'The Football Industry – 1', *Planning*, Vol. 17, 1951, p. 163.
8 See Mason, *Association Football*, Chapter 1; Tischler, *Footballers*, pp. 51–59; Holt, *Sport and the British*, pp. 106–07.
9 Vamplew, *Pay Up*, Appendix 2d; Young, *A History of British Football*, pp. 173–74.
10 Holt, *Sport and the British*, p. 106.
11 Dobbs, *Edwardians at Play*, pp. 45–46.
12 Birley, *Land of Sport and Glory*, p. 36.
13 *Athletic News*, 28 January 1901. Also see *Manchester Evening News*, 24, 26, 28 January 1901.
14 Charles Sutcliffe, letter to the editor dated 1 February 1901, in *Athletic News*, 4 February 1901.
15 'Grasshopper', 'Southern Notes' in *Athletic News*, 28 January 1901.
16 *Manchester Evening News*, 2 February 1901; 'Harricus' (Harry Downs), 'The Football League, 1888–1901' in *Athletic News*, 4 February 1901.
17 *Athletic News*, 24 February 1919.
18 Green, *History*, pp. 404–05; FA Consultative Committee Minutes, 1 February 1899; J. Harding, *For the Good of the Game: The Official History of the Professional Footballers' Association*, London, Robson, 1991, p. 26; Sutcliffe, Brierley and Howarth, *Story of the Football League*, p. 114.
19 Sutcliffe, Brierley and Howarth, *Story of the Football League*, p. 116.
20 Quoted in Harding, *For the Good of the Game*, p. 27.
21 Report of FA AGM in *Athletic News*, 27 May 1901.
22 Sutcliffe, Brierley and Howarth, *Story of the Football League*, p. 116; Green, *History*, p. 409.
23 FA Council Minutes, 29 August, 7 November 1904.
24 FA Council Minutes, 31 March 1905; Report of FA AGM in *Athletic News*, 1 June 1908.
25 Sutcliffe, Brierley and Howarth, *Story of the Football League*, pp. 117–18; SUFC, Football Committee Minutes, 19 August 1908; 9 January, 10 February 1909.
26 SUFC, Football Committee Minutes, 2, 9 February 1908; *Athletic News*, 22 February 1909.
27 Report of FA AGM in *Athletic News*, 14 June 1909.
28 FA Circular on Financial Arrangements Between Clubs and Players, 10 January 1910.
29 FA Extraordinary Committee Minutes, 22 April 1910.
30 Report of Football League 'Coming of Age' banquet in *Athletic News*, 14 June 1909.

31 See I. Sharpe, *40 Years in Football*, London, Sportsman's Book Club, 1954, p. 159; *Athletic News*, 6 March, 29 May, 12 June 1911.
32 *Athletic News*, 30 January 1911.
33 FA Council Minutes, 24 February 1902.
34 Inglis, *League Football*, p. 57; Report of Football League Commission into Middlesbrough FC in *Athletic News*, 4 June 1906.
35 On the Manchester City case, see *Athletic News*, 15, 22 October 1906. On the Sheffield United case, see *Athletic News*, 18 September 1911; SUFC, Football Committee Minutes, 26 April 1911.
36 Agreement between the Football Association and the Football League, 4 December 1911, printed in Green, *History*, p. 401.
37 Football League Minutes, 4 November, 2 December 1912; FA Emergency Committee Minutes, 1 January–31 March 1918; *Athletic News*, 7, 11 June, 26 July 1920.
38 See, for instance, the report on the financial dealings at Arsenal, after which Sir Henry Norris was suspended from future involvement in club management by the FA Commission. Football League Minutes, Management Committee, 13 September, 17 October 1927.
39 Green, *History*, p. 401.
40 Report of FA AGM in *Athletic News*, 2 June 1902.
41 Report of FA AGM in *Athletic News*, 5 June 1905.
42 FA Council Minutes, Meeting of FA Officers, 14 April 1919; FA Emergency Committee Minutes, 1–26 May 1919.
43 Football League Minutes, Management Committee, 12 April 1929.
44 Sutcliffe, Brierley and Howarth, *Story of the Football League*, p. 33.
45 Football League Minutes, Management Committee, 10 May 1929; *Athletic News*, 7 June 1930.
46 A. Hardaker, *Hardaker of the League*, London, Pelham, 1977, pp. 130–31; Inglis, *League Football*, p. 134; B. Dabscheck, '"Defensive Manchester": A History of the Professional Footballers' Association' in *Sport in History*, ed. R. Cashman and M. McKernan, St Lucia, University of Queensland Press, 1979, p. 229. Hardaker's account is inaccurate as well as idiosyncratic, as he claims that Stanley Rous initiated the whole incident. In fact, Rous did not become FA Secretary until 1934.
47 See P. Clark, *British Clubs and Societies 1580–1800: The Origins of an Associational World*, Oxford, Oxford University Press, 2000; R. J. Morris, 'Clubs, Societies and Associations' in *The Cambridge Social History of Britain, 1750–1950: Volume 3 – Social Agencies and Institutions*, ed. F. M. L. Thompson, Cambridge, Cambridge University Press, 1990, pp. 395–443; J. Lowerson, *Sport and the English Middle Classes, 1870–1914*, Manchester, Manchester University Press, 1993.
48 J. Hill, *Sport, Leisure and Culture in Twentieth-Century Britain*, Basingstoke, Palgrave, 2002, p. 131.
49 *Topical Times*, 27 January 1934.
50 Lowerson, *Sport*, p. 22.
51 Quoted in Sutcliffe, Brierley and Howarth, *Story of the Football League*, pp. 4–5. Much of the following is drawn from this work and the Football League Rules and Handbooks.
52 Quoted in Sutcliffe, Brierley and Howarth, *Story of the Football League*, pp. 6–7; Green, *History*, pp. 398–99.
53 For expressions of this opinion, see reports of Football League AGMs in *Athletic News*, 6 June 1904; 5 June 1905; *Athletic News*, 6 March 1911. At the 1902 AGM,

almost all the proposals emanating from the Management Committee were vetoed. Report of Football League AGM in *Athletic News*, 2 June 1902.

54 Football League Minutes, Management Committee, 3 June 1912 (AGM); 28 May 1923; reports of Football League AGMs in *Athletic News*, 10 June 1912; 4 June 1923, 9 June 1924.

55 Football League Handbook, 1937–38, Rule 80.

56 The Football League was converted into a limited liability company in May 1904.

57 *Athletic News*, 2 June 1902. 'Tityrus' (James Catton) similarly accused the League at its 1904 AGM of pursuing 'a policy of do-nothing'. 'No corporate body that I have ever known can demolish an agenda paper with such efficiency, neatness and dispatch, and no society ... can resolutely set a face against all change, and negative all proposals'. Report of the Football League AGM in *Athletic News*, 6 June 1904.

58 See Sutcliffe, Brierley and Howarth, *Story of the Football League*, Chapter 9.

59 *The People*, 4 June 1933.

60 Fishwick, *English Football*, pp. 17–18.

61 Football League Minutes, Management Committee, 5 November 1930.

62 *Sporting Chronicle*, 31 May 1933.

63 Sutcliffe, Brierley and Howarth, *Story of the Football League*, pp. 51–67; Lowerson, *Sport*, p. 23; D. Cannadine, 'The Context, Performance and Meaning of Ritual: The British Monarchy and the Invention of Tradition, c. 1820–1977' in *The Invention of Tradition*, ed. E. Hobsbawm and T. Ranger, Cambridge, Cambridge University Press, 1983, pp. 101–64.

64 The quotation is taken from Clark, *British Clubs*, p. 248.

65 FA Report and Recommendation of the Commission Adopted by the Council, re. Manchester United FC, 30 March 1910; FA Council Minutes, 22 April 1910.

66 Report of Football League AGM in *Athletic News*, 20 June 1910. The 'other things' almost certainly included his decision to support the deletion of the maximum wage rule at the previous FA annual meeting, for which he was publicly criticised by Preston's Tom Houghton. Report of FA AGM in *Athletic News*, 14 June 1909.

67 Football League Minutes, Management Committee, 13 September 1927.

68 For examples and comparisons, see Football League Handbook 1890–91, Rules 2 and 6; Handbook 1900–01, Rules 3 and 11; Handbook 1910–11, Rules 3 and 12; Handbook 1919–20, Rules 2 and 12; Handbook 1937–38, Rule 15.

69 See Football League Minutes, Management Committee, 10 May 1912; Green, *History*, p. 400. In contrast with the Northern Union, the practice of deducting points from clubs for offences was never seriously entertained after Notts County forced the Committee to remit a point deducted from them for fielding an unregistered player in 1899. Sutcliffe, Brierley and Howarth, *Story of the Football League*, p. 6; P. Greenhalgh, '"The Work and Play Principle": The Professional Regulations of the Northern Rugby Football Union, 1898–1905', *International Journal of the History of Sport*, Vol. 9, 1992, pp. 364–69.

70 *Athletic News*, 29 April 1901.

71 For examples, see AVFC, Board Minutes, 7 September 1912; Football League Minutes, Management Committee, 9 August 1912; 3, 24 February 1913; WHUFC, Board Minutes, 28 February, 5 March 1928.

72 See *Athletic News*, 17 April 1917; 14 March 1921; AFC, Catton Folders, A–B, Letter from Fred Rinder to James Catton, 6 October 1919, p. 36.

73 Leavey subsequently argued that his nomination was 'not intended seriously' and that he had intended to withdraw it at the AGM but had been unable to do so. In a

letter to *Athletic News* he suggested that 'the bare idea of any member of our committee opposing the re-election of our president [was] altogether too absurd for one moment's consideration'. *Athletic News*, 13 June 1904.

74 J. Bradley, 'The MCC, Society and Empire: A Portrait of Cricket's Ruling Body, 1860–1914', in *The Cultural Bond: Sport, Empire, Society*, ed. J. A. Mangan, London, Frank Cass, 1992, p. 28; Football League Minutes, Football League Shareholders' Meeting Minutes (First and Second Divisions), 6 March 1931; Report of Football League AGM in *Athletic News*, 8 June 1931.

75 Football League Handbooks, 1910–36.

76 Clegg was Chairman of the FA from 1890 to 1937, while in 1923 he also became FA President (effectively an honorary position). In 1907 William Bellamy, the FA representative for Lincolnshire and one-time Management Committee member, complained that 'for some time ... the work and general policy of the Association have been almost entirely in the hands of Mr Clegg, and this is a state of affairs which I for one do not agree with. My idea of the duty of the Chairman is that he should preside at the Council meetings and not direct and govern the whole business of the Association, and there can be no denying that that is what obtains at present'. AFC, Catton Folders, B–C, W. Bellamy to D. H. Woolfall, 1907, otherwise undated, p. 277.

77 WHUFC, Board Minutes, 21, 28 July 1925; T. Matthews (with L. Smith), *The Wolves: An Encyclopedia of Wolverhampton Wanderers Football Club, 1877–1989*, London, Paper Plane, 1989, p. 29 (although it gives the wrong date for McKenna's visit).

78 Wolverhampton Wanderers FC Programme, 19 September 1925.

79 See S. Gunn, *The Public Culture of the Victorian Middle Class: Ritual and Authority and the English Industrial City, 1840–1914*, Manchester, Manchester University Press, 2000, p. 163.

80 Football League Handbook, 1890–91, Rule 14.

81 For a detailed account of Lockett's resignation see Inglis, *League Football*, pp. 50–52.

82 Report of Football League AGM in *Athletic News*, 2 June 1902; *Barrett's Directory of Preston*, 1904, 1910, 1913, 1922, 1926, 1932, 1940; Football League Minutes, Management Committee, 5 November 1926.

83 Inglis, *League Football*, p. 54; Fred Howarth's obituary in *Lancashire Evening Post*, 12 January 1972.

84 Hardaker, *Hardaker*, p. 36.

85 *Lancashire Evening Post*, 12 January 1972.

86 Hardaker, *Hardaker*, p. 41. For a detailed description of the administration of the League from a much later period, but with inevitable similarities, see Chapter 5 of *Hardaker*. Hardaker argues that the role of Secretary in his era (1957–79) was really more like a 'general manager' (p. 64).

87 These occupational categories are borrowed from G. Routh, *Occupation and Pay in Great Britain, 1906–79*, London, Macmillan, 1980. Routh identifies seven broad occupational categories, two of which are sub-divided: higher professional (1A); lower professional (1B); employers and proprietors (2A); managers and administrators (2B); clerical workers (3); foremen, inspectors and supervisors (4); skilled manual workers (5); semi-skilled manual workers (6); and unskilled manual workers (7).

88 On the role of clerks, see T. Mason, *The Blues and the Reds: A History of the Liverpool and Everton Football Clubs*, Liverpool, Historic Society of Lancashire and Cheshire, 1985, pp. 1–2; Vamplew, *Pay Up*, p. 157.

89 Mason, *Association Football*, pp. 42–49; Tischler, *Footballers*, p. 74. On 'psychic income', see D. Adair, 'Psychic Income and the Administration of English County

Cricket, 1870–1914', *The Sports Historian*, Vol. 14, 1994, pp. 66–72. It has been suggested, however, that both Davies and Norris exerted considerable influence on the Committee through personal nominees, principally John Bentley and William Hall. The assertion is highly debatable in Bentley's case due to his long connection with the Committee before joining United, but the evidence is more persuasive for Hall and Norris, who had been directors together at Fulham before joining Arsenal. See Tyler and Soar, *Arsenal*; D. Turner and A. White, *Fulham: A Complete Record, 1879–1987*, Derby, Breedon, 1987, pp. 45–46.

90 Mason, *Association Football*, pp. 42–49; Tischler, *Footballers*, pp. 72–76; Vamplew, *Pay Up*, pp. 166, 168–70.

91 R. McKibbin, *Classes and Cultures: England, 1918–50*, Oxford, Oxford University Press, 1998, p. 348.

92 Fishwick, *English Football*, p. 27; Korr, *West Ham*, pp. 243–44; Arnold, *A Game That Would Pay*, pp. 201–02.

93 Green, *History*, pp. 194–95.

94 J. Williams, *Cricket and England: A Cultural and Social History of the Inter-war Years*, London, Frank Cass, 1999, pp. 20–25.

95 T. Collins, *Rugby's Great Split: Class, Culture and the Origins of Rugby League Football*, London, Frank Cass, 1998, p. 242 (Table A.7); Greenhalgh, 'Work and Play Principle', pp. 358–59. Also, E. Dunning and K. Sheard, *Barbarians, Gentlemen and Players: A Sociological Study of the Development of Rugby Football*, Oxford, Martin Robertson, 1979, pp. 188, 203.

96 See individual profiles in Gibson and Pickford, *Association Football*, Vol. 3, pp. 149–52, 159–62, 209–10, and in Sutcliffe and Hargreaves, *Lancashire FA*, pp. 58–65, 157–59, 234–35. For Bentley, see the 'Popular People' series in *Lancashire Review*, October 1897, pp. 42–44; *Windsor Magazine*, April 1902, pp. 665–70; F. Wall, *Fifty Years in Football*, London, Cassell, 1935; W. Pickford, *A Glance Back at the FA Council, 1888–1938*, Bournemouth, Bournemouth Guardian, 1938; P. M. Young, *Bolton Wanderers*, London, Stanley Paul, 1961, pp. 43–46. For Lewis, see M. Jackman, *Blackburn Rovers: The Official Encyclopedia*, Derby, Breedon, 1994, p. 145. For Sutcliffe, see William Cuff's appreciation in Sutcliffe, Brierley and Howarth, *Story of the Football League*, pp. 166–67. On sporting images and stereotypes of 'northernness', see T. Mason, 'Football, Sport of the North?', p. 42, and R. Holt, 'Heroes of the North: Sport and the Shaping of Regional Identity' in *Sport and Identity in the North of England*, ed. J. Hill and J. Williams, Keele, Keele University Press, 1996, pp. 138–39. On the historical origins of these northern characteristics, see H. M. Jewell, *The North–South Divide: The Origins of Northern Consciousness in England*, Manchester, Manchester University Press, 1994, p. 208.

97 Jackman, *Blackburn Rovers*, p. 145; McGregor's obituary in *Birmingham Daily Mail*, 23 December 1911; *Preston Guardian*, 15 February 1936; *Lancashire Evening Post*, 12 January 1972.

98 T. Keates, *History of the Everton Football Club, 1878/9–1928/9*, Liverpool, Thomas Brakell, 1929, p. 114; Inglis, *League Football*, p. 171.

99 Section in 'Who's Who' on Brook Hirst in *Huddersfield County Borough Directory*, 1937; *Grimsby Evening Telegraph*, 18 April 1945. The denominational intricacies of education in the West Riding of Yorkshire are discussed in P. Joyce, *Work, Society and Politics: The Culture of the Factory in Later Victorian Britain*, Brighton, Harvester, 1980, pp. 30–32.

100 Mason, *Blues and Reds*, p. 17; Houghton's obituary in *Preston Guardian*, 21 September 1912.
101 McGregor's obituary in *Birmingham Daily Post*, 21 December 1911; Inglis, *League Football*, p. 108; G. C. Miller, *Blackburn Worthies of Yesterday: A Biographical Galaxy*, Blackburn, Blackburn Society of Antiquaries, 1961, p. 229.
102 *Birmingham Daily Mail*, 23 March 1937, and Hart's obituary in *Birmingham Daily Post*, 6 June 1940.
103 Inglis, *League Football*, pp. 392, 393; *Barrett's Directory of Preston and Fylde Districts*, 1901; *Ward's Directory of Newcastle-on-Tyne*, 1924.
104 FA Report and Recommendation of the Commission Adopted by the Council, re. Manchester United, 30 March 1910.
105 West Bromwich Albion FC (WBAFC), Circular to Creditors, 14 December 1905; 16 March 1907; 30 May 1908; List of Creditors, 28 February 1905; December 1909; *Athletic News*, 6 March 1905; B. Goodwin, *Spurs: A Complete Record*, Derby, Breedon, 1993, p. 15.
106 OAFC, Board Minutes, 17 July 1906; 3 December 1907; S. W. Beckett, *Team From a Town of Chimneys – Revisited: The Official Chronicles of the Oldham Athletic AFC Ltd., 1897–1990*, Manchester, Comprehensive Art Services, 1990, p. 15; Dykes, *Oldham Athletic*, p. 10.
107 On the broader connections between sport and alcohol, see T. Collins and W. Vamplew (eds), *Mud, Sweat and Beers: A Cultural History of Sport and Alcohol*, Oxford, Berg, 2002.
108 M. Clapson, 'Playing the System: The World of Organised Street Betting in Manchester, Salford and Bolton, c. 1880–1939' in *Workers' Worlds: Cultures and Communities in Manchester and Salford, 1880–1939*, ed. A. Davies and S. Fielding, Manchester, Manchester University Press, 1992, p. 157; Mason, *Association Football*, pp. 179–87.
109 Both quotations are from M. Clapson, *A Bit of a Flutter: Popular Gambling and English Society, c. 1823–1961*, Manchester, Manchester University Press, 1992, pp. 168–69.
110 *Athletic News*, 14 June 1920.
111 See Football League Minutes, Management Committee, 5 December 1921; 23 October 1922; 5 March 1928.
112 Cited in Inglis, *League Football*, p. 146. Also see *Daily Mirror*, 29 November 1935; Association Football Players' and Trainers' Union (AFPTU) Minutes, 26 August 1935 (AGM).
113 Clapson, *A Bit of a Flutter*, p. 170; Fishwick, *English Fotball*, pp. 128–29; SUFC, Football Committee Minutes, 4 August 1938; OAFC, Board Minutes, 11 May, 27 July 1938; SRO, ITFC, Board Minutes, 2 August 1938.
114 Cuff's obituary in *The Liverpolitan*, February 1949.
115 *Albion News*, 22 October 1921; 18 November 1922; Clapson, *A Bit of a Flutter*, p. 163.
116 *Preston Guardian*, 21 September 1912; Inglis, *League Football*, p. 394.
117 *Birmingham Daily Post*, 21 December 1911; Sutcliffe's obituary in *Rossendale Free Press*, 14 January 1939; Oakley's obituary in the *Wolverhampton Express and Star*, 4 July 1958; Inglis, *League Football*, pp. 108, 109, 391. Other members of the Committee were from families with traditions of involvement in public life. Hart's uncle was an alderman, Keys's father was a prominent councillor in West Bromwich, whilst Brook Hirst's father-in-law was the former Mayor of Huddersfield, an alder-

man, a county councillor and founder member of the Huddersfield and County Conservative Society. *Birmingham Daily Post*, 6 June 1940; Keys's obituary in *Midland Chronicle and Free Press*, 23 August 1929; *Huddersfield County Borough Directory*, 1937.

118 Bassett's obituary in *Midland Chronicle and Free Press*, 9 April 1937. As well as Bassett, Baxter, Tempest and Oakley were local magistrates.

119 McKibbin, *Classes and Cultures*, pp. 89–90; J. M. Roberts, 'Freemasonry: Possibilities of a Neglected Subject', *English Historical Review*, Vol. 84, 1969, pp. 323–35; Joyce, *Work*, p. 37; Lowerson, *Sport*, pp. 21–22; Inglis, *League Football*, pp. 80, 171; Rinder's obituary in *Birmingham Daily Post* and *Birmingham Gazette*, 27 July 1938. Houghton, Tempest and Bach were also freemasons.

120 R. H. Trainor, *Black Country Elites: The Exercise of Authority in an Industrialised Area, 1830–1900*, Oxford, Clarendon, 1993, p. 123; A. Russell, 'Local Elites and Working-Class Response in the North-West, 1870-1895: Paternalism and Deference Reconsidered', *Northern History*, Vol. 23, 1987, pp. 158, 156. McKibbin (*Classes and Cultures*) argues that directors of football clubs 'were often attached to business and social networks which brought them together in several overlapping spheres' (p. 348).

121 Fishwick, *English Football*, pp. 30–32; Korr, *West Ham*, pp. 39–40; Tischler, *Footballers*, pp. 71–72. For a more subtle analysis of the role of football directors in the construction of civic identities outside England, see Johnes, *Soccer*, pp. 146–57.

122 Sutcliffe and Hargreaves, *Lancashire FA*, pp. 58–61; Sutcliffe's obituary in *Burnley Express*, 14 January 1939.

123 Sutcliffe and Hargreaves, *Lancashire FA*, p. 61.

124 Rinder's obituary in *Birmingham Daily Mail*, 27 July 1938; Inglis, *League Football*, p. 64.

125 McKenna retired from his job as a vaccination officer in 1922, while Rinder was forced to resign from the Birmingham City Surveyor's staff on reaching the age limit of 65 in the same year. Barcroft and Cadman also retired while on the Committee, but both took unpaid positions – as Honorary Secretary and Managing Director respectively – of their clubs. *Birmingham Daily Mail*, 26 June 1922; *Blackpool Gazette*, 13 January 1934; letter from A. Porter to the author, 27 November 1994.

126 *Birmingham Daily Mail*, 23 December 1911; Inglis, *League Football*, p. 85. See also Shillcock's obituary in *Birmingham Daily Mail*, 10 October 1940.

127 FA Report and Recommendation of the Commission Adopted by the Council, re. Manchester United, 30 March 1910; Tischler, *Footballers*, p. 74.

128 AVFC, Board Minutes, 11 October 1910; 2 April 1912; Football League Minutes, Management Committee, 3 June 1912 (AGM); Sutcliffe and Hargreaves, *Lancashire FA*, p. 61; OAFC, Board Minutes, 24 July 1906.

129 *Rossendale Free Press*, 18 January 1939.

130 Gibson and Pickford, *Association Football*, Vol. 3, p. 159; Jackman, *Blackburn Rovers*, p. 145; Miller, *Blackburn Worthies*, p. 229.

131 Sutcliffe, Brierley and Howarth, *Story of the Football League*, pp. 163–65; Sutcliffe and Hargreaves, *Lancashire FA*, p. 61; Gibson and Pickford, *Association Football*, Vol. 3, p. 186; *Wolverhampton Express and Star*, 4 July 1958.

132 *Lancashire Review*, October 1897, p. 43; Gibson and Pickford, *Association Football*, Vol. 3, pp. 160, 165; letter from A. Porter to the author, 27 November 1994.

133 *Windsor Magazine*, April 1902, p. 668.

134 C. Francis, *History of the Blackburn Rovers FC, 1875-1925*, Preston, Toulmin, 1925, p. 195; Gibson and Pickford, *Association Football*, Vol. 3, p. 161; *Burnley Express*, 14 January 1939; Mason, *Blues and Reds*, p. 5.
135 Football League Minutes, 3 June 1912 (AGM); *Athletic News*, 10 December 1906.
136 For parallels with cricket's MCC, see Bradley, 'The MCC', p. 30.
137 See McIvor, *Organised Capital*.
138 Political and Economic Planning, 'The Football Industry – 1', *Planning*, Vol. 17, 1951, p. 163.
139 Morris, 'Clubs', p. 395.
140 McIvor, *Organised Capital*, p. 90.
141 *Athletic News*, 13 May 1901; Sutcliffe, Brierley and Howarth, *Story of the Football League*, p. 65.
142 Report of Football League AGM in *Athletic News*, 1 June 1908; *Athletic News*, 18 May 1903.
143 Report of Football League AGM in *Athletic News*, 24 July 1916.
144 Football League Minutes, Management Committee, 31 May 1920 (AGM); 5 December 1921, 18 December 1922.
145 Football League Minutes, Management Committee, 2 June 1924 (AGM); 10, 12 March 1924 (SGM of Third Division Southern and Northern Sections); Report of Football League AGM in *Athletic News*, 9 June 1924.
146 See Annual Financial Statements of Football League and Football League Mutual Insurance Federation (FLMIF), *passim*.
147 For example, see Football League Handbook, 1893–94, Rule 15.
148 Football League Minutes, Management Committee, 20 December 1920; 11 May, 30 May 1921 (AGM); 29 May 1922 (AGM).
149 Vamplew, *Pay Up*, p. 137.
150 Football League Minutes, Management Committee, 1 March 1913. Also see Simmons, *Tottenham*.
151 Report of Football League AGM in *Athletic News*, 2 June 1913; Football League Minutes, Management Committee, 26 May 1913 (AGM).
152 For a chronological account of events, see G. S. Binns, *Huddersfield Town: 75 Years On*, Huddersfield, Huddersfield Town FC, 1984, pp. 30–69; T. Frost, *Huddersfield Town: A Complete Record, 1910–90*, Derby, Breedon, 1990, pp. 39–46.
153 *Huddersfield Daily Examiner*, 10 November 1919; *Athletic News*, 8 December 1919.
154 Sutcliffe, Brierley and Howarth, *Story of the Football League*, p. 11; *Athletic News*, 12 March 1906. If a club failed to follow the executive's advice and crowd disturbances followed, however, it was obviously liable to ground suspension or other punitive action by the governing body. On this see R. W. Lewis, 'Football Hooliganism in England Before 1914: A Critique of the Dunning Thesis', *International Journal of the History of Sport*, Vol. 13, 1996, pp. 310–19.
155 Football League Minutes, Management Committee, 9 May, 13 January 1913.
156 SUFC Programme, 6 September 1920; Football League Minutes, Management Committee, 10 January, 1–2 July 1921; 8 April 1927 (AGM); Inglis, *League Football*, p. 125.
157 *Topical Times*, 17 March 1928; Football League Minutes, Management Committee, 5 March 1928. The Committee's decision cost many clubs an important source of extra revenue. West Ham was not the only club forced to forgo a substantial offer – £2,500 in this case – to host summer speedway racing at its ground. WHUFC, Board Minutes, 28 February, 6 March 1928.

158 *Athletic News*, 6 February 1905; Football League Minutes, Management Committee, 2 December 1912, 17 January 1921.
159 Football League Minutes, Management Committee, 11 October 1920; *Sheffield Independent*, 20 October 1920.
160 Quoted in SUFC Programme, 30 October 1920.
161 Football League Minutes, Management Committee, 13 November 1913.
162 See, for instance, Football League Minutes, Management Committee, 15 November 1912; 22 September 1922.
163 Football League Minutes, Management Committee, 14-15 June, 6 July 1923.
164 *Athletic News*, 23 April 1906; Football League Minutes, Management Committee, 10 May 1912.
165 *Athletic News*, 26 May 1924; Report of Football League AGM in *Athletic News*, 4 June 1923; 9 June 1924.
166 Football League Commission Report on Middlesbrough FC, printed in *Athletic News*, 5 June 1911; *Athletic News*, 19 June 1911.
167 See Arnold, 'Not Playing the Game?'; M. Jarred and M. MacDonald, *Leeds United: A Complete Record, 1919–1989*, Derby, Breedon, 1989, pp. 344–48.
168 *Athletic News*, 20 October 1919.
169 *Football and Sports Special*, 1 November 1919.
170 Arnold, 'Not Playing the Game?', p. 117.
171 Inglis, *League Football*, p. 101.
172 Report of Football League AGM in *Athletic News*, 26 July 1915.
173 Report of Football League AGM in *Athletic News*, 26 July 1915.
174 Inglis, *League Football*, p. 101.
175 Report of Football League AGM in *Athletic News*, 26 July 1915.
176 Report of Football League AGM in *Athletic News*, 24 July 1916; *Athletic News*, 7 August 1916.
177 Report of Football League AGM in *Athletic News*, 17 July 1917.
178 SUFC, Football Committee Minutes, 4 May 1909; *Athletic News*, 17 May 1909; *Football and Sports Special*, 5 June 1909.
179 Report of Football League AGM in *Athletic News*, 14 June 1909.
180 SUFC, Football Committee Minutes, 29 April 1913.
181 Football League Minutes, Report of Meeting of Football League Clubs, First and Second Division, 4 April 1930.
182 Football League Minutes, Management Committee, 5 December 1930.
183 See *Sporting Chronicle*, 10 May, 3 June 1935; SUFC, Football Committee Minutes, 24 April, 7 May 1935.
184 For detailed accounts of this kind, see S. Inglis, *Soccer in the Dock: A History of British Football Scandals*, London, Willow, 1985, Chapter 7, or an almost identical account in Inglis, *League Football*, Chapter 14. Also see A. Ledbrooke and E. Turner, *Soccer from the Press Box*, London, Sportsman's Book Club, 1955, pp. 70–74.
185 Inglis, *League Football*, p. 149.
186 *Daily Mirror*, 22, 24 February 1936; *The Times*, 26 February 1936.
187 *The Times*, 26, 27 February 1936.
188 *Sporting Chronicle*, 3 March 1936.
189 Inglis, *League Football*, p. 154.
190 *All Sports Weekly*, 11 September 1926.

CHAPTER THREE

Players I: Employment Conditions

Contemporary observers as well as historians have regarded the peculiar employment conditions within the Football League as somehow unique in British industrial relations. In particular, the twin pillars of the League structure – the retain-and-transfer system and the maximum wage – have been seen as tantamount to a form of wage slavery, denying the player the basic freedom enjoyed by any other employee to leave his or her employment when s/he liked, and to sell his or her labour to the highest bidder. Players' Union secretary Syd Owen remarked in 1912 that 'the professional player is the slave of the club and they can do practically anything they want with him'; decades later, in his autobiography, Jimmy Guthrie, a successor of Owen's, referred to the footballer as 'a bondsman, a serf, a slave'.[1] The historian Nicholas Fishwick, meanwhile, chose to describe professional footballers in the first half of the twentieth century as 'obedient servants'.[2] Yet this emphasis on player acquiescence and the master–servant relationship not only provides a rather distorted and partial picture of the complex ways in which the labour market operated until the Second World War, but also has the effect of isolating the experience of employees in the football industry from wider social developments. Hence a dominant theme of this and the next chapter will be the trend towards what Mike Savage and Andrew Miles have described as 'the bureaucratisation of the labour market' from the late Victorian era onwards.[3] In the Football League this took the form of the gradual development of central regulation and formal control over conditions relating to the employment, pay, movement, discipline, standards and welfare of players. Moreover, we need to recognise that the most immediate employment relationship – between player and club – was in fact cross-cut by a complex and often contradictory set of connections involving the player, the Players' Union, the club, the FA and the Football League executive.

This chapter focuses on four important areas of the employment of League footballers: the recruitment of players and their movement between clubs; contracts; transfer conditions; and the payment of professionals. It will explore the extent to which the opportunities of football employees were constrained by the artificially constructed labour market. How free were players to move where and when they wished, and what say did they have in the conditions of their employment? In addition, we shall consider not only how much players were paid, but how this was determined. Did earnings differ substantially from player to player and club to club, and how did this compare to rates of pay in similar occupations?

The recruitment of players

Playing football could be a precarious occupation. Contracts were short and most employees faced the possibility of being released at the end of each season. Even for the best players, injury, loss of form or a change of management could rapidly prompt the end of a contract or even a career. The labour market in the Football League was therefore remarkably fluid and subject to continual change and renewal, with the supply of new talent coming from youth and amateur ranks as well as semi-professional or non-elite football. In view of this, there are considerable difficulties in establishing the precise number of players involved in League football.

The Football League's own figures reveal that 502 players were registered with the 12 member clubs in 1891, a number that had increased to 675 in the 16 clubs by 1896.[4] *Athletic News* listed 997 players registered to 39 of the 40 League clubs in 1911, and by 1925 at least 2,123 players were engaged by the 88 clubs in the League's four divisions.[5] There was relatively little fluctuation in player numbers between the wars. The League reported 2,023 registered players in May 1930 and 2,543 by May 1932.[6] In 1938, the Players' Union reckoned that there were approximately 2,500 top-class professionals, most of whom were attached to Football League clubs; a higher figure of 3,000 was quoted in correspondence between the League and the Union in 1934.[7] Squad sizes varied considerably over time and from club to club. Aston Villa considered that its staff of 30 professionals and 'a few good amateurs' was sufficient for the 1907–08 season, especially as the club had chosen not to run a third team.[8] The average First Division squad in 1911 consisted of 29 part-time or full-time professionals, while clubs in the Second Division employed just over 21. By the 1920s the leading clubs generally signed between 25 and 35 players in May of each year, and often engaged an additional few before the season commenced in September.[9] In 1934, the Secretary Fred Howarth estimated the average squad size of Football League clubs at between 25 and 30. Leading clubs like Manchester City registered between 35 and 43 players each season during the 1930s (see Table 3.2), while Preston North End expanded its staff to some 40 to 50 professionals and part-time amateurs.[10]

Squads were smaller in the lower divisions. Clubs signed fewer full-time professionals and relied more on the services of part-time and amateur players. The Rochdale management struggled through the 1931–32 season with a squad of only 14 full-time and four part-time professionals, but alleged that 'it was impossible to run a club with fewer players'.[11] Third Division Walsall employed a core of between 19 and 31 professional players each season during the 1930s, but could also call on a large pool of local amateurs, mainly to man its second and third teams (see Table 3.1). Durham City was probably less typical in having just nine professionals compared with 20 amateurs on its books in 1925, yet most Third Division clubs, and many in the higher divisions, regularly included a number of amateurs and part-timers, presumably as a means of keeping wage bills low.[12] In 1923 the Management Committee had advised Northern Section clubs in financial difficulties to reduce the number of professionals engaged.[13] With the onset of the Depression, it was not uncommon for players to be given free transfers as a short-term cost-cutting measure.[14]

Official figures of *registered* players, however, are a misleading guide to the numbers actively involved in League football on a regular basis. Not every player who registered with a club and the governing bodies actually signed a contract. Wray Vamplew, with reference to the period before 1914, has pointed out that a large percentage of registered professionals – often over 40 per cent each season – never actually played a League match.[15] This was partly the result of competition within clubs, but can also be explained by the common practice of labour-hoarding. Many clubs retained players who had not received wages at all, or for some time, and had drifted towards a lower standard of football or to different employment entirely. Despite an attempt by the Management Committee in 1899 to introduce a six-month time limit within which a club had to pay or play its registered professionals, clubs continued to hold large numbers of inactive players on their retained lists. In 1901, West Bromwich Albion reportedly held 120 retained players, little more than a quarter of whom were legitimate club employees.[16] Billy Meredith estimated in 1912 that perhaps three-quarters of the names on a club's staff list were 'young amateur lads who have been signed on at some time with a view to being used in a second team in cases of emergency'. The Management Committee recognised 'that many players who have long since finished football are still included in such lists'.[17] In these circumstances, it is difficult to know exactly how many careers followed a path similar to that of Aston Villa's Knight. He had signed for the Birmingham club in 1905 and played a single match for the junior team before spending five seasons in junior football. During this time, Aston Villa neither approached him nor offered him an engagement, but he was nevertheless kept on the club's retained list and was hence theoretically still its player. Eventually, in 1911, a Southern League club offered Knight an engagement, and the Management Committee fined Aston Villa for not removing him from their retained list.[18]

Table 3.1: Player registrations at Walsall FC, 1932/33–1939/40

Season	*Professional registrations*	*Amateur registrations*	*Amateur signing Football League forms*
1932–33	24	45	5
1933–34	21	33	8
1934–35	19	20	3
1935–36	28	25	10
1936–37	29	45	10
1937–38	27	62	13
1938–39	31	73	12
1939–40	24	14	11

Source: Walsall Local History Centre (WLHC), Walsall FC Players' Registration Book, 1932–46.

Table 3.2: Player registrations and transfers at Manchester City FC, 1931/32–1939/40

Season	*Registered players*	*Transfers out*
1931–32	35	10
1932–33	35	9
1933–34	37	9
1934–35	39	11
1935–36	37	6
1936–37	41	10
1937–38	43	10
1938–39	40	4
1939–40*	36	1

*Up to 21 December 1939.

Source: PFA, File 35, statistics required from the Football League in the cases Corbett v. Inland Revenue and Dale v. Inland Revenue, 1939.

The recruitment of players by League clubs underwent significant changes in this period. Football agents and press advertising, both important means of finding players in the early days of League football, seem to have declined by the early twentieth century. Agents, in particular, were increasingly regarded with suspicion by club and League officials, and the FA actually prohibited the engagement of players through agents. However, they did not disappear, continuing to operate surreptitiously as middle men between clubs and players. In January 1909, *Football Chat* printed a circular letter from a London-based agent willing to procure players for any club. Despite affirming that he was 'in no sense an agent' but would act 'in a private capacity … as a friend of the club', the letter included a scale of travelling expenses and charges.[19] References in the minutes of the FA to the suspension of former players H. J. F. Sims of East Ham and C. F. Caswell of Cardiff, and the prohibition of bodies such as Birmingham's Football Players' Agency, indicate that agents continued to operate on the margins of the elite game.[20] Advertisements in the sporting press were still a popular recruitment strategy between the wars, especially for clubs in the lower divisions. *Sporting Chronicle* ran a weekly 'Situations Vacant' column throughout the 1930s, which was frequently used by Second and Third Division clubs in search of 'first-class players'. Darlington advertised in its pages regularly, while in 1934 the club's search for 'players for all positions' was targeted more regionally through the placement of similar advertisements in the *Northern Echo* and *Newcastle Chronicle*.[21] During the 1920s and early 1930s, a successful First Division club such as Sheffield United still occasionally considered it beneficial to advertise in *Athletic News*, although this was increasingly regarded as supplementary to more sophisticated and reliable methods of recruitment.[22]

Advertising declined in importance as clubs began to develop their own scouting networks. Although hearsay and informal recommendations were perhaps still the most important ways of finding new players before 1914, many clubs were beginning to engage itinerant scouts on small fees to scour parts of the country for talent. In its first season in the League, for example, Oldham Athletic paid a local man 30 shillings per week as expenses to scout for players.[23] Scouting networks became increasingly elaborate in the inter-war period. By the early 1930s, Sheffield United had developed an organised and coordinated scouting network covering Lancashire and Cheshire, Birmingham and District, Lincolnshire and the North-east. Each scout was paid £1 per match plus a 10 shilling allowance for lost time if required to watch midweek matches. This was supplemented by the established practice of appointing a number of senior club professionals, including the famous ex-England international Ernest Needham, to 'look out for players', presumably at both local and national levels.[24] Reports were sent to the board of directors for consideration, and generally a director or the club's senior scout would be sent to watch the player again before any attempt was made to sign him. At West Ham United, all such scouting reports were systematically recorded and filed for future reference.[25] The most successful club of the inter-war years, Arsenal, took its scouting system particularly seriously. In 1934, the club appointed Peter McWilliam as its travelling scout and hired the former Bradford City and Rangers player Tommy Cairns to cover Scotland. McWilliam and Cairns joined another retired professional, Andy Aitken, who was responsible for finding players in the Midlands, while the former Charlton Athletic manager Albert Lindon had been appointed to South Wales. One commentator reported in 1938 that Arsenal paid its chief scout £1,000 a year, although by contrast Second Division Burnley relied on directors and 'friends' to find new talent, and employed just two regular scouts at an overall cost of 50 shillings per week.[26] Nevertheless, by the 1930s even some of the less wealthy clubs considered it necessary to organise a national scouting network, enabling them to choose from the widest possible pool of talent. On their elevation to the Third Division South, Ipswich Town appointed four scouts to cover Southern England, the Midlands and the North, Manchester and Scotland respectively.[27]

Few scouting networks were confined to England. The leading clubs certainly regarded international and inter-league fixtures as major recruiting opportunities, but they also kept an eye on regular club games. Aston Villa's representative at Linfield and Glentoran matches in Belfast during March 1925 could inform his board of the presence of scouts from Burnley, Liverpool and Everton.[28] The sporting press likewise kept its readers acquainted with the scouting activities of Football League clubs in the Irish Free State, a number of whom had dedicated Dublin-based representatives.[29] The correspondence files of Aston Villa's Secretary, George Ramsay, reveal that he kept in regular contact with the club's Scottish scout McIlroy, whom he addressed informally as 'Mac'. In February 1922 Ramsay gently censured 'Mac' for his poor rate of successful recommendations ('When the Directors notice so many Scotch players coming this way they ask me when our turn is coming'), and trusted that future suggestions could be made without directors having 'to come down and confirm your view'.[30] Other clubs looked even further afield. Huddersfield Town received occasional recommendations from a contact in Ontario, and sometimes invited guest players over for a trial; Aston Villa, too, benefited from Canadian scouting.[31]

However, clubs could not afford to neglect local players. Junior football remained the most fertile source of new talent for League clubs throughout this period. Former employees, directors, schoolteachers and even local journalists often acted as informal talent spotters and occasionally established personal contacts with League clubs.[32] Aston Villa sent former player Jimmy Logan a cheque for £20 in 1927 'in appreciation of his past services' and instructed him 'to book any junior of the right build etc. he thinks good enough for us'.[33] More importantly, prominent amateur clubs were often adopted formally as nurseries by local professional counterparts. Such agreements, increasingly common by the early 1910s, enabled League clubs to test, and secure priority on, local players in return for financial subsidies. In addition, they would sometimes use nursery clubs to farm out any promising but immature players of their own. Sheffield United, for example, agreed to pay grants of £20 and £50 in 1929 and 1930 respectively to the Norton Woodseats club on the condition that it could 'have first claim on any of their [the Woodseats'] players'.[34] West Ham United established similar agreements with Park Royal and Colchester; Blackburn Rovers did likewise with Victoria Cross; and Aston Villa had a long-standing association with Stourbridge.[35] Non-League Margate's arrangement with Arsenal during the 1930s allowed the Kent club to progress financially and competitively. In 1936 it reached the Third Round of the FA Cup with a team including six players who had arrived via Arsenal.[36] No doubt these relationships could be exploitative. League directorates often regarded nursery club players as their own, even including them on their official retained lists. *Athletic News* accused Villa of occupying 'a position of dictatorship' with regard to its nursery clubs and, in particular, claiming 'little less than actual ownership' over Stourbridge.[37] Yet in general, such agreements were mutually beneficial and continued to be advocated by League officials and sought by amateur clubs in financial difficulties.

Some clubs were particularly keen to assert the local character of their team, and pursued regional recruitment more vigorously than others. The policy of Wolverhampton Wanderers directors to sign only players from within a 50-mile radius might originally have been intended to reduce costs, but came to represent a defining characteristic of the club before the First World War.[38] Barnsley won considerable praise in the press for reaching the 1910 FA Cup Final with an all-English team, while West Bromwich Albion were similarly applauded when it won the 1919–20 First Division championship with a squad composed entirely of Englishmen, all but four of whom were born within a dozen miles of the ground.[39] By the inter-war years, however, predominantly local recruitment of this kind was increasingly recognised as an unobtainable ideal by the most successful League clubs. In 1910, well over half of all League players (54.8 per cent in Division One and 62.1 per cent in Division Two) were born outside the region in which they played. This percentage had increased by 1925 to 61.7 per cent at the top level, 59.2 per cent in Division Two and 71.6 per cent in Division Three (South).[40] Clubs in the Northern Section of Division Three, which had less money to spend and were often located in areas with a tradition of producing professional footballers, made far greater use of local talent. It is in such a context that the decision of the Darlington board in March 1938 to 'use every endeavour to encourage local players' should be seen.[41] In 1925, 30 per cent of Northern Section players were born within 10–12 miles of the club ground (compared to just 16 per cent in the Southern Section), while only 43.2 per cent came from outside the region.

The tendency to look further afield for new players can be partially explained by the growth and increasing importance of the transfer market. The anecdotal evidence suggests that the number of transfers and the amounts involved increased significantly over this period, and rose particularly sharply in the mid-1920s. By 1928, observers could refer to the 'transfer stampede' that took place immediately before the transfer deadline every March: that season it was reported that no fewer than 50 players moved in the last ten days, and that over £30,000 had changed hands in deals involving 40 League clubs. Another correspondent categorised the 1920s as 'the age of transfers', in which long service to clubs was increasingly rare and where players like the Cock brothers, Donald and Jack, could turn out for 12 different League clubs between them in fewer than nine seasons.[42] The available data, however, suggests little change in the total number of annual or seasonal transfers over the period. While the Football League recorded 195 players transferred in 1904, this had risen to 337 by 1910 and stayed at an average of 318 in the five seasons from 1931–32 to 1935–36. At individual clubs like Manchester City in the 1930s, as many as 10 or 11 players might move each season, representing up to 28 per cent of the professional staff, but more generally the figure rarely rose above 20 per cent.[43]

Between the wars, more directors and managers began to adopt the policy of buying established players rather than training and developing their own. Clubs like Arsenal and Newcastle United were especially renowned for spending large transfer fees to help build winning sides. By 1924, Arsenal was not untypical among top division sides in paying over £5,000 per season on transfers, and four years later was responsible for the first £10,000 fee when David Jack was acquired from Bolton Wanderers. Newcastle expended £14,666 on transfer fees in 1925–26, including £6,500 on the Scottish international Hughie Gallacher.[44] Aston Villa's secretary told one of the club's scouts in 1921 that 'we want someone good and experienced enough to go into one of our teams, not to have to *make* them'.[45] The pressure to buy players in order to achieve success on the field was not confined to the highest division. Philip Kelso, manager of Second Division Fulham, remarked in 1922 that his directors lacked the patience to allow youngsters to develop, preferring to resort to the transfer market.[46] As Table 3.3 indicates, by 1939 First and Second Division clubs were spending seasonal averages of £6,545 and £3,682 on transfers, and even those in the Third Division South were net buyers rather than sellers in the transfer market. However, it must be remembered that poorer clubs, especially those in the Third Division North, continued to rely on income derived from transfers to help alleviate financial difficulties.[47]

Table 3.3: Football League transfer payments in 1939 (£)

	Division 1	*Division 2*	*Division 3 (S)*	*Division 3 (N)*	*Total*
Paid out	144,000	81,000	35,000	12,000	272,000
Average per club	6,545	3,682	1,591	545	
Received	55,000	26,000	20,000	22,000	123,000
Average per club	2,500	1,182	909	1,000	

Source: Calculated from data in Political and Economic Planning, 'Football Industry', p. 177.

All these factors contributed to the development of a large and highly regulated internal market for transfers within British football in general, and the Football League in particular, by the Second World War. The circulation of transfer lists, together with informal contacts between clubs, supplemented the work of scouts in this area. Disengaged players were expected to take active roles in this process: like applicants at the recently established labour exchanges, they had to prove 'willingness to work' and 'genuine employability'.[48] League President John McKenna was adamant that players should not 'sit … down and wait … for clubs to come to them', and Charles Sutcliffe noted that it was 'no business of the Management Committee … to find players jobs… The player must make an effort for himself'.[49] What was more, the executive actually informed players that applications for reductions in transfer fees would not be considered before an effort had been made to find employment: it 'considered it was the duty of every player to find a place for himself'.[50] As a result, unemployed players were required to write directly to club secretaries, or advertise in the sporting press, in the hope of being engaged or at least considered for a trial.[51] Clubs also developed independent networks of contact and information regarding players. A club on the look-out for a full-back or an outside-left would often inform other clubs of its requirements and ask for assistance, as in 1933 when the West Ham Chairman received a letter from West Bromwich Albion suggesting one of the latter's inside-rights 'as a likely player for us'.[52] This type of cooperation, though hardly altruistic on either side, certainly saved money on scouting expenses and helped facilitate the recruitment and redistribution of players within the League.

There remained, of course, a vast reserve army of football labour throughout the period. The FA reported in 1939 that there were about 5,000 registered professionals, half of whom were part-timers, and thousands of amateurs played at a high enough level to attract the interest of League scouts.[53] Yet even taking into account places for professional players in other senior leagues, and the expansion of the Football League itself to 88 clubs by 1923, there were always players unable to find work. Some drifted into other types of employment or to the junior leagues, but many simply regarded themselves as unemployed footballers and continued to search for work. A further source of player recruitment that developed in this context was the Employment Bureau organised by the Players' Union, which acted as an intermediary between player and club. The Union had considered one of its roles from the beginning to be that of an informal employment agency. The first set of rules from 1907 declared that a key objective was 'To keep a list of all Members who are on the Transfer list, disengaged, or unsettled, with particulars of their positions on the field of play, their abilities, the clubs they have played for and any other necessary information with a view to obtaining suitable engagements for them.'[54] The correspondence files of the first Secretary, Herbert Broomfield, indicate that the Union did indeed send members' details to Football League, Southern League and Scottish League clubs.[55] Although a relatively minor part of the Union's activities that was dependent upon the time and energy of the Secretary himself, the Employment Bureau was successful enough to have found work for more than 60 players at the end of the 1912–13 season.[56] The Bureau became active again during the Depression, when declining attendances forced some clubs to reduce the size of their playing staffs. By 1934 it was distributing full lists and details of disengaged players to every League member, as well as interested Irish and French clubs.[57] There are no details of the actual number of players assisted by the Bureau, but both the Union and several club managers evidently regarded it as a 'great success … in bringing clubs and players together'.[58]

Players' contracts

When joining a League club, a player became subject to the authority not only of his club but also of the Football League and the FA. As well as signing his particular club agreement, he was required to register with both these bodies before being allowed to play competitively. Moreover, from 1912 onwards the League ordered all agreements between clubs and players to include a clause making the player subject 'to the rules, regulations and bye-laws of the Football League, Football Association … and any other Association, League or Combination of which the club or Football League shall be a member'.[59] Indeed, it was technically the League rather than the club that owned players' registrations. Hence, when a club left the League, for whatever reason, the registration and transfer rights of its players automatically became invested in the Management Committee.[60]

In common with the majority of first-class cricket counties, League clubs were rarely prepared to offer contracts lasting over a year.[61] According to both Tony Mason and Wray Vamplew, the Management Committee forbade longer contracts in 1891, but this may have been merely an informal instruction as there is no trace of a rule to this effect.[62] The archival evidence indicates that a formal ruling on the matter may not have been necessary. Sheffield United gave George Utley a five-year engagement in 1913, but this was part of an exceptional offer to convince the Barnsley player to join United: the board rejected a request by another player for a four-year contract a few months later, and maintained a general policy that 'no player would be signed on for more than 12 months'. After briefly offering one of its senior professionals a two-year contract, local neighbours Sheffield Wednesday took a similar decision.[63] Billy Meredith noted at the same time that the Manchester clubs, Burnley, Aston Villa, Newcastle United, Sunderland and Blackburn Rovers had all signed agreements lasting over a year with certain employees, despite pressure from Wednesday and other clubs to grant only annual contracts.[64] The Players' Union had been arguing for some time that in order to ensure greater job security, contracts should be extended to two years and beyond, but the League considered it 'undesirable that players should be signed for extended periods', and in 1914 limited the contract period to less than two full playing seasons.[65] From 1922 onwards, the length of League agreements was explicitly tied to FA rules, which allowed for three specific time-scales: a trial period of three weeks; a full season or the remainder of a current playing season; and the last three months of a playing season together with the following season.[66]

However, club minute books suggest that the customary one-season contract remained pervasive in each of the League's four divisions.

While there was no standard FA or Football League contract, written agreements between clubs and players were relatively straightforward and rarely differed fundamentally from club to club. They generally stated the inclusive dates of the contract and the weekly wages to be paid, and most included a clause requiring the player to follow training instructions, keep himself fit and serve the club to the best of his ability.[67] Some contracts went further by stipulating where the player could live or, increasingly by the 1920s and 1930s, precluding him from involvement in potentially dangerous pursuits such as motorcycling or aviation. Aston Villa and Sheffield United were probably not the only clubs whose contracts prevented their players from residing in, being employed by or owning a public house (see Chapter 4). Contracts sometimes included conditions relating to specific circumstances, such as the clause in Bernie Harris's 1924–25 agreement giving the Sheffield United board immediate powers to cancel the agreement if the player failed to recover fully from a leg injury sustained the previous season.[68] Yet by this time, contracts had become increasingly standardised throughout the League, as clubs were compelled by League rules to include sections relating to the termination of agreements as well as the payment of wages and benefits. Notwithstanding the legal and administrative significance of contracts, there is fragmentary evidence that clubs continued to employ some players on a casual, non-contractual basis. Derby County was fined £2 by the FA in 1909 for entering into a verbal agreement with a player; the Players' Union was certainly aware three years later that 'certain players had no agreements with their clubs', although it is not clear whether this was regarded as simple negligence or a wilful contravention of League rules.[69] The previous year, a League commission had reported on Middlesbrough's failure to complete and sign all its players' agreements, seeing it as carelessness on the part of the club administration.[70] Such carelessness may well have been eliminated by the increasing tendency of the Management Committee to arrange impromptu inspections of club records.

The breaking or termination of contracts was a facet of professional insecurity experienced by many League players. Although the FA rules from 1894 onwards theoretically protected employees from dismissal during the playing season,[71] the League developed a series of conditions to circumvent these and handed clubs the power potentially to cancel agreements at will. The most significant and contentious of these was the 'palpable inefficiency' clause introduced by the Management Committee in 1910. It allowed clubs to terminate any contract on 14 days' notice 'where a player proves palpably inefficient or is guilty of serious misconduct or breach of disciplinary rules'.[72] As Nicholas Fishwick has noted, this was potentially 'a catch-all clause which might mean anything from missing a penalty to losing a leg'; the Union representative and Newcastle United half-back Colin Veitch opposed it as a one-sided agreement that could lead to the dismissal of a player undergoing a loss of form at the whim of his directorate.[73] In general, clubs used it as a means of ridding themselves of idle or troublesome employees. Any player given notice of dismissal was entitled to appeal to the Management Committee free of charge and, if unsuccessful, to a further appeal before the Appeals Committee on depositing £5. However, the appeals procedure was heavily weighted against the player. Whereas he was denied the right to legal representation, the club tended to support its case with a multitude of witnesses: Stockport County had its Chairman, two directors, trainer, a referee and four other witnesses give evidence in one case.[74]

In the majority of cases, players preferred to accept dismissal reluctantly rather than engage in lengthy and possibly futile appeals, during which time they were jobless and received no wages. The effect that an employer's use of the 'palpable inefficiency' clause could have on a footballer's career is provided by the case of Walter Scott. A goalkeeper with Sunderland in the top division, Scott had been a regular choice for the Wearside club, but after a poor start to the 1912–13 campaign during which his form dipped and he became the target of barracking from sections of the crowd, Scott received his 14 days' notice. In an interview with *Thomson's Weekly News*, he complained that the decision had come 'absolutely as a surprise' and he regarded it as 'altogether unreasonable'. Sunderland's stated reason for ending his contract had been that he had 'not played sufficiently well this season' although Scott claimed he was fitter than ever, had not missed a day's training and got on well with his colleagues and the trainer. 'It appears to me that I am having to bear the brunt of the club's misfortunes, and to appease the crowd I am being fired' Scott wrote, and while he was confident that he could secure a position with another club if Sunderland put a reasonable transfer figure on his head, the goalkeeper admitted to being affected by the 'disgrace' of having his contract terminated.[75] Scott's case was championed by certain sections of the sporting press, but although the player was advised to hold out until his appeal was heard, he had already accepted a contract with Shelbourne in Dublin by the time the commission sat. In common with other players, the accusation of 'palpable inefficiency' had been sufficient to drive Walter Scott out of the Football League altogether.[76]

Nevertheless, as Table 3.4 shows, many of those who actually chose to fight were victorious. In 1913 a Barnsley player, William Hunter, appealed successfully against the club's action in dismissing him on the grounds of his 'failure as a player'. After pointing to his exemplary character and conduct, emphasising that his playing history disproved the allegations and noting that he had received no prior complaint about his play, the Management Committee sustained Hunter's appeal and ordered the club to pay costs.[77] Yet it is unclear what future prospects, if any, a player had in League football under these circumstances. A number of players whose appeals were upheld agreed to leave their clubs on free transfers, but even then the clubs' accusations were unlikely to have made it easy for them to obtain further engagements. In other cases, the Management Committee encouraged the club and player to come to some mutual settlement whereby the latter would be de-registered in return for a lump sum payment.[78]

Table 3.4: Player appeals to the Management Committee against termination of contracts for 'palpable inefficiency', 1912–32

Year	*Appeal sustained*	*Appeal dismissed*	*Mutual agreement*	*Total*
1912*	0	2	1	3
1913	1	0	0	1
1920	1	0	0	1
1921	1	1	0	2
1922	0	1	0	1
1923	2	0	0	2
1924	4	1	0	5
1925	5	0	0	5
1926	2	0	0	2
1927	0	2	0	2
1928	0	1	2	3
1929	0	0	1	1
1930	0	1	0	1
1931	0	0	1	1
1932	0	4	0	4
Total	16	13	5	34

*From May onwards.
Source: Calculated from Football League Minutes.

The League introduced a further clause in 1915, allowing clubs to cancel agreements 'on any reasonable ground on four weeks' notice in writing being given to the player'.[79] Although it was justified as a temporary wartime measure that gave clubs the flexibility to dispense with labour if financial conditions deteriorated, the Players' Union attacked it as 'too drastic' and felt that 'this rule will give clubs, by its vague wording, an opportunity to get out of their contracts should they be disposed to do so, and that it could open the door for unreasonable acts by clubs'.[80] The clause stayed on the rule books throughout the inter-war period, and may have been used by clubs in financial difficulties to break contracts and thus reduce wage costs. The Ipswich Town board was probably more typical in utilising the rule to clear out its unwanted players a couple of months before the end of each season, often with a lump sum payment in lieu of wages.[81] There were also occasional references to such cases in the Players' Union minutes but, on balance, it remained a less popular and controversial 'get-out' clause for clubs than 'palpable inefficiency'.

The retain-and-transfer system

If players faced contractual difficulties with their employers, a more significant problem surrounded the conditions governing the movement of labour and, in particular, the retain-and-transfer system. Historians and contemporary critics have recognised that the system theoretically represented a basic and unique contravention of labour rights by denying the player the freedom to move where he wanted and to chose his own employer.[82] Even President John Bentley acknowledged the fundamental hardship in '[compelling] players to remain with particular clubs'.[83] As all players were registered with the Football League and the FA, the mobility of labour between clubs required the permission of both these bodies, as well as the consent of the player himself and the buying and selling club. However, clubs could not be forced to transfer a player, which meant that the club with whom the player was registered possessed a monopoly over his services. When contracts expired in April and May each year, clubs and players were involved in the complicated process of re-signing. After internal board discussions, clubs forwarded to the League a list of players they intended to retain and a separate list of those 'open to transfer', the latter generally with a corresponding fee that buying clubs were expected to pay. From the early 1890s onwards, the League Secretary began to circulate such lists to all member clubs. Once the board's decision was made, a player had few alternatives and limited bargaining power. If a retained player wanted to leave he could reject the terms offered and apply to the Management Committee to consider the case, but this was often a long process that would mean losing several months' pay with no guarantee that the appeal would be upheld. Indeed, as long as the player had been offered the FA's stipulated retaining wage, or what League rules referred to as 'reasonable wages', the decision was likely to go in the club's favour. Transfer-listed players could similarly find themselves entrapped by the system, especially when unrealistically high prices were placed on their heads. They too were entitled to appeal to the Management Committee to have the fee reduced, but even if successful there was no assurance that another club would be prepared to pay the fee.

In practice, the operation of the system could depend on how flexible the League and the clubs were in their interpretation of the rules. Particularly infuriating to some players was the widespread practice among clubs of retaining players on terms unchanged or even reduced from the previous season. The problem became increasingly acute from the early 1920s onwards, as the maximum wage rose without a corresponding increase in the retaining wage. Indeed, while the maximum wage stood at £8 per week from 1922, pressure from the poorer clubs led in 1923 to a reduction of the retaining fee from £260 per year (£5 per week) to £200.[84] The Players' Union mounted a particularly bitter campaign during the 1920s and 1930s against what it regarded as 'the harsh and unfair treatment' experienced by many of its members as a result of this rule.[85] It claimed that clubs were able to retain long-serving players while drastically cutting their wages. Southampton, for instance, had employed goalkeeper Tommy Allen on the maximum wage for five years – playing in 192 of the 208 matches between 1920 and 1925 – before reducing his terms to the retaining wage. He refused to re-sign, and the club stopped his wages and reported him to the FA, leaving him 'debarred from earning his livelihood' until the case was settled.[86]

High transfer fees, too, could represent a major obstacle to the free movement of labour. The number of players appealing for reductions in transfer fees – approaching 300 annually by 1910[87] – was an indication of the scale of the problem, as was the Football League's recognition in 1911 that 'in many instances fees are fixed that the clubs can never hope to realise'.[88] The Players' Union believed the situation was so bad between the wars that some players were being prevented from earning a living, and were even forced 'to go out of League football, or to leave the country'.[89] Cases like those of Sheffield United's Harold Gough lend support to this view. Gough, an ageing ex-England international, was suspended during August 1924 for breaking his contract with United by running a public house, and was subsequently put on sale for a price of £2,000. Although the fee was certainly too high for a player of Gough's age, and despite the fact that United no longer wanted to employ him, the club refused for over a year to reduce the price, and thus in effect temporarily halted his career. Eventually he was sold in October 1926 – over two years after the cancellation of his contract – to Preston North End for a fee of just £500.[90]

For the older or less talented player, in particular, a transfer fee of any kind made finding another engagement problematic. A fee of £500 was sufficient to keep Ron Viner, a young reserve team centre-half with Leicester City, 'out of employment for weeks on end' during the summer of 1927.[91] In a 1934 article subtitled 'Confessions of an unwanted player', Tom Flannigan blamed the transfer system for forcing him out of professional football at the age of 26. Following a moderate season at Hull City, which ended in a month's suspension for being sent off in a reserve team match, he was placed on the transfer list at a cost of £750. Despite writing to numerous clubs, Flannigan was forced into minor football. Even when the League removed his fee, he could not secure a position back in the elite: 'going into minor labels you as an "outlaw" or an old-ager. Whatever the label, you'd be as well to pack up.' Unable to find employment in football, Flannigan took a job as a labourer. He was hardly alone in arguing that 'a system which lets a club get away with not paying a man a living wage when they think he is worth £750 is just plain crazy'.[92] Officials of the Players' Union regularly made the same point, appealing throughout the 1930s for clubs to give free transfers to players they did not want to retain and the Management Committee to reduce or remove all fees.[93]

Yet the rhetoric of 'slavery' that permeated contemporary criticism of the retain-and-transfer system, especially that of the Union, has led historians to overemphasise the oppressive elements of the system and neglect examples of its practical operation. The cases of Flannigan and Gough show that clubs could be obstructive to players, especially those who broke the rules, but in general they did not stand in the way of employees who were determined to move. It was widely recognised that players were valuable assets and that it was in the club's interests to reach agreed terms or move the player on as quickly and as profitably as possible. No one wanted a discontented player at his club. West Ham United informed one of its transfer-listed players that 'anything possible would be done toward helping him get a job', and in many instances clubs were prepared to voluntarily reduce the original fee, especially if another club had shown an interest in the player.[94] Aston Villa made great play of its policy of placing small fees upon, or granting free transfers to, its players, especially those who had demonstrated 'loyal service and good behaviour'.[95] What is more, the Union's propaganda concerning free transfers seems to have had some effect.

Swindon Town gave 11 of its playing staff free transfers in 1933; Sheffield United similarly freed nine players in 1934, and four years later Oldham Athletic released seven.[96] Moreover, if negotiations with the club were unsuccessful, the Management Committee could step in to help the player. The League's own figures show that the majority of Committee decisions favoured the player. Of the 94 appeals lodged during the summer of 1935, 42 resulted in free transfers and 40 in reduced fees; a year later, 28 players received free transfers and 37 had their fees reduced with no action being taken in just 12 cases.[97] If the official mechanisms failed, it was still sometimes possible for a player to persuade or coerce the board to let him leave. It was not unusual for clubs to accede immediately to a transfer request precipitated by a player's demotion to the second team, or his being generally 'unsettled', although it could take months for a satisfactory move to be negotiated.[98] As we shall see in Chapter 4, clubs rejecting transfer requests were also occasionally faced with absenteeism, non-cooperation or other forms of disruptive behaviour.

Most analyses of professional football have emphasised the unique nature of the employment conditions embodied in the retain-and-transfer system. The usual comparison here is with industries such as coal mining, building, textiles and other occupations traditionally associated with the employment of industrial workers where, regardless of the inherent hardships and dangers, employees were always theoretically free to move between jobs and employers as they pleased. This parallel is hardly surprising given the socio-economic and occupational background of the majority of professional footballers and directors, and the apparent duplication of employer–employee relations from the factory to the football club.[99] Yet as a result, comparisons with the employment conditions in more closely related areas, particularly other sports and sectors of the entertainment industry, have been largely neglected. While it is true that no other industry exhibited such tight and strictly regulated restrictions on an employee's freedom of contract, there were clearly some comparable practices. There is some evidence that rugby league clubs were able to prevent players from moving on, although they had no retaining rights similar to those in the Football League. Players wishing to change allegiance in county cricket were also probably deterred by the qualification rule, which required players to have two years residence in their new county.[100] Looking beyond sport, music hall proprietors similarly attempted to assert ownership over performers by barring them from performing at rival establishments within a certain area and for a specific period before and after each engagement.[101]

The payment of players

The question of how much Football League professionals were paid has not been easy for historians to answer. One of the main problems has been a paucity of systematic data, meaning that conclusions have been partial and largely impressionistic. In view of this, it is surprising that most studies have neglected the considerable data available in football club archives, and that no real attempt has been made to compare the evidence on earnings by drawing on the experience of a range of employers. The aim here is to utilise the material from a number of club minute books, wage books and ledgers, alongside newspaper sources, to examine the issue of payment in more detail and in a broader context than has hitherto been attempted. It also attempts to show the way in which earnings became increasingly regulated centrally by the Football League.

Wages

The absence of hard evidence is less surprising for the period before the introduction of the maximum wage in 1901, when wages, bonuses and other payments were determined by each club individually and could therefore vary substantially. According to the journalist James Catton, the average First Division wage amounted to around £3–4 per week by the late 1890s, while Sheffield Wednesday paid their star players £3 weekly in 1900. Regular second team players, meanwhile, could be guaranteed as little as 10 shillings to £1, with possible increases if picked for the first team.[102] We do know that the pressure of competition was leading to pay increases at the top end of the scale. Few could expect the £7 weekly throughout the year that Tom Baddeley and Billy Beats of Wolverhampton Wanderers were reputed to receive at the end of the decade, but there is enough evidence to suggest that they were not alone.[103] The best players at Aston Villa reportedly made £6 10s just before the wage limit was introduced, while, according to the club's directors, the Liverpool players who won the First Division championship in the 1900–01 season were being paid £7, which with bonuses could reach £10 per week.[104]

The passing of the maximum wage rule has been seen in this context as a significant turning point, heralding a general standardisation and equalisation of wages across the League. Vamplew has argued that the wage limit 'served to reduce the skew in earnings distribution among professional footballers' and that 'for the bulk of League players, especially in the first division, the maximum wage was the effective wage'.[105]

There is much evidence to support this view. Fred Rinder, chairman of Aston Villa and an opponent of the rule, claimed that the maximum wage soon became a standard wage for the top professionals. This certainly seems to have been true at Sheffield United, where the number of players on at least £4 per week leapt from just five in 1899–1900 to 13 by 1901–02, and remained stable for the next few years.[106] By 1913, the Leeds City Captain, Evelyn Lintott, felt confident enough to suggest that 'most of the leading men in the First and Second leagues are £4-a-weekers'.[107] Not all clubs, however, could afford to offer the maximum, even to their best players. The Stoke Secretary revealed that only three players at his club were given the maximum in 1906, while Second Division Blackpool had nobody on £4. Even at a richer club like Sheffield United, the maximum wage was largely restricted to the first team.[108] That the maximum was in fact some way from becoming the standard is testified by a report on the contrasting fortunes of the players of Barnsley and Everton, who met in an FA Cup semi-final in 1910. While every member of the Merseyside team was on the maximum, none of the Yorkshire side were, and one or two allegedly received '£2 10s. a week or less'.[109] According to the FA, just 573 professionals of an estimated total of 6,800, mostly Football League and Southern League players, were receiving the maximum by 1910, suggesting that, at a modest estimation, a little over one-third of all registered League players (there were approximately 1,000 at the time) were on £4 per week.[110]

Vamplew's thesis is less applicable after 1910, when the maximum wage began to develop an internal hierarchy. From that year onwards, players in the Football League could earn an extra 10 shillings per week above the maximum after two years of service, and a further 10 shillings after four years, thus establishing a new elite wage of £5 per week (£260 per year). In 1920, the wage structure was further reformed, partly as a result of pressure from the Players' Union to increase wages 'to cover the extra cost of living' and allow annual wage rises 'according to merit'.[111] Wages were henceforth regulated according to a sliding scale, ranging from a maximum of £5 per week for 'new' players with annual rises of £1 weekly over four years, to a final ceiling of £9 per week. Players could now receive a new annual maximum of £468.[112] The emphasis on payment by length of service ahead of merit, however, caused considerable discontent among certain players. According to the Union, the sliding scale was unpopular: 'We know that is the opinion held by players in the North and Midlands. It is frequently pointed out to us by our members that while men in first teams are receiving £6, others in the second teams are in receipt of £7 to £9'.[113] Two years later, the maximum was reduced to £8 during the 37-week playing season, and £6 in the remaining 15 weeks of the close season. The sliding scale was retained, but clubs were additionally permitted to increase the wages of players picked for the first team and reduce those of players dropped through loss of form.[114]

The sliding scale thus gave clubs a certain amount of flexibility to alter a player's weekly wage, subject to the terms of his contract and the sanction of the League Management Committee. In particular, it was used as an incentive for players to reach the first team and, as such, became a device to intensify competition among the workforce. This could be done by applying to the Management Committee to increase the wages of a reserve player regularly making the first team, although such requests were only accepted if the player had enjoyed a lengthy run – normally at least ten games – at the higher level. Alternatively, wages could be altered on a weekly basis according to the team for which the player was selected. During the 1930s, many clubs adopted the comprehensive incentive scheme pioneered by Grimsby Town and Sheffield Wednesday, in which the best players were guaranteed a weekly wage of just £6, with £2 extra providing they kept their first-team place.[115] In such cases, the maximum remained effectively a first-team wage, a policy made explicit by the West Ham United board in 1927.[116] Some players objected to this, as it increased the pressure to perform consistently each week and denied them a constant and secure wage. *Topical Times* believed that the weekly sliding scale actually created 'a feeling of unsettlement which … upset a team's spirit and efficiency', but this did not prevent its general adoption across all divisions of the Football League.[117]

The available evidence suggests that between the wars, the maximum wage remained far from standard. Indeed, given its central role in the payment incentive schemes of so many clubs, it could not have been. Even at the more wealthy and successful League clubs, the maximum was reached only by a minority, although the precise size of this minority is difficult to gauge. According to the Players' Union, fewer than 10 per cent of professionals were on the maximum by 1939, although the figure may have been higher at more prosperous times, especially the early 1920s.[118] 'For some considerable time many League clubs have been endeavouring to reduce the wages of their players', one journalist noted in August 1926. As a result, he went on to suggest, 'comparatively few professionals are at present in receipt of the maximum wage'.[119] Jimmy Guthrie similarly thought that 'very few players' were on top wages when he was playing during the 1930s, and noted the case of one London club, which paid its first teamers just £4–5 per week.[120] At many

Second and Third Division clubs, the maximum was unattainable even for the best players. The highest possible wage at Ipswich Town during its first season in the Third Division South in 1938–39 was £7, while Bill Ratcliffe, Captain of Oldham Athletic in the Northern Section, was heading the club's wage scale in the late 1930s at just £4 10s. in the winter and £4 in the summer, with an extra £1 when in the first team. Having finished bottom of the Northern Section the previous season, Darlington's first teamers may have considered themselves fortunate to have been offered a basic wage of £3–£4 10s. in May 1937.[121]

Below the top earners at each club were a range of veteran, reserve and youth players moving up and down the scale depending on circumstances. Wage differentials both within and between clubs remained considerable. At the bottom end of the wage scale, many professionals undoubtedly struggled to make a living. Indeed, while wages were limited at the top of the scale there was no stipulated minimum with which League clubs were expected to comply. Sheffield United's lowest terms were offered to part-time nursery or A-team players, who received £1 per week with an increase of £1 if picked for the reserve or first teams. At Sunderland in 1908, wages of £1–2 per week were received by players employed in other occupations throughout the week, and this had risen to £3–4 by the time Raich Carter joined the club in 1931 as a part-time footballer and electrical engineering apprentice.[122] Young players were often employed on the ground staff for minimal wages until they were able to sign professional forms at the age of 17: future manager Ted Fenton was the first to be given such a post at West Ham in 1930, although the practice became commonplace.[123]

Problems of low pay increased with the onset of the Depression and the need of many clubs to economise by reducing wage bills. This often manifested itself in the stoppage of summer wages; players were released in May and re-engaged in August, in time for the new season. The Southport director E. Clayton was adamant that 'No Third Division club could get along and pay summer wages' when he announced the club's policy to the shareholders in 1926.[124] During the Depression, close-season pay was the exception rather than the rule among the League's lower division professionals. *Sporting Chronicle*'s report in late May 1932 that 'approximately a thousand professional footballers who were earning wages with League clubs last season are now out of employment' may have been an exaggeration, but does indicate the scale of the problem.[125] Although those employed by clubs located in the industrial districts of the North-east, Lancashire and South Wales suffered most from this form of seasonal unemployment, the phenomenon was nationwide. Swindon Town, for instance, released all but four of its squad after finishing bottom of the Third Division Southern Section in 1932–33.[126] During the 1931–32 season, the directors of a number of clubs in financial difficulties were forced to temporarily cut players' wages, and the following season the players of Barrow, Gateshead and Bristol City had no choice but to accept short-term reductions to their pay packets of 10 per cent, 20 per cent and 50 per cent respectively.[127] At times, of course, players were simply not paid at all. In May 1933, Clapton Orient, for example, was threatened with expulsion from the League unless it paid the arrears in wages that had mounted up during the season.[128]

Benefits

While the weekly wage was the basic form of remuneration for Football League players, it was increasingly augmented by a number of other financial rewards. The most important of these was the benefit, a practice borrowed most directly from county cricket but also with a long history in the theatre, music hall and other sectors of the entertainment industry.[129] From 1901 onwards, clubs were permitted to grant a benefit match at the end of a player's career, or after five years of continuous service and again after ten years.[130] As in cricket, special matches were set aside for the purpose, but increasingly players were allocated some or all the proceeds of competitive League or cup matches. In addition, directors often guaranteed minimum sums, which guarded footballers from the risks associated with benefits in the theatre, music hall and county cricket, where vast expenses or poor attendances could seriously affect the amount raised.[131] After the First World War, most clubs stopped allocating specific matches and instead guaranteed players a fixed-sum benefit payment. In fact, the footballer's benefit gradually evolved into a contractual right rather than a gift granted by the employer. In this way it was very different from its cricket equivalent, which was more discretionary and a less reliable source of income. The tax authorities certainly treated them differently, taxing benefits in football but not in cricket. In 1923, and again in 1941, the High Court judged that as benefits were specifically provided for in Football League regulations, they should be regarded as a payment for a player's services, just like his wage, bonus and talent money.[132] The benefit had become widely recognised as a basic element of a player's earnings, and probably the main supplement to his weekly wage. Clubs were not compelled to grant benefits, of course, but they were likely to have a dissatisfied workforce if they refused.

The actual sum received via the benefit depended on the status of the player and the financial position of the club. The proceeds of a typical pre-1914 benefit at the two Sheffield clubs was between £150 and £250, although a wealthier organisation like Aston Villa was able to grant sums of £300–450, and even paid £500 to its England inside-left Joe Bache.[133] Charles Sutcliffe testified that £200 was a typical figure, but added that some players were able to get £500 and, in exceptional cases, £1,000.[134] In 1920, Sheffield United allowed club captain George Utley a benefit of nearly £1,100 from a chosen League match, though this angered playing colleagues, who complained of 'preferential treatment', and the board subsequently set the standard benefit at £500 for first-teamers.[135] After 1920, the Management Committee stepped in to limit benefit payments to £500 (increased to £650 in 1924) for regular first-team players, with a proportionately smaller sum for less skilled professionals. In contrast with cricket, there was no possibility of additional revenue from subscription lists or collections until 1930, when clubs could arrange means of supplementing the player's benefit fund in accordance with strict League regulations.[136] Like wages, some benefits were linked to individual or collective performance. Examples include West Ham giving Tommy Hodgson and Billy Moore a definite £300 each, to be increased to £400 if the majority of their performances that season were in the first team; and the same club offering Jimmy Collins £350, 'which could be increased at our discretion if his play and our financial and league position warranted such', or a guaranteed £400. Sheffield Wednesday reserved the full £650 for players who had gained international honours 'and thus done honour to the club'.[137]

Some players increased their earnings substantially as a result of the benefit system. West Ham's Jimmy Ruffell received four benefits of £650, £500 (twice) and £200 in the course of his 18 years with the club, which effectively added £100 to his annual wage.[138] As Table 3.5 suggests, a significant proportion of League players were granted benefits each season, and most of these received £400 and above. These figures could hardly match those in cricket, where sums of £800 were considered extremely poor, even at the less wealthy counties. At Lancashire, the average payment between the wars was £1,500, while wealthy Yorkshire established £1,000 as a guaranteed minimum and aimed for at least £2,000.[139] Yet bearing in mind that cricket professionals were rarely granted a benefit before ten years' service, and that few received a second benefit, footballers did not fare too badly in comparison. Although guaranteed contractually, football benefits were nonetheless subject to delay or suspension. For clubs in financial difficulties, stopping non-obligatory payments like benefits was an obvious means of cutting costs. Sheffield United's decision to suspend benefits from 1933 to 1936 'until the finances of the club improved' was probably not exceptional; and it was also common for clubs in temporary financial difficulties to postpone benefits until the following season. However, non-payment was only tolerated for so long. Stockport County announced in 1921 that it owed £3,000 in benefit monies to players, and issued a public appeal to raise that amount.[140] In 1934, the Wolverhampton Wanderers board ensured its supporters of the inaccuracy of rumours that benefits were being withheld: 'benefits have been paid immediately they were due … and the Directors will follow the same principle in the future'.[141]

Table 3.5: Benefit payments to Football League players, 1931/32–1935/36

Year	*Under £100*	*£100–199*	*£200–299*	*£300–399*	*£400–499*	*£500–650*	*Total*
1931–32	–	15	13	7	3	29	67
1932–33	–	10	11	11	10	30	72
1933–34	3	9	10	12	22	45	101
1934–35	–	1	16	15	10	32	74
1935–36	–	7	11	7	14	38	77
Total	3	42	61	52	59	174	391

Source: PFA, File 35, statistics required from Football League on cases Corbett v. Inland Revenue and Dale v. Inland Revenue, 1939.

Theoretically, the benefit was a reward for loyal service or 'a sign of the bond between [the player] and the club',[142] but in practice it often became a source of conflict between the two. One such case was the dispute between Christopher Buckley and Aston Villa in 1911. Like many players, Buckley signed an agreement entitling him to the proceeds of a League match with a minimum guarantee of £450. A disagreement then arose between the player, who believed he had been promised the lucrative match with FA Cup holders Bradford City, and the board, which repudiated this and offered him a choice of three less attractive games. After meeting with the directors, Buckley decided that 'if he could not have the Bradford match he would have none at all' and refused to play in the next League match. The board subsequently suspended him 'until such time as he expresses regret for his action'.[143] In Buckley's view, the club had consciously restricted his potential benefit income: indeed, 'It was common talk among the Villa players … that nobody got a benefit from the club without a row, and then the player only got what they cared to give him'.[144] Ultimately, the player was powerless in such a situation: three weeks later Buckley backed down, apologised for his action and accepted the match against Sheffield United.[145] Even though clubs increasingly regarded the benefit as a fundamental player's right, there could still be conflict over the amount given. West Ham, for instance, refused Vic Watson's request for a maximum £650 benefit just three weeks after congratulating him on his performance in an international match, and he later accepted the club's standard first-team payment of £500.[146] Moreover, before 1910 certain clubs seem to have avoided paying out altogether by transferring players shortly before their benefits were due.

However, from 1910 onwards League rules entitled a player who had been transferred before completing his five years' qualification for a benefit to receive an accrued share of it: that is, a sum commensurate to the length of his qualifying service and the amount he would have received if not transferred. Initially, the amount the player could receive was regarded as a share of the transfer fee and was given in proportion to the increased fee made by the selling club, but in practice the Management Committee linked such payments to presumed benefits rather than the size of the transfer fee. In ideal circumstances the player was adequately recompensed by his former club for loss of benefit. The West Ham board was happy enough to pay star forward Sid Puddefoot £390 (as a three-year percentage of the expected £650 benefit) on his transfer to Falkirk for £5,000 in 1922 – a new record for a player moving from a Football League to a Scottish League club.[147] Yet where transfer fees were minimal, or the player left the club in acrimony, such amounts were unlikely. Like the benefit itself, the accrued share was a discretionary payment, and the club was within its rights to refuse it. Indeed, players adjudged to have precipitated a transfer had no entitlement to the accrued benefit payment under League rules. Frank Barson's move from Aston Villa to Manchester United was one such example: 'the player, by his conduct and his demands on the club, had practically forced [them] to transfer him' and therefore received nothing.[148] Even when clubs were generous, the moving player could lose out if the Management Committee intervened. This practice became particularly contentious during 1921, when the Players' Union urged the League to reconsider a number of cases in which transferred players had had their guaranteed payments severely cut by the Committee. According to the Union chairman Charlie Roberts, 'the player being transferred is in a blind alley – everything is subject to the consent of the Football League, and they, as representatives of the clubs, keep the amount the player receives down as far as possible'.[149]

Talent money and indirect payments

The 1910 financial package also included the introduction of talent money and the legalisation of bonuses for cup-tie wins. Clubs finishing in the top five of the Football League's top two divisions were henceforth entitled to distribute among their squads sums ranging from £275 for first place to £55 for fifth, and corresponding amounts for FA Cup success. From 1920 onwards, a flat-rate bonus of £2 for a win and £1 for a draw in all League matches and cup ties was adopted, and larger win bonuses of £4 in the semi-final and £8 in the final of the FA Cup were added two years later. Win and draw bonuses of £1 and 10 shillings respectively were permitted for the new Third Division clubs, while smaller bonuses (initially 10 shillings and 5 shillings, doubled in 1921) were also agreed for reserve-team players, although some clubs and reserve leagues refused to sanction such payments.[150] Talent money and bonuses had been advocated partly as a means of rewarding exceptional players 'who received no more … than the mere mediocrity' under the maximum wage rule. Many directors accepted such payments as 'tantamount to a commission in addition to salary in commercial life'.[151] Charles Sutcliffe regarded talent money as 'the reward for honest effort and enterprise on the part of the team to render the best possible service for the club', but others no doubt agreed with the FA's William Pickford that bonuses for match results constituted a form of bribery and meant paying the player twice over for the same work.[152] In 1908, the Players' Union had suggested a marks system based on the 'good conduct and skill' of players, similar to that operated by first class cricket counties, but most clubs opposed the idea of individual rewards in an essentially collective team sport.[153] Notwithstanding initial pockets of opposition, those clubs good enough to win matches, cups and championships were prepared to let their employees share financially in their success. Yet, as the Players' Union pointed out in 1937, only a small minority of the professionals engaged by the 88 Football League clubs benefited from these extra payments. Even at the most successful clubs, talent money was related exclusively to the performance of the first team and, as we have seen, the extension of match bonuses to reserve-team players was only partial.[154]

For the very best players, there were a number of additional opportunities to make money. International match fees for Englishmen were £1 at the turn of the century, rising to £4 in 1907, £6 in 1921 and finally £20 by 1939, but this was still a relatively small sum given the infrequency of such matches – generally fewer than five each season – and the large revenue internationals generated for the respective FAs.[155] Continental tours at both representative and club levels could bring some return, either in the form of extra pay or gifts (like the silver medals given to members of the Nottingham Forest team during their visit to Argentina in 1905).[156] However, from 1912 onwards the Management Committee decided that players 'must not be allowed to make a profit' on such tours, and closely monitored their financial arrangements. Thus while some players had previously been paid as much as £1 per day in addition to their regular wage, daily allowances of only 5 shillings to cover expenses were common between the wars.[157]

Some of the better players could also theoretically boost their incomes through advertising and the endorsement of goods, especially football equipment and new leisure products like cigarettes, as well as by writing newspaper columns.[158] Yet it is misleading to assume that financial benefits inevitably flowed from such commercial contacts. In fact, in many cases players were used to endorse products without their knowledge, let alone any prior agreement, and were therefore unlikely to significantly increase their incomes in this way. Members of the triple-championship-winning Arsenal squad of the 1930s, for instance, were often featured in advertisements for which they received merely a token gift. 'Dixie' Dean, who was alleged by the press to have made large amounts through endorsements, claimed to have actually received just one ex gratia payment of £50 from a cigarette firm for the use of his image in the whole of his career, and hence considered himself particularly exploited by advertisers.[159] In addition, all gifts to players were closely monitored and regulated by the League. Club committees were allowed to award medals or other momentos to cup- or championship-winning sides, provided that this was regarded as part of their talent money. From the early 1920s onwards, wedding presents were given and the payment of removal expenses permitted. Presentations or collections from outsiders, however, were strictly prohibited. Thus 'Dixie' Dean missed out again, when offers to mark his achievement of scoring a record of 60 goals for Everton in the 1927–28 season with 'a momento' were stymied by the authorities.[160]

Historians face obvious difficulties in assessing the significance of illegal or 'under-the-counter' payments. One historian has argued that 'the practice was widespread' in the first decade of the maximum wage at least, and it is indeed likely that the inquiries and commissions instigated by the authorities touched only the tip of the iceberg.[161] Fred Rinder told the FA Council in 1908 that the rules restricting wages, signing-on fees and bonuses 'were being broken daily', and the Players' Union agreed that 'nearly all Football League … clubs had broken the rules for their own advantage'.[162] William McGregor refused to admit 'that the rules are so widely broken as some people would have you believe', but accepted that certain clubs circumvented the FA's restrictions and that 'isolated players are getting more than the maximum wage'.[163] Stars like Billy Meredith could undoubtedly benefit substantially from illegal payments of this kind. As a Manchester City player between 1902 and 1906, Meredith apparently received £6 per week (£2 above the maximum) and more than £50 a year in bonuses. Similar payments seem to have been made to Meredith while he was with Manchester United, through a special account in his name and that of a teammate. An FA commission found that as much as £598 had been paid into the account during a four-month period in 1907 alone. Meredith was fined and suspended in both cases, but other leading players and clubs were evidently more fortunate in escaping detection.[164]

There is no indication that clubs and players stuck to the rules any more in the inter-war period. League and FA inquiries continued apace, with Rotherham, Port Vale, Wolverhampton Wanderers, Bradford Park Avenue and Arsenal among those clubs found guilty of trying to evade payment regulations during the 1920s.[165] However, the absence of quantifiable evidence makes it difficult to be precise about the extent of the practice. Anecdotal and oral evidence is thus particularly useful. The testimonies collected by Rogan Taylor and Andrew Ward suggest that under-the-counter payments or 'backhanders' to players were common ways of circumventing the wage restrictions in the 1950s, and there is little reason to think that things were much different 20 years earlier.[166] That some players received hidden payments for FA Cup success was common knowledge, as one professional noted: 'We knew our Cup opponents were on to a fat fee if they won. We were not. We fought our hardest, but the other fellows fought still harder, knowing the gain to them if they got through.'[167] Jimmy Guthrie, meanwhile, admitted receiving an illegal bonus of £600 when he joined Portsmouth from Dundee in 1938.[168] In his 1957 autobiography, the Charlton manager Jimmy Seed had no doubt that the periodic revelations of illegal payments were not isolated cases, and indicated that on a number of occasions his own attempts to sign international players in the 1930s had been frustrated by demands for 'a bit over the top'.[169] Although necessarily impressionistic, examples of this kind suggest that, for the leading player at least, there was money to be made in excess of his contracted terms. Too much emphasis on the elite of the profession, however, once again runs the risk of marginalising the experience of the majority of players in the lower divisions, whose objective was to attain the legal maximum and were therefore unlikely to have been offered or to have demanded anything extra.

Footballers' pay in context

When all these potential rewards were taken into consideration, the overall earnings of a Football League professional could be significant. According to his autobiography, the Everton and England centre-forward Tommy Lawton made a little over £531 during his club's championship-winning season of 1938–39. Lawton was hardly typical, but his example does reveal what was available for the most successful players by the late 1930s. *The Economist* admitted in 1937 that the 'ablest players' often took home about £420 per year.[170] Average incomes, of course, were much lower. In 1909, *Football Field* calculated that First Division professionals were paid an average of £210 per year, while Second Division players made £150.[171] Just before the maximum was increased in March 1920, the Players' Union estimated that the average weekly income stood at £4 11s 1d in the First Division and £4 2s 3d in the Second, but there is insufficient evidence to attempt a fruitful comparison over time.[172]

How well did footballers themselves think they were paid? In later recollections, Lawton suggested that he had made 'good money' and even 'a fortune' when compared with the income of other workers, but he was evidently less impressed by what he earned at the time. He informed readers of his autobiography that 'top-class players should be paid a great deal more money weekly' and that, while the best were sometimes lucky enough to go on foreign tours and pick up advertising contracts, 'for the majority of players there's little else to be made out of the game, other than a salary that an American baseball or ice-hockey player, or a world-famous boxer wouldn't even look at'.[173] Many players agreed that on the whole, they were inadequately rewarded. Raich Carter was 'frankly disappointed' with his moderate starting wage at Sunderland, especially as he had a mother and two sisters to support.[174] However, it was generally members of the playing elite, rather than the rank and file, who complained about payment. There were manifold expressions of resentment from those who believed they were restricted from making the most of their talent by the wage limit and other regulations. International match fees were a particular bone of contention for players who considered '£6 or a medal' as insufficient reward for those representing their country at the very top of their profession.[175]

In contrast, there were many observers from both inside and outside the game who believed that Football League professionals were well paid. In the opinion of John Lewis, 'a man who gets £4 for five years, and then a £350 benefit, followed by another after a second five years does uncommonly well for himself, and … makes a far better start in life than ninety-nine hundredths of those in a similar situation'.[176] In a similar vein, William Pickford felt that most footballers were 'in a position of financial soundness that might not be attained [in] a labouring or mechanical trade', while even William Bassett, a former England international, believed that 'Professional footballers are a handsomely remunerated set of men, and call for the commiseration of no one.'[177] One *Football Chat* reader, meanwhile, wrote to the editor in April 1909 rejecting the view that the professional player 'is hard done by' and suggesting that 'no footballer, international or otherwise, is worth more than four pounds a week, while 90 per cent now taking the limit wage are barely worth half that amount'.[178] Views of this kind reflected the concentration of the press, and later the electronic media, on the activities of the top players and clubs. Yet while the Players' Union opined in 1939 that distorted media coverage gave the public the impression that 'the player was doing wonderfully well', there were some commentators who expressed sympathy for the financial treatment of players.[179] Writing in 1927, one journalist criticised the restrictions placed on wages and benefits, and went so far as to conclude that 'professional footballers, as a class, are the worst paid of workmen'.[180] Be that as it may, in comparison with other broadly-defined working-class occupations, professional football did indeed offer substantial remuneration. As Table 3.6 indicates, the basic earnings of a First and Second Division footballer on the maximum wage – excluding benefits or other extra payments – easily outstripped the average salary of clerks, skilled and semi-skilled workers and even supervisors and foremen throughout the period. Thus, for instance, a professional with Stoke or Burslem Port Vale in 1906 who earned up to £4 per week was clearly better off than a worker in any part of the region's pottery industry, with the possible exception of those at the peak of the wage hierarchy, such as firemen.[181] Those further down the wage structure or in the lower divisions, like Bert Fletcher and Bill Richmond (Table 3.6), were closer to the foreman category, but even they would probably have taken home more when extra payments are considered.

Comparisons with industrial workers, however, are probably less appropriate than those with employees in other football leagues, and other sports and entertainment industries. For a first-team player at a leading Football League club, there were few opportunities to improve one's earnings. The Scottish League had no maximum wage, but generally only Rangers, Celtic and Hearts offered their players a sum equivalent to the maximum in England.[182] For the more adventurous professional, some overseas clubs offered higher basic salaries. In the mid-1920s, clubs from the professional

American Soccer League were prepared to offer wages of £12–20 a week, often to work during the week in a local factory and play football at the weekend. The soccer section of the New York Giants baseball club reputedly offered 'Dixie' Dean £25 per week to cross the Atlantic in 1928. He resisted, but dozens of other Football League players were tempted to the USA on terms that they could never have hoped to negotiate at home.[183] Similarly, unemployed League players were obtaining agreements with French clubs during the Depression on terms 'far in excess of maximum wages in England'.[184] The maximum wage in the French League was set at 2,000 francs per month, exactly double the wage of a skilled French worker but equivalent to just £5 a week in England. Bonuses and illegal payments, however, could swell this figure considerably. Andy Wilson, Alec Cheyne and Harry Ward were reportedly offered as much as £650 per year to join SC Nîmes in May 1932 (see Chapter 6).[185]

Table 3.6: Comparison of average annual earnings of clerks, foremen, skilled and semi-skilled workers with Football League professionals, 1906–35 (£)

	1906	*1924*	*1935*
Clerks	–	182	192
Foremen, supervisors, inspectors	113	268	273
Skilled workers	97	182	197
Semi-skilled workers*	63	126	134
Football League professional (maxiumum wage)	208	386	386
Bert Fletcher, West Ham United FC	n/a	260	n/a
Bill Richmond, Walsall FC	n/a	n/a	211

*Including agricultural occupations.
Source: Routh, Occupation and Pay, pp. 92, 98, 101, 109; WHUFC, Board Minutes, 28 April 1924; WLHC, Walsall FC, Players' Registration Book, 1932–46.

In cricket, the summer national sport, the earnings of the top players were not markedly dissimilar from those in football. At the turn of the century, a good cricket professional playing for a relatively prosperous county could make about £275 a year, with possible increases in the form of test match pay, benefits and talent money. Lesser players might only receive basic ground staff wages and be deprived of winter pay, though most counties had introduced it in some form by the 1900s.[186] In the inter-war period, the 'big six' counties agreed to limit the annual wages of their professionals to £440, with a maximum of £500 when additional payments were considered. However, benefit payments, test match fees and tour bonuses all easily dwarfed their football equivalents, and meant that the biggest cricket stars were certainly earning more than the top footballers. League cricket could also be lucrative. Learie Constantine apparently received some £800 in 1938 for playing 20 weeks as the professional with Rochdale in the Central Lancashire League. Although Constantine's case was hardly representative – he thought he was 'perhaps the best paid professional cricketer in the world' – there is evidence that weekly wages equal to the maximum in football, and sometimes more, were often guaranteed to the club professional.[187] Even so, in both county and league cricket, as in football, there was a considerable rump of professionals below the highest earners whose pay, conditions of work and job insecurities were much more like those of the average industrial worker. Tony Collins has argued that for the elite of rugby league players, 'wages were comparable with those in the Football League'. Before the First World War, some star players could earn as much as £4 and, without a wage ceiling, earnings such as Billy Batten's massive £14 per match at Hull were possible. Large signing-on fees, particularly for those Welsh players tempted North, also significantly bolstered a professional's career earning capacity. However, rugby league's high earners seem to have been few and far between, and differentials in pay, based on playing position as well as talent, were undoubtedly wider than in football.[188]

Earnings were greater still in highly commercialised sports such as horse racing, boxing and baseball. Top flat jockeys often received several thousand pounds a year in retainers, riding fees and other gifts, and even moderate jockeys at the turn of the century could make £1,000 in a season. National hunt riding fees were even larger – 5 guineas for a losing ride and 10 for winning throughout the period – but retainers were more scarce, and fewer meetings often led to periodic unemployment for some.[189] Purses in major professional boxing contests varied from £100 to £1,500, and more for international and world title fights; the Welsh heavyweight Tommy Farr made £36,000 out of his World Title fight with Joe Louis in August 1937. At the bottom of the scale, the British Boxing Board of Control set £1 as a minimum for six-round preliminary fighters, although some allegedly took home as little as 5 or even 2 shillings.[190] Baseball players in the USA could make substantial sums. The average annual salary was $3,000 in 1910 (equivalent to £617), but rose to $5,000 (£1,091) in 1923 and reached over $7,500 (£1,543) six years later, which compared favourably to the incomes of dentists, doctors, lawyers, professors and other upper-middle-class occupations. The star players, meanwhile, earned much more. Pittsburgh's Honus Wagner was paid $18,000 (£3,703) in 1911, and Detroit's Ty Cobb made at least $20,000 (£4,201) in 1915.[191] At the upper limit, Babe Ruth could command a salary of $80,000 (£16,400) by the end of the 1920s. Writers have used the US star's amazement at the paltry earnings of soccer's superstar 'Dixie' Dean when the two famously met to symbolise the contrasting value attached to sportsmen in the two societies. Yet it must be remembered that even in baseball, there was a large army of low earners: in Ruth's New York Yankees team some players were apparently earning only $2,500 (£514) per year.[192]

As well as other sportsmen, entertainers more broadly were becoming a key reference group for the leading footballers of the period. Yet star footballers' remuneration did not come close to the £50-plus per week that actors in the upper range could earn before 1914. Film work could pay stars as much as £3–5,000 per picture in the 1920s, and even more with the introduction of sound, although stage work might only guarantee £20 per week. However, earnings were extremely uneven in the acting profession, with estimates putting the average weekly income of actors at £2 or even 27 shillings, a level of pay equivalent to the very bottom of the wage scale at most League clubs.[193] Before 1914, the wages of variety artistes also ranged widely, from £3 to over £100 per week. The majority of managers, some operating a minimum wage, ensured that earnings commenced at £3–5 per week, which meant that 'even many less established acts fell within the contemporary lower-middle-class pay bracket'. Middle-ranking acts, on £10–40 weekly, were closer to the upper-middle-class category, while star pay was at a similar level as that of barristers or even Cabinet ministers. *The Perfomer* noted in July 1909 that Harry Lauder was making £500 per week by appearing in vaudeville in the USA.[194]

* * *

The comparison of footballers' earnings with those in other industries does not serve simply as a means of locating the former within an abstract occupational or class category. Most historians agree that the majority of professional footballers in this period were working class, and that they were generally drawn from industrial communities and manual backgrounds. What they have tended to ignore or gloss over are the very real divisions that existed, and which were based on more than transient employer–club loyalties. It is clear from the preceding analysis that the earnings of professional footballers varied significantly, and that the maximum wage never operated as an effective income ceiling. In this, as in many other areas, footballers were not a homogenous group. At the bottom of the pile, where wages were low, extra income was rare and employment was dependent on the vagaries of form, injury and the finances of the club, football was only ever a partial escape from the pit or the shopfloor. However, for the small number of elite players whose weekly wages were supplemented by bonuses, benefit payments and talent money, the entertainment industry represented a more logical point of comparison. Whether footballers were considered wage slaves or labour aristocrats depended not only on who was making the appraisal, but also on who was being appraised.[195]

The role of the Football League in the field of players' contracts, earnings and transfers was vital to the operation of the labour market in top-level football. Clubs, of course, were the employers of players and the first port-of-call in contract or wage negotiations, but directorates themselves were constrained by League regulations and the policy of the executive, which set the boundaries of players' earnings, sanctioned all payments and transfers and, in the final analysis, effectively *owned* players through its control of their registration. By 1939, the autonomy of clubs in all financial matters regarding their employees had been strictly limited: though it hardly controlled the purse strings of its members, the Management Committee had an effective veto on how players were rewarded.

The League therefore acted as both a regulator of the labour market and an arbiter in disputes between clubs and players. The extent to which it was an impartial arbiter remains obscure, although the assumptions of Tischler and Dabscheck that the League was one part of a powerful 'triple alliance' (along with the clubs and the FA) intent on enslaving players and restricting their earning and employment opportunities needs to be discarded.[196] The retain-and-transfer system and other contract regulations were clearly weighted against the player, but it is instructive to note that the League often ruled in favour of the player when disputes arose, and that both the executive and clubs were at times prepared to loosen the restrictive hold of the retain list and lower high transfer fees in order to help players get other jobs. Under their most extreme interpretation, the League's regulations could indeed be highly oppressive, but it must be remembered that committeemen, directors and players worked in a complex environment in which the horizontal allegiances of footballers to their fellow workers had to be accommodated with vertical loyalties to the club and the directors. The nature of the labour–capital relationships that emerged in this context provides the subject for the next chapter.

Notes

1 Green, *History*, p. 419; Preface to J. Guthrie, *Soccer Rebel: The Evolution of the Professional Footballer*, London, Pentagon, 1976.

2 Fishwick, *English Football*, Chapter 4.

3 M. Savage and A. Miles, *The Remaking of the British Working Class, 1840–1940*, London, Routledge, 1994, pp. 48–56. Also see A. J. McIvor, *A History of Work in Britain, 1880–1950*, London, Palgrave, 2001, pp. 93–109; D. Vincent, 'Mobility, Bureaucracy and Careers in Early-Twentieth-Century Britain' in *Building European Society: Occupational Change and Social Mobility in Europe, 1840–1940*, ed. A. Miles and D. Vincent, Manchester, Manchester University Press, 1993, pp. 217–39.
4 Vamplew, *Pay Up*, p. 207; Mason, *Association Football*, p. 89.
5 *Athletic News*, 14, 28 August 1911; 3, 10, 17, 24 August 1925.
6 *Sporting Chronicle*, 7 May 1931; 10 May 1932.
7 Association Football Players' and Trainers' Union (AFPTU) Minutes, 27 February 1939 (EGM); PFA, File 33, Watson Hartley to Jimmy Fay, 21 August 1934.
8 AVFC, 47/82, George Ramsay to Mr Harper, 4 May 1907.
9 SUFC, Football Committee Minutes, 1933–39, *passim*; WHUFC, Board Minutes, 1923–39, *passim*. Based on their published list of players, Bradford City, Chelsea, Newcastle United, Middlesbrough and Sheffield United were all reported in 1912 to have 'more than 30 men but less than 40'. Bolton Wanderers had only 23 'but 30 is a good average'. *Football Echo*, 26 October 1912.
10 *Sporting Chronicle*, 21 April 1934; C. Shindler, *Fathers, Sons and Football*, London, Headline, 2002, p. 35.
11 *Rochdale Observer*, 14 November 1931.
12 *Athletic News*, 3 August 1925. The following season, Durham increased its professional contingent to 13 but still relied heavily on amateur players. *Topical Times*, 11 September 1926.
13 Football League Minutes (Third Division Northern Section SGM), 21 March 1923.
14 See *Daily Mail*, 7 April 1932; *Topical Times*, 17 June 1933; *Daily Mirror*, 4 January 1936.
15 Vamplew, *Pay Up*, p. 207.
16 *Athletic News*, 4 March 1901.
17 *Thomson's Weekly News*, 18 May 1912; *Athletic News*, 8 May 1911.
18 AVFC, Board Minutes, 10 October 1911; *Athletic News*, 9 October 1911.
19 *Football Chat*, 27 January 1909.
20 See FA Emergency Committee Minutes, 13 January–3 February 1910; 23 August–3 October 1921; FA Consultative Committee Minutes, 22 November 1909. On the activities of agents during the 1890s, see Mason, *Association Football*, pp. 92–94.
21 Durham Record Office (DRO), D/XD 97/3, Darlington FC (DFC), Board Minutes, 24 October 1934; 8 May 1935; 6 May 1936; 10 June 1937; 12 June 1939.
22 See SUFC, Football Committee Minutes, 13 April 1927; 10 June 1931.
23 OAFC, Board Minutes, 30 December 1907.
24 SUFC, Football Committee Minutes, 15 August 1934; 16 August 1922; 7 August 1923; 2 October 1928.
25 WHUFC, Board Minutes, 5 December 1932.
26 *Topical Times*, 8 December 1934; 15 March 1938.
27 SRO, ITFC, Board Minutes, 3 January, 5 September 1938.
28 AVFC, Board Minutes, 24 March 1925; 20 April 1926.
29 *Sporting Chronicle*, 11 February 1936.
30 AVFC, Ramsay Correspondence Files, 52/82, letters from George Ramsay to McIlroy, 19 August 1921; 1 February 1922.
31 Huddersfield Town FC (HTFC), Board Minutes, 13, 21 December 1938; AVFC, Board Minutes, 7 September 1920.

32 See Fishwick, *English Fotball*, pp. 6, 41–42.
33 AVFC, Board Minutes, 26 April 1927.
34 SUFC, Football Committee Minutes, 27 March, 15 May 1929; 26 March, 1 April 1930.
35 WHUFC, Board Minutes, 26 March 1935; *Athletic News*, 3 July 1911; AVFC, Board Minutes, 24 August 1911; 2 July 1912; 6 May 1930.
36 *Topical Times*, 20 July 1934; *Sporting Chronicle*, 8 January 1936.
37 *Athletic News*, 9 October 1911.
38 Matthews and Smith, *The Wolves*.
39 *Thomson's Weekly News*, 16 April 1910; *Athletic News*, 5 April 1920.
40 Calculated from data in Vamplew, *Pay Up*, p. 206 (Table 13.2); *Athletic News*, 3, 10, 17, 24 August 1925.
41 DRO, D/XD 97/3, DFC, Board Minutes, 14 March 1938.
42 *Topical Times*, 24 March, 21 April 1928.
43 Vamplew, *Pay Up*, p. 214 (Table 13.5); PFA, File 35, statistics required from the Football League in the case Corbett v. Inland Revenue and Dale v. Inland Revenue, 1939.
44 AFC, Catton Folders, A–B, Arsenal FC Directors' Report 1924, p. 5; Wolverhampton Wanderers FC Programme, 25 February 1933.
45 AVFC, 52/82, letter from George Ramsay to Jack Webster, 7 September 1921.
46 AFC, Catton Folders, E–F, letter from Philip Kelso to James Catton, 27 July 1922, p. 504.
47 Second Division Oldham Athletic's balance sheet for the 1931–32 season included £9,725 from the transfer of players, a figure that was necessary for the club to survive. *Sporting Chronicle*, 24 June 1932.
48 G. Finlayson, *Citizen, State and Social Welfare in Britain, 1830–1990*, Oxford, Clarendon, 1994, p. 184.
49 *Topical Times*, 2, 23 June 1923.
50 Football League Minutes, 8 June 1925 (AGM).
51 For examples of letters from players seeking work, see AVFC, 47/82, 52/82, *passim*. *Sporting Chronicle* had a weekly 'Situations Wanted' column alongside 'Situations Vacant'. A typical entry from 23 May 1932 reads 'FIRST-CLASS CENTRE-FORWARD Seeks Eng. [sic.]; late 2nd Div.; would accept Continental Offer; age 24; Free – Baker, 53 Chevet Street, London, E9.' *Topical Times* advertised a space 'for the use of Senior football players who are looking for clubs', including 'particulars about your past clubs, your position on the field, age, height and weight'. See *Topical Times*, 18 July 1931.
52 WHUFC, Board Minutes, 3 April 1933.
53 Fishwick, *English Football*, p. 70. In April 1914, the Players' Union estimated that there were 4,740 professional players in England, attached to 158 clubs. *Football Players' Magazine*, April 1914.
54 Professional Footballers' Association (PFA), File 11, Rules of the Association Football Players' Union, 1907.
55 See, for example, PFA, File 8, letter from Herbert Broomfield to Dick Allman; letter from Herbert Broomfield to F.C. Metcalf, both 1 July 1909.
56 See the 'Association Football Players' Union: Advantages of Membership' page in *Football Players' Magazine*, 3, 11, October 1913.
57 AFPTU Minutes, 20 August 1920 (AGM), Harding, *For the Good of the Game*, p. 178.
58 AFPTU Minutes, 26 August 1929 (AGM).

59 Football League Handbook, 1912–13, Rule 11.
60 See, for example, Football League Minutes, Management Committee, 3 June 1912.
61 Vamplew, *Pay Up*, p. 72; T. Mason, 'Football' in *Sport in Britain: A Social History*, ed. T. Mason, Cambridge, Cambridge University Press, 1989, p. 161.
62 Mason, *Association Football*, p. 104; Vamplew, *Pay Up*, p. 227.
63 SUFC, Football Committee Minutes, 17 November 1913; 29 April 1914; Vamplew, *Pay Up*, p. 227. On Utley's offer, see Fishwick, *English Football*, p. 77.
64 *Thomson's Weekly News*, 28 June 1913.
65 Association Football Players' Union (AFPU) Minutes, 15 December 1915 (AGM); report of Football League AGM in *Athletic News*, 1 June 1914.
66 See FA Council Minutes, 30 January 1922.
67 Sutcliffe, Brierley and Howarth, *Story of the Football League*, p. 126. For a comparison over time, see PFA, File 2, agreement between Small Heath FC and Edwin Fountain, 5 May 1896; PFA, File 35, agreement between Millwall FC and Leonard Graham, 3 May 1933.
68 SUFC, Football Committee Minutes, 7, 15 October 1924.
69 FA Emergency Committee Minutes, 3 December 1908–13 January 1909; AFPU Minutes, 9 August 1912 (AGM).
70 *Athletic News*, 5 June 1911.
71 See Green, *History*, p. 405.
72 AFPU Minutes, 26 April 1910; Football League Handbook, 1910–11, Rule 11.
73 Fishwick, *English Football*, p. 87; *Thomson's Weekly News*, 19 March 1910.
74 Football League Minutes, Management Committee, 15 November 1912.
75 *Thomson's Weekly News*, 28 September 1912.
76 See *Thomson's Weekly News*, 5, 12 October, 9 November 1912; Football League Minutes, Management Committee, 15 November 1912.
77 Football League Minutes, Management Committee, 13 January 1913; *Football Players' Magazine*, February 1914.
78 See Football League Minutes, Management Committee, 9 November (Figgures of Barrow FC), 14 December (Harry Campling and Tommy Parkin of Coventry City) 1925; 12 January 1931 (James Harris of Rotherham United); DRO, D/XD 97/3, DFC, Board Minutes, 3, 10, 24 February, 3, 10 March 1937 (case of Syd Jarvis).
79 Football League Handbook, 1915–16, Rule 11.
80 AFPU Minutes, 12 April 1915.
81 SRO, ITFC, Board Minutes, 6 March, 1 May 1939.
82 P.J. Sloane, 'The Labour Market in Professional Football', *British Journal of Industrial Relations*, Vol. 7, 1969, pp. 183–89; Mason, *Association Football*, pp. 104–06; Vamplew, *Pay Up*, pp. 126–28, 212–13; Korr, *West Ham*, pp. 171–76.
83 *Athletic News*, 10 June 1901.
84 Football League Minutes (Third Division Southern and Northern Section SGMs), 21, 26 March 1923.
85 AFPTU Minutes, 25 August 1930 (AGM).
86 AFPTU Minutes, 28 September 1925; G. Chalk and D. Holley, *The Saints: A Complete Record, 1885–1987*, Derby, Breedon, 1987, pp. 65–73, 261. The issue was complicated further by the Football League's decision in 1922 to alter its long-standing definition of a 'reasonable wage' as either the maximum wage or the player's previous wage, thereby allowing poorer clubs to legitimately retain players on reduced terms. In a letter to his League counterpart in 1938, the Players' Union Secretary, Jimmy Fay, commented that the 'reasonable wage' rule effectively allowed League

clubs to 'absolutely ignore' the FA retaining wage. See International Football League Board Minutes, 18 March 1922; PFA, File 35, letter from Jimmy Fay to Fred Howarth, 21 January 1938.

87 Vamplew, *Pay Up*, p. 214 (Table 13.5).

88 *Athletic News*, 8 May 1911.

89 AFPTU Minutes, 21 August 1933 (AGM).

90 SUFC, Football Committee Minutes, 13 August, 12 November 1924; 19 August, 3 November 1925; 13 October 1926.

91 *Topical Times*, 6 August 1927.

92 *Topical Times*, 27 October 1934.

93 AFPTU Minutes, 20 April 1931; 8 August 1932; 24 April 1933.

94 WHUFC, Board Minutes, 25 April 1933.

95 See AVFC, 52/82, letter from George Ramsay to Eddy, 9 June 1919; letter from Ramsay to W. Morris, 17 June 1919; letter from Ramsay to R. Black, 17 June 1919; letter from Ramsay to Tom Lyons, 20 June 1919; letter from Ramsay to G. H. Hampton, 24 June 1919.

96 *Sporting Chronicle*, 3 May 1933; SUFC, Football Committee Minutes, 1 May 1934; OAFC, Board Minutes, 4 May 1938.

97 Vamplew, *Pay Up*, pp. 214 (Table 13.5), 241; *Sporting Chronicle*, 7 June 1935; 8 June 1936.

98 See SUFC, Football Committee Minutes, 3 October 1911; 15 January 1931; 25 February 1931; AVFC, Board Minutes, 3 October 1911.

99 Korr, *West Ham*, p. 171, makes a similar point.

100 Vamplew, *Pay Up*, pp. 148, 211–12; R. Sissons, *The Players: A Social History of the Professional Cricketer*, Sydney, Pluto, 1988, pp. 85–89.

101 P. Summerfield, 'The Effingham Arms and Empire: Deliberate Selection in the Evolution of Music Hall in London' in *Popular Culture and Class Conflict, 1590–1914: Explorations in the History of Labour and Leisure*, ed. E. Yeo and S. Yeo, Brighton, Harvester, 1981, pp. 209–40; A. Crowhurst, 'London's "Music Hall War": Trade Unionism in an Edwardian Service Industry', *London Journal*, Vol. 21, 1996, pp. 149–63; L. Rutherford, '"Managers in a Small Way": The Professionalisation of Variety Artistes, 1860–1914' in *Music Hall: The Business of Pleasure*, ed. P. Bailey, Milton Keynes, Open University Press, 1986, pp. 105, 110.

102 W. Vamplew, 'Playing for Pay: The Earnings of Professional Sportsmen in England, 1860–1918' in *Sport: Money, Morality and the Media*, ed. R. Cashman and M. McKernan, Brisbane, University of New South Wales Press, 1981, p. 121; Mason, *Association Football*, pp. 96–98.

103 Matthews and Smith, *The Wolves*, p. 89.

104 Vamplew, 'Playing for Pay', p. 121; *Athletic News*, 27 May 1901.

105 Vamplew, 'Playing for Pay', p. 123.

106 *Athletic News*, 4 June 1906; SUFC, Wage Books, 1899–1900 to 1904–05.

107 *Football Players Magazine*, March 1913.

108 *Athletic News*, 4 June 1906; J. Rawcliffe, 'Blackpool Football Club: From Lancashire League to Second Division' in *Book of Football*, ed. anon, London, The Amalgamated Press, 1906, p. 176.

109 *Thomson's Weekly News*, 12 March 1910.

110 FA Minute Books, Circular on Financial Relationship Between Clubs and Players, 10 January 1910.

111 AFPTU Minutes, 23 February 1920.

112 Sutcliffe, Brierley and Howarth, *Story of the Football League*, p. 123.
113 AFPTU Minutes, letter from H.J. Newbould to J. McKenna, 2 March 1921.
114 Sutcliffe, Brierley and Howarth, *Story of the Football League*, p. 124.
115 *Topical Times*, 2 May 1931. The records of Aston Villa, Darlington, Ipswich Town, Oldham Athletic, Sheffield United, Walsall and West Ham United show that all developed variations of the same basic wage structure between the wars.
116 WHUFC, Board Minutes, 19 April 1927.
117 *Topical Times*, 10 April 1926; AFPTU Minutes, 23 August 1937 (AGM); J. Seed, *The Jimmy Seed Story*, London, Phoenix, 1957, p. 84; Guthrie, *Soccer Rebel*, p. 32.
118 AFPTU Minutes, 27 February 1939 (EGM). Sheffield United signed 11 of its 18-man squad at the £9 maximum for the 1921–22 season, but by 1934 this figure had dropped to four. See SUFC, Football Committee Minutes, 3 May 1921; 1 May 1934.
119 *Topical Times*, 7 August 1926.
120 Guthrie, *Soccer Rebel*, p. 32.
121 SRO, ITFC, Wage Books, 1938–39 Season; OAFC, Board Minutes, 12 April 1939; DRO, D/XD 97/3, DFC, Board Minutes, 3, 24 May 1937.
122 SUFC, Football Committee Minutes, 9 September 1931; 1 March 1933; PFA, File 6, letter from F. Means to H. Broomfield, 25 October 1908; R. Carter, *Footballer's Progress*, London, Sporting Handbooks, 1950, pp. 36, 39.
123 SUFC, Football Committee Minutes, 31 March, 1 June, 5 August 1937; WHUFC, Board Minutes, 25 March 1930. On Fenton, see Korr, *West Ham*, pp. 98–100.
124 *Southport Guardian*, 3 July 1926; *Topical Times*, 17 July 1926.
125 *Sporting Chronicle*, 30 May 1932.
126 *Sporting Chronicle*, 3 May 1933. See also Fishwick, *English Football*, p. 78.
127 *Sporting Chronicle*, 14 December 1931; 28 January, 11 February, 6 April 1933.
128 *The People*, 28 May 1933; *Sporting Chronicle*, 24 April 1933.
129 Sissons, *The Players*, pp. 129–40; Vamplew, *Pay Up*, pp.221–22; K. A. P. Sandiford, 'The Birth of the Professional Cricketer's Benefit Match', *International Journal of the History of Sport*, Vol. 8, 1991, pp. 111–23; N. Baker, *The Rise of the Victorian Actor*, London, Croom Helm, 1978, pp. 122–23; P. Bailey, 'A Community of Friends: Business and Good Fellowship in London Music Hall Management, c. 1860–1885' in *Music Hall: The Business of Pleasure*, ed. P. Bailey, Milton Keynes, Open University Press, 1986, pp. 41–47.
130 FA Consultative Committee Minutes, 17 December 1900.
131 Baker, *Victorian Actor*, p. 123; Bailey, 'A Community of Friends', p. 44; Sandiford, 'The Birth', pp. 113, 121.
132 M. Golesworthy, *The Encyclopaedia of Association Football*, London, Sportman's Book Club, 1957, pp. 25–26; *Athletic News*, 30 May 1927.
133 Vamplew, *Pay Up*, p. 123; SUFC, Football Committee Minutes, 1905–14, *passim*; AVFC, Board Minutes, 23 January, 16 April 1912.
134 *Athletic News*, 22 March 1909, 11 September 1911.
135 SUFC, Football Committee Minutes, 11, 25 February, 2 March 1920.
136 Football League Minutes, Management Committee, 17 October, 4 April 1930.
137 WHUFC, Board Minutes, 19 April 1927, 2 May 1933; *Topical Times*, 30 July 1927.
138 WHUFC, Board Minutes, 13 April 1926, 15 May 1933; Korr, *West Ham*, p. 184.
139 Williams, *Cricket and England*, pp. 170–71; Sissons, *The Players*, p. 234.
140 SUFC, Football Committee Minutes, 22 February 1933; AFPTU Minutes, 26 September 1921 (AGM).
141 Wolverhampton Wanderers FC Club Programme, 3 March 1934.

142 Korr, *West Ham*, p. 186.
143 AVFC, Board Minutes, 14, 28 November 1911.
144 *Athletic News*, 4 December 1911.
145 AVFC, Board Minutes, 19 December 1911.
146 WHUFC, Board Minutes, 7, 29 April, 6 May 1930.
147 WHUFC, Board Minutes, 13 February 1922; Korr, *West Ham*, p. 59.
148 Football League Minutes, Management Committee, 18 December 1922.
149 AFPTU Minutes, 2 February 1921.
150 Sutcliffe, Brierley and Howarth, *Story of the Football League*, p. 119; AFPTU Minutes, 23 February 1920; Football League Minutes, Management Committee, 13 September, 11 October 1920, 12 April 1922 (SGM). An increased scale of bonuses for FA Cup and League success throughout the three divisions was introduced at the 1937 annual meeting. See *Sporting Chronicle*, 3 May 1937.
151 *Athletic News*, 23 May 1904; 15 January 1906.
152 *Topical Times*, 14 April 1934; Report of FA AGM in *Athletic News*, 4 June 1906. Also see the series featuring opinions on the bonus system, *Athletic News*, 8, 15, 29 January 1906.
153 AFPU Minutes, 1 April 1908.
154 AFPTU Minutes, 23 August 1937 (AGM).
155 Green, *History*, p. 415.
156 T. Mason, *Passion of the People? Football in South America*, London, Verso, 1995, p. 18.
157 Football League Minutes, Management Committee, 9 August 1912; WHUFC, Board Minutes, 8 May 1923.
158 See Mason, *Association Football*, pp. 97–98; S. Wagg, *The Football World: A Contemporary Social History*, Brighton, Harvester, 1984, p. 14; M. Hilton, *Smoking in British Popular Culture, 1800–2000*, Manchester, Manchester University Press, 2000, p. 109.
159 J. Harding, *Alex James*, London, Robson, 1988, pp. 165–68; N. Walsh, *Dixie Dean: The Life of a Goalscoring Legend*, London, Soccer Book Club, 1977, p. 69; Nevett, *Advertising*, pp. 159–60.
160 Football League Minutes, Management Committee, 28 August 1925; 29–30 June 1928.
161 Birley, *Land of Sport and Glory*, p. 234.
162 Report of FA AGM in *Athletic News*, 1 June 1908; Minutes of AFPU, 15 December 1908 (AGM).
163 McGregor, 'The £. s. d. of Football', p. 62.
164 *Athletic News*, 4 June 1906; FA Report and Recommendation of the Committee adopted by the Council re. Manchester United FC, 30 March 1910. For detailed discussion of the incidents, see J. Harding, *Football Wizard: The Story of Billy Meredith*, Derby, Breedon, 1985.
165 Football League Minutes, Management Committee, 27 April, 14–15 June, 16–17 November 1923; 13 September, 17 October 1927.
166 R. Taylor and A. Ward, *Kicking and Screaming: An Oral History of Football in England*, London, Robson, 1995, pp. 138–60.
167 *Topical Times*, 5 February 1938.
168 Guthrie, *Soccer Rebel*, p. 30.
169 Seed, *Jimmy Seed Story*, pp. 48–50.

170 T. Lawton, *Football is my Business*, London, Sporting Handbooks, 1946, p. 120; *The Economist*, 17 April 1937.
171 Cited in R. W. Lewis, 'The development of professional football in Lancashire, 1870–1914', unpublished PhD thesis, University of Lancaster, 1993, pp. 404–05.
172 *Daily Mirror*, 17 March 1920.
173 Taylor and Ward, *Kicking and Screaming*, p. 37; Lawton, *Football*, p. 121.
174 Carter, *Footballer's Progress*, p. 36.
175 See, for instance, Carter, *Footballer's Progress*, pp. 73–74; T. Finney, *Finney on Football*, London, Soccer Book Club, 1960; Lawton, *Football*, p. 120.
176 *Football and Sports Special*, 27 February 1909.
177 FA Archives, William Pickford Newspaper Cuttings, *Football Chat*, 1901–06, otherwise undated; W. Bassett, 'Big Transfers and the Transfer System' in *Book of Football*, ed. anon, London, The Amalgamated Press, 1906, p. 160.
178 *Football Chat*, 7 April 1909.
179 AFPTU Minutes, 27 February 1939 (AGM).
180 *Topical Times*, 3 September 1927.
181 R. Whipp, *Patterns of Labour: Work and Social Change in the Pottery Industry*, London, Routledge, 1990, pp. 58–63.
182 Vamplew, *Pay Up*, pp. 213, 224; B. Crampsey, *The Scottish Football League: The First 100 Years*, Glasgow, Scottish Football League, 1990, p. 101; J. A. Hutchinson, 'The development of professional football 1870–1914, with special emphasis on Scotland', unpublished paper, University of Edinburgh, 1977, pp. 252–53.
183 *Topical Times*, 11 August 1928; C. Jose, *American Soccer League, 1921–31: The Golden Years of American Soccer*, Maryland, Scarecrow, 1998.
184 AFPTU Minutes, 26 August 1936 (AGM).
185 A. Wahl and P. Lanfranchi, *Les Footballeurs Professionnels*, Paris, Hachette, 1995, pp. 63–67; *Sporting Chronicle*, 13 May 1932.
186 Vamplew, *Pay Up*, pp. 218–22; K.A.P. Sandiford, *Cricket and the Victorians*, Aldershot, Scholar, 1994, pp. 85–86.
187 Williams, *Cricket and England*, pp. 168–69, 176–77.
188 Collins, *Rugby's Great Split*, pp. 175–77.
189 Vamplew, *Pay Up*, pp. 216–18; R. Munting, *Hedges and Hurdles: A Social and Economic History of National Hunt Racing*, London, Allen Lane, 1987, pp. 130–34.
190 S. Shipley, 'Tom Causer of Bermondsey: A Boxer Hero of the 1890s', *History Workshop Journal*, Vol. 15, 1983, pp. 43, 48; D. Smith, 'Focal Heroes: A Welsh Fighting Class' in *Sport and the Working Class in Modern Britain*, ed. R. Holt, Manchester, Manchester University Press, 1991, p. 207; *Boxing*, 11 July 1934, 6 February 1935.
191 S. Riess, 'Professional Baseball and Social Mobility', *Journal of Interdisciplinary History*, Vol. 11, 1980, pp. 239–40.
192 Harding, *Alex James*, p. 165; L. Lowenfish, *The Imperfect Diamond: A History of Baseball's Labor Wars*, New York, De Capo, 1991, p. 112.
193 M. Sanderson, *From Irving to Olivier: A Social History of the Acting Profession in England*, London, Athlone, 1984, pp. 79–86, 217.
194 Rutherford, 'Managers', p. 109; *The Perfomer*, 1 July 1909.
195 Vamplew, *Pay Up*, pp. 254–56.
196 Tischler, *Footballers*, pp. 105–22; Dabscheck, 'Defensive Manchester'.

CHAPTER FOUR

Players II: Labour Relations

In common with broader historical interpretations of managerial activity, existing accounts of relations between footballers and their employers have tended to apply the notion of 'paternalism' without sufficient explanation or conceptual precision.[1] While there is little doubt that the notion of the individual capitalist 'father' looking after and caring for 'his boys' has an obvious appeal in the environment of male professional sport, it serves nonetheless to simplify the range and variety of managerial strategies that were available to employers in this as in other industries. By the turn of the century, the largely direct and personalised relationships between employers and workers that characterised nineteenth-century paternalism were increasingly being superseded in many industries by more formalised and bureaucratic labour strategies such as scientific management, collective bargaining and the introduction of welfare schemes.[2] Professional football was certainly not immune to these developments. More than this, an emphasis on traditional paternalism ignores the importance of central administrative bodies, such as the Football League and the FA, which as we have seen assumed considerable direct and indirect control over the payment of professionals, the regulation of the labour market and other aspects of capital–labour relations. In this context, the immutable picture of the paternal employer presiding over a deferential workforce is no more adequate as a complete explanation of labour relations in football than it is in the older manufacturing or the emerging service industries.

The concept of workplace control has been a major preoccupation of labour historians, but it still remains rather vague and wide-ranging. In the Marxist variant developed by Braverman, control at work was secured by employers through a gradual process of de-skilling, technological change and the sub-division of work tasks, which led to the subordination of the workforce.[3] While this interpretation has been seriously criticised historically, particularly in the British context, other typologies of managerial control have been put forward that emphasise three distinct categories or stages of development: personal or simple control through the direct supervision of foremen and the use of basic forms of incentive payment; mechanical or technical control via machines or production methods; and administrative or bureaucratic control based on specific rules and procedures.[4] The application of categories of this type to professional football is problematic, but not altogether inappropriate. While the physical environment of football clubs, not to mention the nature of the work undertaken and the production process, was clearly far removed from the factory or the shop floor, this does not mean to say that comparable managerial strategies were not developed. Football employers were as concerned as other businessmen with the need to minimise costs and maximise economic efficiency, and one obvious way this could be achieved was through control of the primary resource: labour.

This chapter will examine the different layers of relationships between employers and workers in the Football League. It will consider, first, the applicability of theories of paternalism to football, before going on to discuss the control and discipline of players at work and beyond. The institutionalised relationship between unionism and management will then be examined, and the final section looks at the development of welfare schemes, focusing particularly on injury compensation and post-career training. It is hoped that this analysis can help broaden and deepen our understanding of what has been described as football's 'essentially feudal set of labour–capital relations'.[5]

Work, control and discipline

Historians searching to understand and explain the nature of employment relationships in professional football have been drawn to the concept of paternalism. Tony Mason has written that before the First World War, football clubs exhibited 'a strange kind of paternalism in which the players were treated rather like some Victorian middle-class wives; stifling their independence perhaps, but cushioning them from some of the natural contingencies of life which most working people could rarely face with equanimity'.[6] Charles Korr has argued that, at West Ham United at least, the club assumed 'the dual role of employer and parent towards its players'.[7] How far these references to paternalism actually take us, however, is not altogether clear. As Warde has observed, the concept is often 'incoherent and overextended' and 'marked by its imprecise usage'.[8] If paternalism is to be used in anything more than a superficial fashion, we need to make some attempt to understand its meanings and define its parameters.

Paternalism was a traditional method of social control in rural society, whereby the landowner provided his subordinates with a secure livelihood and protection against the exigencies of life in return for the right to exercise complete authority and power over production. Newby has defined paternalism in this context as 'a traditional and highly personalised form of "gift relationship"', which arose from the fundamental power inequalities of the eighteenth century agricultural system.[9] The concept has, however, also been applied to the industrial landscape of the mid- to late nineteenth century, most notably in Patrick Joyce's work on the Lancashire cotton towns.[10] Joyce has identified the development of a 'new paternalism', which he sees as crucial in securing the stabilisation of industrial and class relations. Employers encouraged loyalty to management and deference to authority through the arrangement of social events, welfare benefits and other forms of company provision such as schools, libraries and savings and sick clubs. However, in Joyce's cotton towns, paternalism reached beyond the workplace into the daily lives of the townspeople, and even local religious and political life. Deference to the employers meant worshipping in their churches and chapels and voting for them at the ballot box. In this way, Joyce argues that the paternalist ethos was unconsciously internalised by workers and townspeople in general. Employer paternalism was thus not just a managerial strategy; it was an entire social system. In Joyce's words, 'work got under the skin of life'.[11]

Similar forms of employer paternalism have been identified in a range of industrial settings, from Quaker model villages to coal-mining communities and railway towns to pottery districts.[12] Yet it was not universally applicable. For one thing, it depended on the type of direct and personal relationship between employer and employee that simply did not exist in large-scale enterprises with bureaucratic management structures. Nor was paternalism suitable to large urban centres with unstable populations involved in a variety of industrial occupations.[13] What is more, some writers have confined paternalism to particular time periods. For Joyce, Lancashire paternalism declined from the 1890s onwards due to the replacement of the family firm by limited companies and the emergence of commercialised forms of leisure.[14] In her study of the railway town of Crewe, Diane Drummond insisted that railway paternalism 'was only viable for a specific period of history, when workplace relations were highly personalized, the franchise along with local and national government representation was very restricted and local and national economies dependent on one particular industry or firm'.[15] Other writers have argued that paternalism lasted longer in certain industries than the accounts of Joyce and Drummond suggest, or that it evolved into a more sophisticated form of 'welfare paternalism', institutionalised in the employment contract and embodied in pension and medical schemes, company housing and recreational provision.[16]

In many respects, football clubs were far from the ideal-type paternalistic enterprises. They were not run like textile mills and railway workshops. If some clubs were essentially small family firms headed by individual 'paternal' figures, there was nonetheless a lack of personal contact between employers and workers. The positioning of the Secretary, manager and trainer as a link (or a buffer) between the board of directors and the players meant that relations between management and labour tended to be formal and irregular. If paternalism's essential human element existed at all in football, it was increasingly embodied in the manager or secretary-manager rather than the directors. Face-to-face contact was extremely rare, and what Morris and Smyth have termed the 'theatre of paternalism', involving the boss shaking the workers' hands and using their Christian names, was largely absent.[17] Needless to say, football clubs could not possibly have enveloped their surrounding communities in the comprehensive way that other paternalistic employers did. There were also obvious limitations to the extent to which loyalty and deference could be internalised by workers who laboured no more than four hours a day and frequently switched employers at the end of each season. Despite these qualifications, however, there is no question that football clubs did at times resemble paternalistic employers, not least in the methods used to manufacture consent in the workplace and beyond. Paternalism may not explain the labour relations of Football League clubs in full, but it remains a useful concept in understanding the type of managerial strategies adopted.

In League football, as in other areas of industry, the control and discipline of employees was a crucial aspect of labour relations, and here paternalistic strategies were to the fore. Acts of kindness represented one side of the paternalistic coin. The first example of this – the treatment of injured and sick players – will be examined in the final section of this chapter. Another manifestation of benevolence concerned the involvement of clubs in the financial affairs of their players. Loans to players in debt were particularly common, although such applications were always vetted and often rejected. In 1910, for example, the Sheffield United board reluctantly agreed to clear the debts, including those to a money lender, of one of its employees, Joe Walton, 'on condition he disclosed all his liabilities and promised he would not [again] get into debt'. Eighteen years later, the club supervised the repayment from Bert Chandler's wages of subscriptions he had embezzled while acting as Players' Union collector for the club.[18] There were also instances of clubs loaning small sums of money to help players purchase houses or partake in other investments, but these were less common and, in any case, such loans were regarded as an advance of wages to be repaid in weekly instalments at an agreed rate.[19]

Some clubs similarly assisted their part-time professionals in obtaining employment, both directly and indirectly. Club directors occasionally employed players in their own businesses or, more commonly, were assisted by local firms who considered themselves 'supporters' of the club.[20] Charles Buchan was promised a job by Fulham in his chosen profession as a teacher if he signed professional forms with the club; on a grander scale, Alex James was lured to Arsenal by the assurance of a sports demonstrator's job at the famous West End store Selfridges.[21] In 1908, Aston Villa wrote to the owner of the local Ansell's brewery in an attempt to secure a clerkship at about 30 shillings a week for James Logan, one of its Scottish imports. The directors went so far as to issue the following circular to local employers in 1912:

> As several of our players are particularly anxious to obtain some kind of employment, we shall be glad to know whether you or any of your friends could assist us in finding them situations. Some of them can write shorthand, use a typewriter and have had considerable experience in law and commercial work, as well as in travelling. Others are suitable as warehousemen etc.[22]

Though the club's appeal was applauded by most, the Welsh international Billy Meredith was more suspicious, regarding it as a ploy to extend authority over players away from the ground and in the close season.[23]

If paternalism inferred kindness and benevolence, its reverse side was discipline and punishment.[24] Football employers were certainly not averse to adopting tight workplace supervision and discipline. Players could be censured, fined and even suspended for failure to carry out their work, in the form of either training or competitive matches. Most League clubs required their full-time professionals to train mornings and afternoons at least three times a week, and drafted specific training rules with which players were expected to comply. At Millwall, players were required to clock-on by signing a training book each morning and afternoon, and to obtain the manager's or trainer's permission before leaving.[25] Those who neglected training at Sheffield United in the early 1900s received warnings and small fines; at Aston Villa, the trainer was expected to inform the board immediately of 'any transgression of rules and laxity in training', but most players got away with a caution.[26] From 1923 onwards, League regulations formally recognised the club's power 'to suspend or fine players guilty of misconduct or breach of disciplinary rule'.[27] In minor cases, punishments were restricted to 14 days' suspension or an equivalent fine, but prolonged absences and non-attendance at matches were viewed more seriously. When Jim Simmons went absent without leave from West Ham in October 1921, he was immediately suspended *sine die* and reported to both the League and the FA. In late January 1922 the club lifted his suspension and played him in a series of first-team matches, but by April he had gone missing again, forcing the board to effectively sever his connection with the club by suspending him until the end of the season.[28] Birmingham chose to cancel the agreement of Charles Sprigg with 14 days' notice in 1913 for breaching disciplinary rules by failing to report for pre-season training.[29] In general, however, even players who missed games received only small fines – £1 for three West Ham reserves in 1922[30] – or temporary suspensions, and were unlikely to find their career prospects permanently damaged.

More severe punishments were dealt out to players found guilty of dishonesty or insolence. Barnsley's suspension of George Travers *sine die* for 'absence from training and using insulting language to the directors'[31] was fairly typical, but in extreme cases, like that of Aston Villa's Christopher Buckley, the full weight of the punitive system was brought to bear on the player. Buckley had claimed that a Villa director offered him a £250 bonus on re-signing to make up for his disappointing benefit, and when the board refused to pay he threatened not to play for the club again. A League Commission investigating the affair rejected the player's version of events and judged that no bonus had been offered to the player. As Buckley's demand was contrary to League rules, and in view of his general insubordinate attitude, the Commission fined him £24 and suspended him for two seasons – a sentence that remained in force despite numerous protestations by Buckley to both Villa and the Management Committee.[32] The Football League could use other methods to punish players who were believed to be dishonest. For instance, Eugene O'Doherty's application for a reduction of his transfer fee was put on hold until he apologised to the Management Committee and his club 'for deliberately making misleading statements to both Committees'.[33] The most serious penalties, however, were reserved for alleged match-fixers. Billy Meredith was suspended for the 1905–06 season after offering an opponent £10 to let Manchester City win a crucial championship decider, although *Athletic News* considered that Meredith had been treated leniently and that the offence 'ought to have ended his football career'.[34] Fulham's Barney Travers was not so fortunate when he was permanently suspended from taking part in football by the FA after approaching a South Shields player with a monetary offer to throw their Second Division match.[35]

The discipline and control of players on the field of play was also a pervasive concern of club directors and the football authorities. At the beginning of the period, directors or secretary-managers tended to control the selection of professional teams and endeavoured to determine the way they played. At Aston Villa, which did not appoint a manager until 1936, the board of directors issued periodic tactical instructions to players through the Secretary – to mark opponents at throw-ins, avoid giving away needless fouls around the penalty area or to 'place free-kicks to better advantage'.[36] Yet the authority of the employer was often limited once the game began. The Millwall directors acknowledged as much in an application to the National Insurance Commissioners in 1933 (see below), observing that a manager and trainer could only control 'the method of performance of duties' of a player 'as far as possible'.[37] Tactical instructions probably had little impact on footballers who felt they had little to learn: according to one First Division manager, 'You tell the players to do certain things and then when they get on the field they forget all about it'.[38] Indeed, despite the innovations of Herbert Chapman and others, it would seem that tactics, such as they existed, remained largely in the hands of trainers and senior players for much of this period.[39] Perhaps the most significant tactical innovation of the era, the offside trap, was unquestionably introduced and perfected by players: first by the full-back pairing of Herbert Morley and Jock Montgomery at Notts County, and then by Bill McCracken of Newcastle United.[40]

The position of Captain carried with it particular authority. The Captain was normally a senior professional who acted as players' representative and spokesman in negotiations with the board, although his role could also be interpreted as a type of supervisor for management. One clause in the agreement of Small Heath players from the mid-1890s stipulated that: 'The said player shall always obey the Captain of the team in which he is playing, and shall be obedient to his orders and commands.'[41] In 1924, the West Ham board expressly acknowledged the Captain's right to alter the formation and tactics of the team on the field, and the

Millwall players were likewise informed that while the manager and trainer determined the 'general plan of play' before the match, the 'control of tactics on the field is in the hands of the captain'.[42] Irrespective of the relative freedom players enjoyed over the 90 minutes, however, their play and conduct were ultimately subject to close scrutiny by their employers. Improper behaviour on the field often led to a player being warned or brought before the board of directors. In 1911, Aston Villa's Edmund Eyre was summoned to see the directors and severely cautioned 'for dirty play and foul language'.[43] Similarly, West Ham took immediate action by dropping Vic Watson, its England international forward, for the following League match for reportedly kicking an opponent during an FA Cup tie.[44] Nor did indifferent performances go unnoticed. Two of Darlington's forward line for the 1937–38 season, Albert Brallisford and Albert Harris, were interviewed by the chairman and manager and asked to explain their recent poor form. Brallisford never played for the club again.[45] In 1911, meanwhile, James Logan had found himself in trouble with his employer on two occasions. In March, the former professional John Devey reported Logan's 'bad captaincy' during an Aston Villa reserve fixture: 'in many cases his orders were wrong and … his shouting quite upset the players'. Logan was in front of the board again in December, following reports of unsatisfactory performances for the first eleven. In mitigation, he told the board that 'he had been hurt so often that he was trying to avoid mistakes' and that he felt 'some players did not want him in the first team'. Logan's plea was successful, and the board agreed to continue to select him 'if he promised to do his best and play his hardest in all matches'.[46]

Clubs were expected to control the behaviour of their players as far as possible, but even the FA spokesman William Pickford recognised that ultimately, 'a club cannot answer for a player when he has stepped onto the field'.[47] Penalties for foul play became progressively stiffer in the inter-war period, rising from an average of one to two weeks' suspension in 1914 to two to four weeks by 1930–31. Furthermore, the number of players punished almost doubled with the creation of the FA Disciplinary Committee in 1936, leading the Players' Union to protest that players were being suspended for 'trivial offences'.[48] In most cases, this type of discipline again represented no more than a temporary setback for a player, but it could lead to far more serious consequences, as the case of William Cook shows. Cook's refusal to leave the pitch after being dismissed by the referee led to the abandonment of a League match between Oldham Athletic and Middlesbrough in 1915. The FA suspended him for one year because of his 'misconduct on the field and gross misconduct in refusing to leave the ground when ordered by the referee'; in addition, a Football League Commission excluded him from any involvement in League football indefinitely, and ordered him to pay the entire costs of the inquiry.[49]

Attempts to control the off-field activities of players were also common, and it was here that paternalistic strategies, similar to those developed at industrial family firms or department stores, were most evident. In a job where employers worked for only part of the day and consequently enjoyed a great deal of leisure time, the establishment of recreational facilities was regarded as imperative. Aston Villa's plans to build a clubhouse with billiard tables and reading and writing rooms during the 1890s clearly reflected a desire among the directors to control the social lives of their employees, and especially to shelter them from the bad influences that might result from them being left to their own devices. At Sheffield United, the billiard room in the cricket pavilion was utilised for a similar purpose. All players living in the city were required to attend the billiard room on Wednesday, Thursday and Friday evenings; failure to do so without a legitimate excuse could lead to disciplinary action.[50] Rules over players extended beyond the training field. In the 1930s, Millwall required all sick or injured players to be home by 8 p.m. each evening, while squad members were subject to a 10 p.m. curfew before match days. Here, as elsewhere, weekend leave was permitted only under 'very special circumstances'.[51] The players of Hull City, meanwhile, could only attend dances after Tuesdays if they were chaperoned by a club official or had gained prior permission from the club. Probably on the assumption that drinking was more counter-productive to the professional athlete than dancing, players were also banned from visiting pubs after Monday of each week.[52] Not all employers took such a hard line. In 1939, the Middlesbrough right-half Duncan McKenzie compared the attitude of his current club, which trusted the player to look after himself 'when he knows his career depends on it', to that of former employers Brentford, whose restrictive rules were premised on the belief that 'some players have to be saved from themselves'.[53]

Directors also used widely recognised paternal forms of management such as social evenings, whist drives and work outings to improve personal relations between the employers and the workforce, and to encourage collective loyalty and commitment to the club.[54] For a short time, Sheffield United even arranged for a local golf club to take on its players, directors and officials as winter members, and organised regular club visits.[55] By the 1930s, some clubs were also arranging activities for players during the close season, possibly with the dual purpose of keeping them fit and under close supervision. West Ham players, for example, were competing in cricket, tennis and golf tournaments as well as swimming galas, often against rival football clubs, during the July and August of each year.[56] Although it is difficult to know exactly how they reacted to or interpreted these activities, it does appear that, in the main, the social lives of players remained in their own hands. The West Ham board itself recognised that club social evenings were difficult to organise, as 'players have always shown a marked preference for arranging their own social affairs'.[57] Billy Cook's diary of his time at Everton in the late 1930s certainly suggests that professional footballers regularly socialised with one another, and often used facilities supplied by the club, but rarely did so at the behest of their superiors.[58]

Living arrangements were a further area in which clubs sought to exert control over their workforces. Most players were encouraged to live within the immediate district so that they could attend training sessions throughout the week. West Ham preferred their men to live 'within distance of the ground', and Sheffield United actually ruled in 1908 that 'all players signed on in future must reside in the Sheffield district'.[59] Players living within the stipulated area could also find themselves forced to move from accommodation that the club considered unsatisfactory. Aston Villa requested three of its players 'to change their present lodgings forthwith or be suspended', though the board minutes provide no explanation as to why; and the same club reacted to information that seven employees were lodging together in a small double-bedroomed house by pointing out that this 'was not conducive to good health' and ordering some to move.[60] Following the practice of shipbuilding, mining and railway companies, among others, football clubs began to take responsibility for the housing of at least some of their players from the inter-war period onwards.[61] New players were often placed in lodgings with a teammate or, if married, in a rented club house.[62] The Charlton Athletic directors bought six houses in 1934, which they let to players 'at very reasonable rents'. Major Buckley, meanwhile, set up a hostel for his younger charges at Wolverhampton Wanderers.[63] This was certainly a further device for keeping the private activities of employees under close surveillance. Huddersfield Town, for example, required all lodging to be approved by the club, and expected the landlord or landlady to report 'the hours kept and conduct of the players'.[64]

The control of players also involved steering them away from immoral or anti-social behaviour, though the motive was as likely to be physical as moral. Many employers warned their players of the dangers of smoking, gambling or borrowing from loan sharks, but some took more direct action. Possibly as a means of preventing over-indulgence, the Sheffield United committee requested the trainer to monitor weekly changes in the weight of each player.[65] The Aston Villa directors, meanwhile, were so concerned about their players 'drinking and misconducting themselves' during the 1899–1900 season that they employed a private detective to investigate the worst offenders. One player was found to have been drunk several times a week, once with a teammate two days before an important match, and was disciplined accordingly.[66] Two first-team players involved in an assault case also received a 'severe reprimand' from the Villa Chairman; the club likewise discouraged its players from betting on horses or visiting racetracks.[67] Moreover, throughout the 1920s and 1930s the directors continued to employ private detectives to 'shadow' employees and report on their 'movements and habits', often in order to gather evidence against them on the grounds of 'palpable inefficiency'.[68] While the Aston Villa directors were renowned for their uncompromising attitude to indiscipline, other clubs evidently kept less tight reins on their players. Leicester Fosse, for one, received criticism in the press for allowing its team to attend wedding celebrations the night before a match, which it lost 12–0.[69]

Contracted employees at certain clubs were also prohibited from any involvement, as either workers or owners, with drinking or gambling establishments. As we saw in Chapter 2, Football League and FA officials were particularly strict when players became associated with gambling, and stepped in quickly to prevent stars such as Andy Ducat and Ernest Needham (when he was coach at Sheffield United) from taking jobs as newspaper tipsters.[70] The forecasting of match results was not the only right that footballers were denied. During the 1920s and 1930s, the FA cracked down on 'the growing practice of players contributing signed reports and articles containing criticisms of colleagues and opponents, and giving interviews to the press', and encouraged League clubs to 'take the necessary steps' to stop the practice. Though such resolutions did not preclude players from writing for the press, they did seek to influence what was said, a situation that the Union secretary regarded as 'a further curtailment of the players' liberties'.[71] Cecil Hadley of *The People*, a vociferous opponent of 'sportsmen-journalists', was not averse to informing the FA when the 'writing' (or ghost-writing) of footballers contravened the regulations. In the first two months of 1931 alone, Hadley reported Arsenal's David Jack for predicting the results of forthcoming matches and Aston Villa's Billy Walker, who had used his column to criticise the decisions of the referee and the 'rough play' of Chelsea's Hughie

Gallacher in a recent match.[72] The possible threat of injury and the provisions of the club's insurance policy also convinced the West Ham directors to forbid their players from using 'motor cycles, or [indulging] in aviation or any other dangerous pursuit', while Huddersfield Town and Brentford placed similar bans on its employees driving motor cars.[73]

Unionism and labour protest

The need to safeguard and improve the lot of professional footballers led to attempts at industrial action through unionism, strikes and other submerged forms of labour protest. In contrast with other sportsmen and women, football players were relatively successful at establishing a permanent union organisation, which, with the exception of 1915–18, has functioned from 1907 until the present day.[74] The aims of the Association Football Players' Union,[75] formed in December 1907, were basically consistent with those of other trade unions of the period, which acted simultaneously as friendly societies, providing welfare and financial assistance, and as trade societies, seeking to negotiate improved working conditions for their members.[76] Hence, one part of the Union's functions involved giving legal aid and assistance to players, helping members and their families in financial need and assisting transfer-listed or disengaged players in finding employment.[77] Its primary function, however, was undoubtedly to establish freedom of contract for players and abolish the maximum wage.

Recognition by the football authorities was not unconditional, but dependent upon a number of limits being placed on the activity of the Union. First, this involved the monitoring and, to a certain extent, the control of Union finances. The Union was required to submit its balance sheet annually to the FA, while the allocation of funds was subject to veto by the governing body. In particular, the FA became determined to financially separate the Union's welfare activities from its organisational work, and hence in 1910, and again in 1912, stepped in to prohibit the transfer of Union money from the latter's benevolent fund to its general fund.[78] Control could also be exercised over the Union's fund-raising activities. In 1912, the League Management Committee supported the FA's action by withdrawing permission for a benefit match to be played between the English and Scottish Union; in 1921 it was similarly decided that the Union's benevolent finances were not sufficiently depleted to warrant a fund-raising match.[79]

A second and more important condition for Union recognition was the need to conform to the rules and procedures of the football authorities. Hence when the Union threatened in early 1909 to take legal action against clubs for the recovery of wages as well as compensation under the Workmen's Compensation Act without its permission, the FA decided to withdraw recognition 'until they are satisfied that the Union is prepared to carry on its operations in accordance with FA rules'.[80] Writing as editor of the London weekly *Football Chat*, League President John Bentley had no doubt that the Union had been 'ill-advised ... [to] come into direct opposition with the Football Association'. 'If the Players' Union', contended Bentley, 'desires the privileges and the protection of the FA, it must be prepared to abide by its rules – not select those which are suitable and throw the rest to the winds'.[81] Moreover, supporters of the FA pointed out that procedures for the arbitration and settlement of such disputes existed within the laws of the parent body, and that the players were therefore bringing themselves into conflict with an intermediary rather than quarrelling directly with their employers.[82] Such arguments held little sway with the Union Committee, which rejected 'the opinion that a football player forfeits a common legal right on entering into a professional engagement with a football club'.[83] For one of the Union's leaders, Billy Meredith, the issue was essentially about autonomy:

> the Football Association is composed of autocrats who demand that we shall surrender our rights of citizenship. We must not go to law without first obtaining their permission, they themselves clinging like limpets to the privilege of suspending and punishing us ... without allowing us to appear and plead our own cause before them. What [is] the good of belonging to a union that is only recognised provided it observes the rules and practices of the FA[?][84]

The 1909 dispute highlighted a further limit on recognition relating to strike action. In May, the leaders of the Players' Union agreed to affiliate to the General Federation of Trade Unions (GFTU), and inserted a strike clause in its rules whereby members would receive £1 per week strike pay if it were considered necessary to withdraw their labour.[85] Administrators and club directors argued that such a clause was impracticable and unnecessary for League footballers, who benefited from yearly contracts and were not subject to the usual risks of trade and fluctuating wages. Indeed, William Pickford was not alone in pointing out that signing an agreement actually implied a moral duty *not* to strike. In addition to this, there was a diffuse fear that footballers might be called to strike in support of fellow GFTU workers.[86] Football League representatives were particularly vociferous in their objection to the involvement of the GFTU in the dispute. According to John Bentley, 'the League clubs will never agree to players being connected with a union or an organisation of any sort in which there is a strike clause'.[87] In response to pressure throughout the late summer and early autumn to secede from the GFTU, the Union membership continued to resist, even informing the FA that 'the power to withdraw members or to strike is not conceded by the Federation but by the Trade Disputes Act of 1906'. Yet eventually the pressure proved too much. A ballot of members in late October resulted in a majority of 470–172 in favour of disaffiliating from the GFTU, and 'in the interests of peace and harmony' the Union tendered its resignation.[88] Only then was the Union formally recognised again by the FA and the League. A similar approach was taken by the League in early 1919 towards a London-based Professional Football Players' and Trainers' Union, which had met and established preliminary contacts with mainstream union officials. At a joint meeting of players and officials, John McKenna rejected the new union in the following terms: 'So long as you are organising along Trade Union lines the League cannot meet your representatives … [there is] a vast difference between football players and trade unionists. We will not accept a players' union on trade union principles and whose strength lies in the strike clause.' The London union was disbanded, its members joining a revived version of the pre-war Union, which subsequently committed itself to 'deal with the League on proper constitutional lines' without resorting to strike threats or links with the wider labour movement.[89]

The policy of the Football League and the FA was to contain the Union's activities and secure its identification with groups within the football industry rather than outside. For this reason, League officials and supporters placed considerable emphasis on the rhetoric of friendship and loyalty and eschewed references to conflictual employer–employee relationships. During the 1909 dispute, for example, *Athletic News* continually referred to the GFTU as 'the third party', and advised players that it was their 'first duty' to be loyal to the FA:

> If the professional were an ordinary workman, a craftsman or a mechanic, we should be the first to say 'Stand by your Federation'. We have no doubt that the Federation has done and will render much excellent service to the cause of industry, and unionism has accomplished much in its own world. But that world does not happen to be football.[90]

Similarly, in 1919 the paper's London correspondent reminded the Football League player that 'his true friends are in football', and went on to talk of the need for mutual loyalty, harmony and 'friendly cooperation' between the Union and the League.[91] Antagonism and opposition to League decisions were rejected out of hand as inappropriate responses for a players' association. The Union was therefore charged with disloyalty when it encouraged its members to defy League instructions by wearing Union badges during matches. Similarly, when the Union issued a statement in April 1915 criticising alterations of League rules, the Management Committee responded by declaring that the Union had 'adopted a policy and attitude calculated to hinder us in our purpose to keep the game going and complete our Competition' and, furthermore, was 'indisposed to be of any practical assistance to the clubs and the governing bodies'.[92] The Union was thus tolerated as long as it remained acquiescent; working alongside the League rather than against it.

This attempted manipulation of organised labour was exemplified in the Football League's attitude to collective bargaining. In spite of prompting from the Players' Union, formal bargaining procedures were consistently resisted by the executive body. Since its formation, the Union had proposed that it should be entitled to representation on the FA Council, and in 1909 it advocated the creation of a Wages and Claims Board, consisting of equal representation from the FA and the Union, to adjudicate on the claims of players against clubs.[93] Not surprisingly, proposals of this kind involving direct Union influence on decision making were rejected, and the Union was excluded from formal involvement in the settling of players' disputes. Instead, disputes between individual players and clubs – from suspensions, dismissals and unpaid wages to applications for reductions in transfer fees – were normally referred to the League Management Committee and ultimately to an Appeals Committee consisting of three FA Council members. Unlike in rugby league, where a newly-formed Players' Union was briefly represented during the early 1920s on the Board of Appeal, the football Union had no judicial power or influence at any stage in the Football League's procedures.[94] Negotiations over the fundamental issues of wages, contracts and conditions remained largely ad hoc. There were, indeed, no football equivalents of the conciliation and arbitration boards that developed across a broad range of industries in the late nineteenth and early twentieth centuries.[95] In fact, the League frequently rejected Union requests for meetings between the two bodies, leading to a complete breach in formal negotiations between 1923 and 1937. When the bodies did actually meet, Union demands were rarely powerful enough to change the League's obdurate attitude to rule changes.[96]

Strained relations between League and Union officials contributed to the absence of mutual cooperation. This was certainly the case when the two bodies clashed in 1912 as a result of accusations that the Union Secretary Syd Owen had deliberately misled the League executive over a proposed benefit match. To add to the ill-feeling, Owen publicly attacked 'the honour and honesty of the League Management Committee' in communications. The League responded by demanding an official apology and refusing to recognise Owen as the Union Secretary.[97] Billy Meredith thought that Owen had been unfairly treated by the League, which had shown 'a very unkind feeling towards the Union secretary and a desire to humble him'. For the Union Chairman Colin Veitch, the incident reflected that body's lack of support among football legislators: 'there seems to be a strong influence working in a way inimical to all matters connected with the Players' Union'.[98] Owen was eventually forced to resign, and a year later the League could publicly acknowledge that the appointment of his successor, Harry Newbould, had contributed to an improvement in relations between the two bodies.[99] But by the end of the First World War, these had again deteriorated. In his annual report of 1920, Newbould complained of the 'austere attitude of the Football League', particularly its Secretary Tom Charnley, and resolved that the Union viewed 'with dissatisfaction the tendency of the Football League to ignore the official, and other, communication forwarded in connection with the alleged grievances of players, and requests that in every case prompt replies should be forwarded to the secretary of the Union in order that a satisfactory relationship can be maintained'.[100] Not all League officials were overtly hostile to the Union – Veitch even admitted in 1912 that 'we have a few friends amongst the legislators'[101] – but the leading figures at Preston were invariably viewed with distrust by their Union counterparts. Charles Sutcliffe, in particular, regularly crossed swords with Union representatives, and was often accused of attempting to undermine its position. In 1923, the Union executive publicly condemned an article by Sutcliffe in *Topical Times* that it believed 'was written with the object of damaging the status of the Union'; and it even considered a libel action against Sutcliffe and the co-authors of the League's golden anniversary history for a passage accusing the Union of dishonesty.[102]

How prevalent was unionism within the Football League, and how did this compare with the wider union movement? Membership levels fluctuated significantly before 1914, from a reported high of over 1,300 in December 1908 to 510 by September 1910, before a further increase to 853 in April 1912 and a dip to 467 a year later. However, Football

League players accounted for only about two-thirds of the total registrations, while approximately a quarter of League clubs were unable to contribute a single Union member.[103] While unions generally underwent rapid growth during the First World War, the Players' Union was forced to disband in October 1915 and was only revived in January 1920. Yet it too benefited from the immediate post-war boom, and more specifically from the wage rises of 1920, to record a membership of 1,174 in 1921, increasing to 1,481 by 1922. By this point, of course, the expansion of the Football League to four divisions meant the Union had a virtual monopoly on League professionals. The general slide in union membership from 1920 onwards, though slightly delayed, was equally pronounced in the Players' Union, chiefly due to the wage reductions of April 1922. By February in the following year, Newbould had to report a 'falling off' in membership to 994 from 39 clubs, and appealed to First and Second Division players particularly to renew their support;[104] the appeal was evidently unsuccessful, as membership slumped to a low of 398 in 1924. Yet despite the Depression and the overall decline in union membership during the late 1920s and early 1930s, a successful membership drive led to a growth of over 60 per cent, to 1,040 registered members by 1932. From this point onwards, membership rose gradually to nearly 1,400 by 1937 and then more rapidly, so that in April 1939 the Players' Union could claim 1,850 Football League members and an extra 80 or so forced out of the League by excessive transfer fees.[105] What is more, by now all but a handful of clubs were represented in the Union, normally by at least half a dozen players. Yet on balance the Union remained a fairly weak and marginal organisation in numerical terms during this period. It could only confidently claim to represent the majority of League footballers for short periods in 1908–09, 1921–22 and from the mid-1930s onwards. For the rest of the period, union membership rarely topped 40 per cent, and even dipped to below 20 per cent in the mid-1920s. Jimmy Guthrie later admitted that even at its pre-war peak, the Union's spirit was at 'a low ebb' with many of the players 'members in name only'.[106]

In certain ways, the labour market and the nature of employment in the Football League was incompatible with strong union organisation. Though employment for most players was guaranteed for at least a season and was thus more secure than in casualised trades like docking and building, labour mobility within the League was nonetheless substantial as the importance of the transfer market increased between the wars.[107] Because playing staffs constantly changed, it was difficult to ensure long-term stability in membership, especially when collectors, the focus of union organisation within clubs, moved. This could produce erratic membership levels from year to year and, in extreme casers, the Union could lose a club's entire membership almost overnight, as happened with Aston Villa in 1938–39.[108] Careers, moreover, were relatively short – lasting perhaps ten to fifteen years if the player was particularly lucky – and thus the Players' Union could rarely rely on the type of permanent employees who became crucial to the growth of many other unions in this period.[109]

In common with other professional sports, the inherent pressures of football competition could lead to divisions among players both within and between clubs. One of the Union's perennial headaches during the inter-war years was its failure to attract players associated with the more wealthy and successful clubs. The Union was aggrieved that some players 'connected chiefly with the richer clubs ... take a very selfish view, and have no consideration whatever for their Brother Professionals', a statement borne out by the fact that in 1936, only 271 of its total League membership of 1,250 were from First Division clubs. By contrast, the Second Division could boast 480 and the Third Division South had 413 members.[110] This lack of involvement at the elite level may have been because such players considered themselves reasonably well paid and well treated, and thus saw no need to join a union. However, it can also be partly explained by the individual nature of contract negotiations and other forms of bargaining. Each player's agreement with his club was conducted independently of his fellow workers and remained, theoretically at least, confidential. This probably encouraged selfishness and even envy at times; it could certainly preclude the development of solidarity among players. For example, when Scottish international Alex James refused to re-sign for Arsenal at the end of the 1930–31 season, he did so not 'to right the wrongs of the oppressed brothers of my profession' but to convince the club to increase the terms offered. For James, 'football – off the field ... of course – must always be each man for himself. And professional footballers didn't invent that rule.'[111]

Many contemporaries certainly believed that professional footballers lacked collective strength. *Athletic News* remained convinced that 'The footballer is not naturally inclined to be an ardent and staunch trade unionist' on the very eve of a threatened players' strike in August 1909.[112] Writing at around the same time, Meredith bemoaned the tendency of players 'to live a kind of schoolboy life and to do just what they are told'.[113] Another member of the Union executive, Charlie Roberts, was similarly critical of the fundamental apathy and docility he had witnessed among League players:

> I know of no class of workpeople who are less able to look after themselves than footballers; they are like a lot of sheep. A representative from the Union could go and speak to them on the why and wherefore they should join the Union, and they would immediately decide to join. Two minutes after, a manager could go and say a few words to them, and then they decide not to join.[114]

Conventional forms of collective action, such as strikes, were therefore extremely rare. The only major national dispute during this period took place in 1909, significantly at the beginning of a period of widespread labour unrest and soaring strike activity in which vast numbers of unskilled workers became organised for the first time.[115] The events of that year indicated the difficulties and risks involved in attempting an all-out strike. In the context of a dispute over the Union recourse to law, the FA had ordered both officials and rank-and-file members to resign from the Union by the beginning of July or have their registrations cancelled; those who failed to do so also faced the possible loss of summer pay and prospective benefits. Hence players had a great deal to lose by remaining defiant, and the majority – as many as 800 of a 1,200 membership according to the FA – complied with the parent body's wishes.[116]

The letters received by Herbert Broomfield, the Union Secretary, over the critical months of May, June and July provide a clear insight into the attitudes of the membership. Most resigned reluctantly: though they supported the Union and its demands, they were not convinced that they had the collective strength to withstand a protracted dispute. An Oldham Athletic player, for instance, wrote to Broomfield declaring that he was prepared to 'stand out' but thought it useless to do so alone: 'One in a team will not do much good'.[117] Jack Carr of Newcastle United similarly believed that the Union's case was doomed to failure because 'the players won't stick together and a handful's no good whatever'. Although Broomfield tried to convince him to cancel his resignation, Carr was unable to see 'why I or a few should risk our livelihood for the sake of a lot of football players who haven't pluck enough to fight for themselves'.[118] Self-interest was a clear motivation for Carr's seven teammates, and many others who broke with the union to protect their arranged benefits. Additionally, the numerous requests for guidance and information on whether team colleagues had resigned illustrates the difficulties of collective action in the close season when players were necessarily scattered across the country.[119] In view of these circumstances, it is hardly surprising that the players of only one club, Manchester United, withdrew their labour collectively, though other 'militant' sides like Sunderland and Newcastle

United agreed to rejoin the Union in time for the start of the season. Even so, Broomfield still believed that the Union was 'absolutely assured of success' if 'a few players in a few of the Principal Clubs' stood out for a fortnight, and remained convinced 'that every man was a Unionist at heart, and would belong to us if no coercion was used to make them act differently'.[120] Eventually, however, a compromise was reached on the eve of the new season, which saved the Union from testing the League's belief that players would be unable to withstand even a month-long strike.[121] After 1909, the Union's general retreat from conflict with the authorities and the effective outlawing of conventional strike action by the latter diminished the likelihood of another national dispute.[122]

Tony Collins is doubtless right to point out that, unlike the earliest footballers of the Northern Rugby Union who were required to work outside the game and were thus more prepared to act, full-time soccer professionals 'ran the risk of losing their livelihoods if they went on strike'.[123] However, the absence of industry-wide strikes and other combative forms of industrial action did not mean that labour relations in the Football League were stable and free of conflict. Despite the criticisms of unionists like Meredith and Roberts, it is clear that many footballers did recognise that individual interests were best served by acting together. Collective action and mutual support among players, though difficult to uncover, did take place in spite of the individualism encouraged by employers. At the end of Luton Town's 1897–98 campaign, the board's decision to reduce players' wages led to a strike involving ten first-team players, all of whom refused terms and were subsequently transferred to other clubs. 'Not wishing to blackleg, although I was opposed to the principle of striking, I left with the others, and in so doing sacrificed a benefit match', recalled John McCartney, one of the Luton strikers.[124] When Sheffield United suspended Alec Kay in 1902, his fellow workers contributed, against the club's wishes, to a common fund to ensure that he received his normal income. Indeed, according to Sutcliffe, it was 'common knowledge that the [suspended] players go round with the hat and make up their loss of wages'.[125] In 1920, nine first-team players at the Sheffield club joined together to send a letter of protest to the board of directors against the 'preferential treatment' given to the Captain over his benefit match. While this may be interpreted as a collective show of jealousy as much as unity, it did persuade the management to grant benefits that had previously been refused to a number of the protesters.[126]

More often, however, unrest was expressed through individual and submerged forms of protest. The most common example involved contract disputes, in which players would avoid signing in the hope of gaining an improved offer. While the less talented players could be in a weak position in such disputes, club records indicate that bargaining was relatively common and reluctantly accepted by directors as part of the signing-on process.[127] Often, the club would refuse to make improved offers, as was the case at Sheffield United in 1930 and at Arsenal during Alex James's close season strike a year later; in some cases, players refusing to sign on risked being placed on the transfer list.[128] The Aston Villa board was similarly reluctant to accede to demands for extra wages or benefits, as Frank Barson and Frank Moss were both to discover in 1922; a dispute over benefit payments led Stanley Matthews to delay re-signing at the end of both the 1936–37 and 1937–38 seasons, leading to what essentially became a three-week strike on the latter occasion.[129] Yet many players were able to successfully negotiate better terms. West Ham agreed to pay four of its players up to an extra £1 per week for the 1935–36 season; George Raynor, Jack Smith, Bernard Oxley and Jack Pickering similarly secured amended terms at Sheffield United in 1931.[130]

Grievances might also be expressed through absenteeism, go-slows, and other forms of non-cooperation or dissent. Potentially the most powerful weapon footballers possessed was simply the refusal to play, although again it was generally only the most talented who could afford to aggravate their employers in this way. In 1931, 15 of Southampton's professionals refused to play in a charity match following wage cuts, but most were eventually persuaded to accept the new terms.[131] When two of Aston Villa's senior players, the aforementioned Barson and Clem Stephenson, declined to play in a League match because of a dispute involving residency outside Birmingham, they were initially suspended for a fortnight by the club, but eventually achieved a board climbdown.[132] Historians of industrial relations have recognised that such expressions of dissent can reasonably be interpreted as conscious forms of protest. Hence it is not implausible to speculate, as Tony Mason does, that the England international forward Stephen Bloomer's persistent insobriety and neglect of training during 1901 may have been an individual response to the restrictive maximum wage rules passed that year.[133]

Perhaps the best example of what might be called industrial sabotage in League football involved 'playing for one's papers' – the practice of intentionally playing badly in order to get a transfer. It is hard to know how widespread this was, though the press seemed to regard it as something of a phenomenon for much of the period.[134] Certainly, Jimmy Seed noted that it was not uncommon in the 1930s for a player to suddenly lose form if his transfer request had been rejected, and the *Sunday Express* in 1931 similarly exposed what it referred to as the 'scandal' of directorates 'tapping' players at other clubs by offering them inducements, usually through a third party, to play badly and thus facilitate a transfer.[135] One obvious instance, involving Sheffield United's Stan Fazackerley, can be gleaned from club records. Fazackerley had evidently been unsettled for some time at the club, and in October 1920 he put in a transfer request, which was refused. In response, the player not only stopped training but generated considerable discontent among both teammates and supporters by 'not doing his share of the work' during matches. Not surprisingly, the club chose to transfer 'with reluctance' a player who had become a disruptive influence, and by November Fazackerley had moved on to Everton.[136]

Football welfare

Welfare provision in the Football League at the beginning of the twentieth century can be described as rudimentary and sporadic. Without government or League intervention, there were no legal obligations upon club employers to provide for the sick or injured player who 'ran risks which often cost him his job and his capacity to earn a living'.[137] In practice, however, many clubs did make certain financial and medical arrangements to look after players who found themselves in such unfortunate circumstances. In minor cases, the player received his normal wage until he was declared fit; part-timers would likewise be paid for earnings lost owing to a footballing accident. Medical treatment was also necessary to get a man fit and playing again as quickly as possible. Hence, clubs increasingly employed their own doctors, masseurs and other specialists to treat injuries and, with a few exceptions, paid for the costs of surgery and convalescence. West Ham United established specific arrangements with a local hospital for treating its players. Others might send employees to hospitals specialising in football injuries, like the renowned Matlock House in Manchester, which was run by Mr Allison, a director of the City club, and was widely recommended by John Bentley in his dual role as League President and editor of *Athletic News* and *Football Chat*.[138] This concern with the physical wellbeing of players sometimes extended to the organisation of recuperative visits to seaside resorts. This was especially popular with the Sheffield United committee, which agreed to send Alf Common to Skegness for two weeks during the summer of 1902, and gave Lewis a similar fortnight's holiday on medical advice the following season. It is unclear whether this practice was followed at other, poorer, clubs, but at United it certainly lasted well into the 1930s.[139]

In common with many employers, Football League clubs preferred informal welfare arrangements that allowed for discrimination and control. Only as the costs and scale of activities rose did they consider more institutionalised and formal schemes designed to financially protect themselves against the threat of injury to employees. As Joseph Melling has argued, such welfare programmes 'were devised by employers with a rational concern for efficiency and profitability in the enterprise, rather than being the result of spontaneous and altruistic gestures'.[140] Aston Villa had taken out an insurance policy against accidents to players even before joining the League, and West Bromwich Albion had its players insured with Lloyds from the early 1900s.[141] These initiatives were prompted by the introduction of government measures such as the Employers' Liability Act of 1880 and the Workmen's Compensation Acts of 1897 and 1900, which, under certain conditions, made employers liable to compensate workers injured in the course of their employment.[142] In 1902, the Football League took legal advice on the application of these laws to employers of football labour, but were told that no such liability was attached to member clubs.[143] However, the authorities were forced to seek counsel's opinion again following the introduction of a wider-ranging Workmen's Compensation Act in 1906, which extended its application from a limited number of 'dangerous trades' to 'virtually all employments'.[144] The original decision was reversed: professional footballers were deemed 'workmen' under the new act. League officials and club directors envisaged being inundated with claims for compensation, and it was this fear, rather than any emerging sense of moral responsibility, which convinced them to seek more comprehensive insurance cover.[145] An article printed in *Football Chat* in August 1907 went so far as to suggest that 'the risks attached to the insurance of a footballer may be as serious as in the case of any ordinary worker', and warned any club which failed to insure its players over the coming season that it risked a financially crippling legal dispute and possibly bankruptcy.[146]

The response to this was the creation in 1907 of the Football Mutual Insurance Federation (FMIF), a joint body composed of Football League, Southern League and Scottish League representatives, which attempted for the first time to provide a comprehensive, self-funding insurance scheme for clubs. In opting for mutual insurance, the League's actions were in keeping with those of employers' associations in a range of industries.[147] Premiums began at £1 per player, subsequently reduced to 10 shillings in 1910–11, and were supplemented by additional levies to cover any possible loss on the season. Membership was not compulsory, but by 1911, 32 Football League clubs had joined, along with 20 each from the Southern and Scottish Leagues. In the preceding year, the FMIF settled 22 claims, mostly concerning Football League clubs and players.[148] Those clubs that chose not to join the FMIF generally took out private insurance policies. Sheffield United, one of the eight League members going it alone, insured its entire playing staff from 1908 with the Essex and Suffolk Accident Indemnity Society, and despite higher premiums of up to £3 per player, preferred to make separate arrangements outside the aegis of the FMIF.[149]

A further development came in 1912, and concerned the position of League footballers under the National Insurance Act of 1911, the cornerstone of the Asquith government's social legislation.[150] Following an inquiry by the League Management Committee – and based on the Walker and Roberts v. Crystal Palace FC case of 1909, which had reinforced the status of the footballer as a 'workman' within the meaning of the Workmen's Compensation Act – the National Health Insurance Commissioners ruled that 'a professional *is* employed by way of manual labour', and thus had to be insured under the Act 'whatever his remuneration'.[151] In effect, the ruling extended a club's involvement with the welfare of its employees beyond the football ground. Firstly, claims under the National Insurance Act were concerned with sickness and injury outside the course of one's employment, and hence covered cases to which the Workmen's Compensation Acts did not apply. Secondly, football clubs, like other employers, were now responsible for making small weekly contributions (initially 3 pennies per player) along with the employee and the government, as well as arranging for players to join approved societies and stamping their insurance cards.[152] Initially, the League and most member clubs had opposed the scheme, despite the fact that it cost them little time or money. According to *Athletic News*, 'League clubs do not take kindly to insurance'; players, it was argued, were already employed throughout the year and given free medical attendance. There was also a feeling that the act threatened the autonomy of clubs in looking after their own players, along with broader reservations, shared by many employers, 'about the potential costs of a state system for social insurance'.[153] Even after the Commissioners' verdict was given, Sheffield United recommended that the Management Committee test the opinion of the Court, but was overruled by the executive body.[154] In 1920, League players 'who are under a contract with their clubs and are not in civil employment' were also included in the government's unemployment insurance scheme, which was funded, like health insurance, by mixed contributions from the worker, employer and state.[155]

This legal clarification of the footballer as a manual worker, together with the unsatisfactory operation of the FMIF, persuaded the League in late 1912 to set up a new Football League Mutual Insurance Federation (FLMIF) 'with the object of insuring the clubs in membership with the Football League against all claims under the Workmen's Compensation Acts'.[156] Yet although the restriction to League clubs was intended to lessen the financial burden, the FLMIF was actually to be troubled throughout this period with financial and organisational difficulties that were never adequately resolved. Its major dilemma was to keep premium rates affordable for all clubs, while ensuring that sufficient funds remained to cover all claims in this notoriously unpredictable profession. Over the next decade, the FLMIF struggled to pay its way, with claims often outstripping premiums and extra levies on members required to make up the deficit. By the end of 1920–21 a £1,800 shortfall was reported, and the executive made a renewed appeal to persuade all outside clubs to join the Federation.[157] Finances deteriorated still further, however, and so in 1924 the Management Committee constructed a new scheme to be funded by percentages of gate revenue rather than the previous system of individual premiums for each player. Clubs were now effectively compelled to join. First and Second Division members were to contribute 1 per cent, and Third Division South and North clubs 1.5 and 2 per cent respectively, of the net gate from each League match (extended in 1925 to include cup ties). It was envisaged that this would raise between £10,000–11,000 per annum, of which just over half was to be set aside to cover the insurance of every professional player contracted to the clubs, and the remainder used for the general running of the League.[158]

The 1924 scheme also ironed out some of the anomalies that had previously existed in both individual club and Football League insurance schemes. Henceforth, players and trainers were covered 'from the commencement of training to the end of the season', including all recognised first- and second-team fixtures, practice matches and training sessions.[159] Clubs could no longer claim that a player injured during non-competitive football was not in fact working, as Manchester City had in 1902 following the death of one of its employees from an injury sustained in a pre-season trial match.[160] The risk of travelling to and from matches was also covered by the FLMIF. However, players on continental club tours were not included and, in fact, it was not until 1930 that the FA established a formal system for insuring all players chosen for international and representative matches, with the Scottish, Irish and Welsh FAs also agreeing to insure Football League players a year later. The FA's scheme was precipitated by the serious injury sustained by Sheffield Wednesday's Billy Marsden in an international fixture against Germany. Following a claim by Wednesday, the FA paid the club £2,000 to cover the loss of the player and a further £700 'for the benefit of Marsden and his family'. All players were then systematically insured for a minimum of £2,000, a sum that was doubled in 1934.[161] Nevertheless, some clubs evidently considered this cover inadequate, choosing to take out separate ad hoc policies for their international players. In 1932, for example, Sheffield United arranged accident and sickness insurance amounting to £5,000 each for Jack Pickering in an inter-league match, and Robert Barclay and Jimmy Dunne in international games.[162] The risk of accidents to employees away from the football field also convinced many clubs to take out extra insurance protection. West Ham arranged a policy in 1930 with the Motor Insurance Company covering all players and officials 'whilst on club business', but when the company denied liability for an accident to first-team goalkeeper George Watson three years later, the club took out a more comprehensive policy covering all activities except aviation, motorcycling and football playing.[163]

In theory, then, an injured or sick player in the 1920s was not forced to rely on his employer's benevolence alone. As well as state health benefits, he was entitled to weekly compensation until he regained fitness or was forced to retire. Yet in practice, players could often face a long and arduous struggle with the FLMIF before receiving compensation payments. As the work of Bartrip and Burman has demonstrated, the operation of workmen's compensation legislation was seriously hampered by the difficulties of pressing a claim and by delays in settlement, and even then the worker and his dependants were rarely adequately compensated.[164] The League Management Committee often portrayed itself as sympathetic to players, even exhorting them 'to trust the Committee as friends',[165] but there is no doubt that its chief concern was to limit the financial liability of its clubs to a minimum. The vast majority of claims were conducted on the player's behalf by the Union, and more specifically by its solicitor from 1909, Thomas Hinchcliffe. Normally an injured player would receive full wages up until the end of his contract and then compensation of 30 shillings per week (£1 before the First World War, and briefly 35 shillings just after), but by the early 1920s Hinchcliffe and Sutcliffe, who acted as FLMIF solicitor, had established a standard procedure for settling claims by lump sum payments. In certain cases, the FLMIF chose to contest the player's claim by denying liability for the injury, or reducing, and even stopping, compensation payments when it considered the player had recovered. In 1922 it advised every club 'to take an interest in its injured players and to see that there is no malingering' but, despite such concerns, liability was eventually admitted in the majority of cases, even if this sometimes had to wait until the eve of county court decisions.[166]

The procedure for settling claims set up an adversarial relationship between the FLMIF and the club on one side, and the Union and the injured player on the other. During one set of negotiations, the Union was informed by the FLMIF that 'on no account will compensation be paid unless and until they are compelled to do so after a fight', and employer liability was certainly challenged in cases where it was believed – often with justification – that players had given dishonest information or made fictitious claims.[167] The problems of re-registering players who had already received compensation exacerbated these conflicts. In 1926, the Management Committee notified clubs that it would neither register nor insure players who had received lump sum settlements unless they could prove complete recovery from their injuries, and later ruled that those receiving over £100 compensation could not be registered for at least a year after the settlement date.[168] Following the application of this rule to a player seeking to resume his career with a month's trial at Darlington, the Union strongly attacked the League's treatment of injured players. It complained that the player, Cook, had got compensation of just £125, which the FLMIF said should cover two years, but that his injury prevented him returning to his former occupation of mining. It was considered 'disgraceful that any man should be debarred from earning his livelihood' in both occupations. Jimmy Fay complained bitterly that with the Federation's final payment, 'the door is locked, bolted and barred to the player should he recover and be fit to take his place in the game once more'.[169] On the other hand, the Union was forced in 1934 to condemn the action of another member who had represented himself as fit to play League football less than two months after being awarded £400 compensation by the FLMIF.[170] Tensions between the Union and the FLMIF over claims procedures, however, probably peaked in 1927 over a case where a member settled his claim directly with the League after initiating proceedings through the Union. Hinchcliffe considered this a calculated move to marginalise the influence of the Union:

> It is quite evident that the Football League are going to go behind our backs wherever they can, and not only deprive the Union of proving to players (non-members) of the brilliant

The Football League representative team photographed before their match against the Irish Football League at Belfast in October 1932. The team line-up is (players only): Back row – Dickie Rhodes (Wolverhampton Wanderers), Lew Stoker (Birmingham), Tommy Cooper (Derby County), Frank Moss (Arsenal), Sam Weaver (Newcastle United), Peter O'Dowd (Chelsea), Charlie Keetley (Leeds United). Front row – Fred Worrall (Portsmouth), Ernie Hine (Huddersfield Town), Ernie Blenkinsop (Sheffield Wednesday), George Brown (Aston Villa), Jack Pickering (Sheffield United), Stan Wood (West Bromwich Albion). The Football League won the match 5–2.

The Football League Management Committee, 1910–12. Left to right: John Cameron, Harry Keys (Vice-President), Dr James Baxter, Charles Sutcliffe, Tom Charnley (Secretary), John McKenna (President), John Lewis (Vice-President), William McGregor (Founder), Arthur Dickinson, Tom Harris, John Bentley.

William McGregor, the founder and 'father' of the Football League. © *Popperfoto*

John McKenna, President of the League from 1910 until his death in 1936. © *Empics*

Tom Charnley, the League's Secretary from 1902 until 1933, when his son-in-law Fred Howarth took over.

John Lewis, Vice-President of the League from 1901 until his death in 1925. Lewis was known as the 'Prince of Referees' and was probably the best-known match official of his day. © Popperfoto

Harry Lockett, Secretary of the League in its formative years, working at the first offices of the organisation. Lockett was forced to resign in 1902 after admitting to embezzling League funds to bankroll the printing business he was also running.

John (or J. J.) Bentley, President of the Football League between 1894 and 1910. Bentley was a full-time sporting journalist and edited the League mouthpiece Athletic News *up until 1900 and* Football Chat *during the 1900s. While still President of the League, he was also employed to run the football affairs of Manchester United.*

Charles Sutcliffe, a lawyer from Lancashire who became the most influential figure in the administration of English football before the Second World War.

The Management Committee at work in 1926–27. Around the table from left to right: Will Cuff, John Oliver, Fred Rinder, Arthur Dickinson, Harry Keys (Vice-President), John McKenna (President), Tom Charnley (Secretary), Charles Sutcliffe (Vice-President), William Hall and Tom Barcroft.

The Chesterfield players admire the new numbers to be worn by all Football League sides from the beginning of the forthcoming (1939/40) season. Harry Shepherd/Hulton Archive © Getty Images

The West Ham United team line up for the camera in April 1923, the month they were to compete in the first FA Cup final at Wembley. From left to right: L. Richards, G. Ruffell, W. Moore, G. Tresadern, W. Brown, Vic Watson, G. Young, W. Henderson, G. Kay, S. Bishop, A. E. Hufton and Charlie Poynter (trainer). Gill/Hulton Archive © Getty Images

Circuit training at Fulham's Craven Cottage ground in November 1935. The practice of lapping the ground to harden muscles was well-established at many League clubs although rarely popular with the players. On the bicycle is the footballer/cricketer John Arnold, who had been advised to take up cycling in order to heal a knee injury. H. Allen/Hulton Archive © Getty Images

Danish amateur international Nils Middleboe, one of the first foreign players in English football, before a match for his new club Chelsea at Stamford Bridge in November 1912. Hulton Archive © Getty Images

Scottish international centre-forward Hughie Gallacher scoring for Chelsea against Liverpool in February 1932. Gallacher was one of a number of high-profile players approached by French clubs to join their newly professional league that April. Gallacher declined but 43 British players, including team-mates Andy Wilson and Alex Cheyne, made the move. Central Press/Hulton Archive © Getty Images

Middlesbrough goalkeeper Hiller punches the ball away from Alex James, one of the stars of the Arsenal side, during a League match in April 1935. Arsenal won the game 8–0 and went on to take the First Division Championship for the third consecutive season. J. A. Hampton/Hulton Archive © Getty Images

> services rendered by the Union, but also depriving me of your valuable work and making it more costly for the Union from a legal point of view.[171]

It would be wrong to assume, however, that incapacitated players were always paid the minimum possible compensation by clubs and discarded when they ceased to be of immediate use to the team. At a purely financial level, it may often have been less expensive to treat and compensate an injured player than to buy a replacement. This perhaps explains Coventry City's 'good treatment' of Alf Widdowson, who received his full weekly wage in addition to weekly compensation during his injury lay-off and, after an operation, was signed on full wages despite not yet being fully fit.[172] Players forced to retire through injury were similarly sometimes treated generously by football employers. Benefit matches and/or payments were generally granted by the better-off clubs. Blackwell received £500 from Sheffield United, even though the club was not legally liable, after abdominal trouble had 'rendered him incompetent to fulfil the terms of his contract'; Fulham similarly granted John Dudley a benefit match, which raised £280 in addition to the FLMIF's ex gratia payment of £150, while strenuously denying liability for the player's heart trouble.[173] The death of an employee provided the best opportunity for League and club to publicly assert their philanthropic tendencies. A good illustration of this was the collective response engendered by the death of the Chelsea player Tommy Meehan in August 1924. The League immediately donated £50 from its own benevolent fund, established a benefit fund for the player's dependants and organised a Football League team to play Chelsea in a benefit match in aid of the fund. By December the Meehan fund had raised over £1,800, including almost £600 subscribed separately by League members.[174] Meehan's relatives undoubtedly benefited from his having been a prominent representative player, appearing three times for the Football League XI between 1922 and 1924, because in most cases such public fund-raising was restricted to deceased League or club officials or the victims of colliery disasters, rather than players. Indeed, by contrast, Henry Cunningham's elderly parents received just the minimum £300 from the FLMIF in 1929 when their son died from a football-related injury sustained in training, while the widow of another Cunningham, Peter of Crewe, was afforded small grants of only £10 each from the FA and the League to cover wages owed to her late husband after his entry into a sanatorium.[175] In the majority of cases, then, even a seriously ill player could expect no more than a small discretionary grant from his club, and perhaps from the benevolent fund of the FA, League or Union. In the event of death the Union also provided a £100 burial grant for members' families, but even this was rudimentary compared with the financial protection offered by an organisation like the actor's Royal General Theatrical Fund or the National Hunt Accident Fund.[176]

Notwithstanding the FLMIF's determination to limit compensation payments wherever possible, the Union achieved a gradual increase in sums received by injured players during the inter-war period. As Table 4.1 indicates, seasonal figures were prone to fluctuation, but the general trend was upwards, with over seven times more compensation being paid to players overall in the late 1930s than during the early 1920s. It appears that this was mainly due to increases in the number rather than the size of settlement claims, though the precise data on this question are unavailable. In 1926, lump-sum settlements ranged from £50 to £300 and stayed fairly consistent throughout the late 1920s and 1930s, even during the 1928–29 season, which witnessed a substantial leap in total compensation. Yet by 1932, some players on higher earnings were able to secure up to £600, and there were signs that by this point, the FLMIF was actively searching for ways to reduce compensation payments.[177] The first such attempt was Sutcliffe's controversial contract clause, which was considered, but eventually rejected, by the League clubs in 1934. The proposed clause threatened the established practice of players receiving full wages until their contract expired: henceforth, the full salary was to be paid only for the first fortnight or month after the injury or sickness, followed by one half of the salary for the same period. After a maximum of two months, the club was to be permitted to stop the players' wage and put him on compensation. In Sutcliffe's view, the change was in keeping with broader employer practice: 'In every phase of work … as soon as a workman is injured he is at once put on compensation, but in football, not so'.[178] However, critics responded angrily to the idea that the proposal was intended to 'stop the malingerer' and bring an end to the 'sham injury'. The Union, in particular, condemned the proposal and demanded its immediate withdrawal, resolving

> that the Football League Management Committee, for reasons best known to themselves, seem to be intent upon making the lives of players as difficult as possible; that the attempts to impose upon players such conditions are tantamount to slavery; that, should players have the misfortune to be stricken with illness or crippled physically, they also wish to cripple them financially.[179]

Table 4.1: Payments made by FLMIF to Union members for compensation under the Workmen's Compensation Act, 1920/21–1938/39

Season	*Total compensation* (£)*	*Season*	*Total compensation* (£)*
1920–21	760	1930–31	5,101
1921–22	1,250	1931–32	5,134
1922–23	895	1932–33	4,087
1923–24	1,132	1933–34	6,035
1924–25	900	1934–35	7,583
1925–26	2,876	1935–36	6,508
1926–27	1,015	1936–37	5,637
1927–28	1,360	1937–38	9,476
1928–29	5,187	1938–39	7,154
1929–30	4,365		

* Lump sum payments and weekly compensation.
Source: Annual Solicitor's Reports of the AFPTU.

Underpinning Sutcliffe's scheme was the assumption that injuries received during play were primarily the responsibility of the players themselves. In 1932, the League Vice-President had announced his wish to 'diminish accidents by reducing if not eliminating rough or dangerous play'. He went on:

> Injuries to players are in many cases due to careless recklessness and, therefore, avoidable. If players would appreciate that by lack of reasonable care, or worse still, by their venturing into a reckless spirit, they will do financial harm to opponents, I think that respect and care would be far more apparent in their play.[180]

For the majority of players and Union representatives, however, increased injuries were the direct result of the quickening pace of the game, or what might be considered the intensification of football work. Many commentators identified the 1925 change in the offside rule as crucial to this (see Chapter 7). According to Jimmy Fay, players were henceforth trained to be faster on the pitch, the result being that 'the strain becomes greater and greater' and 'leads to players becoming more susceptible to knocks, injuries, breakdowns'.[181] In this view, an injury to a football employee was proof not that he had been careless in his duties, but quite the opposite: that he was 'playing his part, and doing his best for the club'.[182] For this reason, critics of Sutcliffe's scheme argued that if compensation were denied, players would simply not give of their best: 'They would shirk tackles, and certainly no goalkeeper in his senses would dive at a forward's feet. Not when he saw his wages going "up the spout" along with his dive.' One player had no doubt that the scheme would change the way he approached his work:

> If I thought I was going to lose money by taking risks, would I chance it? I'd take bloomin' care that, whatever happened to the club, I was safe. As it is, I take these risks, knowing that my club will have to stand by me if I get smashed up. If that faith went my 'courage' would go with it.[183]

A few months before Sutcliffe presented his scheme, the basic principles underlying both private and state insurance cover had been undermined by Justice Roach's verdict that professional footballers were no longer considered to be employed by way of manual labour.[184] The whole question had been re-opened by the Ministry of Health, and its direct relevance was to the health insurance of players by the state, although it also had profound implications for the rights of players under the Workmen's Compensation Acts. Those League players who received over £250 per year in wages and bonuses – undoubtedly a considerable majority – were now denied compulsory insurance and health, pension and unemployment benefits, although the Ministry did make concessions to allow them to continue contributing to the scheme voluntarily.[185] More significantly, any professional footballer whose annual remuneration exceeded £350 had no future claim against his club under the Workmen's Compensation Acts. Initially, the FLMIF agreed to continue 'to treat all players alike' regardless of income, but from 1935 onwards it began to refuse compensation to a number of players forced to retire through injury. Sutcliffe informed the Union of the FLMIF's change of policy by stating that 'owing to the many calls during recent years it would not be possible in future to deal with any injured players who were outside the Workmen's Compensation Acts'.[186] Considerable opposition from the Union and club directorates, however, led the FLMIF to refer the question directly to the clubs, who agreed by a large majority to treat players receiving £350-plus salaries as if they came under the provisions of the Acts and make ex gratia payments accordingly.[187] Though this represented a partial victory for the better-paid players, the FLMIF continued to attempt to limit its liabilities by reducing weekly compensation payments when injuries had improved sufficiently to allow those players unable to play football again to engage in some form of light work. Again, the Union responded angrily by pointing out that 'whilst the Federation are entitled to do this legally, at the same time it is unfair and unjust to take advantage of the Workmen's Compensation Act as though the player were an industrial worker'.[188] Indeed, the Union's general dissatisfaction with the levels of compensation led to an unsuccessful proposal in March 1939 that weekly compensation be increased from 35 shillings to £3 per week and lump-sum settlements fixed, with a maximum pay-out of £1,000.[189]

Despite the FLMIF's attempts to reduce costs and the accusation that players were inadequately compensated for their loss of employment, the League's insurance scheme continued to suffer financial problems in the years preceding the Second World War. In March 1937, the FA Finance and General Purposes Committee actually paid off the FLMIF's deficit of £5,446, which had built up over the previous ten years, and agreed to contribute £660 annually for the following four years to cover its average deficit.[190] The compensation of injured players was still the major financial burden for the Football League in 1939 that it had been when the FLMIF was established in 1912, and remained throughout a significant source of conflict between the axes of player–Union and club–League.

Another important aspect of welfare provision involved the treatment of players after their footballing careers had ended. Typically, League clubs, in common with most private companies, were discriminatory in arranging for the future wellbeing of retired employees. Ex-players who were destitute or down on their luck were sometimes able to secure ad hoc grants from the benevolent funds of the Union or governing bodies. A former Burnley player called Wallace, for instance, who 'found himself in distress' after being forced to stop playing through illness and failing to find other work, received grants totalling £25 from the Union in addition to £50 grants from both the League and the FA. The Aston Villa directors particularly prided themselves on their record of assisting old players 'in poor circumstances'.[191] When Stephen Bloomer, the famous ex-Derby County and England forward, became seriously ill with asthma and bronchitis 23 years after his retirement, a public fund was established by the Derby manager George Jobey and other local figures, raising £558 to send him on a cruise to Australia.[192]

Notwithstanding occasional instances of this kind, however, the League made no attempt to develop formally constituted schemes to provide financially for players on their retirements, or facilitate their movement towards other careers, until the very end of the 1930s. Professional footballers, as insured workers, were included in the provisions of the 1925 Old Age and Widows and Orphans Contributory Pensions Act, but as the pension was to start at the age of 65 it was clearly of little immediate benefit to the player who retired in his twenties or thirties.[193]

Occupational pensions for footballers, however, were not considered until 1934, when Watson Hartley, a Liverpool solicitor, approached the League executive with a series of proposals, including a pension fund, which would be financed by his scheme to copyright the Football League fixture list. According to Hartley, the fund would enable all players 'with five or more years of service to be entitled to a pension, graded according to the years of service, payable on retiring from the game, and terminable by the League in the event of the player re-entering the game'. Yet the executive 'refused point-blank to consider the scheme', partly because the funding involved connections with the pools industry but also, as both Hartley and Fay recognised, because of its obstinate opposition to any suggestions emanating from outside Preston.[194] This attitude had evidently changed by 1939, when a London insurance firm contacted the League and the Players' Union with plans for an endowment insurance policy for players. Although details of the proposed scheme were sketchy, it appears that the League, the Union, clubs and players were all expected to contribute to an endowment policy that was to mature when the player reached 32. Both the League and the Union executives agreed to proceed with the scheme before the onset of hostilities left it in abeyance.[195]

There were opportunities to remain within League football at some level after finishing playing, mainly as a trainer, coach or scout, and increasingly by the 1920s as a manager, or what was contemporaneously called a 'players' manager'. Many trainers were former professionals, and were often promoted directly from the playing to the training staff. Yet it must be understood that in terms of both income and status, a training job was not markedly dissimilar from a playing engagement and was equally insecure. For example, the Irish international Billy Gillespie was engaged as a coach by Sheffield United in 1930 while still playing first-team football. He then took up the coaching position full time, but within two seasons was informed that the club 'had no further use for his services owing to the appointment of a new manager'.[196] There was a discernable trend from the 1920s onwards for clubs to appoint former players as professional managers in place of the directors or secretaries who had previously been responsible for team affairs. Though this transformation was gradual and uneven, by 1923 Sutcliffe was able to justify the introduction of players' managers at Preston North End, Stoke and Hull City 'not on the principle of set a thief to catch a thief, but because they have, or seem to have, the necessary qualities to make good'.[197]

Like management posts, which were only open to the few, fully-fledged coaching positions – as opposed to training jobs, which involved simply maintaining the physical fitness of players – were extremely scarce at Football League clubs even by the end of this period. As Stephen Wagg has shown, many League clubs, administrators and even players remained ideologically opposed to the concept of coaching football skills, and the continent therefore offered far more, and better, opportunities for former League players who wished to coach.[198] It is impossible to calculate exactly how many took this route but, as we shall see in Chapter 6, by the Second World War ex-League players were to be found coaching throughout most of Europe and beyond. As one former goalkeeper who had been coaching in France since 1911 wrote in a letter to James Catton in 1920, 'it would not be possible to obtain a living wage in England for my services'.[199] The first step towards the professional training and regulation of coaches in England was eventually taken by the FA, which from 1934 began to organise annual coaching courses attended by League trainers, managers and players, though amateurs also took part. Those who passed received FA coaching certificates, which were intended to help them secure positions in schools, colleges or even within the professional game: in fact, the FA's list of regional coaches in 1935–36 included a number of former elite players such as Tommy Sampy in the Sheffield and Hallamshire area and Jesse Pennington in Worcestershire, whose job it was to coordinate and supervise schoolboy coaching in their regions.[200] Wagg has suggested that this initiative encountered considerable resistance at League and club level, but there is little evidence to support this claim. In a newspaper article written in 1938, Tom Mitchell sang the praises of the FA course and revealed that he had introduced many of its methods to the York City players, as well as the local schoolboys he coached.[201] The directors of Sheffield United and Oldham Athletic must also have been impressed, as they sent their entire training staffs on the coaching course. Huddersfield Town, among others, also encouraged its players to attend. Even so, no comparable initiatives came from Preston, despite the fact that Hartley's 1934 scheme had included a proposal to establish several regional centres for the coaching of young footballers under the supervision of 'well-known players of other years'.[202]

Training in areas outside football was also slow to develop, with League and club officials tending to leave such matters to the individuals concerned. Occasionally, clubs would assist players in acquiring businesses or other interests, such as when Sheffield United arranged for its Captain, George Utley, to become a tenant of a local sports shop with a five-year contract to supply equipment to the club; but generally, players were given no help in providing for their lives after football.[203] In 1936, the FA contacted the Board of Education and London County Council in order to arrange educational classes for professional footballers in the capital. While the reaction of clubs was poor, with only Charlton Athletic and Clapton Orient agreeing to cooperate, it did represent a turning point as regards management's awareness of its responsibility for something more than the football education and training of employees. Nine Clapton players were able to attend courses in commerce, general education and woodwork, while Charlton organised for courses in elementary accounts and business methods to be conducted in its ground, and enrolled other players interested in learning technical subjects at the local Woolwich Polytechnic.[204] It was not until 1938, however, that the League accepted some responsibility for the educational and vocational training of players, with the launch of its Jubilee Trust Fund. The object was to raise £100,000 for the purpose of financially assisting players, ex-players and club officials in times of need, and also developing arrangements for the re-training of former professionals in new trades and professions. To this end, each First Division club was compelled to contribute £1,000, with those in the Second and Third Divisions giving £500 and £250 respectively, while a series of pre-season derby matches in August 1938 raised a further £27,443, although even with extra donations and another series of Jubilee derbies the following year, the fund was still some way short of the £100,000 mark.[205] Moreover, the League's delay in deciding how the money was to be distributed, and its reluctance to include the Players' Union on the fund committee, led to accusations by early 1939 that the fund had proved 'a flop'.[206] Indeed, arrangements for the vocational element of the fund's activities were clearly only at the planning stage by September 1939. Club directorates had been asked in January to inquire into the suitability of local facilities for vocational training, and the Management Committee had embarked on talks with the Players' Union as well as with teaching and educational authorities, including the Chief Inspector of the Board of Education. Free classes in 'commerce, industry or the professions' were arranged if 12–15 players signed up in a particular area, but in the event no professional was able to benefit from the fund until League football proper resumed after the war.[207]

* * *

In many respects, the change in the status of the professional player in the Football League between the turn of the century and the Second World War was considerable. It is possible to argue that elite players were beginning to acquire 'professional status', defined by Harold Perkin as 'a career with security of tenure, rising scales of pay, and the customary white-collar fringe benefits'.[208] Clubs were less likely to dismiss players at short notice as often occurred in manual work. Almost all players had annual contracts and, if incapacitated through injury or sickness, were paid until at least the end of their contract and sometimes longer. Moreover, the majority of players in the top two divisions (and many below) enjoyed what effectively amounted to 15 weeks of paid holiday during the close season and, though a scheme for occupational pensions was still being planned, they were given other customary rewards related to loyalty, such as benefit payments. There were, additionally, indications that the League professional of the 1920s and 1930s had acquired a respectability that his predecessors lacked. He seems to have stayed more sober, to have been more disciplined and even occasionally to have taken on some of the habits of the inter-war middle class, like playing golf and driving motor cars.[209]

Yet for all this, League players were still treated by management as subordinate employees who had little control over their own career structures. With the possible exception of the few star players whose outstanding talent gave them a degree of freedom in the labour market, Pickford's description of the professional footballer from 1906 could be equally applied to 1939: once registered, he remained 'tied up, "cribbed, cabined and confined"' and was ultimately forced 'to obey club instructions and do what he is told'.[210] While English football's controllers were some way short of establishing the 'all-encompassing system of labor serfdom' characteristic of US baseball at the time, clubs still endeavoured to 'rule' players, and remain masters over their men in every possible area of their employment.[211] Indeed, we have seen that most of the benevolent and welfare arrangements that benefited players by the late 1930s had not been gained by players through their Union, but were the product of the enlightened self-interest of their employers. In the Football League, as in other industries, the extension of welfare schemes to cover accidents, pensions, illnesses or deaths was not the work of idealistic paternalists, but of hard-headed employers intent on maximising the efficiency and ensuring the dependence of their workforces at the lowest possible cost.[212]

In spite of the institutionalisation of welfare arrangements and the faltering growth of unionism, Football League players in the 1930s were subject to many of the same forms of discipline and techniques of control established in the late nineteenth century. Most clubs continued to treat their employees like troublesome children who needed at different times to be punished, praised or protected. In and out of work, players were subject to harsh discipline and rigid supervision. While the professional footballer was probably more independent than the average industrial worker, what he did on the football field and in his free time was nevertheless closely monitored and constrained by management. In time, this older strand of paternalism was supplemented by more bureaucratic systems of control. By the inter-war period at least, the structure of the labour market, payments systems and even disciplinary rules were organised centrally by the League and the FA. Managerial strategies at individual clubs were increasingly standardised, and professional footballers found that employment conditions were more or less the same wherever they worked.

Collective action among footballers was limited. The Players' Union was never more than a marginal body before 1939, its effectiveness ultimately restricted by the football authorities' unwillingness to recognise it as a union rather than a trade association. It was not until the post-war years that the Union was able to take advantage of increased support from the government and the popular press, along with a more militant membership, to make significant gains. Yet it would be mistaken to conclude that labour relations within professional football were entirely quiescent, that players were merely the passive, obedient servants of management. The various strategies developed by individual clubs and the central authorities to control labour were never completely successful. Players did indeed employ a range of informal, often individual, forms of resistance to managerial control, although it tended to be established professionals such as Alex James and Stanley Matthews who had the self-confidence to do so. Labour relations in the Football League were thus far from straightforward. Dissent and unrest existed alongside the more common examples of obedience and deference. Historians in this field should take heed of the great body of work in labour history more generally, which recognises the complexity and diversity of workplace relationships, instead of relying on a one-dimensional account of football labour as akin to feudalism or slavery.

Notes

1 J. Melling, 'Employers, Industrial Welfare and the Struggle for Work-Place Control in British Industry, 1880–1920' in *Managerial Strategies and Industrial Relations: An Historical and Comparative Study*, ed. H. F. Gospel and C. R. Littler, London, Heinemann, 1983, p. 56.

2 H. F. Gospel, 'Managerial Structure and Strategies: An Introduction' in *Managerial Strategies and Industrial Relations: An Historical and Comparative Study*, ed. H. F. Gospel and C. R. Littler, London, Heinemann, 1983, pp. 1–24; R. Fitzgerald, *British Labour Management and Industrial Welfare, 1846-1939*, London, Croom Helm, 1988, pp. 4–12.

3 H. Braverman, *Labor and Monopoly Capitalism: The Degradation of Work in the Twentieth Century*, New York, Monthly Review, 1974.
4 See S. Tolliday and J. Zeitlin, 'Introduction: Employers and Industrial Relations Between Theory and History' in *The Power to Manage?: Employers and Industrial Relations in Comparative-Historical Perspective*, ed. S. Tolliday and J. Zeitlin, London, Routledge, 1991, pp. 8–9; Gospel, 'Managerial Structure', pp. 4–5. For criticisms of Braverman's thesis, see N. Kirk, *Labour and Society in Britain and the USA: Volume 2–Challenge and Accommodation, 1850–1939*, Aldershot, Scholar, 1994, pp. 46–49; J. Turner, 'Man and Braverman: British Industrial Relations', *History*, Vol. 70, 1985.
5 Russell, *Football*, p. 93.
6 Mason, *Association Football*, pp. 106–07.
7 Korr, *West Ham*, p. 171.
8 A. Warde, 'Industrial Discipline: Factory Regime and Politics in Lancaster' in *Skill and Consent: Contemporary Studies in the Labour Process*, ed. A. Sturdy, D. Knights and H. Willmott, London, Routledge, 1992, p. 103.
9 H. Newby, 'The Deferential Dialect', *Comparative Studies in Society and History*, Vol. 13, 1975, p. 118.
10 Joyce, *Work*.
11 Joyce, *Work*, p. xv.
12 P. Ackers, 'On Paternalism: Seven Observations on the Uses and Abuses of the Concept in Industrial Relations, Past and Present', *Historical Studies in Industrial Relations*, Vol. 5, 1998, p. 174; D. Drummond, *Crewe: Railway Town, Company and People, 1840–1914*, Aldershot, Scholar, 1995; Whipp, *Patterns*, pp. 139–43, 169–72.
13 On the limitations of paternalism as a strategy of social control in the Scottish context, see W. W. Knox, *Industrial Nation: Work, Culture and Society in Scotland, 1800–Present*, Edinburgh, Edinburgh University Press, 1999, pp. 106–10.
14 Joyce, *Work*, pp. 186, 331–42.
15 Drummond, *Crewe*, p. 208.
16 See Fitzgerald, *British Labour*, pp. 10–11; S. Jones, 'Cotton Employers and Industrial Welfare Between the Wars' in *Employers and Labour in the English Textile Industries, 1850–1939*, ed. J. A. Jowitt and A. J. McIvor, London, Routledge, 1988, pp. 64–83; D. Wray, 'Paternalism and its Discontents: A Case Study', *Work, Employment and Society*, Vol. 10, 1996, pp. 701–15.
17 B. Morris and J. Smyth, 'Paternalism as an Employer Strategy, 1800–1960' in *Employer Strategy and the Labour Market*, ed. J. Rubery and F. Wilkinson, Oxford, Oxford University Press, 1994.
18 SUFC, Football Committee Minutes, 14 December 1910; 31 October, 4 November 1928.
19 SUFC, Football Committee Minutes, 30 August 1905; 9 November 1910; 1 February, 9 May 1928; AVFC, Board Minutes, 9 November 1926.
20 SUFC, Football Committee Minutes, 17 September 1902; Durham Record Office (DRO), D/XD 97/3, Darlington FC (DFC), Board Minutes, 17 July 1939. Sunderland's success during the 1890s has been partly explained by the club's ability to find employment for their players. See Tischler, *Footballers*, pp. 95–96.
21 C. Buchan, *A Lifetime in Football*, London, Phoenix, 1955, p. 16; Harding, *Alex James*, pp. 100–01.
22 AVFC, 47/82, letter from George Ramsay to Mr Ansell, 16 August 1907; *Huddersfield Weekly Examiner*, 31 August 1912.
23 *Thomson's Weekly News*, 7 September 1912.

24 D. Roberts, *Paternalism in Early Victorian England*, London, Croom Helm, 1979, pp. 4–5; Russell, 'Local Elites', pp. 154–55; W. Licht, 'Fringe Benefits: A Review Essay of the American Workplace', *International Labor and Working-Class History*, No. 53, 1998, pp. 164–78.
25 See OAFC, Board Minutes, 7 August, 4 September 1906; Professional Footballers' Association (PFA), File 35, Millwall FC Rules to Players, 1933.
26 SUFC, Football Committee Minutes, 6 January, 11, 18 February 1903; AVFC, Board Minutes, 3 April 1928.
27 Report of Football League AGM in *Athletic News*, 4 June 1923
28 WHUFC, Board Minutes, 4 October 1921; 18 January, 18 April 1922.
29 Football League Minutes, Management Committee, 1 September 1913.
30 WHUFC, Board Minutes, 6 November 1922.
31 Football League Minutes, Management Committee, 2 February 1914.
32 AVFC, Board Minutes, 7, 10 September, 1 October, 17 December 1912; Football League Minutes, Management Committee, 26 May, 3 November 1913.
33 Football League Minutes, Management Committee, 26 July 1920.
34 *Athletic News*, 4 June 1906. On this incident and Meredith's career more generally, see Harding, *Football Wizard*, especially pp. 93–115.
35 FA Emergency Committee Minutes, 21 March–22 April 1922.
36 AVFC, Board Minutes, 8 January 1929; 14 January 1930.
37 PFA, File 35, application to National Health Board Commissioners in the case of Leonard Graham, 21 November 1933.
38 *Topical Times*, 4 August 1934. Herbert Chapman admitted that prior to the introduction of his Friday team meetings at Arsenal, players would 'just nod, say "yes", then not follow his orders'. T. Say, 'Herbert Chapman: Football Revolutionary?', *The Sports Historian*, Vol. 16, 1996, p. 91.
39 Fishwick, *English Football*, p. 35.
40 Buchan, *Lifetime*, pp. 29–30; Sharpe, *40 Years*.
41 PFA, File 2, Small Heath FC Players' Agreement, 1896–97.
42 WHUFC, Board Minutes, 11 February 1924; PFA, File 35, Millwall FC Players' Weekly Diary, 1933. This arrangement seems to have been the norm. Raich Carter, a captain with Sunderland from the start of the 1936–37 season, discussed the role in his post-war autobiography: 'Generally a manager gives brief instructions before the game, but the captain must be allowed to think for himself and alter them according to the run of the play.' Carter, *Footballer's Progress*, p. 114. Similarly, Stan Cullis recounted that as a young 18-year-old Captain of Wolverhampton Wanderers reserves, he had countermanded the instructions of a travelling director with the words: 'I am captain of this team … and I am the one who gives the orders on the field'. S. Cullis, *All For the Wolves*, London, Sportsman's Book Club, 1961, p. 14.
43 AVFC, Board Minutes, 3 January 1911.
44 WHUFC, Board Minutes, 2, 9 March 1925.
45 DRO, D/XD 97/3, DFC, Board Minutes, 6 October, 10 November, 1 December 1937.
46 AVFC, Board Minutes, 7 March, 21 December 1911.
47 *Athletic News*, 15 March 1909.
48 Fishwick, *English Football*, pp. 84–85; AFPTU Minutes, 8 February 1937.
49 AFC, Catton Folders, C–D, Report on Suspension of William Cook, 19 April 1915, p. 291.

50 Mason, *Association Football*, p. 107; SUFC, Football Committee Minutes, 10 September 1902; 6 December 1904. From Tottenham Hotspur's Southern League days, the club room at White Hart Lane served a similar purpose, and was allegedly used as a model by other clubs. J. Cameron, 'The Tottenham Hotspur: Its Story and Progress' in *Book of Football*, ed. anon, London, Amalgamated Press, 1906, p. 82.
51 PFA, File 35, Millwall FC Rules to Players, 1933.
52 Cited in R. Holt and T. Mason, *Sport in Britain, 1945–2000*, Oxford, Blackwell, 2000, p. 69.
53 *Topical Times*, 7 January 1939.
54 Whipp, *Patterns*, pp. 140–41; J. Griffiths, '"Give My Regards to Uncle Billy…": The Rites and Rituals of Company Life at Lever Brothers, c. 1900–c. 1990', *Business History*, Vol. 37, 1995, pp. 33–35.
55 SUFC, Football Committee Minutes, 5, 18 August 1937.
56 WHUFC, Board Minutes, 31 July, 14 August 1934; 13 August 1935.
57 WHUFC, Board Minutes, 3 December 1934.
58 See 'A Footballer's Weekly Diary', *Topical Times*, January 1938–May 1939, *passim*.
59 WHUFC, Board Minutes, 28 March 1922; SUFC, Football Committee, 19 August 1908.
60 AVFC, Board Minutes, 4 January 1900; 31 October 1911.
61 On the provision of company housing more generally, see J. Melling, 'Employers, Industrial Housing and the Evolution of Company Welfare Policies in Britain's Heavy Industry: West Scotland 1870–1920', *International Review of Social History*, Vol. 26, 1982.
62 AVFC, 52/82, letter from George Ramsay to G. N. Robinson, 22 July 1919; WLHC, Walsall FC, 522/1/66, letter from W. Askew to Mr Lowes, 8 June 1937; AVFC, Board Minutes, 2 May, 27 June, 18 July 1922; G. Allison, *Allison Calling*, London, Staples, 1948, p. 76.
63 *Topical Times*, 27 October 1934; 16 April 1938.
64 HTFC, Board Minutes, 12 April 1939.
65 SUFC, Football Committee Minutes, 10 February 1904.
66 AVFC, Board Minutes, 28 December 1899; 8 March 1900.
67 AVFC, Board Minutes, 11 January 1900; 8 November 1910; 5 September 1911.
68 See AVFC, Board Minutes, 2, 9 November 1920; 23 September, 21 October 1930.
69 *Athletic News*, 10 May 1909.
70 See AVFC, Board Minutes, 16 February 1921; SUFC, Football Committee Minutes, 8 December 1926; 4 January 1927; PFA, File 35, Millwall FC Rules to Players, 1933.
71 FA Council Minutes, 20 December 1920; FA Emergency Committee Minutes, 21 June–19 August 1929; FA Finance and General Purposes Committee Minutes, 27 June 1936; AFPTU Minutes, 24 August 1936 (AGM). Also see SUFC, Football Committee Minutes, 20 March 1929.
72 *The People*, 25 January; 15 February 1931.
73 WHUFC, Board Minutes, 15 August 1933; HTFC, Board Minutes, 12 April 1939; *Topical Times*, 7 January 1939.
74 The history of the Players' Union is well covered in Harding, *For the Good of the Game*. More academic treatments are to be found in Dabscheck, 'Defensive Manchester'; Mason, *Association Football*, pp. 110–17; Vamplew, *Pay Up*, Chapter 15; Fishwick, *English Football*, pp. 86–90. However, none of these explicitly examine the nature of the Union's changing relationship with the governing bodies, or its broader role in structuring labour relations in the Football League.

75 Billy Meredith, one of the Union's founders, had originally preferred the title Players' Union and Benefit Society. Harding, *For the Good of the Game*, p. 46. In 1919, the name was altered to the Association Football Players' and Trainers' Union, and in 1958 it became the Professional Footballers' Association. It was best known, however, by its shortened title (which will be used here), 'the Players' Union'.

76 P. S. Bagwell, *Industrial Relations*, London, Irish University Press, 1974, p. 31; N. Whiteside, 'Social Welfare and Industrial Relations' in *A History of British Industrial Relations, Volume 2: 1914–1939*, ed. C. J. Wrigley, Brighton, Harvester, 1987.

77 See PFA, File 11, Rules of Association Football Players' Union, 1908; 'Association Football Players' Union Advantages of Membership' page in *Football Players' Magazine*, October 1913.

78 AFPU Minutes, 21 March 1910; 14 October 1912; *Thomson's Weekly News*, 26 October 1912.

79 Football League Minutes, Management Committee, 22–23 October 1912; AFPU Minutes, 29 April 1912; AFPTU Minutes, 5 December 1921.

80 FA Council Minutes, 8 March 1909.

81 *Football Chat*, 3 March 1909.

82 For expressions of this opinion see *Athletic News*, 15 March, 10 May 1909.

83 *Athletic News*, 22 February 1909.

84 Quoted in Mason, *Association Football*, p. 132.

85 AFPU Minutes, 7 May 1909.

86 See the editorials and the articles by Pickford and Charles Sutcliffe in *Athletic News*, 11, 18 October 1909.

87 *Athletic News*, 11 October 1909.

88 AFPU Minutes, 7 October, 2 November 1909 (AGM); FA Minutes, Further Report of FA Officers, 1 December 1909.

89 Report of Football League SGM in *Athletic News*, 20 January 1919.

90 *Athletic News*, 18 October 1909.

91 *Athletic News*, 13 January 1919.

92 Sutcliffe, Brierley and Howarth, *Story of the Football League*, pp. 119, 122.

93 PFA, File 11, Rules of Association Football Players' Union, 1908; Minutes of AFPU, 1 April 1908; PFA, File 6, letter from Herbert Broomfield to James Ashcroft, 24 March 1909; *Athletic News*, 30 August 1909.

94 G. Moorhouse, *A People's Game: The Centenary History of Rugby League Football*, London, Hodder and Stoughton, 1995, p. 136.

95 J. Lovell, *British Trade Unions, 1875–1933*, London, Macmillan, 1977, Chapter 4; N. Kirk, *Change, Continuity and Class: Labour in British Society, 1850–1920*, Manchester, Manchester University Press, 1998, p. 173; V. Gore, 'Rank-and-File Dissent' in *A History of British Industrial Relations, Volume 2: 1914–1939*, ed. C. J. Wrigley, Brighton, Harvester, 1987, pp. 64–67.

96 See AFPTU Minutes, 10 February, 10 November 1930; 9 October 1933; 20 April 1938; 27 February 1939 (AGM); Sutcliffe, Brierley and Howarth, *Story of the Football League*, p. 125.

97 Football League Minutes, Management Committee, 22–23 October, 15 November 1912; Minutes of AFPU, 28 October 1912.

98 *Thomson's Weekly News*, 16 November 1912.

99 AFPU Minutes, 2 December 1912; 10 February 1913; Football League Minutes, 26 May 1913 (AGM). Owen resigned in February 1913 and took up a coaching post in Budapest.

100 AFPTU Minutes, 23 August 1920 (AGM).
101 *Thomson's Weekly News*, 16 November 1912.
102 AFPTU Minutes, 12 February 1923; 23 January 1939; Harding, *For the Good of the Game*, p. 189. The offending *Topical Times* article, entitled 'Is Players' Union a Useless Body?', was printed in the 10 February 1923 issue.
103 The first figure is from Mason, *Association Football*, p. 111; the others are taken from the Union's subscription figures tabulated in Vamplew, *Pay Up*, p. 248 (Table 15.1). The inter-war membership figures are recorded in the annual reports and minutes, though it must be remembered that membership could vary significantly at different stages of the season.
104 AFPTU Minutes, 12 February 1923.
105 AFPTU Minutes, 7 April 1939.
106 AFPTU Minutes, 1 November 1948 (AGM).
107 H. A. Clegg, A. Fox and A. F. Thompson, *A History of British Trade Unions since 1889, Volume 1: 1889–1910*, Oxford, Oxford University Press, 1964, p. 88.
108 Harding, *For the Good of the Game*, pp. 170–71; *Manchester Evening News*, 1 March 1939.
109 Dabscheck, 'Defensive Manchester', pp. 135–36; Clegg, Fox and Thompson, *History of British Trade Unions*, pp. 87–88. For data on career lengths in the Football League during the 1890s and early 1900s, see Vamplew, *Pay Up*, Chapter 14.
110 AFPTU Minutes, 6 February 1933; 24 August 1936 (AGM).
111 Quoted in Harding, *Alex James*, p. 136. James was already in receipt of the maximum wage, but his contract with Selfridges had ended, bringing his salary back to the basic £8 per week. He was therefore effectively asking Arsenal to make illegal payments. Eventually, however, Selfridges made a new, improved offer and James re-signed for Arsenal in time for the start of the new season.
112 *Athletic News*, 30 August 1909.
113 *Thomson's Weekly News*, 1 January 1910.
114 *Football Players' Magazine*, April 1914.
115 J. Hinton, *Labour and Socialism: A History of the British Labour Movement, 1867–1974*, Brighton, Harvester, 1983, pp. 83–95; R. Devlin, 'Strike Patterns and Employers' Responses: Clydeside in Comparative Perspective' in *Roots of Red Clydeside, 1910–1914? Labour Unrest and Industrial Relations in West Scotland*, ed. W. Kenefick and A. McIvor, Edinburgh, John Donald, 1996, pp. 66–85. For detailed accounts of the 1909 crisis, see B. Dabscheck, '"A Man or a Puppet?": The Football Association's 1909 Attempt to Destroy the Association Football Players' Union', *International Journal of the History of Sport*, Vol. 8, 1991, pp. 221–38; Dabscheck, 'Defensive Manchester', pp. 237–41; Harding, *For the Good of the Game*, Chapters 7–9; Tischler, *Footballers*, Chapter 6.
116 FA Council Minutes, 10 July 1909.
117 PFA, File 6, letter from H. Butterworth to Herbert Broomfield, 1909, otherwise undated.
118 PFA, File 7, letters from Jack Carr to Herbert Broomfield, 29 June, 2 July 1909.
119 See PFA, File 7, letter from J. Johnson to Herbert Broomfield, 22 June 1909; letter from W. McCrombie to Herbert Broomfield, 29 June 1909; File 8, letter from Jack Carr to Herbert Broomfield, 2 July 1909; letter from Herbert Broomfield to A. Young, 5 July 1909.
120 PFA, File 8, letter from Herbert Broomfield to A. Collins, 24 July 1909; letter from Herbert Broomfield to Harry Mainman, 1 September 1909.

121 *Athletic News*, 8 March 1909; *Football Chat*, 10 March 1909.

122 According to Charles Buchan, a strike had been called by Union delegates at the end of the 1919–20 season, but this position soon became untenable when several teams re-signed with their clubs en bloc. Similarly, the possibility of striking in response to the wage cuts of 1922 was briefly debated at that year's annual meeting, but the consensus was that the risk remained too high. One delegate pointed out that, as in 1909 and 1920, players 'would not stand out in the close season'. Buchan, *Lifetime*, p. 64; AFPTU Minutes, 20 August 1922 (AGM).

123 Collins, *Rugby's Great Split*, p. 175.

124 *Topical Times*, 17 September 1927.

125 SUFC, Football Committee Minutes, 7 October 1902; *Topical Times*, 5 January 1935.

126 SUFC, Football Committee Minutes, 25 February, 2 March 1920.

127 Hutchinson, 'Development', p. 253.

128 SUFC, Football Committee Minutes, 30 April 1930; Harding, *Alex James*, pp. 135–39. Bennett suffered the latter fate at Walsall in 1935. WLHC, WFC, Board Minutes, 28 May, 2 July 1935.

129 AVFC, Board Minutes, 2 May, 13 June, 21 November 1922; *Sporting Chronicle*, 27 May 1936; 1 May 1937; T. Mason, 'Stanley Matthews' in *Sport and the Working Class in Modern Britain*, ed. R. Holt, Manchester, Manchester University Press, 1991, p. 163.

130 WHUFC, Board Minutes, 2 April, 9 April 1935; SUFC, Football Committee Minutes, 9 May, 29 July 1931.

131 *Sporting Chronicle*, 7 May 1931.

132 AVFC, Board Minutes, 14 September, 22 September, 16 November 1920; *Topical Times*, 2 October 1920.

133 Gore, 'Rank-and-File Dissent', p. 60; T. Mason, '"Our Stephen and Our Harold": Edwardian Footballers as Local Heroes' in *European Heroes: Myth, Identity, Sport*, ed. R. Holt, J. A. Mangan and P. Lanfranchi, London, Frank Cass, 1996, p. 80.

134 See *Athletic News*, 4 December 1911; Sutcliffe's comments in *Topical Times*, 17 March 1928. Also see Tischler, *Footballers*, p. 106.

135 Seed, *Jimmy Seed Story*, p. 118; *Sunday Express*, 25 January 1931.

136 SUFC, Football Committee Minutes, 15 March, 13 October, 20 October, 2 November, 10 November 1920; *Sheffield Independent*, 6 November 1920.

137 Sutcliffe, Brierley and Howarth, *Story of the Football League*, p. 126.

138 See WHUFC, Board Minutes, 31 January 1931; PFA, File 9, M. Randal Roberts, 'A Footballer's Hospital', *Windsor Magazine*, 1904 (otherwise undated), pp. 511–16; J. Hutchinson, *The Football Industry: The Early Years of the Professional Game*, Glasgow, R. Drew, 1982, p. 40; *Thomson's Weekly News*, 16 April 1910.

139 SUFC, Football Committee Minutes, 20 August 1902; 11 March 1903. Also see Minutes, 9 November, 16 November, 23 November 1932.

140 J. Melling, 'Employers, Workplace Culture and Workers' Politics: British Industry and Workers' Welfare Programmes, 1870–1920' in *Culture in History: Production, Consumption and Values in Historical Perspective*, ed. J. Melling and J. Barry, Exeter, Exeter University Press, 1992, p. 112. The earliest expression of this argument can be found in R. Hay, 'Employers and Social Policy in Britain: The Evolution of Welfare Legislation, 1905–14', *Social History*, Vol. 4, 1977, pp. 435–55.

141 Mason, *Association Football*, p. 107; *Athletic News*, 6 November 1911. Tony Collins has shown that rugby clubs were taking out insurance policies for players from the early 1880s onwards: Collins, *Rugby's Great Split*, pp. 126–27.

142 On the development of Employers' Liability and Workmen's Compensation legislation, see P. Bartrip, *Workmen's Compensation in Twentieth Century Britain: Law, History and Social Policy*, Aldershot, Ashgate, 1987; P. Bartrip and S. B. Burman, *The Wounded Soldiers of Industry: Industrial Compensation Policy, 1833–1897*, Oxford, Clarendon, 1983; V. Markham Lester, 'The Employers' Liability/Workmen's Compensation Debate of the 1890s Revisited', *The Historical Journal*, Vol. 44, 2001, pp. 471–95.
143 Sutcliffe, Brierley and Howarth, *Story of the Football League*, pp. 126–28.
144 Bartrip and Burman, *Wounded Soldiers*, pp. 210–11.
145 *Athletic News*, 29 April 1907; SUFC, Football Committee Minutes, 1 May 1907.
146 *Football Chat*, 6 August 1907.
147 See McIvor, *Organised Capital*, pp. 79–81; R. Johnston, *Clydeside Capital, 1870–1920: A Social History of Employers*, East Linton, Tuckwell, 2000, pp. 70–74; P. Bartrip, 'The Rise and Fall of Workmen's Compensation' in *The Social History of Occupational Health*, ed. P. Weindling, London, Croom Helm, 1985, p. 172.
148 Sutcliffe, Brierley and Howarth, *Story of the Football League*, p. 129; *Athletic News*, 25 September 1911.
149 SUFC, Football Committee Minutes, 13 May 1908; 12 August 1909; 6 August 1912.
150 See E. Midwinter, *The Development of Social Welfare in Britain*, Buckingham, Open University Press, 1994, pp. 76–78; D. Fraser, *The Evolution of the British Welfare State*, second edition, Basingstoke, Macmillan, 1984, pp. 154–55; H. A. Clegg, *A History of British Trade Unions, Volume 2: 1911–1933*, Oxford, Oxford University Press, 1985, pp. 101–02.
151 Football League Minutes, Management Committee, 9 September 1912.
152 *Athletic News*, 9 September 1912.
153 *Athletic News*, 12 August 1912; A. Russell, *The Growth of Occupational Welfare in Britain*, Aldershot, Avebury, 1991, p. 57.
154 SUFC, Football Committee Minutes, 3 September 1912; Football League Minutes, Management Committee, 9 September 1912.
155 Football League Minutes, Management Committee, 10 November 1920; Clegg, *History*, pp. 243-44.
156 Sutcliffe, Brierley and Howarth, *Story of the Football League*, p. 130.
157 Financial Statement of FLMIF, December 1922; Football League Minutes, Management Committee, 23 October 1922.
158 Football League Circular to Clubs, 31 August 1923; Football League Minutes, Management Committee, 4 February, 2 June 1924 (AGM); Report of Football League AGM in *Athletic News*, 9 June 1924.
159 Football League Minutes, Management Committee, 2 June 1924 (AGM); Report of Football League AGM in *Athletic News*, 9 June 1924.
160 Harding, *For the Good of the Game*, pp. 38–39.
161 Green, *History*, pp. 416–17; Sutcliffe, Brierley and Howarth, *Story of the Football League*, pp. 131, 138–39.
162 SUFC, Football Committee Minutes, 28 September, 12 October 1932.
163 WHUFC, Board Minutes, 28 October, 1 December 1930; 3, 11 April, 8 August 1933.
164 Bartrip and Burman, *Wounded Soldiers*.
165 Quoted in AFPTU Minutes, 22 August 1927 (AGM).
166 Football League Minutes, Management Committee, 8 September 1922.
167 AFPTU Minutes, 22 August 1927 (AGM).
168 Football League Minutes, Management Committee, 13 March, 13 December 1926.

169 AFPTU Minutes, 22 August 1927 (AGM); PFA, File 35, James Fay, 'Star player's career ended by injury: Offered £200 compensation', draft of fourth newspaper article, 1938–39 (otherwise undated), p. 2.
170 AFPTU Minutes, 8 October, 10 December 1934.
171 AFPTU Minutes, 22 August 1927 (AGM).
172 AFPTU Minutes, 26 August 1929 (AGM).
173 SUFC, Football Committee Minutes, 24 September, 2 October, 7 October 1924; AFPTU Minutes, 24 April 1933.
174 Football League Minutes, Management Committee, 5 September, 15 December 1924.
175 AFPTU Minutes, 26 August 1929 (AGM); 11 March, 26 August 1935.
176 See Sanderson, *Irving to Olivier*, pp. 87–91; W. Vamplew, 'Riding for a Fall: The Health Hazards of Professional Jockeys in Nineteenth and Twentieth Century British Horse-Racing', paper presented at ISHPES Congress, Lyon, July 1997.
177 AFPTU Minutes, 1 March 1926; 26 August 1929 (AGM); 18 January 1932; *Topical Times*, 25 June 1932.
178 *Topical Times*, 9 June 1934.
179 AFPTU Minutes, 20 August 1934 (AGM).
180 *Topical Times*, 25 June 1932.
181 PFA, File 35, Jimmy Fay, 'Too Old at Thirty', draft of eighth newspaper article, no date, p. 2.
182 PFA, File 35, Jimmy Fay, draft of newspaper article (untitled), 1934 (otherwise undated), p. 1.
183 *Topical Times*, 16 June, 15 September 1934.
184 See report of Ministry of Health v. Leonard Graham (Footballer) in *Sporting Chronicle*, 21 April 1934.
185 AFPTU Minutes, 24 April 1933, 20 August 1934 (AGM); Sutcliffe, Brierley and Howarth, *Story of the Football League*, pp. 39, 131–32.
186 AFPTU Minutes, 26 August 1935 (AGM).
187 Sutcliffe, Brierley and Howarth, *Story of the Football League*, pp. 129–30; AFPTU Minutes, 14 October 1935.
188 PFA, File 35, Jimmy Fay, 'A Job for Parliament', draft of third newspaper article, 1938–39 (otherwise undated), pp. 2–3; AFPTU Minutes, 22 August 1938.
189 AFPTU Minutes, 13 March 1939 (EGM).
190 FA Finance and General Purposes Committee Minutes, 8 March 1937.
191 AFPTU Minutes, 23 November 1936; 10 May 1937; AVFC, Board Minutes, 15 August 1922; 25 August 1926.
192 Mason, 'Our Stephen', p. 82; P. Seddon, *Steve Bloomer: The Story of Football's First Superstar*, Derby, Breedon, 1999, pp. 199–200.
193 On the broader development of state and occupational pensions, see L. Hannah, *Inventing Retirement: The Development of Occupational Pensions in Britain*, Cambridge, Cambridge University Press, 1986; Fitzgerald, *British Labour*; Russell, *Occupational Welfare*, pp. 72–78, 85–88.
194 PFA, File 33, letter from Watson Hartley to Jimmy Fay, 21 August 1934; letter from Jimmy Fay to Watson Hartley, 24 August 1934.
195 See AFPTU Minutes, 8 May, 22 May, 21 August 1939 (AGM). The creation of such a scheme had to wait until 1949, when the Football League set up a Provident Fund in collaboration with the Players' Union. The Fund was financed by a 4 per cent levy

on gates, out of which the player received a lump payment (calculated as 10 per cent of his career earnings) when he reached 35. By the end of the 1949–50 season, 3,618 players, present and past, had signed up to the fund. See Inglis, *League Football*, pp. 181, 183. On the Union's proposed rival scheme and its reluctant acceptance of the Provident Fund, see Harding, *For the Good of the Game*, pp. 228–30.

196 SUFC, Football Committee Minutes, 26 February, 30 July 1930; 8 June 1932. Gillespie was subsequently appointed manager of Derry City. *Topical Times*, 21 January 1933.

197 *Topical Times*, 7 April 1923. On the development of professional managers, see Wagg, *Football World*, Chapter 5; Fishwick, *English Football*, pp. 35–38.

198 Wagg, *Football World*, pp. 12, 32–33, 60–61.

199 AFC, Catton Folders, B–C, letter from Charles Bunyan to James Catton, 2 December 1920, p. 201.

200 See Report of the FA Instructional Classes for Boys in Association Football (ICBAF) Committee, 1935–36.

201 Wagg, *Football World*, p. 33; *Topical Times*, 12 February 1938.

202 SUFC, Football Committee Minutes, 1 June 1937; OAFC, Board Minutes, 29 June 1938; HTFC, Board Minutes, 24 May 1939; PFA, File 33, letter from Watson Hartley to Jimmy Fay, 21 August 1934.

203 Cited in Fishwick, *English Football*, p. 77.

204 Report of FA ICBAF Committee, 1936–37; Green, *History*, pp. 418–19.

205 *Football League Jubilee Souvenir Booklet*, Preston, Football League, August 1938. On the fund's finances, see Inglis, *League Football*, pp. 159, 164.

206 PFA, File 33, letter from Watson Hartley to Jimmy Fay, 6 February 1939; *Manchester Evening News*, 1 March 1939; *Topical Times*, 16 April 1938.

207 OAFC, Board Minutes, 18 January, 25 January 1939; AFPTU Minutes, 8 May 1939; 26 April 1948.

208 H. Perkin, *The Rise of Professional Society: England Since 1880*, London, Routledge, 1989, p. 314.

209 See M. Taylor, 'Work and Play: The Professional Footballer in England, c. 1900–1950', *The Sports Historian*, Vol. 22, 2002, pp. 16–43.

210 Gibson and Pickford, *Association Football*, p. 200.

211 The quotation is from Burk, *Never Just a Game*, p. 238.

212 Perkin, *Rise of Professional Society*, p. 307; Hay, 'Employers', pp. 439–40.

CHAPTER FIVE

League Football and the Question of Equality

Competition is an inevitable and essential prerequisite for the survival of any modern sports club: without opponents there would be no product, no audience, and consequently no revenue. Even in the early stages, prior to the creation of cup competitions and leagues, clubs were necessarily dependent upon one another and had established economic as well as sporting ties that were crucial to their continued existence. At the most basic level, the creation of a league merely formalised these relations. However, economists of sport have gone a step further by arguing that professional sports leagues operate in the same fundamental way as industrial cartels. They can be seen as 'a coalition of teams with restrictive practices in both product and labour markets designed to protect the interests of member clubs' with 'a central structure … for developing rules and enforcing controls'.[1] Where sports cartels arguably differ from industrial ones, however, is in their basic functions and objectives. P. J. Sloane has observed that while conventional firms usually combine in order to prevent potentially damaging price wars, the objective of combination among sports firms is to ensure both the production of the common product and the equality of playing competition between clubs.[2]

Modern economists and contemporary observers have stressed the economic value of preserving a relative equality between clubs on a match-by-match and longer-term basis. In short, it is assumed (though it has never been convincingly proven) that attendances are higher when the result of a match is uncertain, and thus that a league's viability depends on keeping clubs as equal as possible in terms of playing strength.[3] Many League officials, club directors and football writers certainly subscribed to this 'uncertainty of outcome' hypothesis, and positively encouraged the adoption of measures designed to minimise inequality. Compared with the elite county cricket and rugby league tournaments, the Football League remained a highly competitive and relatively open competition throughout this period.[4] Yet it is argued in this chapter that equalisation policies, though generally accepted and promoted at Management Committee level, encountered considerable resistance from clubs that were inclined to put self-interest before group-interest. Individual clubs were perhaps quite naturally concerned with improving their own ground facilities, attendances, playing squads and bank balances: the finances of other clubs remained a secondary consideration, so long as sufficient opponents existed to maintain the viability of the league. Only gradually, and largely through the necessary implementation of cross-subsidisation policies during the First World War, were the major clubs persuaded to accept the concept of equality as a central plank of League policy. It is also stressed that the support for equalisation policies was not simply motivated by economic concerns. Existing accounts have ignored the possibility that notions of 'fair competition' could continue to influence the conduct and values of professional sport years after the presumed heyday of the gentleman amateur in the late nineteenth century. For Charles Sutcliffe, John Bentley, John Lewis and other important League administrators, an equal league competition was both economically and morally justifiable. In their view, every club should have a fair chance to reach the top of the table regardless of resources, and if a club struggled it should be helped along by its fellow members.

Competition and equality in the Football League

The theoretical ideal of an equal and competitively balanced sporting league has never been achieved in reality. Economic analyses show that even North American sporting leagues, which have adopted equalisation policies throughout their histories, have been unable in practice to prevent competitive imbalance and the concentration of championships. This has been most apparent in baseball, where the New York Yankees dominated the League from the 1920s to the 1970s by winning 29 of the 50 available pennants, but is evident in all the major US professional team sports. Weak or 'problem' clubs also cause perennial difficulties for league administrators, though these have been eased in the long term by changes in ownership or franchise moves to more viable cities.[5] Restrictions in the distribution of playing talent – mainly through the reserve clause, player drafts and salary caps – have been combined in these leagues with various income-sharing arrangements between clubs, with the intention of achieving some degree of playing equality. However, these arrangements have been largely ineffective in balancing playing strengths, essentially because franchises are necessarily situated in cities with vastly differing populations.[6] Playing equality has therefore proved to be an unobtainable ideal.

No club in the Football League reached the level of dominance achieved by the New York Yankees. In the 34 official seasons during the period under review, only one club – Arsenal – won the First Division championship five times, while the Merseyside neighbours Liverpool and Everton did so on four occasions each; 13 clubs held the title at least once. As Table 5.3 shows, the most consistently successful club over the whole period, Sunderland, achieved just 15 top-five finishes in 34 seasons; a poor record when compared with the leading Scottish League clubs, Celtic and Rangers, who were never out of the top five. Moreover, Sunderland was the only leading English side (those in Table 5.3) to avoid spending at least one season in the Second Division, suggesting that even the most successful clubs suffered periodic setbacks. This is not to deny, of course, that certain teams enjoyed short periods of dominance. One can point to Huddersfield Town's three championship victories from 1923–24 to 1925–26, and Arsenal's repeat of this in the early 1930s. Nevertheless, Tables 5.1 and 5.2 indicate that long-term domination of the highest positions by a single club or group of clubs was rare. Only Sunderland, Aston Villa and Sheffield Wednesday appear on both the pre- and post-1914 tables and, though this suggests that they enjoyed a disproportionate share of playing success, it hardly equates with a sustained period of superiority. Tony Arnold's analysis of competition dominance, based on clubs finishing in the top three positions of the First Division or reaching an FA Cup Final, similarly suggests a leading group whose size and composition was subject to change over time.[7] Indeed, it might be argued from this evidence that no core group of elite clubs existed in the Football League before 1939.

Variations in championship distribution and top-five places are not the only methods of assessing league equality. In his economic history of professional sport, Wray Vamplew attempted to calculate the degree of equality between clubs in each season from 1888–89 to 1914–15 by measuring the extent to which winning percentages deviated from the 50 per cent ideal.[8] His calculations revealed that the Football League was considerably more competitive than the major football leagues in Scotland, as well as cricket's County Championship and the Northern Rugby Football League. Vamplew's work also showed that the First Division of the Football League exhibited greater equality over time than did other leagues, which, in turn, supports the view that long-term ascendancy was rare and the constituency of the League elite variable. Another method of measuring equality has been employed by Michael E. Canes in an analysis of US professional and college leagues.[9] His focus on the winning percentages of each championship club and the percentage of successive

Table 5.1: Championship record of the most successful Football League clubs, 1900/01–1914/15

	1st	*2nd*	*3rd*	*4th*	*5th*	*Top five*
Newcastle United	3	0	2	3	0	8
Aston Villa	1	5	0	1	1	8
Sunderland	2	1	3	0	1	7
Blackburn Rovers	2	0	2	2	1	7
Everton	1	4	1	1	0	7
Sheffield Wednesday	1	0	2	0	3	6
Total	**10**	**10**	**10**	**7**	**6**	**43**
Possible maximum	**15**	**15**	**15**	**15**	**15**	**75**

Table 5.2: Championship record of the most successful Football League clubs, 1919/20–1938/39

	1st	*2nd*	*3rd*	*4th*	*5th*	*Top five*
Huddersfield Town	3	3	2	1	1	10
Arsenal	5	2	1	0	1	9
Sunderland	1	2	3	1	1	8
Sheffield Wednesday	2	0	4	0	0	6
Liverpool	2	0	0	3	1	6
Aston Villa	0	2	1	1	2	6
Total	**13**	**9**	**11**	**6**	**6**	**45**
Possible maximum	**19**	**19**	**19**	**19**	**19**	**95**

Table 5.3: Competition domination of Football League and Scottish Football League clubs, 1900/01–1938/39

Football League club	*Top five finishes*	*Scottish League club*	*Top five finishes**
Sunderland	15	Celtic	38
Aston Villa	14	Rangers	38
Newcastle United	12	Hearts	19
Sheffield Wednesday	12	Motherwell	16
Everton	11	Airdrie	11
Liverpool	10	Falkirk	10
Huddersfield Town	10	Aberdeen	8
Total	**84**		**140**
Possible maximum	**170**		**190***

* Scottish League continued for four seasons during the First World War.

championship victories has been applied (where possible) in Table 5.4 to each division of the Football League, along with the Scottish First Division and the rival Southern League. Again, the Football League First Division championship emerges as the closest competition, although champions of the lower divisions were able to win slightly more often. The clearest contrast is with the Scottish League champions, who between 1900–01 and 1938–39 recorded a mean winning percentage of 81, compared with just 68.1 for their English counterparts. This relative inequality is also reflected by the fact that the Scottish champions were able to repeat their success in the subsequent season more than 50 per cent of the time, while this was achieved just 20 and 13.3 per cent of the time, respectively, in the top divisions of the Football and Southern Leagues.

Table 5.4: Winning percentages* of championship clubs and successive championship victories in British football, 1900–39

League/Division	*Period*	*Mean winning percentage*	*Highest winning percentage*	*Lowest winning percentage*	*Percentage of successive championship seasons*
Football League First Division	1900/01–1938/39	68.1	79.4	60.5	20
Football League Second Division	1900/01–1938/39	71.9	86.8	63.1	n/a
Football League Third Division South	1920/21–1938/39	70.6	81	64.3	n/a
Football League Third Division North	1921/22–1938/39	71.4	79.8	66.7	n/a
Scottish League First Division	1900/01–1938/39	81	90.5	72.4	51.3
Southern League First Division	1900/01–1915/15	71	80	65.8	13.3

* Draws classed as a 50% win.

Sources: Calculated from data in J. Mallory (ed.), *Football League Tables: 1889 to the Present*, London, Collins, 1977; Harrison, *Southern League Football*.

The relative equality of competition in the Football League when compared with its competitors in football and other team sports has generally been explained by the success of four initiatives: the retain-and-transfer system, the maximum wage, central control over league quality, and pooling or income-sharing arrangements. Certainly, the lack of some form of stipulated maximum payment for players and the absence of a system for controlling the size and quality of the competing group – such as the promotion and relegation systems in the League – have both frequently been posited as reasons for the inequalities of the Scottish football, county cricket and rugby league championships.[10] Yet empirical studies concerned with whether such arrangements actually bring about greater competition within leagues have often proved inconclusive. Economists have cast considerable doubt, for instance, on the utility of the reserve clause and other restrictions on player mobility in US team sports as a means of increasing sporting competition, an argument that has also been applied to the League's transfer system.[11] According to H. F. Moorhouse, for example, the notion that the transfer system 'is a "vital" element of the finances of association football, "crucial" to its continuance, that it "automatically" redistributes cash between "rich" and "poor" clubs … is confirmed only by easy anecdote, obvious confirming example, or statistics of dubious authenticity'.[12] There is also little conclusive evidence that these Football League initiatives had a significant equalising effect before 1939. Measurements of the effectiveness of the retain-and-transfer system in this respect are especially troublesome, as it operated from the early 1890s onwards. Some attempt can be made, however, to assess the impact of the maximum wage, introduced for the 1901–02 season. Table 5.5 shows that for the First Division, the championship winning percentage was lower in the five seasons following the wage rule than before, suggesting a more equal competition. The contrast was less marked in the Second Division, where the winning percentage of the first-placed club actually increased after 1901–02;[13] even in the First Division, there were seasons, such as 1904–05, in which equality of competition was worse than the pre-maximum wage period.

Sloane has suggested that an 'equal distribution of income is no less important than an equal distribution of playing talent in ensuring equality in terms of sporting competition'.[14] However, while approaching nothing like the ideal of pooling all gate receipts and club income, the introduction of income-sharing arrangements in the Football League from the First World War onwards seems to have been relatively ineffective in this respect. There was, for example, no marked change in the winning percentages of First and Second Division champions in the inter-war period compared with those before the war: in fact, the mean First Division figure (68.5 per cent as against 67.6 for the 1900/01–1914/15 period) actually suggests a marginally less equal competition after the 20 per cent payment to visiting clubs was established (see below). There is more convincing evidence to suggest that the promotion and election systems encouraged competition and equality. Tables 5.6 and 5.7 show that the majority of promoted or elected clubs performed well in their new positions and managed to survive for at least two seasons, and often much longer. The fact that both Liverpool and Everton were able to win the First Division championship at the first attempt after promotion (in 1905–06 and 1931–32 respectively) supports the belief that the lower divisions acted as a reservoir of quality clubs capable of increasing competition at the higher level by replacing weak sides that dropped down. The election system in the lower divisions also worked in this way, although Cardiff City's achievement in the early 1920s of gaining promotion to the First Division in its first season and subsequently finishing fourth at the top level was rare.[15]

Notwithstanding the limited and unsophisticated nature of this statistical approach, the success of equalisation policies between 1900 and 1939 has been shown to have been mixed. With the possible exception of the promotion system, there is little evidence that these policies substantially assisted the attainment of equality within the Football League. However, the important point for our purposes is that key figures within the League hierarchy were convinced that they did.[16] The remainder of this chapter will thus concentrate on the attitudes and debates surrounding the introduction and development of policies designed to promote equality. It will also trace the evolution of what might be regarded as an ideology of equality within League circles, formed around notions of fair competition, mutual support and the ambivalent concept of friendship.

Table 5.5: Relative equality of Football League First and Second Divisions before and after the introduction of the maximum wage rule in 1901–02

Season	*First Division: winning percentages of championship clubs**	*Second Division: winning percentages of championship clubs**
1896–97	78.3	70
1897–98	70	80
1898–99	66.2	75
1899–1900	73.5	79.4
1900–01	66.2	72.1
Mean total	70.8	75.3
1901–02	64.7	80.9
1902–03	61.8	79.4
1903–04	69.1	73.5
1904–05	70.6	85.3
1905–06	67.1	86.8
Mean total	66.5	81.2

* As measured in Table 5.4.

Source: Based on data in Vamplew, *Pay Up*, p. 134 (Table 9.12); Table 5.4 (above).

Table 5.6: Average finishing position of newly promoted and elected clubs in the Football League, 1900/01–1938/39

	First division			*Last division**		
Period	*Clubs promoted*	*Clubs in division*	*Average position of promoted clubs in first season*	*Clubs elected*	*Clubs in division*	*Average position of elected clubs in first season*
1900/01–1904/05	10	18	10	6	18	12
1905/06–1914/15	20	20	12	13	20	9
1919/20–1928/29	21	22	14	15	22**	13
1929/30–1938/39	20	22	11	7	22	13

* Second Division from 1900/01–1919/20, Third Division for 1920/21 and Third Divisions North and South thereafter.
** In its first two seasons (1921–22 and 1922–23), the Third Division North had just 20 clubs.
Source: Calculated from data in Mallory, *Football*. Based on Table 9.7 in Vamplew, *Pay Up*, p. 127.

Table 5.7: Performance over two seasons of promoted and relegated clubs in the Football League, 1900/01–1937/38

	First division		*Last division**		
Period	*Clubs promoted*	*Remained in division at least two seasons*	*Clubs elected*	*Remained in League at least two seasons*	*Promoted within two seasons*
1900/01–1909/10	22	19	15	13	2
1910/11–1919/20	13	12	9	9	0
1920/21–1929/30	18	16	10	10	1
1930/31–1937/38	18	17	5	5	0

* Second Division from 1900/01–1919/20, Third Division for 1920/21 and Third Divisions North and South thereafter.
Source: Calculated from data in Mallory, *Football*. Based on Table 9.7 in Vamplew, *Pay Up*, p. 127.

Equality of playing talent: the transfer system and the maximum wage

In most sports, the principal step taken to attain equality of competition has involved the distribution of the major resource – playing talent. The US sports of basketball and football have traditionally used direct methods like the college or rookie draft, which attempts to equalise performance by giving teams with weaker playing records first choice of players.[17] However, indirect measures to control the mobility and payment of players have been more common on both sides of the Atlantic. First-class cricket developed a system of county qualifications from 1873 onwards, which allowed a player to compete either for his county of birth or his county of residence, although he was required to complete a two-year qualifying period before playing for his residential county. However, it has been recognised that this did little to reverse the fundamental disparity between counties with vastly contrasting population sizes and financial resources, and even led to an increased concentration of playing talent.[18] In 1919, Major Frank Buckley advocated residential qualifications as an alternative to the maximum wage in order to protect poorer clubs,[19] but the fact that clubs were based around towns and cities rather than counties, and that football players were more mobile from the very beginning, probably precluded serious discussion on this point. Rugby league authorities chose to impose a maximum player roster similar to the team player limits in US baseball and ice hockey, but there is little indication that the 75-man limit prevented the monopolisation of talent by the wealthier clubs.[20] In the Football League, however, the retain-and-transfer system and the maximum wage became the cornerstones of equalisation policy before the First World War.

For contemporaries, these measures served a dual purpose: they enabled clubs to control their employees, and prevented the wealthier clubs buying up the best players. Many supporters of the transfer system believed its primary aim from the beginning was to maintain some degree of competitive balance within the League. *Athletic News* argued in 1895 that 'it will be a bad day for the League, the clubs, and the players when freedom all round is given. Teams must be comparatively level to sustain the interest – if they are not, receipts fall off, and without receipts players cannot be paid wages'.[21] When a club signed a player, he remained its property 'for League purposes forever, unless an arrangement is made for his transfer'.[22] Placing a prohibitive fee on the player's head could deter interested parties but, if this proved unsuccessful, clubs still received compensation in the form of a transfer fee, which could be used to replace the lost player and improve the playing squad. By the 1900s, League officials regarded the system as a fundamental and highly successful contribution to equalisation. Writing in 1901, President John Bentley suggested that:

> The chief object of the League is … to provide for an equality of strength as far as is practicable, and it is just here that the transfer law is of value, for anyone interested in the game knows perfectly well that if half a dozen wealthy organisations snapped up all the best players, the interest in the League Championship would be reduced to a minimum.[23]

William Bassett was convinced that without the considerable sums received from selling players, clubs like West Bromwich Albion, Barnsley and Bury would have been forced out of business.[24] Indeed, few commentators in the period doubted the orthodox view that the transfer system encouraged the levelling of playing performance. In response to the Southern League's decision to grant freedom of contract to its players in 1920, Charles Sutcliffe reaffirmed the League's commitment to equality. 'Freedom of contract', he argued, was 'contrary to the true League spirit. The strong must help the weak. Each for all and all for each. The gospel of the survival of the fittest is rotten in sport.'[25]

Limits on transfer fees were also recommended at various times by officials and club directors, but the idea never received sufficient club or Committee support and, in fact, opinion was mixed as to whether such a limit would be an obstacle or an aid to equality. In 1905, dissatisfaction with escalating transfer prices had provoked the FA to introduce a £350 maximum fee, but this was easily evaded when it came into operation in 1908, and lasted just three months.[26] *Athletic News* advocated a fixed limit in 1911 on the grounds that high transfer prices negated the League's existing measures to equalise playing ability. 'The present system of allowing the highest bidder to capture the best player is a menace to the protection of the weaker club that has been the policy of the League for years.'[27] Yet it was richer clubs such as Arsenal and Everton who supported a limit in the 1920s, primarily in order to reduce transfer expenditure.[28] Arsenal's chairman, Sir Henry Norris, admitted that 'some of the poorer clubs could not exist without large transfer fees' but, in direct opposition to the rhetoric of Sutcliffe and others, suggested that 'football was not organised with that object, and those that could not carry on should cease'. In contrast, Derby County's W. Bendle Moore outlined the orthodox viewpoint that 'Players were assets to small clubs and they should be paid for'.[29] Most clubs evidently agreed with him: Arsenal's proposals to set a transfer limit of £1,650 received only five votes out of 40 in 1922, and ten the following year.

From its introduction for the 1901–02 season, the maximum wage (initially £4 per week) was a far more contentious measure within League circles. More than any other rule it polarised the rich and poor clubs, who fought an annual battle over the issue at the FA annual meeting for most of the ensuing decade. As we have seen, the wage limit was technically an FA rule, but Football League clubs were instrumental in its establishment and subsequent defence. Chief among these were representatives of Preston North End and Wolverhampton Wanderers, who could also rely on the support of League officials like Bentley and Sutcliffe. Fred Rinder, the leading opponent of the maximum, argued that initially neither the rich nor the poor clubs really wanted the rule; it had, in his view, been created in the interests of ten or so middle-sized clubs 'who could pay about £3 per week to a man'.[30] There is little evidence to support this claim. Early attempts to rescind the rule were easily defeated, and though no systematic data exist to indicate the voting patterns of clubs on the issue, it seems that most League members were prepared to experiment with the maximum wage during the early 1900s. By the middle of the decade, however, criticisms of the operation of the wage rule were mounting. Many believed the rule had failed in its two basic objectives of reducing wage bills and encouraging equality of competition. According to Rinder, big city clubs were still able to dominate the championship by accumulating large squads and paying each player the £4 maximum.[31] Writing in 1907, the former England international John Goodall lauded the rule's 'charitable object of putting the smaller clubs on a more equable [sic] basis as regards competition with the larger', but remained unconvinced of its effectiveness. 'I am really very doubtful', he admitted, 'whether the smaller fry have to any extent benefited much [from the maximum wage], if at all'.[32] All this was enough to convince Charles Clegg, FA Chairman and a director of both the Sheffield clubs, that even under the maximum wage wealthy clubs were still able to 'get the players they wanted' and hence that 'the inequality between the two classes of clubs [rich and poor] would not be greatly increased by the removal of financial restrictions'.[33]

A very different interpretation of the maximum wage was offered by other Committee members and club directors. John Lewis, for instance, had become convinced by 1907 of the direct link between the wage limit and increased public interest in League football. Though he had always objected to the rule in principle, there was little doubt in his mind that the clubs had collectively benefited from

> the practical equality of the sides engaged in League combat. I don't say that the play is better than it was, or as good, but the teams are more equal, and therefore the games are more exciting than they would be if they were runaway affairs in the favour of a few clubs … those who agitate for a return to the pre-limit days should consider whether concentration of playing talent would lead to unattractive games.[34]

Sutcliffe agreed that the maximum wage 'has done something to equalise opportunity and level up and strengthen interest in competition', while Tom Sidney of Wolverhampton Wanderers noted in 1908 that 'clubs were of a much more equal playing strength than ever they were before'. The wage rule by this stage was considered fundamental to the survival of the so-called weaker clubs in the short term, and the League itself in the long run. Equality here had both ideological and economic value: it gave clubs like Wolves 'a chance to carry off the highest honours in the football world', and ultimately saved them from financial ruin.[35] Although the advocates of the maximum wage eventually won through, they did not do so without mounting opposition from within the League circle. When the issue was debated at the FA annual meeting of 1909, only 14 of the 40 League clubs (six from the First Division and eight from the Second) voted to keep the wage limit. Six months later, the FA Council balloted the 75 clubs in the Football and Southern Leagues, and found from the replies that 12 clubs favoured the abolition of wage restrictions and 19 opposed it.[36] For the first decade of the twentieth century, then, the League remained divided on the maximum wage issue, giving it neither unanimous support nor condemnation. By 1910, however, the richer clubs appear to have been prepared to tolerate its continuance, and redirected their energies towards the introduction of bonus payments.

Sporting leagues have generally chosen to avoid more direct forms of control over the playing strengths of their members that 'would require the league to act as a multi-plant firm which allocated staff to various parts of the country as circumstances dictated'.[37] In the Football League, as we noted above, belief in the ideology of equality meant the exclusion of clubs with consistently sub-standard playing records through the relegation and re-election systems. Yet when clubs were weakened through long-term suspensions or financial problems, League officials could encourage a more direct form of equalisation. The position of Manchester City in 1906 provides a case in point. In the summer of that year, an FA Commission found the club guilty of illegal payments to its players over a number of years and suspended 17 of its squad from playing football until the following January, while banning them permanently from appearing for the club. Given this situation, Bentley wrote to all First Division clubs explaining that City had 'been permanently deprived of the services of the majority of its players' and that he thought it 'unfair for the board to start the season without … funds and with but few players'. He then issued an unprecedented appeal on behalf of the 'unfortunate' club:

> League clubs ought, according to the first rule of the League, to support each other. This is their opportunity, and I would seriously and with the greatest confidence, ask them to assist Manchester City to the extent of offering the transfer of players nominally free, with the proviso that when the City is in a position to negotiate, the … Management Committee should be allowed to fix an equitable fee… I sincerely hope your directors will favourably consider the matter, and thus show that the Football League is not merely a name, but a body of clubs loyally banded together to assist and support each other, especially in times of need… Manchester City just now is greatly in need of assistance and encouragement. Let them have it.[38]

Although a majority of clubs offered players or other assistance, some were highly critical of Bentley's intervention. An anonymous director of a League club from Sheffield regarded Bentley's appeal as 'one of the most remarkable letters which ever has been written by one who holds a high position in football legislation'. The President was accused of acting as a 'special pleader' for a dishonest, rule-breaking club while 'to clubs who loyally carried out the rules as they stand, and who owing to misfortune are on the bottom rung of the League table … he turns a deaf ear, and no helping hand in the shape of an appeal is issued, and he leaves them to sink'. Significantly, Bentley responded to this criticism by pointing out that there were economic as well as sentimental reasons behind his appeal, because a club with novice players would be unable to compete at the required level and 'anyone conversant with club management is aware that a team beaten week after week ceases to be a drawing power, especially away'.[39] In general, however, the League steered away from this type of centralised control over player movement, leaving the transfer system and the maximum wage to limit the concentration of football talent that might otherwise develop in a free and unregulated labour market.

Subsidising the poor: income sharing and mutual support

Like the maximum wage, income sharing became a highly contentious issue that tended to divide the wealthy big city clubs and their less well-off colleagues. The original Football League scheme drawn up by William McGregor and a small band of club representatives in March 1888 had included a rule stipulating that all gates be pooled, but this was subsequently rejected in favour of home clubs keeping the gate receipts and providing a small guarantee of £12 to the visitors.[40] This arrangement was abandoned within two years due to the massive increases in gate money, and a series of proposals in the early 1890s and then again in 1901 and 1908 for gate receipts to be equally divided were similarly dismissed.[41] Indeed, prior to the First World War there were relatively few calls to introduce income redistribution. James Catton certainly believed that the absence of gate-sharing was the League's primary weakness, but even McGregor could accept by the mid-1900s that the pooling of gates would probably in the early days have created 'friction and unrest' between the richer and poorer clubs, and that it would now 'lead to badly managed clubs being bailed out by the well-managed'.[42] The Scottish League, in contrast, had adopted gate-sharing arrangements from its foundation, although the two-thirds home to one-third away distribution it initially settled for was evidently insufficient to save clubs with near-village populations, like Dumbarton, Renton and Vale of Leven, from extinction. By 1905 it had opted for an equal division of gate money in order to subsidise the clubs with low attendances and provide some competition for the dominant trio of Celtic, Rangers and Hearts.[43] No doubt the relative equality in the Football League because of wage and transfer restrictions persuaded the executive not to intervene in this sensitive area for the time being.

Opposition to the principle of gate-sharing was based largely on the assumption that this form of income was purely the product of the home club's endeavour. In this view, people came to watch the home side play, and thus it was logical that it should keep its own gate receipts as reward for investments in players and ground facilities, and other good management practices. The issue of ground facilities was particularly sensitive for those clubs that were beginning to erect covered stands and make other improvements (see Chapter 7). As a Liverpool director pointed out in 1901, 'clubs which have provided covered accommodation … should reap the rewards. Why should they be called upon to divide with, say, Bury, who have little or no covered accommodation?'[44]

W. R. Clayton of Everton – a club which had spent over £50,000 on two new stands and other developments between 1907 and 1909 alone to create 'by far the best equipped ground in England'[45]– similarly objected to the idea of enterprising and modernising clubs paying 'out of their gates for the up-keep of the so-called weaker organisations'.[46]

It took the outbreak of war in 1914 to force the richer clubs to accept income redistribution, initially through the mechanism of the Relief Fund. The intention was that each club would pay 2.5 per cent of its gate, and players between 5 and 15 per cent of their wages, to a central fund administered by the Management Committee 'for the purpose of assisting necessitous clubs' who had particularly suffered from the drop in attendances. The architect of the scheme, Sutcliffe, estimated that £8,000 was needed to help 14 clubs in financial difficulties, and indeed 18 of the 40 League members applied for assistance from the fund at some point during the 1914–15 season.[47] In introducing the scheme, the executive had returned to the established rhetoric of solidarity and mutual support:

> The loyalty of the League clubs cannot be questioned. At heart we are faithful adherents to the League spirit. In a critical period in the history of the game, devotion to the League is of paramount importance. Our personal and individual interests must be sacrificed to the common good… The strong clubs must come to the help of the weak.[48]

The Relief Fund was dissolved at the end of the 1914–15 season and, for the first time, a system of pooling gate receipts was introduced in the newly organised Lancashire and Midland sections.

In the Principal Competition, which lasted the first half of the season, clubs retained their own gate receipts as before, but the Subsidiary Competition from January to April was formulated on a more equitable basis, with the Midland section deciding to split the gates equally between the home and away clubs, and the Lancashire group requiring each member to contribute half the gate to a common pool, to be shared equally by the 12 clubs at the end of the season. *Athletic News* applauded the willingness of clubs to help 'each other to survive in times of peril', and enthusiastically backed such schemes, which exemplified the 'true League principle of mutual support'.[49] There is little doubt that the less wealthy clubs benefited substantially from these pooling arrangements. In the Lancashire Competition, two-thirds of the members derived more income through pooling than they would have gained under the previous system. Blackpool publicly thanked its richer neighbours for 'falling into line with the pooling system', while the Preston chairman admitted that his club would have had to leave the League without the money received from the pool.[50] Everton, Liverpool and Manchester City, each of whom lost over £450 as a result of the pooling arrangement, were less favourable. At the 1916 annual meeting, these clubs masterminded a return to the pre-war system, partly by threatening to establish a breakaway competition if pooling was continued. For Clayton, pooling was contrary to established League principles, whether its purpose was equality or survival:

> from the inception of the League there has never, until the war started, been any pooling of gates. When clubs have applied for membership of the League, they have always been asked about the support they can guarantee, financial or otherwise. Had they for any moment expressed the slightest doubt as to the support on which they could rely they would not have secured admission... Under these circumstances why should these clubs come to us now and ask for a proportion of our takings[?][51]

By January 1917, however, a series of extremely low gates led Bury to organise a conference of 'clubs with inadequate support' in Lancashire in an attempt to convince their wealthier rivals to agree to the re-introduction of gate-pooling. They failed, but the big three Lancastrian clubs did make voluntary contributions of £200 each into a fund administered by League President, John McKenna, to provide financial aid 'as occasion requires, to clubs in need'.[52] In the Midland section, Birmingham donated £100 while Rotherham County, Chesterfield, Sheffield Wednesday and Sheffield United gave £50 to a similar central fund for clubs 'in financial difficulties'.[53]

Despite this, the pressure to return to some form of pooling or division of gate money for the 1917–18 season mounted. Although the Sheffield clubs, among others, obstinately maintained that there 'should be no pooling whatever',[54] the poorer clubs were able to enlist the support of McKenna and other members of the executive to their cause. In fact, it was McKenna who devised a scheme for 20 per cent of the home club's net gate (including stand charges) to be paid to the visitors in the main competition, and for the same percentage to be pooled in the supplementary matches. While expressing 'his confirmed objection to pooling as a principle', Clayton accepted 'that the rich were consenting parties to the President's plan because it was wartime'; the Sheffield

United committee also assented to the scheme 'as a temporary arrangement'.[55]

Notwithstanding the self-help philosophy of Everton and others, the ideology of mutual support and cooperation was cemented as official League policy when the competition proper resumed after the war. This became evident, first of all, in the arrangement established by Sutcliffe to enable the doubling of players' expenses to £2 in January 1919. The League executive was convinced that only a handful of clubs could afford such an increase, but persuaded its members to accept a scheme whereby the ten best-supported clubs sent in weekly contributions to subsidise 17 of the 'needy clubs'.[56] According to Simon Inglis, this was 'the typical Sutcliffe formula: the rich helping the poor, to keep the family strong'.[57] Of greater significance was the insistence of Sutcliffe and others that the division of gate money should become both a permanent measure and, importantly, a visiting club's right rather than an act of benevolence on the part of the richer clubs. Sutcliffe certainly believed that 'the visiting team provided half the attraction. They do as much to draw the gate as the home team.'[58] When, in early 1920, a Birmingham director proposed the creation of a 'charitable pool' administered by the Management Committee instead of the 20 per cent pool to visitors, the idea was rejected outright. *Athletic News* summed up this change in attitude: 'Clubs do not ask for charity. Every team that visits Birmingham helps Birmingham to draw its gate, and it is the acknowledgement of this right that clubs ask for.'[59]

By the mid-1920s, the principle of gate-pooling had become enshrined as Football League policy. There was some pressure to abandon the system in 1923, but McKenna was adamant that 'they ought to see the industrial cloud raised before they took away that assistance which the poorer clubs were wanting'.[60] At the next annual meeting, the Management Committee formally proposed the continuation of the 20 per cent allocation to visiting sides and there was no concerted attempt to remove the rule during the remainder of the period. It may be that the richer clubs were prepared to put up with the system because they were paying out relatively small sums. The account books of Sheffield United, for example, show that the club rarely paid out or received a balance of more than £500 during the course of a season, and even a poorly-supported club like Oldham Athletic – which spent time in the First Division, Second Division and Third Division North between the wars – only made a profit of over £1,000 on the pool exchange once.[61] After dropping into the Third Division in 1923–24, Wolverhampton Wanderers could bemoan the fact that it had to send out cheques to visitors twice as large as it received in return, but such instances were rare, not least because pooling operated strictly within divisions and there was no attempt to redistribute income across the League as a whole.[62]

These limitations contributed to proposals in the early 1930s aimed at extending the scope of the pooling system. In both 1931 and 1932 Derby County attempted to have the 20 per cent increased to 40 per cent to help clubs suffering from reduced attendances as a result of industrial depression, and as a general means of 'levelling things up in more ways than one'.[63] The idea was greeted favourably in the sporting press. Ivan Sharpe of the *Sporting Chronicle* regarded the increase as 'a timely and reasonable procedure' entirely in keeping with the League's historical status as 'a brotherhood of clubs'.[64] Although the Derby President considered his proposal 'both democratic and fair', it was withdrawn in 1931 for technical reasons, and when put to the next annual meeting, Arsenal issued a counter-proposal to abolish pooling altogether. Doubtless in agreement with Derby's contention that the need for pooling was greater than ever, the Management Committee stepped in with a conciliatory resolution to preserve the 20 per cent pool.[65] In his *Topical Times* column the following year, Sutcliffe floated a more ambitious idea, reminiscent of the Lancashire wartime scheme, by which home clubs would pay their 20 per cent not to the away side but into a central pool to be distributed equally every month between each club in each division. Sutcliffe saw the scheme as an 'equitable adjustment' of a system that penalised clubs who were unable to draw good gates either at home or away: it 'would indeed be a mutual help society, and a practical instance of the rich helping the poor'.[66]

Although this idea was shelved, plans to extend pooling arrangements continued to find support among the associate members in the Third Division sections. As well as advocating the doubling of visitors' percentages in order to help out the 'poorer brethren' and keep the competitions going, both the Northern and Southern sections agreed to pool the expenses of match officials so as to reduce the burden on clubs like Plymouth Argyle and Carlisle United, which were geographically isolated.[67] Pooling was also fundamental to the working of the Third Division Cup competitions, which were created in 1933 primarily to generate extra funds, especially for clubs whose crowds fell drastically towards the end of each season. Gate receipts were pooled up to the semi-final stage and shared equally among competing clubs, although perpetually low crowds compromised the impact of this form of mutual aid.[68] In addition, clubs were always entitled to make individual pooling arrangements. This tended in practice to be restricted to local rivals of corresponding wealth and support. Aston Villa and West Bromwich Albion, for instance, agreed to pool receipts from their derby matches during the 1911–12 season, while Arsenal and West Ham United made similar arrangements in 1925–26. Rather surprisingly, given their close relations in most areas, the Sheffield clubs chose not to pool gates, but instead made sure that home fixtures on holiday dates were alternated each season.[69]

Pooling aside, there was no formal mechanism for subsidising financially weak clubs. No attempt was made to adapt the Relief Fund to peacetime conditions and, unlike in the Northern Rugby Union, financial assistance to clubs in need continued to be resisted during the economic slump of the early 1920s and the depression of the 1930s.[70] In general, the executive agreed with Clayton's view that each club should support itself financially, but cross-subsidisation could also take spontaneous forms, such as direct financial assistance via cash transfers between League members.[71] Appeal funds organised by clubs with money problems were a particular feature of the period before 1914. The Aston Villa minute books indicate that that club was among the keenest philanthropists, donating £50 to Wolves in 1901 and 20 guineas to Burslem Port Vale a year later, although similar appeals by Bolton and Leicester Fosse fell on deaf ears.[72] When Second Division West Bromwich Albion launched an appeal in early 1905, a local correspondent wrote that it was 'the duty of every wealthy club in the League to assist the Albion to turn the corner'. Villa had, by this point, already sent its neighbour a cheque for 100 guineas with the wish that 'your good old club once more places [itself] upon a sound footing financially'; Everton later donated 20 guineas, while Small Heath, which was unable to afford a donation, contributed its share of the Birmingham Senior Cup Final gate receipts.[73] Sheffield United, on the other hand, refused to fund Albion, a stance the committee maintained when faced with similar appeals from struggling clubs up to the 1930s.[74] In different ways, the actions of each of these clubs lent support to N. L. Jackson's assertion that 'only self-interest or self-preservation will persuade the richer clubs to devote a portion of their wealth to keeping their poorer brethren alive'.[75] Indeed, the apparent selflessness of Aston Villa undoubtedly betrayed a fundamental economic logic: matches against local rivals drew some of the highest crowds, and by subsidising Wolves and Albion, Villa was hoping to secure future financial rewards for itself.

Self-interest was certainly behind Arsenal's attempt in 1931 to help out its neighbour, Clapton Orient. The plan of the First Division champions to gain financial and administrative control over Orient and turn it into a nursery club for its young players was initially well received in certain quarters. Sutcliffe, who had for some time suggested that lowly clubs in a parlous financial state 'might well be helped out by neighbouring First and Second Division clubs to the mutual advantage of both', applauded Arsenal's actions in assisting Orient 'through its difficulties'. It was for him a perfect example of the responsibility of more fortunate clubs to 'stand godfather for the poor'.[76] However, his colleagues on the Management Committee were less sympathetic. They rejected Arsenal's proposal for the reconstruction of the bankrupt Orient club, and, with FA assistance, formulated a new scheme ensuring that the debts were paid off and the club was managed independently by its own board of directors.[77]

Clubs often helped to relieve the financial burdens of fellow members less directly by loaning players or money, staggering the payment of transfer bills or agreeing to play fund-raising matches. In 1910 Aston Villa, for example, was prepared to loan its neighbour Birmingham £250 while taking 'one or more' of Birmingham's players as a form of security until the loan was repaid.[78] Other clubs that were unable to afford large transfer fees were occasionally loaned players for short periods, or offered favourable terms, although such arrangements were again generally between those in the same city or district. In 1933, Manchesters City and United agreed to temporarily transfer some of their professionals free of charge to nearby Oldham Athletic in order to strengthen the latter's playing squad.[79] Later the same season, the Orient chairman F. W. Snewin issued an appeal to 'millionaire clubs, whether neighbours or otherwise, to play the Good Samaritan' by loaning players to the cash-strapped Third Division outfit. The manager Jimmy Seed distanced himself from the request by informing the press that not only was the club unable to pay any new players, but League regulations prevented their registration so late in the season. Two months later, however, Seed did agree to donate £50 to the Clapton Orient Trust Fund on behalf of his new employers, Charlton Athletic.[80] In cases where direct assistance was considered improper or impracticable, clubs often followed Small Heath's example in donating a proportion of gate receipts to struggling neighbours, or playing a friendly match for fund-raising purposes. In 1928 Burnley, for example, assisted Nelson by playing one of its prestigious close season ties against Scottish League opposition at the Third Division club's ground, and donating all the proceeds to the survival fund.[81]

'Friends and rivals': friendship, mutuality and the League spirit

Such examples of financial assistance between Football League members must also be interpreted in the context of the wider expressions of mutual support and friendship that permeated the private and public relationships between club officials and directors. In many ways, the equalisation policies themselves, and the language used by officials to justify and defend them, can be tied in with the philosophy and practice of the friendly societies of the eighteenth and nineteenth centuries.[82] Certainly the friendly society idea of pooling resources to protect all members of the group was popular among the League executive – if not with all its clubs – from the early part of the century, and the rhetoric of the rich and strong helping the poor and weak was a common feature of the public statements and newspaper columns of Sutcliffe, Bentley, McKenna and others. To this extent, Alan Tomlinson's metaphorical description of the Football League as a 'family and friendly society' driven by a 'philosophy of mutual protection' has some validity.[83] Yet the sentiments of friendship and mutuality that undeniably existed between clubs were rather more ambivalent than this suggests, and were never simply imposed on clubs from above.

In his account of an annual dinner of League managers and secretaries from the late 1930s, the FA councillor and former Secretary William Pickford noted the importance of sociability and fellowship:

> Here were gathered together in the old British fashion some hundreds of men who run the clubs, the sergeants, orderlies and corporals of the League, plus a mixture of officers i.e. directors and rank and file. It was the 'close season' and these henchmen of the game … were greeting each other like old friends, club rivalry temporarily suspended, slapping one another on the back and exchanging jokes and reminiscences… I really got a better idea of what the League meant than ever before during the many years in which I have watched the start and growth of that gigantic organisation.[84]

Peter Bailey has analysed the significance of similar occasions involving displays of friendship and its associated rhetoric in the business of music hall management during the late nineteenth century. The benefit night, in particular, developed partly as 'a great celebration of fraternal good feeling' at which rival proprietors could meet, renew long-standing friendships or reconcile differences.[85] In League football there were parallel social events after Cup or League successes, or to mark the anniversary of a club's foundation. Thus the West Ham directors attended a Jubilee dinner at Tottenham Hotspur in 1927 and celebratory dinners hosted by Arsenal in 1933 and 1934, as well as a banquet in 1935 following the north London club's third consecutive championship success.[86]

The language of friendship was also used in the letters of congratulation sent to the champions of each division, to the cup winners and even in the notes of condolence to relegated sides. Aston Villa's congratulatory message to Newcastle United following the Tyneside club's victory over Villa in the 1924 FA Cup Final had a heightened significance due to the fact that relations had been soured by Newcastle's decision to send out a weakened team for a League fixture at Villa Park on the Monday before the final tie. The Secretary of the cup winners wrote back to assure his counterpart that 'through no fault of Newcastle United will our friendly relations be severed', and that 'friendly feeling will only be more cemented through the courteous action of your Club'.[87] West Bromwich Albion included a public message to Stoke – at the time second from bottom of the First Division – in its official programme of 27 January 1923: 'Stoke have our sympathies – we are hoping to see them rise considerably in the League table, for Stoke and Albion have been friends and rivals for very many years, and we do not like to see any of our Staffordshire or local clubs in distress.'[88] Such expressions of friendship were clearly important in emphasising the close ties and relations between clubs that, as we have seen, were both sporting competitors and economic partners.[89] Friendship was also publicly displayed at times of bereavement: representatives of Liverpool, Blackburn Rovers, Manchester United, Oldham Athletic, Manchester City, Bury, Blackpool, Woolwich Arsenal and Fulham all attended the funeral in 1912 of Preston director and Management Committee member Tom Houghton, while five of these plus a further nine clubs sent wreaths. Similarly, in spite of the history of personal animosity between the two directorates, when Liverpool Chairman John Houlding died in 1905, the Everton players wore black armbands during their next fixture.[90]

Some local clubs developed even closer links through mutual arrangements, regular meetings of directorates and even joint policy decisions. Thus the major Birmingham and Black Country League clubs – Aston Villa, Wolves, Birmingham and West Bromwich Albion – established an agreement that all officials and players were to have entry to each other's ground if they wished on match days.[91] The Merseyside rivals went further by publishing a joint match programme called the 'Everton and Liverpool Official Football Programme', which lasted from 1904 until 1935.[92] Relations between Sheffield United and Wednesday were perhaps closer still. Not only did they share the same Chairman – FA president Charles Clegg – for most of the period, but they tended to take joint decisions on the questions of bonuses and wages, voted together at League meetings, and ensured that entrance fees and season ticket prices were uniform.[93] Hence Wednesday's decision in 1922 to depart from the mutual agreement on season ticket prices and reserve match admission brought forth immediate criticism from the United committee. The club's minute books indicate that it was unable to understand its neighbour's action in making such a change 'without instructing … us', and embarked on a series of negotiations to restore the status quo. Good relations were quickly resumed, and in 1932 the two clubs actually made enquiries into the possibility of joint United–Wednesday season tickets, although the idea was soon dropped as impracticable.[94]

The rhetoric of friendship, however, could not disguise occasional disagreements or the breakdown of club relations. When even neighbouring clubs came into conflict over issues like player transfers or compensation claims for rearranged fixtures the philosophy of mutual protection could appear illusory, while the language of friendship could be easily discarded. Aston Villa and Birmingham could not hide their ill-feeling towards each other during a dispute over fixture allocation in 1907. At Birmingham's annual meeting, W. W. Hart accused Villa of being inflexible in insisting that his club should not play on Christmas Day afternoon when Villa had a morning fixture; Fred Rinder countered by sarcastically referring to Hart as 'the man who wants peace'. The dispute moved a local journalist to ask if it was not 'too much to expect [the two clubs] to be neighbourly'.[95] Enduring friendships also depend on mutual trust, and this became an important element in inter-club relations, especially in cases where one club relied on the word of another regarding the character or fitness of a new player. In most instances, cooperation between clubs on matters of this kind ran smoothly. Aston Villa, for example, always wrote to the club that was releasing a player in whom it was interested in order to gain insights into his suitability. One letter to Sheffield United relating to its former goalkeeper Joe Mitchell read: 'As we know nothing of his ability or habits I am writing to you to find out all I can about him and whether you consider he would suit us.' It added that 'anything you care to say will be esteemed a favour and treated in strict confidence'.[96]

An interesting example of how this type of trust between clubs could break down is given by a prolonged dispute between Nottingham Forest and Sheffield United in 1911. The acrimony began when the Forest board accused certain United directors of misleading them 'both as to the ability and character' of Jack Smith, an ex-United player whom Forest had bought without seeing play and on the basis of the recommendation of his former employers. After United had denied Forest's claim, the latter club refused to pay the agreed transfer fee and the matter was taken to an FA Commission, which eventually ruled in favour of the Sheffield club. Relations became further embittered when the Forest secretary made public statements 'affecting the honour of the [United] directors', in response to which United demanded a formal withdrawal and apology. After months of public and private feuding, the Forest board eventually withdrew its accusations and paid Smith's fee.[97]

* * *

The record of the Football League in establishing a balanced and equal competition has been mixed. Szymanski and Kuypers have suggested that rather than developing in 'a highly cartelized form', English professional football has been characterised by a lack of cooperation, a failure to coordinate policies and a fragmentation into its constituent parts of club, league and association. 'Traditionally', they argue, 'the football authorities have shown little interest in maintaining a competitive balance and have done little to promote it actively'.[98] By contrast, Dobson and Goddard contend that regulations constraining player mobility and ensuring gate-pooling helped create 'an element of cross-subsidy (explicit or implicit), which has undoubtedly been crucial in ensuring the survival of many of the smaller clubs'.[99] During its first 50 years, the Football League enacted a series of measures – from the maximum wage, promotion and election and retain-and-transfer systems to the 20 per cent rule and other forms of income redistribution – which were justified, at least in part, as a way of ensuring that competition remained as close, and clubs as evenly matched, as possible. In this, it achieved some success. We have seen that no club or group of clubs dominated the championship in this period. In comparison with other major football leagues in Britain and with its counterparts in county cricket and northern rugby, the League was a relatively open and balanced competition. Even with the unprecedented success of Huddersfield Town and Arsenal between the wars, and the financial difficulties of the newly-founded Third Division, the League could still claim to represent a competition in which the big city and small town club, the strong and the weak, the rich and the poor were capable of vying each season for the major honours.

The question of equality was only partly a matter of economics. The central debate between those who extolled policies of mutual support and those who thought each club should look after itself was underpinned not so much by conflicting economic theory as by different understandings of what membership of a sporting league meant. Wealthier clubs were often prepared to accept policies that constrained their economic dominance and to give directly to their poorer brethren precisely because the existence of these clubs as competitive rivals remained vital to their own long-term financial security. In this sense, such philanthropy might have been essentially self-interested. However, there was also a fundamental sporting objective in assisting or supporting the weak. The League's policies of economic mutuality were not designed primarily to increase profits, individual or collective, but rather to ensure the viability of competing clubs within the context of a fair competition. As such, they need to be understood in light of the idea of collective self-help, which had led to the creation of the Football League in the first place. For Sutcliffe, the greatest test of good sportsmanship was the willingness 'to eliminate personal and individual considerations for the common good of the clubs forming the League'.[100] In spite of periodic resistance to such policies, most members ultimately recognised that clubbing together offered a better chance of financial and sporting success than standing alone.

Notes

1 J. A. Schofield, 'The Development of First-Class Cricket in England: An Economic Analysis', *Journal of Industrial Economics*, Vol. 30, 1982, p. 338.

2 Sloane, 'Restriction', p. 6. See also S. Dobson and J. Goddard, 'Performance, Revenue and Cross-Subsidization in the Football League, 1927–1994', *Economic History Review*, Vol. 51, 1998, pp. 763–85.

3 See S. Szymanski and T. Kuypers, *Winners and Losers: The Business Strategy of Football*, London, Penguin, 2000, pp. 277–80; P. J. Sloane, *Sport in the Market?*, London, Institute of Economic Affairs, 1980, pp. 25–26; J. Cairns, N. Jennett and P. J. Sloane, 'The Economics of Professional Team Sports: A Survey of Theory and Evidence', *Journal of Economic Studies*, Vol. 13, 1986, p. 17; J. Quirk and R. D. Fort, *Pay Dirt: The Business of Professional Team Sports*, Princeton, Princeton University Press, 1992, p. 243; Arnold, 'Rich Man', pp. 50–51; K. Sandiford and W. Vamplew, 'The Peculiar Economics of English Cricket Before 1914', *British Journal of Sports History*, Vol. 3, 1986, p. 314.

4 See Vamplew, *Pay Up*, Chapter 9 for the pre-First World War period.

5 Quirk and Fort, *Pay Dirt*, Chapter 7; Sloane, 'Restriction', p. 15.

6 See J. Quirk and M. El Hodiri, 'The Economic Theory of a Professional Sports

League' in *Government and the Sports Business*, ed. R. G. Noll, Washington, DC, The Brookings Institute, 1974, pp. 35–48; S. Dobson and J. Goddard, *The Economics of Football*, Cambridge, Cambridge University Press, 2001, pp. 129–30; Szymanski and Kuypers, *Winners and Losers*, pp. 268–70.

7 Arnold identifies an elite of ten clubs (based on reaching the top three or the FA Cup Final at least four times) in the period 1895–1915. In 1919–39, the elite included 11 clubs, six of which were new. See Arnold, 'Rich Man', pp. 58–59. For a similar analysis of competition dominance in the Football League, Dobson and Goddard, *Economics*, pp. 42–49.

8 Vamplew, *Pay Up*, Chapter 9.

9 M. E. Canes, 'The Social Benefits of Restrictions on Team Quality' in *Government and the Sports Business*, ed. R. G. Noll, Washington, DC, The Brookings Institute, 1974, pp. 85–92.

10 Sandiford and Vamplew, 'Peculiar Economics', pp. 314–17; Schofield, 'Development', pp. 341, 357; Vamplew, *Pay Up*, pp. 139–44, 148–51.

11 See especially various essays in R. G. Noll (ed.), *Government and the Sports Business*, Washington, DC, The Brookings Institute, 1974, pp. 85–92; R. G. Noll, 'Professional Basketball: Economic and Business Perspectives' in *The Business of Professional Sports*, ed. P. D. Staudohar and J. A. Mangan, Urbana, University of Illinois Press, 1991, pp. 18–47; Quirk and Fort, *Pay Dirt*, pp. 268–93; Sloane, 'Restriction', pp. 14–17.

12 H. F. Moorhouse, 'The Economic Effects of the Traditional Transfer System in European Professional Football', *Football Studies*, Vol. 2, 1999, p. 91.

13 The maximum wage probably had less impact in the Second Division as fewer clubs were able to pay £4 to players either before or after 1901 (see chapter 3).

14 Sloane, 'Restriction', p. 10.

15 It could be argued, however, that the 'closed shop' that developed in the Third Division Northern and Southern Sections for much of the inter-war period impeded the equalisation of competition, as consistently weak playing sides were generally not replaced by stronger clubs outside the League (see Chapter 1).

16 As Vamplew has noted, 'it is not calculated truths which determine a club's [or a League's] policy; what they believe to be true is far more significant'. Vamplew, *Pay Up*, p. 174.

17 A. J. Arnold and I. Benveniste, 'Cross-Subsidisation and Competition Policy in English Professional Football', *Journal of Industrial Affairs*, Vol. 15, 1988, p. 2; Noll, 'Professional Basketball', p. 36.

18 Sandiford and Vamplew, 'Peculiar Economics', p. 314; Sissons, *The Players*, pp. 85–89.

19 See AFC, Catton Folders, B–C, newspaper cutting, 13 January 1919, p. 196.

20 Vamplew, *Pay Up*, p. 148.

21 Quoted in Tischler, *Footballers*, p. 62.

22 Bassett, 'Big Transfers', p. 160.

23 *Athletic News*, 29 April 1901.

24 Bassett, 'Big Transfers', p. 160.

25 Quoted in Sheffield United FC Programme, 17 April 1920.

26 Green, *History*, pp. 409–10.

27 *Athletic News*, 13 November 1911.

28 See AFC, Catton Folders, A–B, Arsenal FC Directors' Report, 1924, p. 21.

29 Reports of Football League AGMs in *Athletic News*, 5 June 1922; 4 June 1923.

30 Report of FA AGM in *Athletic News*, 27 May 1901.
31 Report of FA AGM in *Athletic News*, 6 June 1904; Mason, *Association Football*, pp. 99–100.
32 *Football Chat*, 12 March 1907.
33 Report of FA AGM in *Athletic News*, 1 June 1908.
34 *Athletic News*, 4 March 1907.
35 *Athletic News*, 8 February 1909; report of FA AGM in *Athletic News*, 1 June 1908. The idea of equality having 'economic value' is taken from Vamplew, *Pay Up*, p. 174. The case of Wolves was particularly apt as it had won the FA Cup in 1908 as a Second Division side by beating reigning League champions Newcastle United in the final.
36 FA Council Minutes, 17 January 1910; *Athletic News*, 13 September 1909.
37 Sloane, 'Restriction', p. 17.
38 John Bentley, circular to Football League clubs, quoted in *Athletic News*, 11 June 1906.
39 *Athletic News*, 18 June, 2 July 1906.
40 Sutcliffe, Brierley and Howarth, *Story of the Football League*, pp. 3, 5.
41 Catton, *The Real Football*, p. 87; report of Football League AGM in *Athletic News*, 20 May 1901; Football League Minutes, Management Committee, 29 May 1908.
42 AFC, Catton Folders, E–F, James Catton, notes for a speech on 'The Football League', undated, p. 500c; McGregor, 'The Origin and Future', p. 5.
43 R. M. Connell, 'The Scottish Football League and its History' in *Book of Football*, ed. anon, London, The Amalgamated Press, 1906, p. 267.
44 Report of Football League AGM in *Athletic News*, 10 May 1901.
45 S. Inglis, *The Football Grounds of Great Britain*, London, Collins Willow, 1987, p. 214.
46 *Athletic News*, 7 August 1916.
47 Sutcliffe, Brierley and Howarth, *Story of the Football League*, pp. 85–86; Inglis, *League Football*, p. 95.
48 Sutcliffe, Brierley and Howarth, *Story of the Football League*, p. 83. This rhetorical solidarity could at times appear flimsy given the behaviour of clubs like Derby County, which was forced by the committee to pay back a sum of £350 received from the Relief Fund when it had actually made a profit that year of over £500. SUFC, Football Committee Minutes, 28 June 1915; Report of Football League AGM in *Athletic News*, 26 July 1915.
49 *Athletic News*, 21 February, 17 January 1916.
50 *Athletic News*, 12 June, 29 May 1916.
51 *Athletic News*, 7 August 1916.
52 *Athletic News*, 1, 15, 22 January 1917.
53 SUFC, Football Committee Minutes, 14 February 1917.
54 SUFC, Football Committee Minutes, 14 March 1917.
55 Report of Football League AGM in *Athletic News*, 17 July 1917; SUFC, Football Committee Minutes, 25 June 1917. Nottingham Forest's more radical plan for one common pool for both sections was rejected by the Lancashire members, who professed themselves unprepared to extend financial aid to the Midland clubs.
56 Report of Football League SGM in *Athletic News*, 20 January 1919.
57 Inglis, *League Football*, p. 112.
58 *Athletic News*, 13 January 1919.
59 *Athletic News*, 22 March 1920. At the same time, however, the visitors' share of the

gate was modified so that the 20 per cent applied only to the ninepence basic admission fee for each spectator, and not to the stand and enclosure receipts as had operated previously, a move aimed to pacify those clubs who had spent heavily on stand accommodation. This came as a major blow to clubs like Bury, who estimated that they were only likely to draw £150 per season from the new system, compared with the £750 received the previous season. Home clubs were subsequently required to pay a small fee (initially one pence) per head for all season tickets issued. Sheffield United FC Programme, 3 April 1920.

60 Football League Minutes, 28 May 1923 (AGM).

61 SUFC, Revenue Accounts Book, 1900–39; OAFC, Ledger, 1921/22–1938/39; Szymanski and Kuypers, *Winners and Losers*, pp. 265–66.

62 Woverhampton Wanderers FC Programme, 6 October 1923.

63 *Athletic News*, 25 May 1931.

64 *Sporting Chronicle*, 6 June 1932.

65 Football League Minutes, 1 June 1931 (AGM); *Topical Times*, 11 June 1932; report of Football League AGM in *Sporting Chronicle*, 7 June 1932.

66 *Topical Times*, 13 May 1933.

67 Sheffield United FC Programme, 5 March 1932; Football League Minutes (Third Division Southern Section), 26 March 1923; Football League Minutes, 8 June 1925 (AGM).

68 On the Third Division Cups, see *Sporting Chronicle*, 6 June 1932; report of Football League AGM in *Sporting Chronicle*, 30 May 1933; *Topical Times*, 3 February 1934; Inglis, *League Football*, pp. 141, 426.

69 WHUFC, Board Minutes, 9 June 1925; SUFC, Football Committee Minutes, 1 September 1926; *Athletic News*, 3 July 1911.

70 Moorhouse, *A People's Game*, p. 179.

71 See Arnold and Benveniste, 'Cross-Subsidisation', p. 15.

72 AVFC, Board Minutes, 18 May 1900; 14 March, 9 May 1901; 26 March 1902.

73 AVFC, 1905 File (uncatalogued), George Ramsay to West Bromwich Albion directors, 2 February 1905; *Athletic News*, 13 February 1905.

74 SUFC, Football Committee Minutes, 7 February 1905; 24 September 1913 (appeal by Bury FC); 15 June 1936 (appeal by Notts County).

75 Quoted in Tischler, *Footballers*, p. 65.

76 *Topical Times*, 21 March, 10 October 1931.

77 Football League Minutes, Management Committee, 24 August, 14 December 1931; 11 January 1932; FA Emergency Committee Minutes, 17 March–16 April 1931; Seed, *Jimmy Seed Story*.

78 AVFC, Board Minutes, 8 February, 15 February, 1 March 1910.

79 *Sporting Chronicle*, 30 March 1933; *Topical Times*, 29 April 1933.

80 *Sporting Chronicle*, 29 March, 30 March, 27 May 1933.

81 *Topical Times*, 10 March 1928.

82 See E. P. Thompson, *The Making of the English Working Class*, London, Penguin, 1968; E. Hopkins, *Working-Class Self-Help in Nineteenth-Century England*, London, Macmillan, 1995; Morris, 'Clubs', pp. 416–17; Clark, *British Clubs*, Chapter 10; D. M. MacRaild and D. E. Martin, *Labour in British Society, 1830–1914*, Basingstoke, Macmillan, 2000, pp. 125–30.

83 A. Tomlinson, 'North and South: The Rivalry of the Football League and the Football Association' in *British Football and Social Change: Getting into Europe*, ed. J. Williams and S. Wagg, Leicester, Leicester University Press, 1991, pp. 35, 38.

84 Pickford, *A Glance Back*, p. 52.
85 Bailey, 'A Community of Friends', p. 43.
86 WHUFC, Board Minutes, 31 May 1927; 2 May 1933; 24 April 1934; 29 April 1935.
87 AVFC, letter from Newcastle United FC to George Ramsay, 1 May 1924.
88 *Albion News*, 27 January 1923.
89 Vamplew, *Pay Up*, p. 112.
90 Tom Houghton's obituary in *Preston Guardian*, 21 September 1921; Mason, *Blues and Reds*, p. 18.
91 AVFC, Board Minutes, 6 September 1910.
92 Mason, *Blues and Reds*, p. 18.
93 SUFC, Football Committee Minutes, 9 September 1908; 20 August 1912; 3 June 1919; 1 July 1932.
94 SUFC, Football Committee Minutes, 16 August, 13 September 1923; 23 November 1932.
95 *Athletic News*, 10 June 1907.
96 AVFC, 52/82, letter from George Ramsay to J. Nicholson, 13 June 1919. There is no record of Sheffield United's reply, but we do know that Mitchell was passed over by Aston Villa and instead joined South Shields.
97 SUFC, Football Committee Minutes, 4 April, 26 April, 2 June, 6 June 1911.
98 Szymanski and Kuypers, *Winners and Losers*, p. 250.
99 Dobson and Goddard, 'Performance', p. 782.
100 *Athletic News*, 18 October 1920.

CHAPTER SIX

Away from Home: The League and International Football

Although the Football League defined itself from the beginning as a self-contained, inward-looking and 'a frankly selfish organisation',[1] its very success spawned imitators in other countries and necessitated the development of international relationships. Before 1914 these were generally restricted to the home countries of Britain, especially Scotland and Ireland, whose leagues were both established in 1890. In the inter-war period, however, the growing international popularity of the game led to the creation of regional and national competitions based on the league model throughout Europe, South and North America. The influence of English (as well as Scottish) teams, players and coaches was undoubtedly central to these developments. Nevertheless, the English football authorities themselves have been portrayed as aloof and marginal in this respect, paying little attention to the continental game and establishing only intermittent contact with international bodies. In his history of British football, James Walvin described the years from 1915 to 1939 as the era of 'the insular game'.[2] The Football League, in many ways, exemplified this insularity. While it developed a formal dialogue, as well as administrative links, with other British associations and leagues, it made no such contacts outside Britain and did little to encourage its members to do so. The Management Committee tended to regard international football as an irrelevance at best, and to perceive non-British clubs and associations in the first instance as rivals rather than friends, posing a potential threat to the League and its players.

This chapter is not concerned solely with the Football League's international relations at a formal, administrative level. In the context of the FA's self-imposed exclusion from the Fédération Internationale de Football Association (FIFA) before 1905, between 1919 and 1924 and then again from 1928 until the Second World War, Football League clubs were obliged to develop their own contacts and form individual networks of relationships on the international stage. This was facilitated through the practice of close-season club tours to the continent and sometimes beyond, and was increasingly complemented between the wars by the staging of international club and representative fixtures on home soil. It was the issue of labour migration, however, which remained the primary concern of the League and its clubs throughout this period, and shaped their perceptions of the international game. The flow of football talent from the other nations of the United Kingdom to English clubs had been a distinctive feature of the game prior to the creation of the Football League, and Scottish players, in particular, became overrepresented at many League clubs even before the turn of the century. While the movement of football labour within the United Kingdom tended to be a one-way flow towards England, the process was reversed as professional leagues developed outside Britain from the 1920s onwards. The loss of registered players to the emerging leagues in the USA during the 1920s and France in the 1930s became a highly contentious issue among club and League officials, mainly because no agreement or transfer payment was necessary. In this way, international developments threatened to undermine the Football League's control over its labour force and compromise its much-vaunted autonomy.

The League and British 'international' football

Association football in the late nineteenth and early twentieth centuries was emphatically not a purely English product, even if the administrative structures of the game developed there first. The structural anomaly of four separate associations and three individual (and nominally national) leagues within a single political state has naturally led most students of the game to adopt a type of 'four nations' approach and to reject as misleading the very concept of *British* football.[3] Yet it is noteworthy that in football's rudimentary stage, prior to the League's formation in 1888, associations and competitions in Britain were not separated according to national boundaries. From its formation in 1863, the FA regarded itself as much more than an English national body. In the same way as colonial clubs and associations were incorporated, the FA allowed Scottish, Welsh and Irish clubs to affiliate, a situation which led in 1881 to a firm rejection of the proposal to rename it 'The English Association'. Non-English clubs were also included in early FA Cup competitions. Scotland's premier club, Queen's Park, entered the inaugural 1871 edition and Scottish clubs continued to participate until

1887, while Irish clubs withdrew only after the creation of their own league in 1890. Welsh clubs, by contrast, continued to enter English competitions and were even awarded a direct seat on the FA Council up until the late 1880s.[4]

The Football League was likewise never conceived by its founding fathers as a national and a strictly English competition. The absence of the epithet 'English' in its title is instructive in this respect, as it indicated the League's willingness to include non-English, particularly Scottish and Welsh, members. The creation of the Scottish Football League in 1890 precluded the entry of clubs north of the border, but for Welsh clubs there was no national league to divert their attention and many continued to look towards English competition. For clubs from the larger towns and cities in the principality this initially involved membership of the Southern League. However, with the League's expansion after the First World War, Cardiff City were elected to the Second Division while Merthyr, Newport, Swansea Town and Wrexham became associate members in the new Third Division sections.[5] In 1921 the Management Committee was forced to insist 'that it was time their clubs ceased advertising matches as English League matches' and accepted the competition's multinational identity.[6] The national constituency of these leagues remained fluid enough to encourage Newcastle United to volunteer the inclusion of its reserve team along with another English club, Berwick Rangers, when two members withdrew from the Second Division of the Scottish League during the 1932–33 season.[7] What is more, the earliest League teams were composed of a mixture of indigenous talent and players from the other British nations. Clubs from Lancashire, the North-east and the Midlands were engaging Scots in considerable numbers throughout the 1880s and 1890s, and the most successful teams in the first decade of the League championship – Preston's 'Invincibles' of the 1888–89 and 1889–90 seasons, Aston Villa's double winners of 1896–97 and Sunderland's 'Team of All the Talents', which lasted from 1889 to 1898 – invariably included at least three or four non-English members.[8]

The establishment of administrative relations

The Football League's recognition of its counterparts north of the border and across the Irish Sea was marked initially by the arrangement of Inter-League fixtures. The first in this series of annual games, against the Scottish League, took place at Bolton in 1892, and by 1894 the Irish League had also been granted a match. Such fixtures came to serve a dual function: they consolidated good relations between the competing bodies, and generated additional income for administrative purposes. As Inter-League matches developed in the twentieth century into major sporting events, they also acquired important social and ritual dimensions. They became a means of acknowledging the administrative links and mutuality between the different leagues, with the arrangement of joint meetings and even luncheons to which representatives of clubs and the relevant national associations were invited.[9] Nonetheless, the Inter-League fixture was primarily a money-making venture. During the 1890s and well into the twentieth century, the receipts from Inter-League matches constituted the major source of Football League income; for the Scottish and Irish Leagues, they were indispensable in financial terms. Attendances were always higher when the fixture was held in Scotland, establishing it as probably 'the second most important game in the football calendar' north of the border, surpassed only by the England–Scotland international itself.[10]

Inter-League matches aside, during the 1890s the Football League's relations with other British leagues remained unresolved and in a state of flux. The constant movement of players between the English and Scottish leagues created considerable difficulties, especially when a particular player was registered by a club in each country. These problems were partially resolved in 1897 when the two leagues agreed to 'the mutual recognition of players' registrations and clubs' rights in players'.[11] For the Scottish League secretary William Wilton, the agreement meant 'the practical amalgamation of two Leagues, involving 56 clubs and almost 2,700 players'.[12] At the same time, the International Football League Board (popularly known as the Inter-League Board) was founded with the objective of settling disputes and coordinating joint policy. The Board's constitution allowed for an equal representation of four officials nominated by each league, while the presidency was to alternate between England and Scotland on an annual basis.[13] Agreement with the Irish League, always a more detached and antagonistic body in the mind of Football League officials, was slower to arrive. Following the agreements over player registration with the Scottish and Southern Leagues (in 1910), increasing numbers of both disengaged and retained players crossed the Irish Sea. Belfast, in particular, became known as 'a city of refuge for discontented footballers'.[14] So in 1914, with the intention of closing the Irish door, an Anglo–Irish Football League Board was established on the Scottish model, incorporating the same recognition of club registration and transfer rights.[15] As spokesman for the Management Committee, Charles Sutcliffe explained that the objective was:

> to protect their clubs against the migration of players who had been offered reasonable terms...It would prevent players holding a gun to their heads. They may have occasion to suspend players, and the latter, in such circumstances, had no right to leave the country, play for clubs in Ireland, and then return when their suspension was at an end. Under the agreement this would be stopped... The agreement would put an end to the friction [between the two leagues] which had existed.[16]

There was, as we have seen, no equivalent Welsh senior national league, although regional leagues comprising clubs from North and South Wales respectively emerged as early as 1890. A Welsh Football League was in fact formed in 1912, and it soon made tentative requests to establish a working relationship with the Football League. Yet, possibly due to its minor status and the limited interaction of its labour force with those of League clubs, the formal agreements and consultation machinery arranged with the Scottish and Irish bodies were not to be repeated in the Welsh case. There is no indication that the League Management Committee even debated the Welsh League's 1920 proposals to arrange Inter-League fixtures and allow the automatic promotion of its two leading clubs into the newly-founded Third Division.[17]

Controlling the import and export of players

Illegal poaching and the consequent administrative tensions did not cease with the creation of the Inter-League boards. Despite the 1914 agreement, the major threat to the Football League's control over its labour force continued to come from Ireland. The modified wartime regulations operative from July 1915 accentuated these problems, as players were partially freed to turn out for a club other than their own. In these cases, however, they were obliged either to join a club close to their residence or work, or to seek permission from their contracted club to play elsewhere.[18] Difficulties soon arose when Irish clubs, particularly the newly-formed Belfast United, began to sign Football League players without the agreement of their clubs. The League believed that one such player, Manchester United's George Anderson, had been induced to move overseas with the promise of accommodation and a job from the Belfast club, and this at a time when professionalism was outlawed. Another former professional from Birmingham wrote anonymously to the President of the League, the FA and sections of the press informing them that he had been engaged for a season as a professional in Belfast under a pseudonym, and challenging them to uncover his identity.[19] In August 1916 the Irish FA finally suspended Belfast United when another League player, Grimsby Town's Tom McKenna, was revealed to have been operating as a professional under the name 'McGuiness'. In response, the Football League banned its professionals indefinitely from playing in Ireland and the Irish FA, incensed by the hypocrisy of the English, accused Manchester United of signing a registered Linfield player, and insisted in future on sanctioning the movement of all Irish players to English clubs.[20] Although the veto was soon rescinded, the two bodies clashed again in 1920 over Crystal Palace's signing of Robert McCracken from Distillery of Belfast. The League argued that as Palace had not been a member of the Football League when it engaged McCracken the previous June (and that, even then, as a Third Division club it was an associate rather than a full member), the club was not bound by the Anglo–Irish agreement to respect the registration of players. Significantly, the Irish representatives rejected not only the League's argument but also its supporting evidence, and sought to refer the matter to the Scottish League for an independent judgement. This action was regarded as an 'unwarranted attack' in Preston, the Management Committee announcing that it would 'have no further negotiations with an organisation which declines to accept the truth and accuracy of official documents, but challenges them as if they were forgeries and fraudulent'.[21] For one observer, the open hostility of the McCracken case signalled that the 'two Leagues have virtually severed their friendly relations'.[22]

Contact between the two bodies was resumed when the Irish League eventually accepted the position of the Football League's new associate members, but the situation was complicated further with political partition in 1922 and the creation of an Irish Free State in the South. Ireland now had two separate football associations, and those clubs incorporated within the new Football Association of Ireland (FAI) and the League of Ireland were no longer covered by the Anglo–Irish agreement.[23] A potential 'open door' had thus been created for discontented League players otherwise constrained by the Scottish and Irish settlements. As the conditions and wages of many League professionals deteriorated during the Depression, so Free State clubs took the opportunity to reverse the migratory trend by raiding their English counterparts. During the summer of 1931 alone, for example, Leicester's Albert Harrison and Burnley's Irish international Andrew McCluggage both joined Dundalk, while the Sheffield United centre-back Vincent Matthews signed for Shamrock Rovers. While McCluggage regretted leaving an employer that had treated him well, he was adamant that the poor terms offered 'make it impossible to stay any longer'.[24] Such decisions impelled *Athletic News* to proclaim the Irish 'open door' as 'a menace, particularly to English clubs who have paid big sums of money for the transfer of players, and then find they have little control over them at the end of the season'. It went on to advocate that players who refused 'reasonable' terms with their employer and signed for an Irish Free State club should be prohibited from returning to League football.[25] Proposals of this type proved untenable, but the Football League remained hostile to League of Ireland clubs, refusing to recognise player registrations or even to organise representative fixtures until after the Second World War.[26]

Even though Football League squads had always contained a mix of nationalities, the importation of non-English professionals became an increasingly contentious issue. Even if the numbers increased over the period, the overall percentage of non-English players engaged by League clubs stayed remarkably consistent, at 22.6 per cent in 1910 and 22.5 per cent in 1925 (Tables 6.1 and 6.2). Nevertheless, many clubs were genuinely British in their recruitment campaigns.[27] Few were as cosmopolitan as Leeds City, whose squad for the 1911–12 campaign contained 11 Irish footballers, two Scots, two Welshmen and only two native Englishmen. Seven of the Irish contingent had been recruited from Belfast and Dublin that summer, and three came directly from cup-winners Shelbourne. Other clubs such as Preston North End, Sunderland, Newcastle United and Chelsea established traditions for hiring Scotsmen on a regular basis.[28] The most consistently multinational workforce of all was probably that of Arsenal, which in 1925–26 included seven Scots, two Irishmen and one Welshmen; Liverpool went a step further at the beginning of the 1934–35 season by fielding a team containing just two Englishmen. One journalist referred to the Merseysiders as 'the League of Nations club'.[29] On the other hand, whether motivated by financial or ideological concerns, certain clubs undoubtedly preferred to stick to English products. We saw in Chapter 3 that Black Country rivals West Bromwich Albion and Wolverhampton Wanderers, for instance, rarely had more than one or two non-English players on their books, while Sheffield United's 1925 FA Cup-winning side was entirely English, with the exception of its Irish captain, Billy Gillespie.[30]

The role of Scottish players in the Football League was particularly significant. As Tables 6.1 and 6.2 show, in 1910 Scots accounted for 168 of the 870 players in the Football League, a figure which had risen to 302 in four divisions by 1925. The Scottish presence especially was felt in

Table 6.1: Nationality of Football League players, 1910

*Nationality**	*First Division* No. (%)	*Second Division* No. (%)	*Total* No. (%)
English	382 (72.5)	291 (84.8)	673 (77.4)
Scottish	124 (23.5)	44 (12.8)	168 (19.3)
Welsh	11 (2.1)	4 (1.2)	15 (1.7)
Irish	7 (1.3)	2 (0.6)	9 (1)
Non-British	3 (0.6)	2 (0.6)	5 (0.6)
Total number traced	527	343	870

*Birthplace.
Source: Adapted from Vamplew, *Pay Up*, Table 13.1, p. 205.

Table 6.2: Nationality of Football League players, 1925

*Nationality**	*First Division* No. (%)	*Second Division* No. (%)	*Third Division (South)* No. (%)	*Third Division (North)* No. (%)	*Total* No. (%)
English	379 (74.9)	404 (76.4)	341 (75.6)	387 (83.6)	1,511 (77.5)
Scottish	82 (16.2)	96 (18.1)	74 (16.4)	50 (10.8)	302 (15.5)
Welsh	25 (4.9)	22 (4.2)	25 (5.6)	18 (3.9)	90 (4.6)
Irish**	16 (3.2)	5 (0.9)	10 (2.2)	7 (1.5)	38 (2)
Non-British	4 (0.8)	2 (0.4)	1 (0.2)	1 (0.2)	8 (0.4)
Total number traced	506	529	451	463	1,949

*Birthplace.
**Including Irish Free State nationals.
Source: Athletic News, 3 August, 10 August, 17 August, 24 August 1925.

qualitative as well as quantitative terms. One commentator noted towards the end of 1926 that at least 70 'front rank players' (presumably meaning those with international or representative experience) and many more with emerging reputations had journeyed south since the First World War. Two years later the famous Scottish team that beat England 5–1 at Wembley was dominated for the first time by Anglo-Scots, with only three 'home' players chosen.[31] The 1920s witnessed a salient trend towards the acquisition of Scottish players, often for large transfer fees. Four of the 'all-tartan' (entirely home-based) Scottish side that met England in 1925 had by 1926 been sold to League clubs for fees of between £4,500 and £5,000.[32] This activity, however, provoked a backlash among some Football League officials and club directors who wished to restrict the number of Scottish imports. In a series of newspaper articles written at the beginning of 1928, Charles Sutcliffe outlined a scheme to impose a £1,000 tax on each transfer from Scottish

League to Football League clubs, with a reduced tax when players were acquired from Scottish junior clubs. The fund thus created by this taxing system could be used to aid the parlous finances of Third Division members. In this way, Sutcliffe argued, the leading clubs would be persuaded 'to turn their attention to the English players on their doorstep, and the English clubs needing help and encouragement'. In addition, he raised the possibility of limiting the number of non-English professionals registered by Football League clubs, though the idea of prohibiting Scots from competing in FA Cup competition was firmly rejected.[33] In the event, no such limitation was imposed and by 1929 the Scottish element in the League had reached its inter-war peak of 362.[34] Whether or not Scottish players subsequently fell out of favour with English directors, as Sutcliffe claimed in 1933, there is little doubt that Scotland continued to represent the 'great football emporium' for League recruiters up until, and indeed beyond, the Second World War.[35]

Club versus country: the League and the British national associations

The hegemony of the Football League within British football was most clearly demonstrated in its relations with the national associations and the whole debate involving the release of players for international fixtures. At the centre of this debate were the competing claims to the player's services of the club who employed him and the national association to which he was registered. Both assumed an effective ownership over labour, but increasingly it was the League and its clubs that came to dictate which players could be released, and even when international fixtures could take place within the football calendar.

The origins of the debate can be located in the 1890s with the growing status of Football League clubs and their ability to attract the best Scottish, Welsh and Irish talent. Between 1890 and 1899, they contributed almost half of the players in the Welsh national team and smaller proportions of the Irish (1.2 per cent) and Scottish (4.6 per cent) national teams. Hence, the English body was implicated in the organisation of international matches almost from its foundation.[36] Teams selected by these national associations for representative and trial matches – especially in the International Championship involving the four home nations – were open to the influence of Football League clubs, which were often not prepared to release players from important League fixtures on the same day. The Scottish FA responded in 1898 by recommending to the International Board comprising all four British associations that a player should be placed 'directly under the jurisdiction of the Association selecting him' while the FA of Wales claimed 'the right … to call on Welsh players with English clubs'.[37] Both proposals were checked by the FA, as was a similar joint Welsh–Scottish suggestion the following year that would additionally have enabled the selecting association to cross national boundaries of jurisdiction by punishing those clubs or players from other associations who failed to comply. The four associations instead constructed a less rigid agreement proclaiming that each should 'use their influence with Clubs to ensure to other National Associations the service of Players in International Matches'.[38]

While the FA of Wales, and increasingly the money-strapped Irish FA too, made habitual efforts to persuade its more powerful sister organisations to ensure the service of selected players, the League began to take steps to make sure that its programme remained free from the disruption of international and representative fixtures. In 1911 the Management Committee was instructed to arrange Inter-League matches – and to ask the FA to play all international games – on weekdays rather than the customary Saturdays. The proposal's sponsor, Tom Harris of Notts County, argued that international calls on players often had 'a very prejudicial effect' on League fixtures, while the playing of representative matches on a Saturday also prevented those clubs with town or city rivals from staging such fixtures.[39] Though Inter-League matches were henceforth often moved to midweek, the national associations were less willing to allow the Football League to intervene in their schedules, and so the antagonism between League clubs and the minor British associations continued to build. In 1921 the Irish FA accentuated the existing tensions by unilaterally inserting a clause in the registration agreement of every Irishman moving across the Irish Sea, allowing it to appropriate the player's services whenever required. The Management Committee publicly opposed this initiative, though as the registration of players was technically beyond its jurisdiction it was left to the FA and the Scottish FA to force their Irish counterpart to back down.[40]

By the late 1920s, the increased number of British internationals playing in the Football League had rendered the existing arrangements untenable for England's elite professional clubs and football authorities. Over the course of that decade, as many as 62.2 per cent of Irish, 58.5 per cent of Welsh and 27.4 per cent of Scottish international caps were awarded to employees of English League clubs.[41] In a letter to the Irish FA written in February 1929, the FA agreed that the next England–Ireland fixture should be played on a Saturday but intimated that 'in view of the many complaints from Clubs of being deprived of the services of players in important matches' it would have to reconsider in the future.[42] The Irish body rebuffed this suggestion on the grounds that 'it was extremely unwise, and against the interests of the game all over the Country [Ireland], to relegate International Matches to a subsidiary position'.[43] Meanwhile, Arsenal had issued a circular to each national association advocating that all international fixtures should be played midweek. Arsenal could by now count on the backing of some 45 League members as well as the Management Committee, which – while proclaiming the loyalty of its clubs to their respective governing bodies – was nonetheless determined to see that each national association selected players strictly from within its own jurisdiction.[44] Thus, at the next annual meeting, the Management Committee altered its rules so that 'A Club shall not release any player for International games on the day on which it has a League fixture, except at the call of the National Association of which the Club is a member.' The decision was not unanimous, however, as ten members voted against this interference in the international sphere, and a twin proposal to change the FA's rules by prohibiting Saturday and holiday internationals was withdrawn. One opponent, Derby's W. Bendle Moore, described the rule change as 'a retrograde step' and appealed to fellow members 'to consider the matter from the standpoint of the game and not the League position of Clubs'.[45]

The impact of the Football League's decision on the selection of Welsh and Irish teams was particularly significant, as they now had to pick mainly from players engaged in their own less competitive leagues and tournaments. The Welsh elevens that took the field against Scotland in October 1930 and England in November included a number of inexperienced footballers drawn from minor organisations such as Cardiff Corinthians, Colwyn Bay, Llanelli, Nunhead and Oswestry Town alongside those with the Welsh Football League clubs. By that time the FA had been informed of 'the serious plight in which the FA of Wales has been placed by the recent action of the Football League', and was asked to organise a conference with the League and the four national associations so as to reach a compromise 'in a final effort to save the International Tournament'.[46] In January 1931 the League drafted a new set of proposals, which were accepted unanimously by the associations as 'a satisfactory solution to the International question'. The agreement consisted of three basic requirements for the release of players. First, Saturday fixtures were accepted so long as they took place before 14 December each season, with the exception of the customary end-of-season England–Scotland match. Second, the national associations were to apply to the executive 21 days in advance to obtain League players, and even then the clubs were at liberty to refuse permission. Finally, a recognised insurance policy was to be taken out on each registered League player by the national association, which, in addition, was to pay his weekly wage if the match took place on a Saturday.[47] While the concession of Saturday internationals generated opposition from some clubs, which regarded it as representing a significant disruption of the League programme, the agreement was nevertheless widely recognised as a clear sign of the Football League's dominating influence over British football as a whole.[48]

In practice, however, the agreement offered no permanent solution, as the discretionary release of players continued to cause friction between the League and the national associations. League clubs had always been entitled to block the release of players, but before 1914 few were prepared to disrupt the primacy of home internationals for purely selfish club purposes. The 1920s, in contrast, witnessed a significant change in club directors' perception of the status of internationals vis-à-vis the League programme. Clubs with hopes of winning the championship or gaining promotion or, conversely, those in danger of relegation, regularly pulled their employees out of international squads. Where fixtures clashed many clubs claimed to allow the player to choose between club and country, but there is plentiful evidence to suggest that this was not an altogether free choice. It may not be a coincidence, for instance, that West Ham United's Welsh international Dick Richards opted to assist his club rather than his country during its promotion campaign in March 1923, or that in the midst of relegation worries Billy Gillespie 'preferred to play for [Sheffield] United and not in the International match' for Ireland scheduled for the same day.[49] The pressures to decide in favour of the employer were undoubtedly pervasive. Harry Duggan was certainly not the only player to refuse an international cap 'because, having got his place in the [Leeds] first team, he was not prepared to risk losing it'.[50] We know that Alex James was pressurised by the Preston North End directors on a number of occasions to chose club over country: when Scotland's match with Ireland in February 1928 clashed with a vital Second Division game against Manchester City, he reportedly left 'his' decision in the hands of the directors, who predictably elected to keep him.[51] The Huddersfield Town directors were more candid than most when, in response to a request to release their forward Bill Hayes for a match against Hungary, they informed the FA of Ireland that 'we should do all in our power to help … but it would depend entirely on our [League] position'.[52] Despite these examples, it was rare for players to admit that their employers precluded them from representing their country, as the Irishman Billy Halligan did of his manager Scott Walford at Leeds City in 1910. Sutcliffe stopped short of revealing whether it was the Management Committee, the club or the player who made the final decision, but was prepared to disclose that the rights of the 'master' were at least as important in this matter as those of the 'servant'.[53]

It is clear, then, that by the late 1920s and early 1930s the Football League exercised an effective veto over international selection, with the notable exception of the England team. In March 1930 the Management Committee took the step of explicitly outlawing those club agreements which gave the player 'the right to elect to play in International games'.[54] Players hoping to establish international careers were thus forced to rely entirely on the benevolence of their board of directors. Those whose clubs ruled them out of regular international duty, including James at Preston and Irishman Jimmy Dunne at Sheffield United, often attempted to find themselves employers that were more committed to international football, or else had a squad strong enough to deal with such absences.[55]

In view of this general reluctance to release players, it is hardly surprising that the agreement of January 1931 was short-lived. In April 1932, the FA of Wales informed the League and its sister associations of its decision to break from the agreement because of the 'unjust manner' in which it had been carried out.[56] According to a *Sporting Chronicle* reporter, it was well known that the existing arrangement 'has no friends either in Scotland, Ireland or Wales'. The circumstances surrounding the Scotland–Ireland encounter in Glasgow the previous September had clearly aggravated this sense of disquiet, with rumours circulating that the Management Committee put 'very considerable pressure' on Cardiff City, Leeds United and Sheffield United to prevent Tom Farquharson, Duggan and Dunne respectively from representing the visitors; suggestions were also made that League policy precluded the release of more than one player from any member club.[57] A recent historian of Scottish football captured this mood of frustration when he noted that while 'Anglo-Scots were usually released … the record of English clubs in so far as Irish and Welsh players were concerned was nothing short of disgraceful'.[58] The Management Committee, in response, defended the action of its members, arguing in the face of considerable evidence that international releases had in fact been 'liberally given'.[59]

The Welsh body was persuaded before the summer meetings to withdraw its initial complaint by an assurance from the English authorities of a more open policy to the release of players, but the disagreements over the international tournament were far from resolved.[60] Indeed, by 1934 the central issue of midweek matches had surfaced again, and in the course of a series of conferences with the four associations at the beginning of that year, the will of the Football League and its leading clubs finally won through. Significantly, both the FA and the Scottish FA had become convinced that Saturday matches throughout the season were now an impracticality, and the latter body issued its own scheme for all internationals, except England–Scotland, to be played during the week. In a summary report to the FA Council, Vice-President William Pickford lucidly identified the League's principal objections to the existing arrangements:

> Their contention is that their commitments are too serious to permit them to supply, particularly Wales and Ireland, with the bulk of their players for Saturday International Matches. Both these Associations make heavy demands on their nationals playing in England. If all International games were played on Saturdays the League clubs would, if compelled to release players, provide an average of 40 players for Scotland, Wales and Ireland in addition to 33 and six reserves to travel, for England. In practice, until a few years ago, the clubs, asked by the Associations for players, were reasonable, but held their right to refuse. They are the employers of the players and insist on that right. A Club cannot be compelled to release a player for another Association, and what one Club may do a combination of Clubs may do.[61]

These sentiments were echoed by the Management Committee's own statement to the FA:

> Players are sought and signed on by clubs for the purpose of their own Competitions, and it must be readily appreciated that the players fit for International duty are the most attractive players on the clubs' books and, in these days of keen competition, cannot be replaced except after considerable negotiation and expense, if at all.[62]

Though the FA of Wales was now prepared to accept midweek matches, the Irish delegates refused and, with the League clubs intent on collectively withholding their players for internationals during the coming season, the negotiations appeared to have reached a deadlock. However, at the Football League's annual meeting John McKenna and the executive persuaded member clubs to compromise by allowing both the smaller associations one home Saturday fixture each season. To compensate for this additional loss of players, all future Inter-League games were to be moved to weekdays from the weekend. The decision was justified as an act of benevolence on the part of the League: against their own wishes, the clubs were prepared to help out the smaller national associations by loaning players and accommodating international fixtures within the dominant League schedule.[63]

As the foregoing discussion demonstrates, the hegemony of the Football League over the professional game in Scotland, Wales and Ireland was established and consolidated over the first four decades of the twentieth century. In the first place, these nations provided significant percentages of the League's labour force and, as a result of the establishment of mutual agreements with the Scottish and Irish Leagues for the registration of players, with administration boards to settle disputes, the control over footballers had been extended throughout the United Kingdom. Furthermore, once large numbers of non-English players had become employees of Football League clubs it was possible for Preston to dictate the timetabling of international matches, the selection of international teams and, indirectly, to control the finances of the Welsh, Irish and (to a lesser extent) Scottish national associations. This power remained latent until the 1920s, when the influx of greater numbers of top quality footballers from these countries led the executive and its leading clubs to adopt a number of policies that were successful in asserting the primacy of the League competition over international fixtures. By 1939 there is little doubt that the decisions made at the headquarters of the national associations in Glasgow, Cardiff and Belfast were increasingly subject to confirmation and agreement from Preston.

The League and overseas football

The relationship between British football and the game in the rest of the world involved some fundamental contradictions. Formally, the British played a relatively marginal role in the development of football as a 'world game'. The isolation, insularity and sheer arrogance of the British authorities are generally taken as read. In his recent history of world football, Bill Murray has noted that 'much of the progress on the continent was passing unnoticed' in the 'home' of football;[64] the action of the British governing bodies in distancing themselves from FIFA appeared to symbolise this position. However, the notion that British football in this period was deeply anti-European and isolationist is both simplistic and erroneous. On a less formal level, British clubs, players and coaches were instrumental in the development of the administrative and playing side of football in continental Europe, the Americas and parts of the Empire. The inter-war period witnessed numerous club and representative sides touring abroad each year, and the cementing of institutional and personal relations that in some cases proved to have remarkable longevity. That influential figures in British football kept more than an eye on events across the Channel is clear from the memoirs of the most successful manager of the inter-war era, Herbert Chapman, and journalists such as the former amateur footballer and *Athletic News* editor Ivan Sharpe, as well as the private archives of his predecessor James Catton.[65] Nor were leading figures at the FA as parochial as they are sometimes portrayed. It is well known that Stanley Rous, who became FA Secretary in 1934, was a dedicated Europhile who had been advocating closer contact with overseas football some time before he spearheaded Britain's return to FIFA during and after the Second World War.[66] Rous's was hardly a lone voice in this respect. Even his predecessor Frederick Wall, the embodiment of the nineteenth-century amateur gentleman, who ran the governing body well into the twentieth century, was less prepared to dismiss international competition as an irrelevance by the 1930s.[67] The close links with the British game established by 'the presiding geniuses of European football in the 1930s',[68] the Austrian manager and administrator Hugo Meisl and the Italian manager Vittorio Pozzo, also serve as a corrective to the idea that having given the game to the world, Britain then bolted the door and ventured out only reluctantly.[69]

The Football League and its officials appear to have epitomised the isolationist, 'Little Englander' strain of British football. Not only was it an essentially selfish body, concerned with the interests of its members and little else, it also exhibited a parochial and inward-looking sense of superiority, which (as we saw in Chapter 1) rendered even the inclusion of clubs from the South of England a long drawn-out and highly contested process. With football in London marginalised for so long, it is hardly surprising that the game in Vienna, Budapest, Paris and New York was largely overlooked. Unlike the FA, the League was no football missionary. The Management Committee felt no moral duty to popularise the game outside its own territory, and thus tended to regard representative matches and tours as trivial distractions from the realities of competitive club football. It was the League and its representatives who most powerfully articulated the archetypal isolationist stance – based in Peter Beck's words 'on a strong concept of Britishness, a belief in the fundamental superiority of British football, and the primacy of the domestic league programmes' – normally associated with the British game as a whole.[70]

With the possible exception of John Lewis, who was a well-known international referee and propagandist of the sport in Europe and the empire, few League officials showed much interest in overseas developments, and many were positively contemptuous of the continental game in particular.[71] The most ardent of these anti-Europeans was Charles Sutcliffe. Throughout the 1920s and early 1930s, the League Vice-President used his newspaper columns to disparage non-British football and challenge the increasing, and undeserved, significance he felt was being allocated to overseas fixtures. 'I don't care a brass farthing about the future of the game in France, Belgium, Austria and Germany' Sutcliffe wrote in January 1928; he had earlier claimed not to know the name 'of a club or a single individual on the Continent'.[72] For Sutcliffe, like many others, 'international football' was synonymous with the annual home international championship. Consequently, he had little time for the increasing frequency of matches between British and foreign national sides during the 1930s; such games, in his view, were 'a waste of time and money' and ought not to be treated as internationals 'in the full sense of the word'.[73] Similarly, while Frederick Wall was prepared to admit that the 1934 World Cup was 'not cheaply won' by the Italian hosts, Sutcliffe referred to the same competition as 'a joke': 'I am not … interested in the World Championship and I think the national associations of England, Scotland, Wales and Ireland have quite enough to do in their own International Championship which seems to me a far better World Championship than the one to be staged in Rome'.[74]

The relationship between the FA and FIFA had important implications for the Football League. The issues on which the two sides parted company in 1920 and 1928 – contacts with the defeated nations in the First World War, the question of 'broken time' payments and the definition of amateurism – shrouded a more fundamental threat to the autonomy of the British associations.[75] The persistent suggestion that the four British associations should have just a single vote at FIFA meetings had embittered relations since the FA joined FIFA in 1905, and gained a resurgence in the mid-1920s. British authority was also threatened by suggestions that Britain's majority vote on the International Board – a body with complete control over changes in the laws of the game – might be brought to an end. In such circumstances, there was some apprehension that the Football League might become subject to overseas interference and control. The possible repercussions, in the view of *Athletic News* at least, were momentous: 'We might have to accept fantastic alteration[s] of the laws of the game emanating from Thibet or Timbuctoo [sic] – a development which our traditions and heavy financial commitments could not risk.'[76] Not surprisingly, therefore, League officials played an important part in shaping FA policy towards the world governing body. In his position as Vice-President of the FA, John McKenna became a member of the International Board just in time to be involved in the exclusion of the two FIFA representatives in June 1920;[77] Sutcliffe, meanwhile, was one of the five FA representatives who voted to withdraw once more from FIFA at a conference of the United Kingdom associations in February 1928. Sutcliffe, without doubt, was more dismissive of FIFA than his FA colleagues, but his brand of stubborn anglocentrism can nonetheless be detected in the association's formal letter of withdrawal. While hoping to maintain 'friendly relations' with FIFA and 'cooperate with them on all suitable occasions', the associations indicated their determination 'to conduct their affairs in the way their long experience has shown desirable'. In a typically patronising tone, Wall informed his FIFA counterpart Carl Hirschmann that as most of the associations affiliated with FIFA were relatively young and untested, they could not possibly 'have the knowledge which only experience can bring'.[78] Sutcliffe's high-minded disdain for FIFA was underlined later the same year when, in response to the rumoured prohibition of British tours on the continent, he declared that by 'parting from the Federation we lose nothing, in slamming the door in our face they have lost wisdom, guidance and help'.[79]

As far as the growth of leagues in continental Europe and North and South America was concerned, the Football League provided no material or technical assistance. Yet in almost every case the League was used as a model of structure and policy. Few league competitions deviated much from what Pierre Lanfranchi has called the 'British model of championships', with promotion and relegation and movement up and down divisions or sections based on sporting merit. Those that did, like the American Soccer League, were influenced by an established national tradition of sporting competition based on the principle of a 'fixed elite'.[80] The French League was one which consciously 'borrowed' from the Football League in its formative stage, from regulations such as a maximum wage to the acquisition of many of its players (see below). However, while the League may have provided a structure, the substance and style of the emerging continental competitions both nationally and internationally were filled in with almost no English assistance. In the Central European nations of Austria, Hungary and Czechoslovakia, in particular, the parlous finances of the new professional clubs meant that domestic competition never dominated the fixture list as it did in England. Instead, international competitions such as the Mitropa Cup (featuring club sides from the Danubian nations alongside those from Yugoslavia and Italy, and by the late 1930s Switzerland and Romania) were developed, alongside schedules of international fixtures and tours; an autonomous style of play known as '*calcio Danubiano*' even emerged.[81] The English authorities in general, and the Football League especially, played no part in the creation of this nascent international football system. While continental nations played each other, disseminated ideas and exchanged talent, the English 'put themselves ... outside a vast, unprecedented network of exchanges'.[82]

Overseas contacts and foreign tours

To dwell on the institutional isolation of the Football League and its apparent hostility towards overseas football, however, would be to ignore the multifarious activities existing below the surface at informal club and individual level. The close-season tour was the earliest and most important aspect of this. The pioneers here were the Southern amateur clubs, who began arranging individual exhibition matches and even full-blown tours of continental Europe towards the late 1890s. League clubs were slower to take up the challenge, not due to worries about the cost but because prospective tours coincided with the signing-on process in late April and early May, and many players were unwilling to travel abroad after a long domestic season. Some clubs, such as Sheffield United, were simply unable to raise a touring party because many of their players were engaged either in first-class cricket or in other business pursuits during the summer.[83] Nevertheless, by the late 1900s a number of League clubs were making annual or biannual visits to the continent. Austria-Hungary appears to have been the most popular destination in these formative years. In the decade before the First World War, Everton, Manchester United, Sunderland, Barnsley, Blackburn Rovers, Oldham Athletic, Tottenham Hotspur and Burnley all played there.[84] Others travelled further afield. Nottingham Forest followed the initiative of Southern Leaguers Southampton and the amateur Corinthians when it played a series of matches in Uruguay and Argentina in 1905. Everton and Tottenham made the same journey in 1909, playing games against local clubs, Uruguayan and Argentinian League teams and even against each other in two exhibition matches.[85]

Tours of this kind received neither official promotion nor condemnation from the Football League executive. While the FA would often act as a go-between, receiving offers from foreign associations and clubs which were then passed on to selected League members, the Management Committee remained uninvolved. In fact its first intervention came in 1912, when it responded to Newcastle United's action in paying players £1 per day expenses when on tour by ruling that, in future tours, players 'must not be allowed to make a profit'. In addition, the Committee was to be notified of the terms, conditions and arrangements for any proposed tour and furnished with a thorough financial statement within two weeks of the club's return.[86] However, it remained the duty of the governing body and not the League to officially sanction or veto overseas tours, even if Preston sometimes intervened to modify certain details and continued to set maximum limits on the tour expenses given to players.

By the 1920s, overseas tours were increasing in frequency and becoming more significant in the sporting calendars of the leading League clubs.[87] Minute books reveal that offers to tour the continent were received almost every winter from overseas clubs or associations, and tended to be accepted more often than before the war. In 1922, Arsenal and Everton visited Sweden and Denmark respectively, while Newcastle United played in both these countries; Burnley and Liverpool, meanwhile, travelled to Italy, and Notts County, Durham City and Hartlepools United undertook tours in Spain. Two years later, the Management Committee provisionally sanctioned continental tours by eight First Division, three Second Division and three Third Division South clubs.[88] West Ham United was one of the most regular tourists, travelling to the Basque region of Spain in 1921, Austria and Czechoslovakia in 1923, Germany, Switzerland and France in 1924, Holland in 1925 and Spain again a year later. A contemporary source described the East London players as 'football missionaries' who by 1936 had 'played matches in most of the important Continental towns'.[89] The primary motivation for this increased continental activity, however, was less proselytising than financial. If efficiently arranged, a close-season tour could often turn a disappointing season's deficit into a profit. Everton's 1909 excursion to South America reportedly made a £300 profit, which was dwarfed three years later by the profit of over $20,000 made on a similar trip by Southern League club Swindon Town.[90] European tours generally grossed smaller but not insignificant sums. West Ham received £900 for the five matches on its 1923 post-FA Cup Final trip to Central Europe, while Aston Villa was guaranteed £2,000 for a six-match tour of Scandinavia in 1926.[91]

In the process of arranging tours and individual matches, some clubs built up a network of institutional contacts on the continent.

Individuals like Hugo and Willi Meisl – the latter was based in London for part of the 1930s – were important in facilitating such links and organising matches, in their case with Austrian and Hungarian clubs; the League referee R. G. Rudd performed a similar function with the Scandinavian clubs.[92] Elsewhere, matches were arranged through British exiles associated with foreign clubs as officials or coaches, such as when Wolverhampton Wanderers played Charlie Bell's Nice side as part of its 1933 French tour, with a return fixture at Molineux organised the following year.[93] Some close and long-standing relationships were formed. We know that the idea of regular fixtures had been raised before the First World War: Sheffield United, for instance, declined FC Bruges' suggestion to inaugurate an annual Easter match between the two sides in 1912.[94] The best-known series of matches was Arsenal's annual Armistice Day fixture against Racing Club de Paris, which began in the mid-1920s and lasted through to the 1960s. These matches were considered extremely successful on both sides of the Channel, with crowds regularly topping the 50,000 mark.[95] Furthermore, by the 1930s visits of club sides were no longer exclusively in one direction, as more continental teams were invited to play on Football League grounds. London clubs took the lead here, especially Arsenal and Tottenham Hotspur, whose grounds also began to be used for England international matches at this time.[96] Others soon followed, and not only those clubs from the highest division. As a Second Division club, West Ham staged matches against AIK Stockholm, Austria FC and a Hungarian XI during the first half of the 1935–36 season. The Swedish club had visited Upton Park the previous season, an event which was recorded in the club's minutes as 'a most happy occasion'. Representatives of the FA, the London FA, Swedish and English diplomats and even Prince Carl of Sweden were entertained at the match and an after-match dinner, which for the club 'marked a further step in Diplomatic and Sporting relations' and 'would ever remain a delightful memory at Upton Park'.[97]

It would be wrong, however, to assume that matches between Football League clubs and continental opposition were always occasions for the expression of international friendship. There were in fact as many voices calling for clubs to withdraw from the continent as to extend and strengthen relations. The perceived benefits of overseas excursions, which were never fully appreciated at executive level, were coming to be increasingly undermined by the late 1920s, primarily as a result of the damage done to the League's prestige by regular defeats. The large and easy victories recorded by English teams before 1914 became more rare between the wars, as superior coaching methods and administrative nous enabled continental sides to close the quality gap. Sunderland's 2–1 defeat by Vienna AC in 1909 after finishing third in the First Division championship was the first Football League failure on the continent, but was regarded as little more than an aberration: the superiority of the masters over the pupils was still taken for granted.[98] Things changed slowly but significantly after the war. Defeats became more common at club level, even if the ramifications of the 'Versailles mentality' in international football and the withdrawals from FIFA meant that England's national side was spared possible defeat by the stronger Central European nations, particularly Austria and Germany, during the 1920s.[99] Under these circumstances, tour matches gained an added resonance, offering as they did the only chance for aspiring continentals to pit their skills against the English masters.

Football League clubs treated these encounters rather differently, often sending weakened sides that were accused by the continental and British press alike of not treating such matches as proper competitive fixtures. After a series of defeats in the summer of 1927, *Athletic News* mounted a campaign aimed at informing League clubs and the football authorities of 'how British prestige was suffering by the defeats of tired and holiday-making touring teams'.[100] A year later, the exit of the British associations from FIFA resulted in a retaliatory attempt by the latter to prohibit British tours of the continent. Sutcliffe's reaction to this probably reflected that of many League and club officials:

> I have always taken a very definite stand against Continental tours. They serve no good purpose to our football or footballers. The only description is Continental picnics, where football is very secondary. At times the games are played on grounds, and under conditions, with so-called referees, which reduce the game from that of contest to one of farce. Our players have got to face a keen effort on the part of their opponents determined to win, and players are subject to serious risk which may have an effect on the playing ability of some players in the next season… The close season should be a period of rest and recovery, and if the International Federation ban the visits of our clubs to meet Continental clubs, I shall be delighted.[101]

FIFA did subsequently issue a ban, but this was quickly rescinded due to pressure from clubs in England and abroad that had already entered into tour contracts. That summer, League prestige was further dented when the FA Cup holders Blackburn Rovers recorded five defeats in six games while touring Austria, Hungary and Czechoslovakia. At that year's annual meeting, McKenna 'expressed hope that the League Clubs touring the Continent would maintain the prestige of the League' but, in concert with Sutcliffe, added that if clubs continued to be beaten match after match 'it would be better not to go'.[102] Certainly, the League hierarchy was reluctant for its clubs to assume an ambassadorial role, especially if this adversely affected the smooth running and status of its own competition.

The debate intensified further during 1929 as Football League clubs suffered ever more embarrassing tour defeats. Huddersfield Town lost four of its five matches in Austria, Hungary and Czechoslovakia. Upset by poor refereeing standards, Joseph Barlow, the director in charge of the party, decided not to 'go on tour again against professional Continental teams'.[103] Cup-winners Bolton Wanderers, meanwhile, were trounced 4–0 by a Catalan Select XI at the opening of Barcelona's new 65,000 all-seater stadium in front of the Spanish King.[104] The most bitter criticism was reserved for Newcastle United, which was beaten 8–1 by a 'second-rate Austrian team' called Pozsony, and also lost matches in Bratislava and Prague.[105] After the club's 2–0 defeat by Vienna AC, the local *Neues Wiener Journal* claimed that '10,000 spectators were deceived of their money' and declared that: 'We need no more games with English teams. That is the net result of the match with Newcastle and of most displays given by English teams in Vienna since the war.' The Prague correspondent of the *Berliner Zeitung am Mittag* broadened the criticism by suggesting that:

> The English professional teams have so far only brought disappointments, as practically all their matches in Vienna, Budapest, Prague and Leipsic [sic] etc have suffered from the indifference shown by these guests in carrying out their fixtures, with the result that they have been defeated almost everywhere. For the organisers, at all events, an expensive and an unprofitable pastime, and for the Englishmen a well-paid pleasure trip![106]

The Hungarian federation even made a formal complaint to the FA about the performances of Newcastle, and an FA Commission (including McKenna) judged that because of the 'indifferent displays given by the Newcastle United players during the tour … the Hungarian FA was justified in endeavouring to cancel the contract'.[107] 1932 witnessed a further series of poor overseas performances, with Newcastle again criticised during a visit to France, along with the reigning First Division champions Everton, who won only two of their four tour games. Moreover, the scale of press criticism at home both deepened and widened: British (and particularly Football League) clubs were now accused not only of damaging the prestige of the sport but of the nation as a whole. 'The people who let British football down are letting Britain down. There is no question about that.'[108]

Despite such criticism, the overseas fixtures of club sides were marked by a lack of interference from outside bodies. In his meticulous study of international football and politics, Peter Beck has outlined the increasing intervention, subtle and sporadic though it was, by the Foreign Office in the fixtures of the British (particularly the English) national teams between the wars. The acknowledgement by inter-war governments that football could be used to support British interests and project a favourable image of the nation abroad undoubtedly impacted upon the organisation of England fixtures by the FA, especially high-profile matches such as those with Germany in 1935 and 1938 and Italy in 1934. The Foreign Office may not have 'ordered' English teams to win games abroad, as a sensationalist story in the *Daily Express* claimed in late 1928, but there was an increasing recognition in Whitehall 'that international football was too important to be left entirely to sporting bodies'.[109] Yet government officials were evidently less concerned with the staging of club matches. Although the FA secretary acknowledged that most complaints from abroad involved Football League sides and that 'individual clubs who have toured Europe have not put up such good performances' as the national team, no official action was taken.[110] One writer to *Athletic News* felt that the Foreign Office should refuse passports to those teams unable to uphold national prestige abroad, while Derby County's W. Bendle Moore informed his fellow League secretaries and managers that 'no one – whether it was the FA or the smallest club in the country – had the right to send a team abroad unless it was a competent team accompanied by plenty of reserves'.[111] Despite prompting from various quarters, neither the League nor the FA took any steps to prohibit or regulate continental tours, as the Scottish League had when it ruled that clubs touring Europe could play district teams but not national representative teams, while those visiting the colonies or dominions could meet both.[112] In 1931, Arsenal, perhaps the most willing and successful of foreign travellers, proposed that the Football League's prestige abroad could be best protected by paying bonuses to players for matches considered sufficiently important.[113] Bonuses, one director argued, would help motivate their employees, most of whom 'did not want to go on the Continent. They would rather be playing golf in Scotland.' The proposal was narrowly defeated: President McKenna, ever mindful of the League's reputation, was concerned that 'it would be said on the Continent that we could not win matches without paying. The Arsenal had won their matches, and all players should be loyal to their country and their clubs.'[114]

By the 1930s, most of the leading professional clubs in England had experienced football on the continent of Europe, if not further afield. Even the Sheffield United directors, who in the 1920s resolved not 'to entertain the idea of any Continental Tour', finally agreed to venture overseas when a tour party was sent to Sweden in 1938.[115] 'Never before in the history of football have so many British clubs indulged in international rivalry with foreign opponents as they are engaging at present', wrote *Sporting Chronicle* columnist and Chelsea director W. Capel-Kirby in February 1933. Inspired by the England–Austria international at Stamford Bridge the previous December, matches against national and club sides from the home of football were more sought after than ever, and English clubs were increasingly prepared to arrange continental fixtures when blank dates appeared in their schedules. The ubiquity of continental competition among Football League clubs was evident from the fact that Clapton Orient, Gillingham and Northampton of the Third Division South had all played abroad that season. Even at the time of writing, Capel-Kirby noted, Bristol Rovers (another Third Division side) was on a week-long trip to Holland, with fixtures in Amsterdam and The Hague, while Portsmouth was due to entertain Racing Club de Paris at Fratton Park, with a return match a few weeks later.[116] The fact that the League executive took relatively little interest in such developments reveals an important point about its attitude towards international football. Unlike the leading clubs in Central Europe, most Football League outfits did not need to tour extensively for financial or political reasons. They were not, except in the view of a rather nationalistic metropolitan press and some government officials, seen as ambassadors of the nation in the way that the clubs of Vienna, Budapest, Prague and Bologna often were.[117] Everything considered, overseas engagements were always regarded as a temporary or seasonal distraction from the real business of life – domestic competition – and thus whatever happened abroad did not really matter too much. 'Whether we can play as well, better, or worse, than Austrians, Frenchmen or Spaniards is of no moment', wrote Sutcliffe in 1931. 'As a nation, we have more pressing difficulties, and our clubs have quite enough serious and competitive football'.[118]

Foreign leagues and alien players

Defeats while playing abroad, though damaging to the prestige and reputation of the Football League and its clubs, could easily be rationalised or swept under the carpet. When overseas progress impinged upon the League's domestic authority, however, the response was quite different. The growth of professional clubs and then leagues abroad represented a potential danger to the Football League only during the inter-war years, when clubs from two nations – the USA and France – endeavoured to recruit its players. There had been precursors to this type of activity. As early as 1894, eight players broke professional contracts in England and sailed to the USA, where they were employed by the Baltimore Orioles club in the baseball-financed American League of Professional Football Clubs (ALPFC) on comparatively generous terms of £10 as a signing-on fee and £4–5 per week.[119] However, despite favourable press attention, attendances were poor and the ALPFC immediately found itself under scrutiny from the US immigration authorities over the foreign imports. As a result, the venture was abandoned within a month and the English players returned home, having discovered, according to one writer, 'that in the New World disillusionment was the consequence of insubstantial promises'.[120] We know little of the Football League's reaction to the incident, although Andrei Markovits and Steven Hellerman claim that the defection of the players 'was met with contempt and anger' at home.[121]

A more important forerunner to the export of Football League players, however, was the diffusion of ex-players as coaches. In the absence of any precise data on the number employed in coaching posts at any one time, the fragmentary evidence supports Mason's view that these former League footballers 'were to be found everywhere, from Spain to Hungary, to Italy and Uruguay', and often in considerable numbers.[122] The best-known British coach of the period, Jimmy Hogan, left Bolton Wanderers for Holland during 1911 and continued to coach national and club sides in Austria, Hungary, Germany, France and Switzerland throughout the inter-war period, including the Austrian team which gained the silver medal at the 1936 Berlin Olympics. William Garbutt followed Hogan abroad, in his case to Italy where he managed Genoa, Naples, Roma and Milan (with a brief move to Bilbao) over a 36-year career.[123] The highpoint of the British coach abroad was probably immediately after the First World War and during the 1920s. Men who were relatively unknown as players in England, such as Ted Magner, Curtis Booth, G. S. Kimpton and Fred Pagnam, enjoyed successful careers as coaches in a variety of continental nations between the wars.[124] Manchester United's former full-back Herbert Burgess enjoyed a similarly lengthy spell in Hungary, Spain, Italy, Austria, Denmark and Sweden from 1920–32, and even applied for positions in Canadian football. In 1927, *Athletic News* could report that Germany's two most powerful clubs were both coached by former League players: ex-England internationals Fred Spiksley at Nuremberg and Will Townley at Fürth.[125] The Dutch federation employed a coterie of ex-League coaches in the 1930s, including Bob Glendenning (Barnsley, Bolton Wanderers), Gus Smith (Sunderland), Billy Marsden (Sheffield Wednesday), Jimmy 'Sprinter' Marshall (Oldham Athletic) and Peter Donaghy (Bradford City). Yet by 1933 there had been a discernable move away from British coaches across much of the continent, with only two out of some 500 in Germany and Garbutt as the loan British representative among 45 Hungarians in Italy.[126]

The migration of former players – or those approaching retirement – as coaches caused little disruption in League circles. It was when offers arrived for contracted footballers to *play* abroad, however, that the League really stirred. The initial threat came from the USA, when the American Soccer League (ASL) was formed in 1921. Based around a number of established clubs and company teams in the North-east, the ASL drew heavily on immigrant communities as well as Scottish, Irish and other European personnel.[127] With the British associations outside FIFA regulations, ASL clubs were able to sign retained League players free of charge and without reference to their English clubs. By late 1923, the activities of US scouts had generated minor panic among League clubs, even though it was the Scottish League that was particularly targeted. By this point, *Topical Times* could report the presence of a number of English professionals in New York, Philadelphia, Boston and Fall River, many of them receiving wages equivalent to £10 per week for playing football. They were likely to take home substantially more – perhaps £20 according to some estimates – when subsidiary industrial work was taken into account. The attraction of the US game was not difficult to understand under these circumstances: 'The lure of adventure, employment and bigger money for football are reasons why so many players are talking of going to America.'[128] Some observers regarded this as a real menace to the ability of Football League clubs to hold on to their players and demand transfer fees. Others, like Sutcliffe, believed the 'American menace' would be short-lived and that players would come to realise 'that to leave England with its definite benefits for America with its promises is taking a leap in the dark'.[129]

Despite a significant increase in the movement of players across the Atlantic between 1924 and 1928 (see Table 6.3), Sutcliffe's prognosis proved to be fairly accurate. Many of those who emigrated, though nominally associated with Football League clubs, were not in fact even active professionals. What the ASL offered them was an opportunity to rebuild or prolong professional careers in an entirely new cultural and sporting environment. Fred Morley moved from Brentford to Philadelphia in 1921, specifically to heal a knee injury that had forced him to quit the English game; Bob Perry's emigration was the result of his having been suspended for life by the FA for his part in 'fixing' competitive matches. Less typical was Alex Massie, who at just 22 became one of the youngest direct imports to the ASL when he moved to Bethlehem Steel in 1928, even if his decision to leave First Division Bury was largely explained by the prohibitive £1,000 transfer fee that had been placed on his head.[130] Billy Hibbert, Sam Chedgzoy and James Wood were representative of a more significant group of players who arrived in the USA in their thirties to play for a few extra seasons before retirement.

Table 6.3: Movement of Football League players* to the ASL, 1921–31

Season	*Total players from League clubs*	*New arrivals from League clubs*
1921–22	3	2
1922–23	4	1
1923–24	6	3
1924–25	13	6
1925–26	20	10
1926–27	25	11
1927–28	26	10
1928–29	27	8
1929 (autumn)	14	2
1930	11	1
1931	9	0

*Defined as those employed or retained by a Football League club prior to playing in the ASL.
Source: Drawn from data in Jose, *American Soccer.*

Even if this potential transatlantic stream rarely developed into more than a trickle, the capture of prominent internationals such as Manchester City's Mickey Hamill in 1924 and Arsenal's Scottish goalkeeper Bill Harper in 1928 were considered serious enough for the League executive to enact deterrent measures. The Management Committee declared in 1926 that any player leaving a club for the USA or the continent would be prohibited from re-registering until the League 'has had ample opportunity to investigate the circumstances under which the Player left and the reasons for and conditions attendant on his return'. A few months later, a former Bradford Park Avenue player engaged in the

New Bedford City Football League was suspended by the Committee for trying to induce contracted League players to go to the United States. The executive also issued a warning that it would 'entirely prohibit all Tours to the United States so long as any American Club improperly attempts to interfere with any of our League clubs'.[131] Yet despite widespread fears of players being permanently suspended, the League did in fact leave the door open, and few of its US exiles stayed away for long. Even for many of the older players, the US experience was never intended to be permanent, and return migration was common.[132] Harper, for instance, came back to Arsenal within two seasons before moving on to Plymouth Argyle, while even Jerry Best, who spent seven years away in the ASL, was able to pick up his Football League career with Clapton Orient in 1931. Disillusionment with the 'primitive' and 'farcical' conditions of US football were sufficient to persuade the Irish centre-half Mick O'Brien to return to England after only seven matches, although the tightening of US immigration controls during the first half of the 1920s was probably more important in encouraging European players to visit rather than settle.[133] The ASL challenge really subsided when it was revealed in August 1928 that Everton's record goal-scorer 'Dixie' Dean had refused a move to the New York Giants for a reported wage of £25 per week. One correspondent concluded that 'the American menace has been grossly exaggerated by the scare-mongers' and that Dean's decision could 'be taken as a symbol of defeat for the plans of our friends on the other side of the Atlantic'.[134] From 1928 onwards, US soccer was ravaged by an internal dispute which, combined with the impact of the Wall Street Crash, caused a significant drop in football immigration. In any case, the English and Scottish associations had already plugged this particular labour market hole by establishing a 'working agreement' with the United States Football Association (USFA) in January 1929 to respect each other's registrations and suspensions.[135]

While the threatened exodus of players to the USA failed to materialise, the French 'menace' of the 1930s proved to have more substance. In 1932, a professional league was created in France, and from its beginnings it employed a policy of importing foreign footballers.[136] The quality of British footballers, demonstrated through numerous international encounters and club tours, made them particularly attractive to French scouts, especially as the British exclusion from FIFA ensured that transfer fees would not be a hindrance. During the spring and summer of 1932, the possibility of League footballers being tempted to join French clubs dominated the press on either side of the channel. The catalyst for all this was the shock announcement on 13 April that Chelsea's Scottish international pairing of Hughie Gallacher and Tommy Law had been approached to join SC Nîmes as player-coaches, with David Jack of Arsenal apparently receiving a similar offer from Racing Club de Paris.[137] The financial package offered to Gallacher and Law was based on a weekly wage of £18–20, more than double the Football League maximum. Though the French salary limit was set at 2,000 francs a month (just over £21 or £5 10 shillings per week), Nîmes proposed to overcome this by paying the Scots a 5,000-franc (£54) monthly fee for coaching the team.[138] Gallacher was certainly tempted, telling one journalist that the offer was 'too good to be turned down without consideration'. In another interview, he suggested that:

> it would be a good thing for football here if something like 50 or 60 players received a like offer. It is not fair that players with years of experience in first-class football should be allowed to draw only £208 a year... My feeling is that the conditions in France would be preferable to those obtaining here, and I know what I am speaking about, for I have played in every country in Europe with the exception of two.[139]

Gallacher, Law and other potential emigrants faced considerable pressure from the football authorities and the press in England. The Football League issued a resolution stating that players leaving the country would be prohibited from registering with English clubs in the future, while continental clubs trying to sign players 'will be regarded as having committed an unfriendly act and all friendly relations will cease'.[140] The League President, John McKenna, told reporters that professionals going to France without consent 'would cease to have the right to play again in this country'. One official warned that clubs had learned lessons from the US menace and would 'act much more stringently' than when Bill Harper had been fined just £10 in 1930 before being re-registered with Arsenal. FA Secretary Frederick Wall, meanwhile, wrote to the French federation reminding it of an 1894 agreement which recognised the registration of players in both countries.[141] French football itself was also vilified. 'Spotlight' agreed that if the players did decide to go overseas 'it is not *au revoir*, it's goodbye', and admitted to *Topical Times* readers that: 'I wouldn't go within 25 miles of French football as a professional player. Ask some of the continental teams about bad legs, violent spectators, rotten referees and one-man clubs!'[142] Under the headline 'French Football – The Truth', the *Daily Herald* printed a letter from the father of a British footballer who had played for four years at Alès in Southern France. He catalogued a range of problems with language, customs, food and travel, together with the poor standard of play and refereeing and the excitability of the spectators. The letter closed by saying that '[The] Cost of living is on the expensive side, and my son's advice to those about to travel to France is, roughly, DON'T.' A few days earlier, the same newspaper had published details of a letter allegedly written by Hughie Gallacher's mother, urging him not to leave his home for France.[143]

In the event, Gallacher and Law's demand for financial security – a £2,000 deposit and £20 per week on a four-year contract – was refused, and the players re-signed for Chelsea. Nonetheless, Nîmes succeeded in contracting two other prominent Chelsea players, Andy Wilson and Alec Cheyne. Wilson had spent the previous season on loan to QPR, was out of condition and at 37 probably past his best, but Cheyne was a 25-year-old current Scottish international. Warning potential exiles of the immigration problems that they could face and the financial limitations of French clubs, Capel-Kirby urged his two employees to change their minds. Cheyne, in particular, was 'a young man with a fine football future, and, though he has not been too comfortable at Stamford Bridge, there are many clubs who would be glad to pay Chelsea for his signature.'[144] A stream, though hardly of flood, of British players followed Cheyne and Wilson to France during the summer. Few of these were elite players. Although several of the Bolton Wanderers staff given free transfers had apparently considered 'sampling' French football, the club's former captain Bob Haworth admitted that the wages quoted 'would not pay a married man to take his family out there'. There was to be no mass exodus, although Haworth felt that the limited opportunities in England ensured that 'some of the lesser lights will not be exactly tempted, but more or less compelled to examine the possibilities of the situation'.[145]

The British were the dominant non-French national grouping during the first two years of professional football in France. Forty-three Britons (over 40 per cent of the 'foreigners') played for the 20 league clubs in 1932–33, and while this figure dropped to 26 the following season, there were an additional 21 British footballers employed in the new Second Division. How many of these arrived from Football League as opposed to Scottish, minor or amateur clubs is hard to tell. As with the US migrants, many of those who travelled to France were on the margins of the professional game in England. George Harkus had retired in 1930 from a successful career with Aston Villa and Southampton to become a publican, but returned to play a season with Sporting Club Fives. Fred Kennedy was still on Oldham Athletic's transfer list, but was turning out for Northwich Victoria when he signed a contract with Racing Club de Paris.[146] Hugh Vallance was erroneously described in the French press as a 'regular international', but in reality had drifted away from elite football after falling out with his employers Brighton and Hove Albion in October 1930. He was playing for Kidderminster when he joined Alès in 1932.[147] As Capel-Kirby had predicted, most of those who left in August were back by May. Indeed, data gathered from the French press show that 58.2 per cent of the British imports stayed in France for less than a year, while only 22.4 per cent remained for more than two years.[148] Many were signed for trial periods or on month-to-month contracts and some, like Bill Fraser at Marseilles, were home in time for the start of the English season. Others ran into difficulties in obtaining labour permits; such troubles forced Tom Flannigan to return home after only three months with St Etienne in 1933.[149]

By the mid-1930s, then, migration had slowed and the better players, such as Cheyne and Wilson, returned home. From 1934 onwards, most British players were engaged in the second rather than the first tier of French football, and from a peak of 11.9 per cent in the first professional season the British presence in the top division had dwindled to 1.5 per cent (five players) by 1938–39.[150] The problems of adapting to a different style of football and a new way of life were undoubtedly important in explaining this decline. Few of the exports were integrated into French society, and many gained reputations for behaving badly, drinking and, most importantly of all, playing poorly. Peter O'Dowd, for example, the only English international to play in France, failed to secure a first team place at Valenciennes, faced press criticism and was even accused of attempting to 'throw' a match.[151] Within a season and a half he had returned to League football with Torquay United. Andy Wilson certainly settled better than most and admitted being 'treated well' at Nîmes, but he too became disillusioned with the poor conditions and the lack of discipline among the players he was employed to coach: 'They are temperamental and do not treat their job in the workmanlike manner which the average Britisher adopts.'[152] The increasing availability of Central European professionals willing to accept lower wages than those paid to their British counterparts was a further factor diminishing this migratory flow.

Moving to France represented an overseas sojourn rather than the end of a Football League career for most players. Fraser indicated that his return to England was motivated by 'the danger of falling out of touch with football in this country' and, more specifically, by the FA and League warnings that players who deserted their clubs would never be allowed back.[153] In reality, however, the governing bodies placed no major obstacles in the way of the return of these exiled footballers. Even when complications arose, the door was never closed entirely. In one telling case from 1937, George Gibson returned to England in violation of his contract with Racing Club de Roubaix and, though the FA instructed him to go back to France to complete his agreement, Roubaix refused to remove the suspension or to reinstate him. Under these circumstances, the FA chose to protect the interests of the player by refusing the French federation's demand for a transfer fee and allowing Gibson to register with any English club he wished. The Irish centre-forward Thomas Davis was less fortunate, receiving a three-month suspension from the FA after breaking a contract with FC Metz in 1935 and signing for Oldham Athletic.[154] However, even his career was halted only temporarily. Despite the rhetoric of exclusion, League footballers faced no blacklists and the majority moved home to new engagements of one kind or another. As with the USA in the previous decade, French football in the 1930s offered a new job opportunity for the journeymen, and increasingly peripatetic, footballers who numerically dominated Football League dressing-rooms; men like Tom Devlin, whose short spell with Roubaix in 1935–36 amounted to his eleventh engagement in five different countries over 11 years.[155] For a short time, the French league managed to expand the geographical boundaries of employment for the British professional footballer.

While the Football League struggled to prevent its employees leaving Britain, it was more successful in its efforts to keep 'foreign' players out. To this end, it was aided by the anti-alienism characteristic of much of the period, which in turn was reflected in the restrictive policies of the Ministry of Labour and the attitudes of the FA and the Players' Union.[156] With the exception of a handful of colonial-born players, non-British footballers rarely featured in League sides before 1914. Like many African migrants, Arthur Wharton and Hassan Hegazi arrived in England as students, but both briefly became League footballers. Wharton had travelled from the Gold Coast in 1882 at the age of 17 to complete his education at colleges in Staffordshire and County Durham. An accomplished athlete and cricketer, he also became a top-class goalkeeper for Preston North End, Rotherham Town and Sheffield United during the late 1880s and early 1890s. Hegazi, meanwhile, became the League's first Egyptian player when he turned out as an amateur for Fulham and Millwall during his time at London University between

1911 and 1913.[157] The most successful continental import was Nils Middleboe, the Danish international captain who played as an amateur for Chelsea between 1913 and 1922. Middleboe had competed against Great Britain at the 1908 London and the 1912 Stockholm Olympics, and so his initial appearances in Chelsea colours generated considerable interest. *Athletic News* regarded the Dane's presence as 'a vindication of the progress of the Continental nations in football', praising his 'skill and coolness' and 'deft and intelligent placing of the ball' during his debut game. The famous amateur international Vivian Woodward was even said to be an admirer. While some commentators bemoaned the presence of foreigners such as Hegazi and Middleboe and argued that clubs ought to stick to British players, the football establishment made no protest. Indeed, William Pickford noted with pride that no line had ever been drawn on the basis of nationality in English football: 'If a capable Colonial or foreigner is able to get a place in an English club, why should anybody object?'[158]

This distinction between the 'colonial' and the 'foreigner' was to become crucial in understanding attitudes to immigration during the inter-war years. Those born in the colonies or dominions of the Empire were classified juridically as British subjects, and their traditional freedom to enter and settle in the home country was consolidated by the British Nationality and Status of Aliens Act of 1914.[159] With no immigration controls, players from the overseas empire were thus regularly scouted and brought over to leading English and Scottish clubs. White South Africans were the most popular recruits. Boksburg, a small town in the Transvaal, contributed nine players to the English and Scottish leagues between the wars. Liverpool was the most conspicuous importer of South Africans: by the early 1930s there were six on the books. Players like Gordon Hodgson, Arthur Riley and Berry 'Nivvy' Nieuwenhuys became celebrated and senior figures in League football, their success stimulating a consistent flow of South African talent throughout the 1930s.[160] A number of leading First Division clubs followed Liverpool's example. Huddersfield Town, for one, signed the South African goalkeeper Dennis Leary and right-winger George Wienand for the 1937–38 season.[161] The Football League may not have been able to match either the numbers or the impact of the Australian, New Zealand, Indian and West Indian cricket professionals who played in the Lancashire League between the wars, but its own exploitation of imperial sources of labour has undoubtedly been underplayed.[162] That most of these colonial footballers were easily integrated into the English professional game is explained by the fact that the majority were recent emigrants with obvious British backgrounds. The same was true of the handful of US imports who turned out for Football League clubs. A Scottish schoolboy international, Alex Wood had represented the USA in the inaugural World Cup in 1930 but spent most of the following decade across the Atlantic as a full-back with Leicester City and Nottingham Forest.[163]

While the arrival of colonial and North American footballers could be interpreted as a form of return migration, the importation of continental footballers was less easily rationalised. Between 1905 and 1920 the government enacted a series of laws that overturned Britain's tradition of free entry and established strict guidelines for the employment of aliens. The 1919 Aliens Act and the subsequent Order in Council of 1920 were particularly significant, heralding a new system of work permits that laid down conditions for the employment of foreign workers. Potential immigrants had to prove that they could support themselves; employers were required to justify the acquisition of foreign labour, showing that reasonable efforts had been made to find indigenous labour. Final decisions, meanwhile, were left in the hands of immigration officials.[164] From this point on, then, any attempt to import players from abroad faced considerable obstacles.

Attitudes towards foreign imports crystallised in relation to a series of incidents during the late 1920s and early 1930s. During the summer of 1930, Arsenal attempted to sign the Austrian goalkeeper Rudy Hiden, a member of the famous *Wunderteam* that was to sweep all opponents aside (with the exception of England) in a series of international fixtures during 1930 to 1932. Negotiations between Arsenal's manager Herbert Chapman and Hiden's club Vienna AC were successful; a fee was agreed for an initial two-month contract with the possibility of renewal, and Hiden was guaranteed a supplementary job in London as a chef. Yet on his arrival at Dover, immigration officials denied the Austrian entry.[165] Some years earlier, the Belgian centre-forward Raymond Braine faced similar obstructions when he signed for Clapton Orient but was forced to return to Belgium before his League registration could be completed.[166] Hiden returned to Austria but, incensed by the decision, Chapman was not prepared to let the issue die. Arsenal had also signed a Dutch-born goalkeeper, Garard Pieter Keyser, whom Chapman provocatively picked to play for the first team during the opening game of the 1930–31 season, only a week after the FA had publicly expressed its opposition to the import of alien players. Unlike Hiden, Keyser had lived in England for three years, having played semi-professional football for Margate, but Arsenal still decided that it was safer to cancel his professional forms and sign him as a 'permit' player (effectively, a professional playing as an amateur). *Athletic News* considered him the 'outstanding personality' in the match 'not so much by his brilliant goalkeeping as by his daring tactics', but his appearance generated widespread criticism and he never played for the first team again.[167]

Reactions to these events were mixed. The Ministry of Labour had written to each of the British football associations asking for their opinions on its established policy of refusing entry to foreigners whose presence would have restricted the employment opportunities of British workers. It received overwhelming support. The FA announced its opposition to the 'granting [of] permits for alien players to be brought into this country', while the Players' Union informed the ministry of 'its disapproval of allowing Alien Professional Footballers into the country' and trusted that the ministry would 'continue to follow its present principles'.[168] For Peter Hodge, a director of Manchester City, the resort to overseas markets was unnecessary: 'my view is that we have enough players in the British Isles to supply our needs and keep up the standard of football that is required'. Hodge's views were echoed by the England international Eddie Hapgood, one of Hiden's prospective teammates, who admitted in his autobiography that he had applauded the exclusion of Hiden as there were 'enough good players in this country to go round without importing them from abroad'.[169] Such attitudes were driven by something more than xenophobia. The effects of the Depression and the specific problems of unemployment in professional football sharpened opposition to continental imports. For Cecil Hadley of *The People*, it was scandalous that football's governing bodies should consider allowing a foreign footballer to enter the country and take British jobs when there were two million unemployed, or that Arsenal could think of sending money in transfer fees abroad – 'money, remember, made in the bulk out of the working-class patrons of the game'.[170] Despite his criticisms of the inactivity of the FA and the League, Hadley's campaign against the Hiden transfer could rely on the support of one influential administrative figure: Charles Sutcliffe. The League Vice-President raised many of the stock objections to the employment of 'foreigners': that it would deprive Britons of jobs, discourage local talent and, no less seriously for Sutcliffe, raise insurmountable language problems, leading to anarchy in dressing-rooms and on the field of play. 'The idea of bringing foreigners to play in league football', Sutcliffe argued, 'is repulsive to the clubs, offensive to the players and a terrible confession of weakness in the management of the club'.[171] Implicit in all this was the same sense of superiority, prejudice and mistrust of the 'foreigner' reflected in his attitude to overseas tours, combined with a strong defence of British football's traditional self-sufficiency in recruitment and an antipathy towards any suggestion of outside control or exploitation.

Sutcliffe's point of view was influential and widely shared in football circles. In October 1930, C. Wreford-Brown, a former amateur international and representative of Oxford University, proposed to the FA Council that a two-year residential qualification should be imposed on non-British players wishing to compete in the FA Cup. His primary object was to nip in the bud a possible wave of continental imports: 'with talent becoming so highly developed on the Continent, no one knows what may happen in the future'.[172] Backed by the League Management Committee, however, Sutcliffe submitted a more comprehensive scheme by extending Wreford-Brown's residential qualification to 'all clubs and all competitions'.[173] While the balance of opinion favoured restriction of some kind, there were those who took a more moderate and liberal view. William Struth, manager of Glasgow Rangers, regarded the policy of the Home Office as draconian and 'entirely inconsistent' given that 'none of the first-class players [were] unemployed' and that no similar prohibitions were placed on theatrical performances from overseas. Under Ivan Sharpe's stewardship, *Athletic News* was particularly sympathetic to Arsenal's attempts to field continental footballers: 'really great footballers are scarce, and … the average supporter would give a warm welcome to any man who could play first-class football, whether he be English, Scottish, German, Dane, or Jap, if it comes to that'. In the present economic slump, it supported a temporary ban on imports but warned football's bosses not to 'shut the door to the many splendid players who are now being produced overseas'. A club should not be prevented from 'adding to its attractions the world's best players', thus keeping England at the pinnacle of world football.[174] Such platitudes had little impact on the FA Council, which at its 1931 annual meeting voted for the Sutcliffe resolution. His determination to 'stand by British players for British games' had won through.[175] The new measure represented an effective veto on the importation of professional footballers from the continent, and a further sealing off of the Football League from foreign influence.

* * *

For the Football League and its predominantly English membership, international football consisted of two distinct and fundamentally contrasting relationships. Close contacts between the FA and its sister associations in Scotland, Ireland and Wales preceded the creation of the

League, while non-English players and administrators were instrumental in the foundation and early progress of its leading clubs. Thus the League emerged in an environment where national footballing distinctions were fluid and boundaries largely ignored. From the beginnings, the Football League's perspective was British rather than strictly English, and its horizons soon stretched beyond the territory of its membership and towards Glasgow, Cardiff and Belfast. The process of expansion, in which the League developed into the premier competition not only in England but also in Britain, reinforced the basic inequalities in the relationship between the British football organisations. By the inter-war period, Football League clubs were employing the most talented players throughout the British Isles and, with their greater financial clout, were able to dictate the terms on which players would be released to play for their countries of birth. The League's mastery over British football was widely acknowledged. W. E. Maley, a Celtic director, admitted that these players 'belong to English clubs, and Scotland has not the slightest claim over them. Self-preservation is what matters now first and last in English professional football'.[176]

While self-preservation encouraged Preston to extend its control over the British game, it led to the opposite impulse in relation to overseas football. Historians have rightly emphasised the 'administrative isolationism' of British football, especially in the inter-war period, which was undoubtedly associated with a wider perspective of 'splendid isolation' in the British economy, society and culture.[177] In concert with the FA, the Football League was able in the main to seal off Britain from the interchange of playing talent between different nations and leagues that was a feature of football's development in continental Europe and the Americas. Notwithstanding the importance of informal links between League clubs and their continental counterparts, the League remained insulated from overseas developments and only glanced beyond British shores when its administrative or sporting authority became threatened. In contrast to its view of British 'international' football, the League considered the game overseas as a fundamentally alien affair that it neither wanted nor needed to involve itself in.

Notes

1 Comment of John Lewis in *Football and Sports Special*, 16 January 1909.

2 Walvin, *The People's Game*, Chapter 6.

3 H. F. Moorhouse, 'One State, Several Countries: Soccer and Identities in a "United" Kingdom' in *Tribal Identities: Nationalism, Europe, Sport*, ed. J. A. Mangan, London, Frank Cass, 1996, pp. 55–74. For broader reflections on 'British' and 'four nations'

history, see J. G. A. Pocock, 'The Limits and Divisions of British History: In Search of the Unknown Subject', *American Historical Review*, Vol. 87, 1982, pp. 311–36; A. Grant and K. Stringer (eds), *Uniting the Kingdom? The Making of British History*, London, Routledge, 1995; R. Samuel, 'British Dimensions: "Four Nations History"', *History Workshop Journal*, Vol. 40, 1995, pp. ii–xxii. This chapter adopts the extensive definition of 'British history' suggested by Pocock, regarding pre-partition Irish football alongside the Scottish, Welsh and English game as part of a corporate 'British' football structure.

4 Green, *History*, pp. 76, 90.

5 For the development of the professional game in Wales and its relations with English competition, see Johnes, *Soccer*, especially Chapters 1 and 2.

6 Football League Minutes, Management Committee, 30 May 1921.

7 Crampsey, *Scottish Football League*, p. 95. Both applications were rejected and the leaving clubs not replaced. Berwick was eventually admitted for the 1955–56 season, and remain the only English-based club competing in the Scottish League.

8 See Appleton, *Hotbed*, pp. 175–84.

9 See report of John McKenna's speech prior to the Inter-League match against the Irish League in *Athletic News*, 23 October 1911; FA International Selection Committee Minutes, 29 March 1920; WHUFC, Board Minutes, 28 October 1930.

10 Crampsey, *Scottish Football League*, p. 245.

11 Sutcliffe, Brierley and Howarth, *Story of the Football League*, p. 134.

12 Quoted in Crampsey, *Scottish Football League*, p. 39.

13 Rules of International Football League Board, Football League Handbook, 1899–1900, p. 25.

14 *Athletic News*, 16 January 1916.

15 Rules and Bye-Laws of Anglo-Irish Football League Board, Football League Handbook, 1915–16, pp. 59–62. The only variation was that the Anglo-Irish Board consisted of two rather than four representatives from each league.

16 Report of Football League AGM in *Athletic News*, 1 June 1914.

17 Johnes, *Soccer*, p. 194; A. Evans, 'Football on the edge: the relationship between Welsh football policy-making and the British International Championship', unpublished MA dissertation, De Montfort University, 1996, pp. 29, 34.

18 Sutcliffe, Brierley and Howarth, *Story of the Football League*, pp. 89–90.

19 *Athletic News*, 16 January, 31 January, 6 March 1916.

20 *Athletic News*, 14 August, 11 September 1916.

21 Football League Minutes, Management Committee, 6 December 1920.

22 *Athletic News*, 13 December 1920.

23 See Moorhouse, 'One State', pp. 58–64; J. Sugden and A. Bairner, *Sport, Sectarianism and Society in a Divided Ireland*, Leicester, Leicester University Press, 1993; M. Cronin, *Sport and Nationalism in Ireland: Gaelic Games, Soccer and Irish Identity Since 1884*, Dublin, Four Courts, 1999. On the origins of the creation of the two Irish associations, see N. Garnham, 'Origins and Development of Irish Football' in *The Origins and Development of Football in Ireland*, ed. N. Garnham, Belfast, Ulster Historical Foundation, 1999, pp. 25-29.

24 *Lancashire Daily Post*, 27 April 1931; *Topical Times*, 11 July 1931.

25 *Athletic News*, 8 June 1931.

26 Sutcliffe, Brierley and Howarth, *Story of the Football League*, p. 142; Football League Minutes, Management Committee, 15 December 1946.

27 These figures are adapted from Vamplew, *Pay Up*, p. 205 (Table 13.1); *Athletic News*, 3, 10, 17, 24 August 1925.
28 *Athletic News*, 14 August 1911; B. Crampsey, *The Scottish Footballer*, Edinburgh, William Blackwood, 1978, p. 33.
29 *Athletic News*, 24 August 1925; Young, *Football on Merseyside*, p. 131; *Topical Times*, 24 June 1933.
30 Young, *Football in Sheffield*, p. 127; SUFC, Football Committee Minutes, 29 April 1925.
31 H. F. Moorhouse, 'Blue Bonnets over the Border: Scotland and the Migration of Footballers' in *The Global Sports Arena: Athletic Talent Migration in an Interdependent World*, ed. J. Bale and J. Maguire, London, Frank Cass, 1994, p. 81; P. Joannou, *Wembley Wizards: The Story of a Legend*, Edinburgh, Mainstream, 1990, pp. 20–23.
32 See H. F. Moorhouse, 'Scotland against England: Football and Popular Culture', *International Journal of the History of Sport*, Vol. 4, 1987, p. 194 (Table 2).
33 See *Topical Times*, 18 February 1928; *Athletic News*, 30 January 1928.
34 Crampsey, *Scottish Footballer*, p. 32.
35 *Topical Times*, 18 March 1933.
36 Players based at English clubs, or 'Anglos' as they were called at the time, were not selected for the Scottish national side until 1896, while the Irish selectors refused to choose 'exiles' based at English or Scottish clubs until 1899. Moorhouse, 'Scotland against England', p. 193; *Ireland's Saturday Night*, 4 March 1899. I am grateful to Neal Garnham for this latter reference and others in this section.
37 International Football Association Board Minutes, 20 June 1898; Evans, 'Football', p. 37.
38 International Football Association Board Minutes, 19 June 1899.
39 Report of Football League AGM in *Athletic News*, 5 June 1911.
40 Report of International Football League Board, 12 March 1921; International Football Association Board Minutes, 10 June 1922.
41 Data drawn from J. Rollin (ed.), *Rothman's Football Yearbook, 1989–90*, London, Headline, 1989.
42 FA International Football Association Board Minute Book, 1886–1956, letter from F. J. Wall to C. Watson, 22 February 1929.
43 FA International Football Association Board Minute Book, 1886–1956, letter from C. Watson to F. J. Wall, 18 April 1929.
44 SUFC, Football Committee Minutes, 30 October 1929; Football League Minutes, Management Committee, 29 November 1929; Moorhouse, 'One State'.
45 Football League Minutes, 2 June 1930 (AGM).
46 FA International Selection Committee Minutes, 13 October 1930.
47 Football League Minutes, Management Committee, 12 January 1931.
48 See Football League Shareholders' Meeting Minutes (First and Second Divisions), 6 March 1931.
49 WHUFC, Board Minutes, 12 March 1923; SUFC, Football Committee Minutes, 23 February 1921.
50 *Topical Times*, 31 October 1931.
51 See Harding, *Alex James*, pp. 84–85; *Topical Times*, 3 March 1928.
52 HTFC, Board Minutes, 6 February 1939. Hayes's release was eventually blocked by the club Chairman and League Committee member Amos Brook Hirst.
53 *Thomson's Weekly News*, 26 February 1910; *Topical Times*, 31 October 1931.
54 Football League Minutes, Management Committee, 11 March 1930. Such release

clauses seem to have been rare, but the Irish FA revealed that John Kirwan had one written into his Tottenham Hospur contract while playing in the Southern League during the early 1900s. Irish Football Association, Finance Committee Minutes, 25 August 1924.

55 Harding, *Alex James*, pp. 93–94; Young, *Football in Sheffield*, p. 138. Both James and Dunne were transferred to Arsenal following disputes over their availability for international matches.

56 FA International Selection Committee Minutes, 22 April 1932.

57 *Sporting Chronicle*, 11 April 1932; *Topical Times*, 10 October 1931.

58 Crampsey, *Scottish Football League*, p. 97.

59 Sutcliffe, Brierley and Howarth, *Story of the Football League*, p. 139.

60 Report of International Football League Board Meeting in *Sporting Chronicle*, 13 June 1932.

61 FA Minute Books, International Matches Memorandum: summary of position by W. Pickford of matters discussed at 9 January and 16 March 1934 conferences.

62 Sutcliffe, Brierley and Howarth, *Story of the Football League*, p. 140.

63 Report of Football League AGM in *Sporting Chronicle*, 5 June 1934; Sutcliffe, Brierley and Howarth, *Story of the Football League*, p. 141.

64 Murray, *Football*, p. 93.

65 See H. Chapman, *Herbert Chapman on Football*, London, Garrick, 1934; Sharpe, *40 Years*, especially Chapters 9, 16 and 24. The James Catton Folders and Archives are held at Arsenal FC, Highbury Stadium, London.

66 On Rous, see S. Rous, *Football Worlds: A Lifetime in Sport*, London, Faber and Faber, 1978; J. Sugden and A. Tomlinson, *FIFA and the Contest for World Football*, Cambridge, Polity, 1998.

67 T. Mason, 'Defeat of the Soccer Exiles', *BBC History Magazine*, Vol. 1, 2000, pp. 33–34.

68 Murray, *Football*, p. 93.

69 On Hugo Meisl, see the later account of his journalist brother W. Meisl, *Soccer Revolution*, London, Phoenix, 1955. On Pozzo, see his autobiography, V. Pozzo, *Campioni del Mondo. Quarant'anni di storio del calico italiano*, Rome, CEN, 1960.

70 P. Beck, *Scoring for Britain: International Football and International Politics, 1900–1939*, London, Frank Cass, 1999, p. 102.

71 After retiring as a League referee in 1905, Lewis was recalled to officiate at the 1908 London Olympics and also took control of the controversial 1920 Olympic Final at Antwerp, in which the Czech side left the field following a sending-off and he awarded the game to Belgium. In his later years, Lewis undertook overseas trips as a travelling official with FA representative sides to South Africa and Australia. Sutcliffe described Lewis as a 'missionary for football' who devoted 'time and money to a ceaseless propaganda in our Colonies where football was in its infancy'. Sutcliffe and Hargreaves, *Lancashire FA*, p. 158; Miller, *Blackburn Worthies*; Jackman, *Blackburn Rovers*, p. 145.

72 *Topical Times*, 14 January 1928; 2 July 1927.

73 *Topical Times*, 3 July 1926; 3 June 1933.

74 Mason, 'Defeat', p. 34; *Topical Times*, 18 March 1933.

75 On the rise of FIFA and its evolving relationship with the British governing bodies, see P. Beck, 'Going to War, Peaceful Coexistence or Virtual Membership? British Football and FIFA, 1928–46', *International Journal of the History of Sport*, Vol. 17, 2000; A. Tomlinson, 'Going Global: The FIFA Story' in *Off the Ball: The*

Football World Cup, ed. A. Tomlinson and G. Whannel, London, Pluto, 1986, pp. 87–93.

76 *Athletic News*, 30 January 1928.

77 See International Football Association Board Minutes, 14 June 1920.

78 FA Minute Books, report of the Conference of Representatives of the Associations of the United Kingdom, 17 February 1928.

79 *Topical Times*, 12 May 1928.

80 P. Lanfranchi, 'Exporting Football: Notes on the Development of Football in Europe' in *Game Without Frontiers: Football, Identity and Modernity*, ed. R. Giulianotti and J. Williams, Aldershot, Arena, 1995, pp. 34, 44.

81 M. Marschik, 'Mitropa: Representations of "Central Europe" in Football', *International Review of the Sociology of Sport*, Vol. 36, 2001, pp. 7–23.

82 P. Lanfranchi, 'Bologna: The Team that Shook the World', *International Journal of the History of Sport*, Vol. 8, 1991, p. 338.

83 For these reasons, plus a disinclination to play Sunday matches, Sheffield United declined numerous offers to tour continental Europe and South America before 1914. See SUFC, Football Committee Minutes, 1903–12 *passim*; *Athletic News*, 8 March 1909.

84 Meisl, *Soccer Revolution*, pp. 57–60.

85 Mason, *Passion of the People?*, pp. 17–18; Keates, *History*, p. 132.

86 Football League Minutes, Management Committee, 9 August 1912.

87 Stanley Rous noted that 'only very few English teams had toured the Continent' prior to 1926, and saw the increasing frequency of inter-war touring as the result of 'the breaking down of some of the international reserve' after the Great War. S. F. Rous, 'Football as an International Sport', *The Listener*, 4 May 1938, p. 961.

88 Football League Minutes, Management Committee, 28 April 1922; 11 April, 12 May 1924.

89 D. McDougall, *Fifty Years a Borough, 1886–1936: The Story of West Ham*, London, West Ham County Borough Council, 1936, p. 220.

90 Mason, *Passion of the People?*, p. 23.

91 WHUFC, Board Minutes, 24 April 1923; AVFC, Board Minutes, 16 March 1926.

92 References to the role of Rudd in facilitating tours and matches with Scandinavian club sides can be found throughout the minute books of Aston Villa, Sheffield United, West Ham United and other leading clubs.

93 Matthews, *The Wolves*.

94 SUFC, Football Committee Minutes, 22 November 1911.

95 See Allison, *Allison Calling*, p. 142; G. Jordan, *Football européen*, Paris, Triolet, 1947, p. 88.

96 Arsenal hosted the 7–1 defeat of Spain in 1931, the famous 'Battle of Highbury' against Italy in November 1934 and the 6–2 win over Hungary in 1936. England's victories against France in 1933 (4–1), Germany in 1934 (3–0) and Czechoslovakia in 1936 (5–4) took place at Tottenham's White Hart Lane ground.

97 WHUFC, Board Minutes, 26 November 1934.

98 Murray, *Football*, p. 66.

99 See Beck, *Scoring*, Chapter 4.

100 *Athletic News*, 6 June 1927. On Burnley's 4–2 defeat in Nuremberg in 1927, see T. Riegler, *Als Staulfauth noch im Tor Stand… Ein Buch vom deutschen Fussball*, Munich, Porta Verlag K. G. Schemm, 1953, p. 101.

101 *Topical Times*, 5 May 1928.
102 Football League Minutes, Management Committee, 4 June 1928; Report of Football League AGM in *Athletic News*, 11 June 1928.
103 *Athletic News*, 3 June 1929.
104 J. Garcia Castell, *Història del futbol catalá*, Barcelona, Aymà, 1968, p.191; D. Hayes, *Bolton Wanderers: An A–Z*, Preston, Palatine, 1994, p. 52.
105 F. W. Carter and W. Capel-Kirby, *The Mighty Kick: The History, Romance and Humour of Football*, London, Jarrolds, 1933, p. 64.
106 Both extracts are quoted in *Athletic News*, 3 June 1929.
107 FA Emergency Committee Minutes, 8 October–9 December 1929.
108 Carter and Capel-Kirby, *Mighty Kick*, pp. 66–67.
109 See Beck, *Scoring*, pp. 118–21, 279.
110 *Daily Express*, 1 January 1929, quoted in Beck, *Scoring*, p. 123.
111 *Athletic News*, 20 May 1929; Report of Football League Secretaries' and Managers' Association AGM in *Athletic News*, 10 June 1929.
112 Crampsey, *Scottish Football League*, p. 100.
113 Football League Minutes, 1 June 1931 (AGM).
114 Report of Football League AGM in *Athletic News*, 8 June 1931.
115 SUFC, Football Committee Minutes, 12 November 1924; 9 February 1938.
116 *Sporting Chronicle*, 16 February 1933.
117 Lanfranchi, 'Exporting Football', pp. 35–36. The same can be said of France and Spain, where league matches were not so prestigious or well attended as friendly contests with international opposition.
118 *Topical Times*, 20 June 1931.
119 A. S. Markovits and S. L. Hellerman, *Offside: Soccer and American Exceptionalism*, Princeton, Princeton University Press, 2001, pp. 105–08; N. D. Abrams, 'Inhibited but not "Crowded Out": The Strange Fate of Soccer in the United States', *International Journal of the History of Sport*, Vol. 12, 1995, p. 13; Young, *Football in Sheffield*, p. 73.
120 Young, *Football in Sheffield*, p. 73.
121 Markovits and Hellerman, *Offside*, p. 106.
122 T. Mason, 'Some Englishmen and Scotsmen Abroad: The Spread of World Football' in *Off the Ball: The Football World Cup*, ed. A. Tomlinson and G. Whannel, London, Pluto, 1986, p. 74. Carter and Capel-Kirby, *Mighty Kick* suggested that 'Hundreds of ex-players from England and beyond the Tweed have found lucrative and pleasant employment abroad [as coaches]', p. 140.
123 On Hogan, see Mason, 'Some Englishmen', p. 74; Walvin, *The People's Game*, pp. 110–11; D. Turner and A. White, *Football Managers*, Derby, Breedon, 1993, p. 152. On Garbutt, P. Lanfranchi, '"Mister" Garbutt: The First European Manager', *The Sports Historian*, Vol. 22, 2002, pp. 44–59.
124 Lanfranchi, 'Mister', p. 45; Turner and White, *Football Managers*, pp. 90, 185; *Topical Times*, 18 May 1935.
125 G. Dykes, *The United Alphabet: A Complete Who's Who of Manchester United FC*, Leicester, Polar, 1994, pp. 60–61; AFC, Catton Folders, B–C, letter from Herbert Burgess to James Catton, n.d., p. 206; *Athletic News*, 6 June 1927.
126 Carter and Capel-Kirby, *Mighty Kick*, pp. 132, 140; *Topical Times*, 18 March 1933.
127 A comprehensive account of the history of the ASL has yet to be written. Its statistical history is covered in Jose, *American Soccer*. Also see Markovits and Hellerman, *Offside*, pp. 109–14.

128 *Topical Times*, 19 May 1923; B. Glanville, *Soccer Round the Globe*, London: Sportsman's Book Club, 1961, p. 87.
129 *Topical Times*, 10 May 1924; *Sports Pictures*, 31 May 1924.
130 Jose, *American Soccer*, pp. 483, 487, 490; *Athletic News*, 4 June 1928.
131 Football League Minutes, Management Committee, 13 December 1926; 7 March 1927.
132 As Mark Wyman has pointed out, return and seasonal migration were the norm for many European workers who travelled across the Atlantic during this period. M. Wyman, *Round Trip to America: The Immigrants Return to Europe, 1880–1930*, London, Cornell University Press, 1993; 'Return Migration – Old Story, New Story', *Immigrants and Minorities*, Vol. 20, 2001, pp. 1–18.
133 *Topical Times*, 25 December 1926.
134 *Topical Times*, 11 August 1928.
135 Markovits and Hellerman, *Offside*, pp. 112–14; *New York Times*, 5 January 1929.
136 On the origins and development of the league, see Wahl and Lanfranchi, *Footballeurs*, pp. 57–83.
137 *Daily Herald*, 13 April, 18 April 1932.
138 *Le sports du Sud-Est*, 21 April 1932; Carter and Capel-Kirby, *Mighty Kick*, p. 114.
139 *Daily Herald*, 14 April 1932; *Sporting Chronicle*, 14 April 1932.
140 Football League Minutes, Management Committee, 22 April 1932.
141 *Daily Mail*, 14 April 1932; *Sporting Chronicle*, 27 April 1932.
142 *Topical Times*, 30 April 1932.
143 *Daily Herald*, 29 April 1932.
144 *Sporting Chronicle*, 13 May 1932.
145 *Sporting Chronicle*, 2 May 1932.
146 Chalk and Holley, *Saints*, p. 279; Dykes, *Oldham Athletic*, p. 116.
147 *Le sports du Sud-Est*, 26 May 1932; T. Carder and R. Harris, *Seagulls! The Story of Brighton and Hove Albion FC*, Hove, Goldstone, 1993, p. 95; Carter and Capel-Kirby, *Mighty Kick*, p. 118.
148 *Sporting Chronicle*, 24 February 1933. The data is taken from *Football*, *passim*, 1933–38.
149 *Topical Times*, 13 August 1932; 27 October 1934.
150 Data drawn from Football, *passim*, 1933–38.
151 See P. Hurseau, *L'histoire du Football Nordiste*, Lille, Ligue du Nord du Football, 1977, p. 149; *Les miroir des sports*, 3 December, 10 December, 31 December 1935.
152 *Topical Times*, 12 May 1934.
153 *Topical Times*, 13 August 1932.
154 AFPTU Minutes, 22 March 1937; FA Emergency Committee Minutes, 28 March–19 August 1935.
155 Dykes, *Oldham Athletic*, p. 73; Jose, *American Soccer*, p. 348.
156 D. Cesarini, 'Anti-Alienism in England After the First World War', *Immigrants and Minorities*, Vol. 6, 1987, pp. 5–29; P. Panayi, *Immigration, Ethnicity and Racism in Britain, 1815–1945*, Manchester, Manchester University Press, 1994, pp. 102–25.
157 P. Vasili, *Colouring over the White Line: The History of Black Footballers in Britain*, Edinburgh, Mainstream, 2000, p. 64; *The First Black Footballer: Arthur Wharton, 1865–1930*, London, Frank Cass, 1998.
158 *Athletic News*, 3 November, 17 November, 10 November 1913.
159 See C. Holmes, *John Bull's Island: Immigration and British Society, 1871–1971*,

London, Macmillan, 1988, pp. 95, 309; A. Dummett and A. Nichol, *Subjects, Citizens, Aliens and Others: Nationality and Immigration Law*, London, Weidenfeld & Nicolson, 1990.

160 R. Archer and A. Bouillon, *The South African Game: Sport and Racism*, London, Zed, 1982, p. 99; Young, *Football on Merseyside*, pp. 116, 130–31.

161 See *Topical Times*, 21 May 1938.

162 J. Hill, 'Cricket and the Imperial Connection: Overseas Players in Lancashire in the Inter-War Years' in *The Global Sports Arena: Athletic Talent Migration in an Interdependent World*, ed. J. Bale and J. Maguire, London, Frank Cass, 1994, pp. 49–62.

163 Jose, *American Soccer*, pp. 463–64.

164 Dummett and Nichol, *Subjects*, pp. 92–112; J. Salt and R. T. Kitching, 'Labour Migration and the Work Permit System in the United Kingdom', *International Migration*, Vol. 28, 1990, p. 267.

165 Carter and Capel-Kirby, *Mighty Kick*, p. 121; AFC, Board Minutes, 10 July, 28 August 1930.

166 *Athletic News*, 28 July 1930; Carter and Capel-Kirby, *Mighty Kick*, p. 121.

167 *Athletic News*, 1 September 1930; *Topical Times*, 13 September 1930; AFC, Board Minutes, 7 August, 28 August 1930.

168 FA International Selection Committee Minutes, 25 August 1930; AFPTU Minutes, 25 August 1930.

169 *Athletic News*, 25 August 1930; E. Hapgood, *Football Ambassador*, London, Sporting Handbooks, 1944, p. 70.

170 *The People*, 13 July, 27 July 1930.

171 *Topical Times*, 26 July, 23 August, 6 September 1930.

172 FA Council Minutes, 13 October, 15 December 1930; AFC, Catton Folders, B, newspaper clipping on Wreford-Brown's proposal to ban continental players, 9 October 1930, p. 174.

173 *Athletic News*, 25 October 1930; report of FA AGM in *Athletic News*, 8 June 1931.

174 *Athletic News*, 18 August, 21 July 1930.

175 FA Council Minutes (AGM), 1 June 1931; *Topical Times*, 26 July 1930.

176 *Athletic News*, 9 June 1930.

177 Walvin, *The People's Game*, 143; R. Samuel, 'Introduction: Exciting to be English' in *Patriotism: The Making and Unmaking of British National Identity, Volume 1: History and Politics*, ed. R. Samuel, London, Routledge, 1989, pp. xxii–xxviii.

CHAPTER SEVEN

The League, the Public and the Promotion of Football

While much of the historiography of the commercialisation of sport and leisure has focused on the mid and late Victorian period or earlier, recent studies have confirmed that the first half of the twentieth century represented an equally crucial phase of this commercial revolution.[1] Stephen Jones has observed that while leisure was 'in its prototype stage' in the late nineteenth century, between the wars 'it was radically altered if not transformed' and 'brought into the twentieth century'.[2] In football, the development of a fully regulated labour market, bureaucratic and administrative structures, and large-scale ground improvements were all prominent features of this period. Ancillary services such as the press and gambling also underwent a significant transformation, while the rise of the football pools and radio broadcasting in the late 1920s and 1930s contributed to the widening of the potential football public and increased opportunities for additional club and League income. The contemporary consensus was that elite professional football was 'big business' in the early twentieth century and had become an industry in its own right by 1939. Paradoxically, however, the role of the Football League and its member clubs in this area has tended to be downplayed: inertia, if not obstinate conservatism, has become the orthodox interpretation of the League's response to the commercialisation of the game. According to this view, rising attendances and widespread financial prosperity worked against thorough commercial exploitation: the League did not expand the commercial side of its operations simply because there was no pressure to do so. More than this, the assumption is that the general increase in gates was a direct by-product of rising working-class prosperity and consumer spending.[3] Periods of declining attendances, competition from other sports and entertainments, and the subsequent response of League clubs are rarely brought into the equation.

This chapter will attempt to present a more balanced picture of the Football League's relationship with its immediate spectating public and the broader general public, with whom it connected indirectly through the media, the pools and other activities. The main chronological focus will be the period after the First World War. In particular, we will seek to determine how far opposition to some forms of commercial and popular penetration was modified by other attempts to widen the potential audience and 'sell' the game. This, too, is tied to the whole issue of the League's perception of the product it 'manufactured', and the ostensibly contradictory arenas of sport and entertainment. Was the League competition seen by officials, directors and players as a form of entertainment comparable to the theatre, music hall or the cinema? If so, to what extent did football clubs adopt techniques prevalent in other parts of the entertainment industry in order to stimulate demand and increase audiences? In essence, we will attempt to evaluate the degree to which the game's undisputed popularity at the outbreak of war in 1939 occurred because, or in spite, of the activity of the League executive and its clubs.

Attendances, gate receipts and the popularity of League football

Notwithstanding the significant fluctuations and uneven development of the British economy as a whole, particularly in the inter-war years, the commercial growth of the Football League in this period was undoubtedly significant. The best illustration of this can be found in the rise of attendances and gate receipts. Data on both have proved notoriously patchy and unreliable for most of the period, and historians have thus been forced to rely on press estimates or other impressionistic published material, such as Political and Economic Planning's oft-quoted figures focusing on the 1937–38 season.[4] Rather surprisingly, the clubs' own statistics and those kept centrally by the League from 1925 onwards have been largely neglected, though it must be acknowledged that these too are problematic.[5] Yet taking these limitations into account, it has still been possible to outline the salient trends and to establish the extent to which the period witnessed expansion or contraction in spectator support. Mason has established that the average attendances at First Division matches in 1908–09 was just below 16,000, while Fishwick found that this had increased by approximately 1,000 by the 1911–12 season. Tischler's calculated average of 23,115 for 1913–14 seems rather exceptional, and too high to fit with the gradual seasonal increase before the First World War.[6] The existing orthodoxy has it that, in Jones's words, 'football attendances were high and rising in the inter-war years'.[7] Drawing on a selective range of statistics, this point can be easily supported. We can identify a rise in First Division attendances from approximately 22,000 in the immediate post-war season to over 25,000 in 1927–28 and then 30,000 by 1937–38.[8] The contrast appears to be marked. While six million people watched First Division matches in 1908–09, the figure for 1937–38 was nearly 14 million.[9]

The problem with examples of this kind is that they suggest an uninterrupted rise in popularity by ignoring examples of contraction and focusing solely on the top division. The true picture is not in fact of a uniform upward curve in attendances and gate receipts, but of uneven progress with cycles of rising and falling popular support. Taking Table 7.1 as our guide, we can see that aggregate seasonal attendances dropped after 1921–22 and again from the early 1930s onwards in response to changes in the wider economic environment. A recovery initiated in 1933–34 gained considerable ground from the middle of the decade onwards, reaching a peak in 1937–38 before a slight dip in the final pre-war season. Some clubs were affected more than others by the economic slumps of 1922 and the early 1930s. The Third Division Northern Section suffered particularly in both periods. Inglis has calculated that in comparison to the Southern Section, whose seasonal match receipts averaged £7,625 per club, most northern members in the 1921–22 season could only make between £3,000 and £4,000, while the receipts of five – Halifax Town, Rochdale, Nelson, Stalybridge Celtic and Durham City – actually dropped below this level.[10] Nearly a decade later, Accrington Stanley was surviving on home match receipts of about £95, while during November 1931 Rochdale was attracting gates of 'barely 2,000' and receipts of only £60.[11] As we might expect, the financial position of clubs during the Depression was also regionally differentiated. The *Daily Mail* could report in April 1932 that Middlesbrough, Blackburn Rovers, Bolton Wanderers, Burnley, Preston North End and Oldham Athletic had all 'suffered grievously' during the preceding season in terms of falling attendances and gate receipts, while support for London clubs had held out and in some cases increased.[12] Furthermore, as Tables 7.1 and 7.2 suggest, the uneven distribution of attendances and gate income between divisions meant that the financial advances of the leading clubs were continually offset by the financial struggles of the lower division members, even though the attendance gap between the First Division and the rest of the League undoubtedly narrowed in the last three pre-war seasons.

Table 7.1: Football League attendances, 1921/22–1938/39 (millions)

			Aggregates		
Season	*Total*	*Div. 1*	*Div. 2*	*Div. 3 (S)*	*Div. 3 (N)*
1921–22	25.6	12.5	6.1	4.4	2.5
1922–23	23.6	10.8	6.2	4.2	2.4
1923–24	23.3	10.8	5.9	4.1	2.5
1924–25	23.1	10.4	6.2	4.1	2.3
1925–26	23.1	10.4	6.1	3.9	2.6
1926–27	23.4	10.6	6.5	3.8	2.5
1927–28	23.5	10.6	6.9	3.6	2.5
1928–29	23.9	10.5	6.7	4.0	2.7
1929–30	22.9	10.5	6.3	3.9	2.3
1930–31	21.0	9.5	6.1	3.2	2.3
1931–32	21.8	9.9	5.6	3.9	2.2
1932–33	21.4	9.5	6.1	3.5	2.3
1933–34	22.5	10.4	5.8	3.8	2.5
1934–35	23.1	10.8	6.1	3.8	2.4
1935–36	24.7	11.4	6.9	4.0	2.4
1936–37	26.4	11.4	8.0	4.4	2.6
1937–38	27.9	11.6	8.6	4.6	3.1
1938–39	27.0	11.5	8.6	4.0	2.9

Source: Based on Dobson and Goddard, Economics, p. 57 (Table 2.8).

Table 7.2: Football League gate revenues, 1925/26–1938/39

	Total		*Percentage share*		
Season	*(£ million)*	*Div. 1*	*Div. 2*	*Div. 3 (S)*	*Div. 3 (N)*
1925–26	1.352	46.9	26.8	16.3	10
1926–27	1.373	47	28.2	15.5	9.3
1927–28	1.410	47.2	28.9	14.7	9.2
1928–29	1.419	45.7	28.3	16.1	9.9
1929–30	1.372	47.8	27.5	16.5	8.2
1930–31	1.246	47.4	28.5	15	9.1
1931–32	1.263	48.1	25.8	17.6	8.5
1932–33	1.261	46.9	28.8	15.4	9
1933–34	1.321	48.9	26.2	16	8.9
1934–35	1.373	49.9	26.3	15.3	8.5
1935–36	1.456	48.5	28.2	15.3	7.9
1936–37	1.575	45.2	30.3	16.1	8.4
1937–38	1.661	44.5	30.5	15.6	9.4
1938–39	1.594	45.8	31.1	13.9	9.2

Source: Based on Dobson and Goddard, *Economics*, p. 76 (Table 2.12).

The available evidence indicates that the popularity of the Football League, as measured by attendance figures and gate receipts, did not in fact rise steadily or uniformly after the First World War but fluctuated at the club, divisional and collective League level. This is not to deny that more people watched Football League matches – and paid more to do so – in 1939 than in 1919 (adjusting for the expansion from 44 to 88 clubs), but to qualify the conventional historical assumption that spectators simply 'turned up in droves' at every ground throughout the 1920s and 1930s.[13] Historians themselves are guilty here of being too easily dazzled by the big games and the record attendances of the top clubs to see the wider and more complicated picture.[14] More than this, it is important to relativise the popularity of League football by considering it alongside other sports and forms of entertainment. Jones has emphasised the broader demand conditions that facilitated increases in spending on entertainment and recreation: expenditure on admissions to theatres, cinemas and sporting events rose from £56.2 million in 1920 to £60.9 million in 1930, before dipping to £55.4 million four years later and recovering to £64.9 million by 1938.[15] These conditions benefited the major team sports like cricket and rugby league, which, however, rarely matched the attendance levels of elite football, as well as the more commercialised horse racing, greyhound racing and speedway meetings, which sometimes did.[16] Yet the public support for all these sports was dwarfed towards the end of our period by the growth of cinema; indisputably, in Jeffrey Richards's words, 'the most popular form of entertainment in Britain in the 1930s'.[17] While the Football League was able to attract some 27.9 million spectators paying £1.66 million in entry fees to all its matches during the course of the 1937–38 season (Tables 7.1 and 7.2), British cinema audiences hit 987 million with £41.5 million in gross receipts.[18] It is essential to keep in mind, then, that the League did not develop in a commercial vacuum but as one part of a broader process of recreational expansion from the nineteenth century onwards, and that it could never simply count on a broad base of support in view of the potential and real competition from other sporting activities and entertainments.

Selling the game? The League and popular entertainment

The precise connection between top-level professional football and entertainment was as elusive for contemporaries as it has proved to be for historians. There has been a tendency among academics to perceive 'sport' and 'entertainment' as fundamentally separate spheres of activity, although both are normally located within the broader categories of 'leisure' and 'recreation'.[19] Notwithstanding the crucial importance of the spectating public for the League's financial security, most contemporary observers were keen to distance the game from comparisons with the entertainment industry. This was certainly the case before 1914, when the notions of 'business football' and the importance of the spectators were habitually lambasted in the southern-based press, and often elsewhere, as contravening the basic tenets of sporting practice. Yet even at this point the categorisation of League football as entertainment was widespread. *Athletic News* stood largely alone in 1901 when it objected to the decision of the governing body to cancel a week of fixtures because of the Queen's death by referring to the practice of theatres and music halls: 'Surely there is a strong analogy between professional football and theatricals. Both are entertainments, and, in order to provide those of good class, competent performers have to be engaged so that they can give their patrons a good show for their money.'[20] We have seen that by 1909, FA Vice-President Charles Clegg was confident enough to applaud the Football League as 'a body of entertainers', although the term continued to be used pejoratively, as when one cricket writer condemned League clubs as 'mere "firms" … who simply provide entertainments by the medium of troupes of paid players'.[21] In his work on popular culture in London before 1918, Andrew Horrall has outlined the close links developed between professional football and the music hall, and the numerous interactions between the performers of stage, screen and sport.[22] Under these circumstances, the comment of one columnist that Harry Lauder and George Robey were 'public entertainers in the same way as Meredith, Crompton and Veitch are' was hardly unusual.[23]

Historians have recognised that commercial motives and objectives were less thoroughly developed among Football League clubs than in comparable entertainment businesses. Peter Bailey has described the Victorian music hall as 'a prototype modern entertainment industry, not just because its capital investment allowed economies of scale which secured a mass paying audience, but because of the thorough-going commercialisation which accompanied all facets of its operation'.[24] By comparison, the complex amalgam of club directors' motives and restrictions on shareholders' dividends suggest a different type of commercial orientation in League football. Vamplew and other historians have established that many sports clubs and investors did not fit neatly into the category of profit maximisers, a category more ideally suited to music hall and cinema entrepreneurs. In the Football League, certainly, there is ample evidence of profits being sacrificed for improved playing squads and ground facilities.[25]

There is little doubt that the place of entertainment in football was less easy to identify and define than at the cinema, for instance. For most club directors and supporters, it is likely that winning matches took precedence over entertainment, though it must not be assumed that these two aims were mutually exclusive: a talented team or the acquisition of a renowned player would hopefully ensure both. Entertainment, in short, was regarded not as the essence but a by-product of sporting competition. The Sunderland, Derby County and England international forward Raich Carter commented in his autobiography that:

> An actor, for instance, sets out with the full knowledge that he has to hold and entertain a public audience. With the exception of one or two who deliberately play to the gallery, a footballer is never consciously entertaining his spectators. His business is to win the match with the help of his ten colleagues.[26]

Yet during the inter-war period it became increasingly difficult to deny that at least one aspect of the Football League's purpose was to provide popular entertainment. At a basic level, this was recognised by professional football's inclusion along with other sports in the government's entertainment tax regulations from 1916. The tax was applied to all tickets for entertainment events, and even those clubs struggling to remain viable in the lower reaches of the League ladder were not exempt. The League's acceptance of the measure, albeit initially during the abnormal conditions of war, could be interpreted as a partial acknowledgement of its common interests with the entertainment industry. Indeed, as the tax began to eat into the incomes of clubs after the war, alliances were made beyond the sporting world: hence the support many clubs gave to the Provincial Entertainments Proprietors' and Managers' Association in its attempt to force the Chancellor to repeal the tax in 1930.[27]

More than this, however, there is evidence that the 1920s and 1930s witnessed a subtle change in League attitudes towards the idea of entertaining the spectating public. This can be seen in three main areas: alterations in the laws of the game, changes in ground facilities and the accommodation of spectators, and attempts to improve the football match as a spectacle. First of all, it is important to recognise that the laws of the game throughout the period were under constant re-evaluation and underwent almost annual modification. The body responsible for rule changes was the International Board, consisting of representatives from each of the British football associations and, intermittently from 1913, of FIFA. Thus alterations were not made specifically according to the wishes and concerns of professional football in general, or the Football League in particular, and it is indeed difficult to gauge the precise degree of influence that League representatives or club directors were able to wield. Certainly, there appears to have been relatively little concern in League circles about the need to produce attractive football at the beginning of the century, even though contemporary observations bear witness to the increasingly defensive play adopted by many sides. The pervasive use of the so-called 'one-back game', in which one full-back would drop into a deep defensive position so as to limit long forward passing, generated particular press criticism. Yet in answer to those critics who regarded the tactic as unsportsmanlike and unattractive, League representatives often emphasised a different set of priorities. Addressing the issue in December 1901, John Lewis argued that while 'there was an element of the spectacular' in football and 'those who pay have a right to be considered', the foremost objective for every club was nevertheless to win, and if the one-back game achieved this then there could be no objection to it.[28]

The changing attitudes towards the offside law over the period reflected the way in which the entertainment of spectators shifted from a marginal to a central consideration within League circles. Attempts by the Scottish FA to alter the law so that two rather than three opponents were required to be between the forward and the goal when a pass was made generated strong opposition for more than a decade after an initial proposal had failed in 1913. On that occasion, the presumed advantage of increased goal-scoring failed to convince League directors, who felt that the alteration would give forwards an unfair advantage and penalise good back play; the following season Lewis seconded another motion to oppose the Scottish proposals.[29] The development of defensive tactics including the offside trap, however, led to a change of opinion, fuelled no doubt by the record of goal-scoring in League matches, which by the early 1920s had dropped below an average of 2.8 goals per game in the First Division and 2.3 in the Second.[30] In 1923 the FA Council attempted to amend the offside law by limiting the area in which a player could be caught offside to 40 yards from the goal-line, on the grounds that 'it would largely reduce the number of stoppages and permit of the game being carried on more consecutively and with more satisfaction to spectators'.[31] The proposal narrowly failed at this and the following annual meeting, but by 1925 the support of a vast majority of League officials and club directors had bolstered the movement for change. For many, the problem had now reached a crisis point. Charlie

Buchan claimed that matches were becoming 'a procession of free-kicks', and Sutcliffe agreed that players and referees were 'sick to death of the eternal whistle'.[32] Significantly, for the first time the key interest group used to justify the change in the law from three to two defenders was the spectators. The League had arranged for the proposed new law to be tried as an experiment at a number of representative and practice matches, with the result that the ball was in play longer than under the old rule and that play around the goal area was made more exciting.[33] During the debate at the annual meeting, Sutcliffe emphasised the importance of not discrediting the game 'in the eyes of the public' by continuing with the present unsatisfactory offside law. Fred Rinder employed a similar argument when he told delegates that football 'had attained its world-wide popularity by its attractiveness, its quick movements, its thrills and its minimum of stoppages. These must be maintained to command the support of the public, by which the game existed'.[34] Opposition to the change among mainly amateur clubs and associations was insufficient to prevent its passage. The new rule certainly had the desired effect of improving goal ratios, at least in the short term. The 1924–25 figure of 2.54 goals per game throughout the League's four divisions rose to 3.44 in the first season of its operation, but the gradual introduction of the defensive centre-half, or 'third back', led to another decline to 2.94 goals per game by the 1937–38 season. Writing in 1934, Sutcliffe remained convinced that the change had 'given us more attractive football than ever, and saved us 20 or 30 useless stoppages which always happened under the old rule', even if some observers believed that as a consequence speed had been substituted for skill.[35]

Unlike in rugby league, however, there was no systematic effort to make the game more attractive for spectators. The alterations made in rugby league's rules between 1898 and 1907 – including the abandonment of line-outs, the introduction of the 'play the ball' rule and the reduction of the number of players on each side from 15 to 13 – was motivated partly by the rival attraction of the association code, with its 'potentially flowing simplicities'.[36] For its advocates, football was already established as the premier and most popular winter sport, so the changes that were made in the rules were intended to refine the game's fundamental attractions by reducing unnecessary stoppages and other factors that disrupted or slowed the pace of the game. Even then, it must be remembered that the Football League was not able to change the game's laws unilaterally for its own purposes in the way that the Northern Union was. The FA's broad authority meant that law changes had to be appropriate and acceptable to the amateur and lower levels of the administration, and not just moulded for the purposes of League clubs with big crowds; the machinery of the International Board also made it necessary to gain Scottish, Irish and Welsh approval for any proposed change. Thus even on occasions when its influence appeared to be paramount, as in 1925, the League's control over the rules of the game were really never more than partial.

As well as attempting to enrich the product on offer, there were some signs of Football League clubs trying to improve the manner in which it was consumed. This took the form, first, of better ground facilities and spectating conditions. The first major wave of ground building took place in the 1889–1910 period, with clubs either moving into established recreational and sporting venues or transforming sites of open land. Vast sums were spent in this direction. Everton invested some £41,000 on two large stands between 1907 and 1909, and a further £12,000 improving the terracing and other features of the ground; Middlesbrough spent £10–11,000 on its new Ayresome Park ground in 1903, and Birmingham laid out a similar sum building St Andrews three years later.[37] Such developments often allowed clubs not only to cater for larger numbers of spectators, but also to provide an improved view of the match in more palatial surroundings. Manchester United's new Old Trafford ground, which was opened in 1909 having cost £36,000, was described by one writer as 'a wonder to behold': as well as features designed for players and directors, the ground provided cover for 12,000 in its grandstand and a further 24,000 seats out of a capacity of 80,000.[38] Additionally, the club boasted that the numerous entrances and exits allowed spectators to move easily to the particular section of the ground desired and that, with no cycling or running track, 'the sightseers are brought as near as possible to the playing portion'; the rectangular shape of the ground with curved corners was also designed 'so that everybody will be able to see'.[39] Not every club, of course, had the financial resources to undertake such developments, and those that did often had to convert themselves into limited liability companies or issue debenture schemes to do so. While the Oldham Athletic directors, for example, recognised the importance of 'a well-equipped ground' to the club's future success, they struggled to find the capital needed to finance a new stand, and were forced to hurriedly construct one costing just £1,750 following the club's unexpected admission to the League in 1907.[40]

The extent to which ground improvements were undertaken as a response to demand from spectators remains unclear. Sutcliffe thought that there had been 'an outcry for more comfortable accommodation' prior to the First World War, and that the new imposing covered grandstands at many clubs 'had been erected in answer to popular clamour'.[41] The circumstances that led to the building of Wolverhampton Wanderers' first major stand in 1925 certainly seem to accord with this view. In December 1922, the club admitted that the lack of stand accommodation at Molineux had been 'commented upon and deplored', but encouraged supporters to be patient as the club had recently bought the ground and planned to undertake major ground improvements. A year later Wolves had slipped into the Third Division, finances were tight and the club, backed by the mayor and local dignitaries, launched a share appeal scheme among supporters to help fund the proposed developments.[42] Finally, with the club's promotion in 1925, the stand was opened. Yet the club programme's comments at the time of the official opening illustrate the way in which the rhetoric of service to the spectator was intermeshed with notions of supporter loyalty and financial profit:

> With the opening of the New Stand we are provided with a means to a most desirable end, and so long as the public appreciate it, there are no limitations to its possibilities for affording comfort and enjoyment, recreation and pleasure, and at the same time yielding revenue which in course of time will bring the cost to an irreducible minimum and set it on its mission as a profit-producing concern pure and simple.[43]

In applauding Manchester City's decision in 1931 to erect a cover at its recently built Maine Road ground providing protection for 10,000 supporters from the cold and rain, Sutcliffe similarly argued that 'money spent on public comfort is sure to come back quickly through increased attendances'.[44] There was clearly no altruism at work here: improving facilities was widely regarded as a vital means of improving gates. Despite this, however, it appears that many clubs were reluctant to commit themselves to large-scale ground improvements and that the initiative – and indeed the finance – for such schemes often came from the supporters rather than the club. This is particularly true of the inter-war period and the provision of covered accommodation for standing spectators, who – unlike those sitting in grandstands – were generally offered no protection from the elements. Supporters' clubs were especially active in raising funds for roofs and shelters to be built on 'popular' sides of the grounds.[45] Yet many club directorates remained insensitive and slow to react to appeals for better provision. The minute books of Sheffield United record a number of requests from spectators for more covered accommodation at Bramall Lane during the 1920s and 1930s, but it was not until 1937 that a sub-committee was appointed to consider the question, with the result that a shelter was built on the 'Spion' kop in time for the 1938–39 season.[46] Jimmy Seed, likewise, regretted the decision of his directors at Charlton Athletic not to build better covered and seated accommodation when the club reached the First Division in 1937, a decision that he believed accounted for the club's subsequent poor gates.[47]

Finally, there were efforts to improve the spectacle of visiting a football match, though these were often limited, uneven and differed from club to club. At the majority of League grounds the only entertainment provided besides the match itself consisted of a musical programme by a local band before kick-off and at half-time. Few clubs experimented with alternative methods of drawing spectators: the attraction of football was considered to be the game itself, and so directorates tended to have little time for peripheral distractions. Aston Villa agreed to a local newspaper's request to have community singing at some derby matches, but only with the proviso that it would cost the club nothing.[48] Plans to establish more extensive programmes of entertainment – including athletic and musical events to amuse the standing spectators in the hour or so prior to kick-off – were generally rejected or left undeveloped.[49] It is possible, however, to detect an increased accent on pre-match entertainment from the late 1920s onwards. In 1930, for instance, the Sheffield United Chairman and Secretary interviewed the bandmaster of the resident Imperial Band 'with a view to improving the calibre of the Band and also a more acceptable programme being rendered'. It was subsequently decided that while the band would still receive the annual £20 grant, its continued services would be subject to a month's trial.[50] West Ham United's matchday band was less fortunate in finding itself dismissed due to the installation of public service radio equipment at Upton Park at around the same time. The east London club was not alone in replacing live music with recorded music, though the cost of installation and the acquisition of a phonographic licence turned out to be considerably higher.[51] Indeed, such was the investment in the radio equipment that when public requests were made to replace it with a live band, the directors refused on the grounds that they 'did not consider the extra expense for musical entertainment warranted it'.[52]

Technological advances offered opportunities to enhance the spectating experience in a variety of ways, but here again progress was cautious and partial. The erection of results boards, clocks and floodlighting were all contemplated at different times and yet generated considerable opposition in League circles. The purpose of results or score boards was initially to display the score of the match in progress, but could potentially be used to keep the spectator informed of developments throughout the country. By the early 1920s, advances in telephonic communications together with press cooperation had persuaded some clubs, such as Sheffield United, to build results boards giving the half and full-time scores of selected League matches, although other clubs were reluctant to follow.[53] To boost reserve team attendances, many clubs decided to keep spectators in touch with the progress of the first team in away matches by providing updates every 15 minutes; Walsall did the same with the scores of its more prestigious neighbours Wolves and Aston Villa during first-team games.[54] Another innovation intended to facilitate the crowd's ability to follow the game was the introduction of the 45-minute football clock. While Herbert Chapman, most famously, had a large 12-foot-diameter clock attached to the North Stand at Highbury, other clubs refused similar proposals from watch companies. The FA, in any case, decided in October 1930 that such clocks compromised the time-keeping authority of referees, and therefore ruled that they should be immediately removed.[55]

The potential benefits of floodlit football for both clubs and spectators were also slow to receive official recognition. Experiments took place as early as the late nineteenth century, but until the 1920s artificial lighting could be used only for friendlies, practice sessions or exhibition matches. By this time, however, advances in electrical lighting had proven the viability of floodlit sports events, which were already commonplace in South American and some US sports.[56] However, the immediate inspiration for renewed British experiments came from visits to continental Europe, where floodlighting was developing at professional and amateur levels; after one such trip Chapman installed floodlights on Arsenal's West Stand.[57] This and other examples provoked the FA Council to respond in 1930 by prohibiting its members from taking part in competitive matches under artificial light, apparently on the grounds that clubs might be pushed into spending large sums on floodlighting, which they could ill afford.[58] However, over the next few years a number of club directors and journalists began to suggest that these possible high costs could be more than balanced by the financial benefits. In this view, floodlighting offered above all the chance to diversify the consumption of League football by establishing it as an evening as well as an afternoon event, a particularly important step in the context of the success of dog racing and speedway as evening attractions. By the summer of 1932 James Catton, a leading advocate of floodlighting, could detect a groundswell of support among English and Scottish clubs, especially those who had played under lights during overseas tours. J. G. Hickling, Secretary of Third Division Mansfield Town, believed that a relaxation of the governing body's restriction would be a 'boon' to clubs:

> just imagine the gates we should have if we could have the kick-offs in the evening at 7.30 p.m. in the winter, instead of say 2.30 or 3 when the workers cannot get [out]. If we could have football played under arc light conditions it is my positive opinion that in no less than five years we should nearly double the followers of football, in consequence of which, overdrafts at the banks, the bugbear of nearly all clubs, would sooner or later vanish.[59]

Although few contemporaries shared Hickling's optimistic view of floodlighting as a financial panacea, it was nevertheless widely agreed that spectators would benefit from the greater flexibility and variety it provided.[60] In an attempt to exploit these opportunities, Tottenham Hotspur orchestrated a movement of metropolitan clubs whose lobbying of the FA led to a temporary removal of the ban so as to allow a special exhibition match to be played under artificial lights at White City stadium in early 1933. The match, however, drew a disappointing crowd, and a number of clubs, including West Ham, subsequently withdrew their support for a permanent removal of the ban.[61]

The reluctance of the Football League to embrace innovations that complimented the football-watching experience can be best illustrated by the debate over the numbering of players' shirts. While the idea had been advocated many times since the beginning of the century, and had long been a feature of both rugby codes, it continued to divide clubs and administrators throughout the 1920s and 1930s. Club colours, as we saw in Chapter 2, had to be registered with the League Secretary, but additions to kits were not permitted, so on 25 August 1928 Arsenal and Chelsea agreed to take the field simultaneously in different matches with numbers on the backs of the players' shirts. On the day of the experiment, Catton issued an extended defence of shirt numbering, arguing that it was one aspect of the fundamental obligation that each club had towards its audience:

> Modern football cannot exist without the spectator. The objects of every Association football club, engaged in League football, should be to play the game and give the greatest possible pleasure to those who throng the seats and terraces. Therefore

> let League clubs do all they possibly can for the convenience and comfort of their legions of followers... Hence tip-up chairs, covered accommodation, result boards, programmes, and many other devices that were never dreamed of 40 years ago.

For this reason he found it 'difficult to understand why some clubs are strongly objecting to a proposed change which is of great help to everybody on all occasions. The convenience of the public should be paramount'.[62] The Chelsea directors even conducted their own market research and found that every one of the 700 fans questioned after the club's match at Swansea expressed support for numbering.[63]

Despite the apparent success of the Arsenal–Chelsea experiment, opposition to the idea stayed firm. The League executive stepped in immediately to prevent a repetition of the incident, by 'instructing' clubs not to number shirts until the question had been discussed at a general meeting.[64] At subsequent annual meetings in 1929 and 1933, proposals to introduce compulsory numbering were rejected by large majorities. The FA had agreed to players sporting shirt numbers at the 1933 Cup Final, and the winners Everton repeated the experiment in a subsequent League match, but many clubs continued to consider the cost in terms of money and team spirit too great. Ever mindful of practical obstacles, Sutcliffe argued that each club would probably require eight sets of numbered shirts, that numbers would be difficult to fix onto the shirt and would become impossible to see in muddy conditions. More significantly, he objected to a scheme 'which turns players out like a procession of gaol-birds'.[65] *Topical Times*'s 'Fuse' believed that numbering would make football 'a cattle market display', depriving the game of its 'personal touch': 'You know James by the length of his "skirt". You knew Buchan by his height and his nose. You know Dean by his darkness and his daring and his hitch of the trousers after every attack. You know Billy Walker by the inward slope of the kneecaps.'[66] The claims that numbering emphasised the individual at the expense of the team and was 'unsightly and undignified' failed to impress the popular press, many of whom echoed Catton in criticising the League for its inability to appreciate the interests of supporters.[67] 'In football all their lives', wrote Cecil Hadley, 'they are intimate with all but a few of the players, but their job, as guardians of the game, is to make football attractive and easily understandable to the masses... We want numbers, not for the League legislators, but for the public'.[68] By the mid-1930s, the League stood largely alone in not permitting numbering, as many reserve competitions and junior leagues had sanctioned the idea. It finally relented in 1939, largely due to pressure from a core group of lobbyists and the support of President William Cuff, who dismissed the notion of optional (as opposed to compulsory) numbering and carried the proposal as an instruction to clubs, even though it failed to reach the required three-quarters majority as a rule change.[69]

As the foregoing discussion has indicated, the Management Committee was slow to incorporate and diffuse techniques designed to improve both the intrinsic and the peripheral attractions of football. The majority of innovations, from club programmes to floodlighting, were conceived and refined at club level, and often met with the considerable obstacles of executive conservatism and the in-built inertia of the legislative system. In the eyes of League administrators, football spectators, or the so-called 'football public', were a rather shadowy and ill-defined group upon whom they ultimately relied for financial survival, but about whom they knew very little. There is certainly little evidence that the League made more than token efforts to respond to spectator demands, or that it encouraged its members to make the football-watching public their paramount concern. Beyond ensuring that clubs fielded full strength teams and started matches on time, the League's own regulations made few concessions to supporters. Only when overall attendances began to fall during the Depression was consideration given to the question of League football's popularity in an increasingly competitive product market. Writing before the 1933 annual meeting, Chelsea's Capel-Kirby argued that declining gates were less the result of the economic slump than 'a lack of enterprise' on the part of clubs and the League. He went on to suggest that 'failure to study the comfort, convenience and general well-being of the public is in a very large measure responsible for people staying away… The football follower has become tired of the lack of consideration shown him. He has revolted and shown his displeasure by staying away'.[70] In common with the BBC, the Football League of the 1930s was regularly accused of taking little interest in its audience, but whereas the former was able to react by establishing a sophisticated system of listener research by the end of the decade, the latter appeared only marginally interested in discovering what the public wanted.[71]

Advertising and the press

Away from the game itself and the arena in which it was played, clubs attempted to attract spectators using a variety of methods employed by conventional firms. Difficult as it is to assess its precise impact, advertising came to be regarded as a particularly important means of stimulating demand and thereby increasing crowds. As W. Hamish Fraser has shown, it had developed from its rudimentary stages in the early to mid-nineteenth century into a full-scale industry by the turn of the twentieth century. If football clubs preferred to distance themselves from the overt commercialism of Pears soap or Bovril, they operated nonetheless in an environment where advertising 'had become essential for any firm seeking to break into a market, to move from a local to a national market, or, in many cases, to hold on to its existing market'.[72] Elaborate promotional techniques certainly filtered through to sectors of the entertainment industry. Cinema owners, in particular, often erected huge displays in the foyer or the environs of their building specifically to advertise new features, and incorporated the showmanship and theatrical tactics used by department stores in the inter-war period to pull in customers. All this was then supplemented by carefully constructed newspaper advertisements designed by professional advertising firms and writers.[73]

Unsurprisingly, the use of advertising by Football League clubs was far less sophisticated. Promotional activity was generally based around bill posting and newspaper advertising of forthcoming matches. Directorates tried to keep this form of expenditure within strict limits. Walsall spent just £144 of a total expenditure of well over £8,000 on printing and advertising in 1933–34, and the more successful clubs devoted an even smaller percentage.[74] Money was often saved by arranging a form of mutual advertising with local theatres or other entertainment venues. At the beginning of the century, Sheffield United allowed three local theatres to send sandwich boards around the pitch on Saturdays in return for the announcement of the club's next match on a bioscope or in the theatre programme each evening. Such arrangements lasted into the 1930s, though the increasing competitiveness of football advertising was reflected in West Ham's agreement with the Stratford Empire that it would pay a small fee to have details of forthcoming matches exhibited on a slide, provided that no other club was permitted to advertise.[75] Other popular venues for advertising football matches were railway stations or similar transport facilities. Arrangements were made with railway companies to display bill posters of first-team matches. In preparation for the 1933–34 season, Sheffield United arranged with the London and North Eastern Railway Company to have 50 posters at fourpence each displayed at stations in and around Sheffield.[76] West Ham was one of a number of League clubs in the capital with long-standing advertising rights on the underground railway network, but from 1934 onwards London clubs were no longer entitled to individual advertisements at mainline stations, and paid instead for inclusion on a shared 'Football' notice.[77] Less conventionally, the Darlington directors experimented for a short time with a loudspeaker attached to a van, which toured the town and district days before home matches.[78]

Newspapers, however, continued to be the major outlet for advertising. Clubs had used small newspaper advertisements to publicise matches since before the establishment of the Football League, but the close relationships between many League clubs and their local newspapers had created broader promotional opportunities by the twentieth century. Mutual advertising arrangements were often established between clubs and local newspapers. The *Sheffield Telegraph*, for example, charged United half the usual price for first-team advertisements in return for the display of its sandwich board at these fixtures, a perfect illustration of the symbiotic relationship between sport and the press. By 1932, the Sheffield club had expanded its first-team advertisements from single to double columns in both the *Sheffield Telegraph* and *Sheffield Independent*, and at the same time redesigned its bill posters. The board went further by taking out a special whole-page advertisement in the *Green 'Un* for the opening matches of the 1938–39 season.[79] It must be remembered, however, that while Sheffield United and others were able to advertise throughout the season, clubs with smaller budgets had to target their advertising at specific games.[80]

League clubs did not, of course, gain publicity in the press simply by buying official advertising space. Match reports and results, discussion columns and other features were undoubtedly forms of free advertising for clubs, and this was as true of the local, and increasingly the national, dailies as of the specialist sporting press.[81] In short, by the turn of the century clubs relied on press coverage of League football to generate interest and stimulate demand, and therefore made various efforts to accommodate them. By 1911, Sheffield United was granting free press tickets to local newspapers (the *Telegraph* and *Independent*), to specialist sporting papers (*Athletic News, Sporting News*) and to national dailies and weeklies (the *Daily Mail, Daily Mirror* and *Reynold's News*), although photographic privileges were more tightly guarded.[82] Reporting was also facilitated by the construction of press boxes and the installation of private telephones at the club's expense. Even lower-division clubs were expected to have these facilities: one of the first building projects planned by the Ipswich Town directorate following election to the Third Division was a press box.[83] There is considerable evidence to support Fishwick's view that there existed a cosy, almost 'special' relationship between local journalism and the major clubs in a given area. The inclusion of local journalists in a club's travel party to away matches was common, and there can be little doubt that certain journalists were privy to inside information obtained directly from club directors and officials.[84] West Ham United arranged 'press nights' – rudimentary forerunners of modern press conferences – to officially unveil new stands or new signings during the 1920s. This seems to have been the first step in a new, systematic attitude towards publicity within the club. From January 1931 onwards, members of the press were issued with a 'news bulletin' the day after board meetings by the Assistant Secretary Alan Searles, and by 1933 the new player's manager Charlie Paynter had been given sole responsibility to 'give and seek publicity on *team* matters', with Searles controlling administrative, financial and other publicity.[85]

It would be wrong to assume that changes of this kind were motivated by a new atmosphere of openness and cooperation. Quite the opposite: they were intended to control more tightly the flow of information to the press and to avoid negative publicity. At West Ham, the reorganisation of publicity matters was a reaction to 'the surfeit of publicity' caused by the acrimonious dismissal of long-standing Secretary Syd King, which the board agreed 'should in future be avoided'.[86] The Oldham Athletic directors similarly tried to control the information given to the press about the club's financial problems in 1939 through official statements, but tended instead to be drawn into denying inaccurate stories or misleading articles.[87] The League also attempted to keep certain confidential matters – such as the precise size of transfer fees and the contents of retain-and-transfer lists, together with attendances and gate receipts – from the gaze of the press. Clubs were instructed by the Management Committee not to disclose information to newspapers, and held them responsible for breach of confidence if they did so; they were even encouraged to send communications relating to transfers under sealed cover.[88] However, this did not prevent regular leaks, and so in April 1930 the First and Second Division clubs pledged 'themselves not to divulge confidential matters' and requested the Committee 'to take the strongest measures possible to suppress the practice'. Less than a year later, the President had to admit that the League itself 'could do nothing' to stop the press gathering private information, and instead advised the clubs to prevent this themselves.[89] By the 1930s, however, it was becoming more and more difficult to ration the information given to the press. Newspapers like *The People* and the *News of the World*, increasingly eager to secure transfer exclusives and devoted to 'inside information', were less likely to respect confidentiality than were local journalists.[90]

While the League executive could hardly ignore this mounting clamour for information, its relationship with the press remained restricted and awkward. Press representatives were permitted to attend most general meetings from the 1890s onwards, but the meetings of the Management Committee and gatherings of sub-groups like the Third Division sections and the unofficial conferences of clubs were kept strictly private. Journalists were normally excluded when contentious issues were being discussed, such as during the 'Pools War' meetings in February and March 1936. In a passage from his Jubilee history, Sutcliffe described how, in the course of one of these meetings,

> a shadow was seen to pass across the glass lights on the floor above, where a window was discovered to be open, and investigations resulted in the discovery of a photographer and reporter from a prominent newspaper, who had succeeded in getting shots and notes of what had been transpiring. These gentlemen afterwards appeared in the meeting, apologised for their action, and surrended their notes and plates.[91]

The League was certainly slow to advance public relations at its meetings. The *Athletic News* reporter noted that at the 1930 annual meeting, 'The room was far too small, and the arrangements for the visitors unworthy of an organisation of such importance as the League, who might also remember that it is essential that the Press should be in a position to hear.'[92] Yet close relationships were fostered with favoured sections of the press – particularly *Athletic News* and other Northern sporting papers – as well as with individual reporters. James Catton was certainly in regular correspondence with members of the Management Committee during and after his editorship of the Manchester weekly, while Ivan Sharpe was similarly close to Sutcliffe and other League figures. Sharpe's memoirs reveal that Sutcliffe often discussed future plans with the journalist and trusted him with confidential information. The two travelled to football functions together, and throughout the 1930s met regularly for coffee, when Sutcliffe would provide exclusive stories for Sharpe's column in the *Sunday Chronicle.* Sharpe was also 'among the last of his football friends to talk to Charles Sutcliffe'.[93]

However, close associations of this kind were hardly the norm. The League executive generally distrusted the press, especially those Southern newspapers which remained staunchly critical of its policy and objectives. Periodicals such as *C. B. Fry's Magazine* and *The Rapid Review* continued to regard elite professional football with distaste well into the twentieth century, and to identify the League as the professional game's primary exemplar.[94] Before the First World War, *Thomson's Weekly News* offered a regular platform for Union representatives such as Billy Meredith and Colin Veitch, as well as other players, managers and directors who were often critical of the policies of the League. Fishwick has argued that during the 1930s, *The People* in particular developed an 'anti-establishment' stance in its football reporting, which led to the portrayal of 'the Pickfords, Cleggs and Sutcliffes as buffoons and museum pieces'.[95] Neither publications were in any sense enemies of the League, but both positioned themselves in their contemporary markets as irreverent, 'democratic' voices in opposition to the perceived 'cronyism' of some of their rivals.[96] Even newspapers with established sympathy for the League could at times be critical of its policy. *Athletic News*, which by its own admission had 'stood by the League and done all in its power to support the game, the clubs and the players',[97] was nevertheless prepared to oppose the Management Committee when it saw fit and, under Sharpe's editorship from 1924 onwards (notwithstanding his personal friendship with Sutcliffe and others), it certainly became a less faithful apologist for the League.

Press criticism was also perceived by club directors and committeemen as a perennial problem. Most clubs were highly sensitive to newspaper articles that called into question team selection or financial and administrative decisions. In extreme cases this could lead to reporters being banned from grounds, but more commonly clubs would simply inform the newspaper of their objections. The directors of Sheffield United took criticism particularly seriously, meeting the proprietors of the *Telegraph* in 1913 to discuss a series of adverse reports and actually ensuring in 1930 that the same proprietors agreed to an 'alteration of their attitude to the Club'.[98] Even a brief survey of club minute books reveals that instances of this kind were hardly exceptional. West Ham had similar problems with misrepresentative articles, while Oldham Athletic informed the editor of the *Oldham Chronicle* in early 1939 that it was 'very dissatisfied with the local reporter and his adverse criticisms and reports'. The club's mistrust of the *Chronicle* was compounded three months later, when the Friday evening edition told readers incorrectly that there was no match at Boundary Park the following day.[99]

The League, film and broadcasting

The rapid growth of film and radio broadcasting in the second half of our period generated a further influential medium intent on using top-level football to increase audiences. Unlike with the press, however, the attitude of the football authorities towards broadcasting remained ambivalent, because while it offered unprecedented opportunities to promote the game to larger sections of the public than could feasibly visit a football ground, it carried at the same time the potential to damage existing support. Why, it was widely asked, would people pay to attend matches when they could watch or listen to them elsewhere? In common with most providers of entertainment, the League and its clubs were 'deeply suspicious' of broadcasting, perceiving it more as a danger to guard against than an opportunity to be exploited.[100]

Film companies had used football material from the early days of the Football League, but the role of newsreels in the cinema boom of the 1920s and 1930s increased its importance.[101] By the 1930s, almost all cinema performances were preceded by Pathé or British Movietone newsreels and it has been estimated that some 30 per cent of these featured highlights of sporting events, a significant portion of which we can speculate were football matches. In the main, clubs do not appear to have opposed these developments, mainly because newsreels offered only brief highlights and could only be shown after the match: as Fishwick notes, they 'complemented rather than competed with football'.[102] The major issue for clubs was not the filming itself but payment. As early as 1910, Aston Villa allowed the local Aston Theatre to film a League match as a special privilege, but thereafter established a standard charge of five guineas.[103] The West Ham United board decided to charge three guineas in 1920, but this was essentially to cover the minor costs involved in accommodating the cinematographical equipment. By 1933, the east London club had changed tack by attempting to sell cinema rights to cup-ties for at least £20, again ostensibly because of 'the inconvenience caused by the apparatus'. The board had to reduce the fee to £5 when the newsreel companies refused to pay, and the following year Paramount News even objected to paying this 'as they had been granted free facilities elsewhere'.[104] Huddersfield Town and Sheffield United evidently felt that cooperation could benefit and promote the club, and thus tended to grant unconditional filming permission whenever they were asked.[105]

Radio broadcasting was altogether more contentious, partly because its impact was felt across the four divisions of the League and not just at the leading clubs. Initially, the BBC's educative mandate made it reluctant to broadcast sport in general, and professional football in particular, and the concentration of wireless sets and licences within the broadly-defined middle class underlined this tendency. Things changed, however, as radio came within the grasp of lower-income families, while at the same time the BBC's national profile – together with its attitude to popular entertainment – became more defined. The sale of wireless licences rose from just two million in 1927 to nine million in 1939, and of this number the corporation estimated that some 6.2 million were owned by families with annual incomes of £208 or less.[106] Similarly, pressed by public demand, the BBC extended its transmission of entertainment programmes in the mid- to late 1920s, and although sport was not regarded specifically as entertainment, its national focus made it an ideal target for an organisation anxious to highlight its national credentials and public service ethos. On becoming a corporation in 1926 the BBC developed its first proposals to broadcast live sports events, and within two years the first live outside broadcast of a League match had taken place, closely followed by the 1927 FA Cup Final.[107]

At first, the response of clubs was extremely cautious. The BBC applied directly to the clubs themselves for broadcast rights, and the decision was always left in the hands of the hosts. Sheffield United, which had been the visiting team for the first commentary broadcast at Arsenal in January, agreed to a broadcast from Bramall Lane in February but refused a similar request a month later. Birmingham, too, acceded at first but in October 1927 it prohibited further broadcasts, feeling that 'on wet days at any rate' it could be harmful to gates.[108] Other clubs tried a number of methods to ensure that they would suffer no financial loss. Aston Villa's directors refused to allow the BBC to broadcast from their ground unless the club was paid a fee of £20, while Huddersfield Town attempted unsuccessfully to include a 'no publicity' clause in its agreement with the corporation so that spectators would not be aware of the broadcast and thus attendances would remain unaffected.[109] By early 1929 the Huddersfield board too had informed BBC representatives that running commentaries of matches would cease 'unless a monetary offer was forthcoming'.[110] The BBC recognised the widespread opposition to broadcasting and instructed Gerald Cock, its Director of Outside Broadcasting, to make personal visits to pacify the so-called 'antagonistic clubs'. Influence within the football world was also used in an unsuccessful attempt to convince Huddersfield to rethink its policy towards broadcasting when Herbert Chapman, a personal friend of Cock's, was asked to make an expenses-paid trip to his former club in order to explain the BBC's viewpoint.[111]

Despite such efforts, the BBC was unable to convince the League executive and most clubs of the benefits of broadcasting as a means of popularising the game. As Richard Haynes has pointed out, the BBC's public service rhetoric, emphasising free and shared access to events of national significance, may have been closely attuned to the amateurism and 'Corinthian' sporting ideals of the governing body. However, it had less impact on those for whom the true measure of popularity was the turnstiles.[112] As a BBC representative in Sheffield noted, 'the point of view of the clubs is that we are getting something for nothing at the risk of a falling off in their gate money'.[113] Sutcliffe's opposition to broadcasting was similarly unequivocal:

> I could never understand football clubs having anything to do with broadcasting football games whilst the game is in progress. A few tried it on but soon found that broadcasting football did not … attract … listeners in to becoming supporters of the game [sic]. How could it? When the weather is cold and the elements unkind, a man must be an enthusiast to turn up at the match, but it really needs no enthusiasm to sit at ease with slippers on, peacefully smoking and listening in.[114]

Moreover, in his view it was 'absurd to expect clubs to build stands and spend money to attract the public and then arrange for a broadcast to keep them at home'.[115] The fear of reduced gate receipts was felt most by the poorer clubs, especially those in the Third Division North. By May 1928 they had asked the Management Committee and the FA Council to prohibit broadcasting entirely, and reacted angrily against the FA's decision to allow the transmission of the 1930 Cup Final after a ban in 1929. A spokesman for the Northern clubs protested to the FA that the broadcast 'will cause a very serious loss to our Clubs … as when the Final was last broadcasted [sic] our gate receipts were considerably below the average'.[116] Opposition mounted, until by early 1931 few clubs were prepared to openly condone broadcasts. In March of that year a large majority of League members declared themselves 'against broadcasting', and at the annual meeting it was agreed that 'in the interests of the smaller Clubs, Broadcasting of League matches be prohibited'. At the same time, an official request was sent to the FA Council to likewise prohibit cup-tie broadcasts.[117]

The advocates of broadcasting, led by the BBC, launched a powerful counter-offensive with the aim of pressurising the League into climbing down. Cock wrote to the League and the FA outlining the BBC's principal arguments for a reversal of the ban: that broadcasting provided the blind, incapacitated and elderly with a chance to experience the excitement of the game; that it did not, in fact, affect the gates of the clubs involved in commentaries, those situated nearby or smaller clubs struggling for gate revenue; and, conversely, that running commentaries could actually stimulate interest in the game.[118] He also included a summary of figures purporting to prove conclusively that crowds in all four divisions of the League had not in fact dropped on those Saturdays when matches had been transmitted, although Sutcliffe later argued that the figures were based on newspaper estimates 'which were all wrong and seriously wrong'.[119] In addition, the BBC claimed to have the backing of the general public (in the form of thousands of listeners), regular football spectators and club shareholders. The League was hardly likely to be convinced by arguments stressing its moral responsibility to the public, or by the implication that the BBC, like the League, was fundamentally interested in widening public interest in football. As we have seen, the League's definition of its audience was generally restricted to those who actually attended matches: the committed fan or enthusiast, rather than the casual supporter or listener. Those 'who wanted football', it was argued, 'must go and pay for it, and those who won't must accept such service as the BBC and not football matches can supply'.[120] Significantly, however, there were some voices within the League that defended broadcasting on the grounds of its unique publicity value. At the 1932 annual meeting, a Newcastle United director, Dr Simpson, claimed that broadcasting 'was by no means entirely a disadvantage to football' and that the club's wonderful year 'could be attributed largely to advertising'.[121] Arsenal's George Allison, a veteran of nearly 100 commentaries at the time of the League ban, was probably its leading critic, reminding his colleagues in newspaper columns and after-dinner speeches that:

> any national advertiser would jump at the opportunity of a two-hour talk about his product on a Saturday afternoon. Soccer football … was allowing Rugby Football to steal its advertising medium, because Rugby was getting on the air. Revenues would not be affected, the circulations of newspapers would not diminish, and tens of thousands would be happier for the thrill a soccer broadcast gave them.[122]

However, Allison's propaganda campaign was never powerful enough to alter the obstinacy of the Football League. Not only did the ban on League broadcasting remain operative throughout the 1930s, but both the Management Committee and many of its clubs agitated extensively to end the Cup Final broadcast. Attempts in 1933 failed, and during the 1935–36 season Sutcliffe led another unsuccessful movement through the machinery of the FA Council to prohibit live transmission of the tie or, as an alternative, to enable clubs to re-diffuse commentary at their grounds so that attendances would be less likely to suffer.[123]

For the most part, the relationship between the League and the BBC remained strained throughout this period. In one particularly acerbic editorial in the *Radio Times*, Gerald Cock portrayed the Football League as the 'purely commercial element' of the FA Council and as a body of professionals 'who care not one jot for those not immediately concerned in contributing to their gate money, and who are unable to see that broadcast commentaries actually increase and spread interest in the sports described'.[124] In 1934 Cock reminded the BBC Controller of Programming of the need to distinguish between the FA, who cooperated with broadcasting plans and were thus 'our friends', and the obstructionist 'enemy', the League: 'They will neither allow (nor give reasons for refusing) their matches to be broadcast.'[125] Certain concessions were made by Preston, such as the granting of broadcasts to Empire listeners after 1936, but even here the Management Committee insisted that the BBC should reapply for permission each year.[126] The Committee's insistence on its right to prohibit the broadcasting of any match involving a League club or player, including cup-ties and international fixtures, continually frustrated BBC officials, making it difficult to construct reliable programming schedules. In January 1938, for instance, the League executive stepped in to scupper arrangements to broadcast a number of cup replays on Wednesday afternoons on the grounds that this would clash with rearranged League fixtures. It is significant that this decision appeared to overturn both a previous FA resolution and the wishes of the clubs, who had informally indicated their agreement to the BBC's proposal by a clear majority.[127] Yet while it was generally admitted within Broadcasting House that the League 'have always been difficult', this did nothing to dampen attempts to improve relations. Indeed, it was decided in 1938 that the corporation would donate 100 guineas to the League's Jubilee Fund, although a League request to broadcast part of the Jubilee Banquet was eventually turned down after considerable debate.[128] The outbreak of war finally persuaded the Management Committee to permit broadcasts so as to boost morale at home, but even under these circumstances it was noted that some clubs were reluctant to cooperate, believing 'that this may be the thin end of the wedge and that we [the BBC] shall try to take advantage of the situation after the war is over'.[129]

This type of relationship, it should be noted, was not unique to professional football. As the foremost historian of the BBC has pointed out, to secure sports broadcasting the corporation had to engage in 'the same kind of battles behind the scenes with outside interests as there had been in the case of variety and musical comedy'.[130] As such, the Football League's resistance to broadcasting was mirrored in other sectors of the entertainment industry throughout the inter-war years. Few theatre and variety proprietors were sufficiently far-sighted at first to adopt the equivalent of the Allison position: that broadcasting would stimulate interest in entertainment and lead to an increase rather than a decline in live attendance. As early as 1923, a coalition of theatre managers and employees together with composers, music publishers and copyright owners had been formed to campaign for the prohibition of live broadcasts. Even where agreements were reached, broadcasting was strictly limited so as to avoid damaging audiences. Thus in 1925 a group of West End theatre managers sanctioned brief stage broadcasts at specific times, but banned the transmission of cabaret performances during theatre hours. The industry as a whole remained aloof, and important theatrical agencies, such as Moss Empires and the General Theatre Corporation, along with major theatre chains like Oswald Stoll's, continued to place periodic bans on broadcasts by their contracted artistes or on their stages. In common with the Football League, opposition to broadcasting in general, and the BBC in particular, was rife throughout the 1920s and much of the 1930s, and only declined as the BBC began to develop its own material and star performers within a separate Variety Department, an option obviously less appropriate to the broadcasting of sport.[131]

* * *

The Football League's uneasy relationship with its public reached its nadir during the 'Pools War' of 1936, when Preston's decision to alter fixture lists caused widespread disquiet among clubs and the press, but crucially also among supporters. Even taking into account the skewed coverage offered by the many newspapers that covered the pools extensively, the public reaction was overwhelmingly negative. Charlton Athletic and Bolton Wanderers fans were not the only ones reported to have pledged to boycott matches until the Management Committee restored the original fixture list. Supporters of Sheffield Wednesday and York City were said to oppose the League by ten to one, while George Orwell famously remarked that the action had 'flung all Yorkshire into a storm of fury'.[132] Such objections came partly from those who favoured the pools as a harmless 'flutter' for the working man, but also from those who had come to regard the fixture list as public property. As one writer cogently argued, 'Most of the topics of the moment in the game are based on the fixtures, and if these are not to be available until late in the week what will there be for the football enthusiast to talk about?' The fixture list provided football matches with context and meaning, but also represented the League's main source of advertising. By interfering with it, the Management Committee was accused of keeping supporters 'in ignorance of the common facts of football' and denying the game publicity – 'the life blood of any club'.[133] For McKibbin, the whole incident showed 'how isolated from its popular following were so many of the administrators of English sport'.[134]

Such an observation fits easily with both contemporary and more recent assumptions about League football's inherent parochialism, outdatedness and limited embrace of modernity. Yet it also distorts a more complex reality. The Football League's relationship with the general public was fundamentally contradictory. On the one hand, it was an intrinsically public organisation, engaging with thousands of spectators, wireless listeners and pools punters on a weekly basis through its vast programme of sporting fixtures. Yet, on the other hand, it remained a highly secretive and private body, guarded with the press and outsiders and reluctant to experiment in order to increase revenue for its clubs and itself. It can hardly be denied that by the Second World War, the facilities of grounds, the nature and scope of advertising and other attempts to stimulate spectator demand through broadcasting were rudimentary in comparison with the techniques of retailers, cinema owners and some other sporting enterprises. Club directors and League officials hardly fitted the model of the ideal early twentieth century entrepreneur, who 'sought to increase the supply, reduce the cost and widen the range of goods and services available to the consumer'.[135] Football remained for them a game to be played and enjoyed by its supporters, rather than a product to be packaged, marketed and sold to a broad range of social groups. While there was clearly a considerable demand for League football, it is difficult to see how this was significantly affected by the policies of the executive or the clubs, except inasmuch as winning teams (or close matches) generally brought in bigger crowds.

The attitude of spectators towards the League, and its wider profile among those who never visited football grounds, remain similarly elusive. As the bulk of the football audience were probably supporters of specific teams rather than neutral spectators, their relationships, loyalties and grievances were invariably with the club and not the League. It is more than likely that many were unaware of the League's existence as an autonomous organisation. Yet in another sense, the Football League was synonymous with, and indistinguishable from, top-level professional football: it was, in modern parlance, the game's best-known and most lucrative 'brand'. To those who watched football from the terraces, or followed it through reading newspapers or listening to the radio, there was little doubt that the League represented the best English football had to offer. At the very least, the Management Committee was aware of this distinctiveness and sought to protect the League's name and promote its public image. As Sutcliffe is reported to have told clubs that were advertising their fixtures as 'English League matches': 'They were the Football League and they were proud of their title and what they had accomplished'.[136]

Notes

1 S. Jones, 'The Leisure Industry in Britain, 1918–39', *Service Industries Journal*, Vol. 5, 1985, pp. 90–106; Jones, *Sport*; Hill, *Sport, Leisure and Culture*. The classic texts on the eighteenth and early nineteenth centuries are J. H. Plumb, *The Commercialisation of Leisure in Eighteenth-Century England*, Reading, Reading University Press, 1974; R. W. Malcolmson, *Popular Recreations in English Society, 1700–1850*, Cambridge, Cambridge University Press, 1973; H. Cunningham, *Leisure in the Industrial Revolution*, London, Croom Helm, 1980. On the late nineteenth century, see Vamplew, *Pay Up*. For a more recent restatement of eighteenth and nineteenth-century commercialisation, N. Wigglesworth, *The Evolution of English Sport*, London, Frank Cass, 1996.

2 Jones, 'Leisure Industry', p. 103.

3 The best example of this viewpoint is Wagg, *Football World*, pp. 30, 37.

4 Political and Economic Planning, 'Football Industry', p. 168.

5 It should not be assumed that clubs were always honest about attendances and gate receipts. They may well have kept separate records for League inspection, as many undoubtedly did for other financial matters. The most reliable match attendance statistics are gathered in B. Tabner, *Through the Turnstiles*, Harefield, Yore, 1992, which uses press estimates before 1925 but thereafter makes use of the Football League's attendance books.

6 Mason, *Association Football*, pp. 141–43, 168–69; Fishwick, *English Football*, p. 48; Tischler, *Footballers*, p. 84.

7 Jones, 'Economic Aspects', p. 289.

8 Inglis, *League Football*, p. 430; Fishwick, *English Football*, p. 49. Fishwick's figures may overestimate attendance levels, as they are based on the beginning of each season (September and October) when the largest gates were often recorded.

9 Jones, 'Economic Aspects', p. 289.

10 Inglis, *League Football*, pp. 126–27.

11 *Lancashire Daily Post*, 31 March 1931; *Rochdale Observer*, 11 November, 14 November 1931.

12 *Daily Mail*, 7 April 1932. This is not to suggest that the prevailing economic climate of the locality determined a club's gates. Blackpool, Sunderland and Everton were just three clubs that were able to maintain relatively high attendances despite being

located in areas of high unemployment. As Dave Russell has shown, the link between attendances and unemployment rates was never absolute, mediated as it was by the importance of strong management and, above all, playing success. Russell, *Football*, pp. 82–84; D. Russell, 'Football and Society in the North-West, 1919–1939', *North West Labour History*, Vol. 24, 1999/2000, pp. 5–9.

13 The quotation is from Wagg, *Football World*, p. 37.

14 See Mason, 'Football'; Jones, *Sport*, pp. 45–46. Although based on a detailed statistical study, Stefan Szymanski and Tim Kuypers likewise erroneously argue that 'attendances continued to rise' during the depression years of the 1930s. Szymanski and Kuypers, *Winners and Losers*, p. 42.

15 Jones, 'Economic Aspects', p. 287; J. Sedgwick, *Popular Filmgoing in 1930s Britain: A Choice of Pleasures*, Exeter, Exeter University Press, 2000, p. 42 (Table 2.1).

16 For comparisons with first class and league cricket attendances, Williams, *Cricket and England*, pp. 54–62; on greyhound racing attendances, Clapson, *A Bit of a Flutter*, p. 146; M. Cronin, 'Arthur Elvin and the Dogs of Wembley', *The Sports Historian*, Vol. 22, 2002, pp. 106–07; on speedway, J. Williams, '"A Wild Orgy of Speed": Responses to Speedway in Britain Before the Second World War', *The Sports Historian*, Vol. 19, 1999, p. 6.

17 J. Richards, *The Age of the Dream Palace: Cinema and Society in Britain, 1930–1939*, London, Routledge, 1984, p. 11.

18 Richards, Dream Palace, p. 11.

19 See, for instance, Hill, *Sport, Leisure and Culture*, Chapter 1; Jones, 'Leisure Industry'; G. Jarvie and J. Maguire, *Sport and Leisure in Social Thought*, London, Routledge, 1994.

20 *Athletic News*, 28 January, 4 February 1901.

21 Report of Football League 'Coming of Age' Banquet in *Athletic News*, 14 June 1909; quotation from *Cricket*, 13 May 1913 in Williams, *Cricket and England*, p. 167.

22 A. Horrall, *Popular Culture in London, c. 1890–1918: The Transformation of Entertainment*, Manchester, Manchester University Press, 2001, Chapter 11.

23 *Thomson's Weekly News*, 12 March 1910.

24 P. Bailey, *Leisure and Class in Victorian Britain: Rational Recreation and the Contest for Control, 1830–1885*, London, Methuen, 1987, p. 157.

25 Vamplew, *Pay Up*, Chapters 8–11; Fishwick, *English Football*, pp. 39–44. On music-hall entrepreneurs, see P. Bailey, 'Custom, Capital and Culture in the Victorian Music-Hall' in *Popular Culture and Custom in Nineteenth-Century England*, ed. R. Storch, London, Croom Helm, 1982, pp. 180–208; A. Crowhurst, 'The "Portly Grabbers of 75 per cent.": Capital Investment in the British Entertainment Industry, 1885–1914', *Leisure Studies*, Vol. 20, 2001, pp. 107–23.

26 Carter, *Footballer's Progress*, pp. 50–51.

27 See SUFC, Football Committee Minutes, 26 February 1930. Also see FA Finance and General Purposes Committee Minutes, 22 August 1938.

28 *Athletic News*, 16 December 1901. It is noteworthy that before 1914, League clubs were rarely at the forefront of movements to introduce laws aimed at making goals easier to score, or improving the visual attraction by minimising stoppages in the game. For example, the League had no direct input into the rule changes of 1903, when the International Board permitted a goal to be scored directly from a free kick awarded for a penalty offence or, conversely, in 1914 when an attempt to reduce stoppages caused by injuries was blocked. On the second occasion, W. A. Wilkinson

of Manchester City opposed the proposal because he believed spectators would be more likely to object to seeing 'a man in agony left to pick himself up while play continued' than to frequent halts in play caused by real and imaginary injuries. The spectator was therefore given some consideration, but this did not necessarily equate with a concern for his (or her) entertainment. See Mason, 'Football', p. 155; reports of FA AGMs in *Athletic News*, 1 June 1903; 1 June 1914.

29 Reports of FA AGMs in *Athletic News*, 2 June 1913; 1 June 1924.
30 For figures on goal-scoring, see Sutcliffe, Brierley and Howarth, *Story of the Football League*, p. 287.
31 Report of FA AGM in *Athletic News*, 4 June 1923.
32 Buchan, *Lifetime*, p. 30.
33 Football League Minutes, Management Committee, 12 January, 3 April 1925; Wolverhampton Wanderers FC Programme, 29 August 1925.
34 Report of FA AGM in *Athletic News*, 15 June 1925.
35 *Topical Times*, 17 February 1934.
36 Moorhouse, *People's Game*, p. 65. For a detailed discussion of the changing rules in the Northern Union over this period, see Collins, *Rugby's Great Split*, pp. 208–14.
37 Vamplew, *Pay Up*, p. 64; Allison, 'Rise of Middlesbrough'.
38 Inglis, *Football Grounds*, p. 57; *Athletic News*, 8 March 1909.
39 *Athletic News*, 8 March 1909. The design of League grounds as far as improved visibility was concerned lagged far behind developments in Italy and the Americas. The first major cantilever stands, with no supporting uprights to obscure the supporters' view, were not built until the late 1950s and early 1960s. In contrast, the architect Pier Luigi Nervi built self-supporting cantilever stands at Florence's Berta Stadium in 1933 specifically to allow supporters a completely free view of the pitch. See F. Varrasi, 'Economic, politica e sport in Italia, 1925–35', Tesi di Laurea, Florence, 1996, pp. 353, 360, 503–07; Inglis, *Football Grounds*, pp. 19–20.
40 OAFC, Circular Letter from E. L. Thompson to Oldham Athletic Shareholders, 6 December 1906; Board Minutes, 30 July 1907.
41 *Athletic News*, 9 January 1911.
42 Wolverhampton Wanderers FC Programme, 9 December 1922; 15 December, 29 December 1923.
43 Wolverhampton Wanderers FC Programme, 19 September 1925.
44 *Topical Times*, 21 March 1931.
45 WLHC, WFC, Board Minutes, 28 November 1933; R. Taylor, *Football and Its Fans: Supporters and their Relations with the Game, 1885–1985*, Leicester, Leicester University Press, 1992, pp. 28–31.
46 SUFC, Football Committee Minutes, 6 September 1927; 28 October 1936; 17 March 1937; 24 August 1938.
47 Seed, *Jimmy Seed Story*, pp. 44–45.
48 AVFC, Board Minutes, 15 March 1927.
49 See *Topical Times*, 18 August 1923; 22 September 1934.
50 SUFC, Football Committee Minutes, 2 July, 9 July 1930.
51 WHUFC, Board Minutes, 28 October 1928; 13 September, 19 September 1932; 11 September 1934. Also AVFC, Board Minutes, 27 December 1927.
52 WHUFC, Board Minutes, 5 November 1934.
53 Sheffield United's results board was erected in 1922; Aston Villa's followed in 1923 and West Ham United's two years later. AVFC, Board Minutes, 5 December 1922; 14 August 1923; WHUFC, Board Minutes, 21 July, 28 July 1925.

54 WHUFC, Board Minutes, 26 March 1935; SUFC, Football Committee Minutes, 1 December 1931; WLHC, WFC, Board Minutes, 27 November 1934.
55 S. Studd, *Herbert Chapman, Football Emperor: A Study of the Origins of Modern Soccer*, London, Peter Owen, 1981, p. 109; SUFC, Football Committee Minutes, 2 June 1930; FA Council Minutes, 13 October 1930.
56 Inglis, *Football Grounds*, p. 42.
57 Studd, *Herbert Chapman*, pp. 111–12.
58 FA Council Minutes, 25 August 1930; Studd, *Herbert Chapman*, p. 112.
59 AFC, Catton Folders, E–F, J. G. Hickling to Catton, 5 September 1932, p. 506.
60 See AFC, Catton Folders, E–F, William Struth (Glasgow Rangers) to Catton, 5 September 1932, p. 506.
61 FA Council Minutes, 12 December 1932; WHUFC, Board Minutes, 5 December 1932; 6 March 1933; *Topical Times*, 21 January 1933.
62 AFC, Catton Folders, E–F, newspaper cutting, 25 August 1928, p. 505.
63 Report of Football League AGM in *Sporting Chronicle*, 30 May 1933.
64 Football League Minutes, Management Committee, 27 August 1928.
65 *Topical Times*, 13 May, 25 March 1933.
66 *Topical Times*, 10 June 1933.
67 See *Sporting Chronicle*, 27 March 1933; *Daily Herald*, 30 May 1933; *Daily Mail*, 30 May 1933.
68 *The People*, 4 June 1933.
69 Report of Football League AGM in *Daily Herald*, 6 June 1939; Inglis, *League Football*, pp. 140, 164–65.
70 *Sporting Chronicle*, 5 May 1933.
71 On the BBC and its audience, see P. Scannell and D. Cardiff, *A Social History of British Broadcasting: Volume One 1922–1939, Serving the Nation*, Oxford, Basil Blackwell, 1991, pp. 356–80.
72 W. H. Fraser, *The Coming of the Mass Market, 1850–1914*, London, Macmillan, 1981, p. 146. See also Nevett, *Advertising*.
73 See Richards, *Dream Palace*, pp. 21–22; B. Lancaster, *The Department Store: A Social History*, London, Leicester University Press, 1995, pp. 74, 96–98; Shaw, 'Evolution and Impact', pp. 135–65.
74 WLHC, WFC, Annual Report of Directors for AGM, 1934, 522/1/23.
75 SUFC, Football Committee Minutes, 13 November 1907; 9 September, 21 October 1908; 20 August 1912; WHUFC, Board Minutes, 12 June 1934.
76 SUFC, Football Committee Minutes, 30 August, 5 September 1933.
77 WHUFC, Board Minutes, 17 November 1919; 13 August 1923; 4 September 1934.
78 DRO, D/XD 97/3, DFC, Board Minutes, 25 August 1937.
79 SUFC, Football Committee Minutes, 22 February, 1 March 1911; 30 November 1932; 24 August 1938.
80 See OAFC, Board Minutes, 4 January 1938; DRO, D/XD 97/3, DFC, Board Minutes, 30 December 1935; 16 December 1936.
81 See T. Mason, 'All the Winners and the Half Times', *The Sports Historian*, Vol. 13, 1993, pp. 3–13.
82 Minutes of SUFC, Football Committee Minutes, 23 August, 30 August, 5 September 1911.
83 SRO, ITFC, Board Minutes, 8 August 1939.
84 Fishwick, *English Football*, p. 98.

85 WHUFC, Board Minutes, 28 July 1925; 6 January 1931; 20 December 1932; 24 January 1933.
86 WHUFC, Board Minutes, 15 November 1932.
87 OAFC, Board Minutes, 1 March, 8 March 1939.
88 Football League Minutes, Management Committee, 3 June 1912; 2 February 1914; 11 November 1927.
89 Report of Meeting of Football League Clubs, First and Second Division, 4 April 1930; Football League Shareholders Meeting Minutes (First and Second Division), 6 March 1931.
90 Fishwick, *English Football*, pp. 98, 100–07.
91 Sutcliffe, Brierley and Howarth, *Story of the Football League*, p. 41.
92 Report of Football League AGM in *Athletic News*, 9 June 1930.
93 AFC, Catton Folders, *passim*; Sharpe, *40 Years*, pp. 157–59; PFA, File 33, Hartley to Fay, 6 February 1939.
94 See *Athletic News*, 25 March 1907.
95 Fishwick, *English Football*, pp. 101, 103.
96 Colin Veitch's criticism of 'particular newspapers' that always seemed to be 'in the know' in official matters was a barely concealed reference to *Athletic News*'s status as the League's mouthpiece. See *Thomson's Weekly News*, 7 December 1912.
97 *Athletic News*, 1 May 1916.
98 SUFC, Football Committee Minutes, 25 June 1913; 2 September, 9 September 1930.
99 WHUFC, Board Minutes, 9 April 1923; OAFC, Board Minutes, 4 January, 19 April 1939.
100 Scannell and Cardiff, *Social History*, p. 225.
101 On the use of sport in film from the 1890s onwards, see L. McKernan, 'Sport and the First Films' in *Cinema: The Beginnings and the Future*, ed. C. Williams, London, University of Westminster Press, 1996, pp. 107–16.
102 Fishwick, *English Football*, pp. 107, 110.
103 AVFC, Board Minutes, 23 August, 30 August, 25 October 1910.
104 WHUFC, Board Minutes, 16 August, 24 January, 27 February 1933; 16 January 1934.
105 HTFC, Board Minutes, 13 December 1938; 25 January, 15 February 1939; SUFC, Football Committee Minutes, 16 August 1933; 27 September 1937; 19 January 1938.
106 A. Briggs, *The BBC: The First Fifty Years*, Oxford, Oxford University Press, 1985, p. 113.
107 See A. Briggs, *The History of Broadcasting in the United Kingdom: Volume 2 – The Golden Age of Wireless*, London, Oxford University Press, 1965, pp. 75–121; Scannell and Cardiff, *Social History*, pp. 224–30, 277–79; D. L. LeMahieu, *A Culture for Democracy: Mass Communication and the Cultivated Mind in Britain Between the Wars*, Oxford, Clarendon, 1988, pp. 285–88; R. Boyle and R. Haynes, *Power Play: Sport, the Media and Popular Culture*, London, Longman, 2000, p. 34; Fishwick, *English Football*, p. 107.
108 SUFC, Football Committee Minutes, 9 February, 30 March, 6 September 1927; BBC WAC, Aston Villa Ground, 1927–58, S. D. (Birmingham) to Mr Graves (Programme Executive), 8 October 1927.
109 BBC WAC, Aston Villa Ground, 1927–58, S. D. (Birmingham) to Mr Nicholls (London S. D.), 3 September 1927; Huddersfield Town Ground 1, 1927–41, broadcasting agreement between Huddersfield Town FC and the BBC, 1 November 1927;

programme executive to S. D. (Manchester), 11 November 1927. Also see AVFC, Board Minutes, 8 February, 15 February, 22 February 1927; 30 October 1928.

110 BBC WAC, Huddersfield Town Ground 1, 1927–41, North Regional Director to O. B. Director, 24 January 1929.

111 BBC WAC, Huddersfield Town Ground 1, 1927–41, Programme Executive to S. D. (Manchester), 11 November 1927; Gerald Cock, internal memo, 22 February 1928.

112 R. Haynes, '"There's Many a Slip 'Twixt the Eye and the Lip": An Exploratory History of Football Broadcasts and Running Commentaries on BBC Radio, 1927–1939', *International Review of the Sociology of Sport*, Vol. 34, 1999, pp. 146–47.

113 Quoted in Fishwick, *English Football*, p. 108.

114 *Topical Times*, 19 May 1928.

115 *Topical Times*, 11 June 1932.

116 FA Finance and General Purposes Committee Minutes, 25 April 1930.

117 Football League Minutes, 6 March 1931 (SGM); 1 June 1931 (AGM).

118 FA Minute Books, Gerald Cock to Frederick Wall, 3 September 1931.

119 *Topical Times*, 11 June 1932.

120 *Topical Times*, 21 March 1931.

121 Report of Football League AGM in *Sporting Chronicle*, 7 June 1932. Newcastle's 'wonderful year' was largely the result of winning the FA Cup.

122 Allison, *Allison Calling*, pp. 56–58.

123 FA Council Minutes, 24 June 1933; 7 October, 16 December 1935, 13 January, 30 January 1936; WHUFC, Board Minutes, 18 July 1933; SUFC, Football Committee Minutes, 3 July 1933; *Sporting Chronicle*, 9 January, 10 January, 31 January, 3 February 1936.

124 Quoted in Haynes, 'Many a Slip', p. 147.

125 BBC WAC, Football File 1, 1933–46, Gerald Cock, internal memo, 20 November 1934.

126 BBC WAC, Football League Ltd File 1a, 1936–46, Football League circular, 'Broadcasting of Football Matches', November 1936; Fred Howarth to S. J. de Lotbiniere, 15 December 1936; Fred Howarth to John Snagge, 16 July 1937; SUFC, Football Committee Minutes, 25 November 1936.

127 BBC WAC, Football League Ltd File 1a, 1936–46, S. J. de Lotbiniere to Fred Howarth, 7 January 1938; Howarth to de Lotbiniere, 8 January 1938; de Lotbiniere to Howarth, 10 January 1938.

128 BBC WAC, Football League Ltd File 1a, 1936–46, S. J. de Lotbiniere, internal memos, 18 January, 8 March, 17 June 1938; de Lotbiniere to Howarth, 31 March 1938.

129 BBC WAC, Football League Ltd File 1a, 1936–46, Michael Standing to Fred Howarth, 16 October 1939.

130 Briggs, *History*, p. 120.

131 Briggs, *History*, pp. 76–86; P. Scannell and D. Cardiff, 'Serving the Nation: Public Service Broadcasting before the War' in *Popular Culture: Past and Present*, ed. B. Waites, T. Bennett and G. Martin, London, Croom Helm, 1982, pp. 178–82.

132 *Sporting Chronicle*, 27 February 1936; Fishwick, *English Football*, p. 129.

133 *Sporting Chronicle*, 24 February, 22 February 1936.

134 McKibbin, *Classes and Cultures*, p. 377.

135 J. Benson, *The Rise of Consumer Society in Britain, 1880–1980*, London, Longman, 1994, p. 44.

136 Football League Minutes, Management Committee, 30 May 1921.

Conclusion

Histories of English football have established that the game as we have come to know it was effectively 'made' during the late nineteenth century. In not much longer than a decade, between the mid-1870s and mid- to late 1880s, 'football acquired all the institutional and ritual characteristics with which we are still familiar'.[1] The next 20 or so years witnessed its social and cultural transformation, from the recreation of a largely upper- and middle-class elite to a popular activity indulged in by a small but significant proportion of the English population each week. Through the associated press coverage and the rise of football betting, it seeped into the consciousness of millions more who never played or watched a game in their lives. By the First World War at the latest, it was difficult to deny that football had become the 'national' English winter game. It was clearly coming to mean a great deal to a considerable number of people, representing at the very least a central facet of the cultural experience of many English males.[2]

Yet this chronology fits the professional game much less neatly. As a social and cultural form football may indeed have been 'made' by the turn of the century, but as an industry and a profession it was still very much in its infancy. Professional football's infrastructure was not constructed all at once but built up steadily over decades. In its various guises as a sporting competition, a collective of clubs and an executive body, the Football League was central to this process of 'making'. It was, in Ross McKibbin's view, 'the heart of professional football'.[3] Most of the major landmarks in the game's pre-1945 history – from the record attendances to the expanding transfer fees – took place within the structure of the League. Even the great events that subsequently became mythologised in popular and sporting history – such as the 1923 White Horse Cup Final and the success of Scotland's 'Wembley Wizards' in 1928 – involved League clubs and players. In addition, the transformation of the game from a negative to a positive social phenomenon in the inter-war years, so that 'it was no longer … out of favour with "public opinion" and seemed if anything to stand for much that was good in society', was in reality a transformation in attitudes towards League football and the largely working-class culture that surrounded it.[4] However, there is an evident paradox here: the unquestioned national popularity of football by 1939 was in large part achieved through the activities of a conservative organisation that eschewed attempts both to popularise and nationalise the game. The League decision makers were extremely reluctant to exploit the opportunities provided by the rise of cinema and radio or to promote their 'product' through advertising or other intrinsic methods. The steps that were taken tended to emanate from the clubs themselves, who experimented with improved ground facilities, floodlit matches, shirt numbering and other innovations. As we have seen, the League rarely ventured from its parochial viewpoint and its narrow range of responsibilities, which precluded any involvement in spreading and popularising the game itself, both at home and abroad. This, it was felt, was the job of the governing body, not a self-contained organisation: the League's role was to look after the League, not the game of football.

As James Walvin has noted, football was in an extremely healthy and buoyant state immediately prior to the Second World War. The popular support for the game was visible in the 'packed stadiums, [with] armies of satisfied listeners huddled close to their radio sets, with millions ticking their football pools weekly and with the press replete with footballing interest'.[5] At a lower level, the growth in players and clubs during this part of the twentieth century was enormous. The number of registered players rose from 750,000 before the First World War to a million by the late 1930s, while the number of clubs increased from 12,000 in 1910 to some 35,000 in 1937.[6] The Football League's contribution to these achievements was largely unwitting. It provided the context and the framework for football's mounting popularity, but was rarely consciously involved in the process. In fact, its policies towards the outside world and football in general were usually defensive and reactive rather than proactive.

The development of the Football League was not an uncomplicated or unilinear process. References to the 'rise' or 'progress' of the League in the (mainly official) literature are misleading, as they tend to skate over the various debates and disagreements that accompanied its expansion. On one level, these arguments were strictly concerned with rational issues of economic control and organisational structure. Should the League extend its boundaries by incorporating more clubs and absorbing rival leagues so as to ensure monopolistic and monopsonistic control over English professional football? Or should it remain one of a number of senior organisations which could, nonetheless, establish oligopolistic power through collusion with its rivals?[7] Such debates were not peculiar to football. The major railway companies were confronted with similar questions after 1900, even though they faced the further complications of government intervention.[8] On a more fundamental level, however, the issue of expansion was linked to broader questions of regional and national identity. The Football League was rooted in the North and Midlands of England and developed in its early stages as a parochial organisation, comprising mostly of Northern clubs, players and administrators and backed by a sympathetic sporting press based around Northern weeklies, like the highly influential *Athletic News*. As such, it did not regard itself as a 'national' league, even as its geographical boundaries were pushed back by the election of Woolwich Arsenal and Luton in the 1890s and a coterie of metropolitan and Southern clubs during the 1900s. Opposition to the 'national league' idea informed the staunch resistance of officials and member clubs to the periodic proposals of amalgamation with the Southern League, and it was only after the First World War, in the context of relative prosperity, good gates and a general mood of optimism, that the national league was finally established under the Football League's aegis through the creation of a new Southern-based Third Division.

The transformation of the League into a body with a genuinely national constituency can be seen as part of a broader 'nationalisation of culture' in Britain, in which the variegated, provincial focus of life in the mid-nineteenth century gradually shifted towards 'a more centralised, homogeneous national society'.[9] Accompanied and driven by the growth of national transport and communication networks, the League arguably became one of many factors which contributed to a broadening of horizons and the binding together of various local and regional communities into a national state. While few supporters physically travelled with their teams to away matches, most could follow their progress at grounds located in cities across England and Wales and monitor changing league position in the press. If Eric Hobsbawm could emphasise the importance before 1914 of professional football as a point of reference or a common culture which bound working-class males together 'irrespective of local and regional differences',[10] then this was even more true of the inter-war period, when the League's boundaries spread to encompass communities in almost every region and county in England, and a number in Wales. This is not to say, however, that the growth and consolidation of a national Football League ought to be seen as an 'invented tradition' which contributed to the foundation of an English 'national identity'. English football, at League as at international level, was often too wrapped up in local and regional loyalties to advance perceptions of the nation itself. If football connected with 'Englishness' at all, it was not through the routine of the league programme but the occasion of the FA Cup Final, which firmly entrenched itself between the wars as part of a unified national culture.[11]

Indeed, the League's regional identity, and what might be called its 'Northernness', remained one of its defining characteristics for the whole of this period. This brings us into territory that historians have only just begun to explore. The close relationship between sport and a whole range of national, regional and local identities is now generally accepted, but these identities have tended to be associated with a particular sports team or the individual sportsmen and sportswomen themselves.[12] It certainly appears less evident that a regional identity could be invested in, or constructed around, a sporting organisation, especially one as nebulous as the Football League often seems to have been. It could indeed be argued that what the League really represented was a collection of competing local identities derived from the interconnections of its member clubs, rather than a single identity of its own. There is, moreover, the problem of defining and separating 'Northernness' from other sub-forms of loyalty and identification, built in the League's case around the North-west and Lancashire. As Jeff Hill and Jack Williams concluded in the introduction to their study *Sport and Identity in the North of England*, 'the North and Northernness have had very many meanings. The North is an imagined territory with no fixed boundaries, and the range of qualities which have been seen as characteristic of Northernness are so diverse as to defy neat definition.'[13]

Despite these reservations, however, there is little doubt that the Football League was both objectively and subjectively a Northern organisation. The decision to locate its permanent offices in Preston from 1902 onwards was partly a matter of logistics, given that the new secretary Tom Charnley was based in the town, but it also reflected and reinforced the League's emergent identity as a parochial organisation, fiercely independent of the governing body, whose headquarters remained in the capital. Likewise, the dominance of Northern representatives on the Management Committee, especially in the inter-war period, was both a highly significant symbol and a tangible means of ensuring the hegemony of the provincial North over the metropolitan South at a time when Arsenal's ascendancy was challenging Northern dominance on the field of play. From Bentley and Lewis through to McKenna and Cuff, with the ubiquitous figure of Sutcliffe straddling the entire period, the League's senior administration was essentially a Northern clique, aided by a small supporting cast of officials from Midlands clubs. The 'Northernness' of the League also shone through clearly in its relationship with Southern organisations like the FA. The tensions and antagonism between the two bodies up until 1939 were unquestionably underpinned by North–South rivalries which, as Tony Mason has shown, had their origins in the struggle to legalise professionalism in 1885.[14] However, the League's attitude towards the parent body also drew on a range of wider social resentments and political grievances. The perceived indifference and neglect of the North by central government had a long history, which was only partially modified by the enhancement of its national significance in the course of the industrial revolution.[15] While the FA had rarely shown indifference towards the League and its largely Northern membership, there was nevertheless a powerful feeling that the North had been marginalised in Council meetings, and that the League had been denied the consideration that such a powerful organisation deserved. In this respect, the League's attitude towards the FA fitted into a broader Northern self-image of a people 'whose misfortune it was to be governed by the aristocratic, agrarian South where so much was perceived to depend on public school and family connections'.[16] Between the wars, therefore, the League struggled to reconcile its parochial identity with its national constituency in an effort to represent both the North and the nation.

The Football League was very different in 1939 from the way that it had been in 1900. The changes in its duties and responsibilities completely transformed the nature of the organisation itself. In the first decade or so of the League's existence, it was little more than a representative body of members charged with organising a sporting competition. Only at annual and special meetings, and gatherings of the Management Committee, did the League have real meaning as a tangible organisation. For many clubs, players and spectators it had an almost abstract existence as an entity that bound them together for a common purpose. Even in the inter-war period, few ever visited the offices at Preston: their understanding of the Football League was gained through the fixture list, the signing-on form and the circular letter. However, the League had nevertheless become a powerful bureaucracy with a power-base independent of its constituent clubs. Few aspects of club activity lay outside its ambit and, while there were periodic movements by the leading clubs reaffirming their status as separate enterprises, the overall authority of the

Management Committee was rarely questioned. Previous accounts have all but ignored the growth of the Football League as a central regulatory and administering body – far more important to its professional membership than the FA – and have consequently underplayed its role in the development of the professional game. Reactionary and remote as it may have been from its employees and its audience, Stephen Wagg's description of the League in the 1920s as 'a moribund organisation' whose 'significance … as a bureaucracy' had dwindled, is simply inaccurate.[17]

The League's bureaucratic expansion is connected to a further theme centred on the phenomenon of professionalisation. There are obvious conceptual difficulties in perceiving the football player as a 'professional' in the sense that doctors, lawyers and even actors were by the twentieth century. Footballers did not have the type of job security or long-term career structure enjoyed by many professionals; players themselves were not able to control entry into the profession; and other fringe benefits like pensions were slow to develop. Football was a job rather than a profession, and in most aspects of his employment the player remained associated with the wage-earner and not the salaried professional man. Despite this, it is evident that the increased bureaucratic control of the League regularised the working conditions of football and standardised the relations between player and club. By the 1930s, a player who moved from one club to another was in certain respects only moving between 'branches' in a national company structure. Moreover, the structure of the League professionalised the game by marginalising the amateur and the part-time or semi-professional player at the highest level. Although a paucity of data makes it difficult to be precise about the changing number of amateur and part-time (in relation to full-time) players in the League, the available evidence indicates that by 1939, players who had other jobs were exceptional. One newspaper correspondent noted in 1928 that the strict application of training regulations, together with the mounting intensity of midweek matches, replays and rearranged games during the second half of the season, had made it virtually impossible for most players to have other occupations.[18] This also had fundamental implications for the capacity of League and club employers to control the players, as it inevitably increased the latter's dependence on football as an occupation. In short, the structure of the League and its competition provided the framework for the elevation of the professional footballer and contributed to the development of the close association between professional and elite football in England.

As an industry and a profession as well as a game, football had undoubtedly made a significant mark on the social and cultural landscape of England by the outbreak of war in 1939. It has not been the main intention of this book to use the 'story' of the Football League to shed light on broader historical issues. Certainly, the growth of professional football reveals parallels with other forms of sport, recreation and entertainment, such as theatre, the music hall and the cinema. The nature of the labour market, trends towards industrial concentration and the application of new managerial ideas such as advertising and marketing all seem to suggest a fundamental generic similarity that may have been overlooked by writers intent on analysing the development of a distinct 'football world'. Yet for all this, one of the defining features of the football industry was its peculiarity. For historians and contemporaries, it was often regarded as a separate world in which 'normal' economic and administrative assumptions were inappropriate. In certain crucial respects, the football industry was simply not like other industries: its 'firms' were intrinsically both partners and competitiors; they did not pursue profits above all else; and many were able to survive in the face of the sort of long-term losses and debts that would have meant bankruptcy for any other type of company. Peculiar and unique as it may have been, however, the professional football world was not as closed as it often appeared to want to be. Quite the opposite: it was known to many hundreds of thousands, possibly millions, of English people who shared an interest in its personalities, politics and structure as well as the game itself. To these people at least, the Football League was an institution of no little significance.

Professional football survived the Second World War largely intact. The League reverted to regional groupings, and special wartime cup competitions were established. The players, for their part, had their contracts cancelled and either joined the forces or took up civilian jobs. Most continued to play whenever and wherever they could, often as guest players in competitive matches or in the numerous representative and inter-service games that filled the wartime fixture schedules. In keeping with the prevailing spirit of reconstruction and reform, the League set up a Post-War Planning Committee, which put forward a number of far-sighted proposals, including a reduction in the size of the majority needed for rule changes, the creation of a League Cup and a British Cup and even the suggestion that the League's headquarters move from Lancashire to London. In the event, change was limited and the status quo remained. Despite some criticisms that the pre-war League system had become 'obsolete and moribund', the professional game effectively continued where it had left off, adopting the same divisional structure and fixture list for 1945–46 that had been started in

1939–40.[19] Its popularity was to soar in the immediate post-war decade, with ground records broken throughout the League and aggregate attendances rising to an historic peak of 41.2 million during the 1948–49 season. The foundations for English football's 'golden age' had been laid.

Notes

1 E. Hobsbawm, 'Mass-Producing Traditions: Europe, 1870–1914' in *The Invention of Tradition*, ed. E. Hobsbawm and T. Ranger, Cambridge, Cambridge University Press, 1983, p. 288.
2 Russell, *Football*, pp. 235, 30.
3 McKibbin, *Classes and Cultures*, p. 341.
4 Fishwick, *English Football*, pp. 146–47.
5 Walvin, *The People's Game*, p. 142.
6 Fishwick, *English Football*, p. 1.
7 Vamplew, *Pay Up*, p. 113. A clear explanation of the position of sports monopolies from a North American perspective, but applicable to the English case, is provided in C. C. Euchner, *Playing the Field: Why Sports Teams Move and Cities Fight to Keep Them*, Baltimore, Johns Hopkins University Press, 1994, pp. 35–37.
8 Cain, 'Railways', pp. 117–21.
9 Harris, *Private Lives*, p. 17.
10 Hobsbawm, 'Mass-Producing Traditions', pp. 288–89, 301.
11 See H. Cunningham, 'Leisure and Culture' in *The Cambridge Social History of Britain, 1750–1950, Volume 2 – People and their Environment*, ed. F. M. L. Thompson, Cambridge, Cambridge University Press, 1990, p. 337; Holt, *Sport and the British*, p. 273; D. Russell, 'Associating with Football: Social Identity in England, 1863–1998' in *Football Cultures and Identities*, ed. G. Armstrong and R. Giulianotti, Basingstoke, Macmillan, 1999, pp. 21–22.
12 Holt, *Sport and the British*, pp. 159–79.
13 J. Hill and J. Williams (eds), *Sport and Identity in the North of England*, Keele, Keele University Press, 1996, p. 11.
14 Mason, 'Football, Sport of the North?', pp. 44–45.
15 Jewell, *North–South Divide*, pp. 135–36, 208–10.
16 Holt, 'Heroes', p. 138.
17 Wagg, *Football World*, p. 30.
18 *Topical Times*, 14 April 1928.
19 M. Taylor, 'Leisure and Entertainment' in *The Great World War 1914–45: Volume 2, The People's Experience*, ed. J. Bourne, P. Liddle and I. Whitehead, London, Harper Collins, 2001, pp. 378–94; Inglis, *League Football*, pp. 168–70.

APPENDIX

Management Committee Members, 1900–39

Name	*Positions*	*Club*	*Occupation*	*Occupational class*
William McGregor	Chairman 1888–92 President 1892–94 Life Member 1895–1911	Aston Villa	Draper	2A
John Bentley	Committee 1888–93 Vice-President 1893–94 President 1894–1910 Committee 1910–12 Life Member 1912–18	Bolton Wanderers and Manchester United	Journalist	1A
John Lewis	Committee 1894–95 and 1900–01 Vice-President 1901–26	Blackburn Rovers	Carriage builder	2A
David Haigh	Vice-President 1895–1901	Sheffield United	Not known	Not known
William Bellamy	Committee 1896–1900	Grimsby Town	Partner in mineral water business	2A
Tom Sidney	Vice-President 1897–1905	Wolverhampton Wanderers	Corporation official	2B
Harry Radford	Committee 1898–1905 Vice-President 1905–08	Nottingham Forest	Corporation official	2B
Charles Sutcliffe	Committee 1898–1902 and 1903–27 Vice-President 1927–36 President 1936–39 Life Member 1938–39	Burnley and Oldham Athletic	Solicitor	1A
Walter Hart	Committee 1899–1903	Small Heath	Metalware manufacturer	2A
George Leavey	Committee 1901–04	Woolwich Arsenal	Men's outfitter	2A
John McKenna	Committee 1902–08 Vice-President 1908–10 President 1910–36 Life Member 1923–36	Liverpool	Vaccination officer	2B
James Baxter	Committee 1904–19	Everton	Doctor	1A
Henry Keys	Committee 1905–10 Vice-President 1910–29	West Bromwich Albion	Bicycle agent	2A
John Cameron	Committee 1907–16	Newcastle United and Leeds City	Clothing trader and publican	2A

Name	*Positions*	*Club*	*Occupation*	*Occupational class*
Arthur Dickinson	Committee 1909–29 Vice-President 1929–30	Sheffield Wednesday	Cutlery salesman	2B
Tom Harris	Committee 1909–17	Notts County	Football club secretary	2B
Tom Houghton	Committee 1912–13	Preston North End	Brewery agent	2A
William Hall	Committee 1913–27	Arsenal	Metal merchant	2A
John Peel Oliver	Committee 1917–28	Newcastle United	Wine spirit merchant	2A
Fred Rinder	Committee 1917–30 Vice-President 1930–38 Life Member 1938	Aston Villa and Bristol Rovers	Corporation surveyor	2B
Tom Barcroft	Committee 1919–25 and 1927–43	Blackpool	Retired banker and football club secretary	2B
William Cuff	Committee 1925–36 Vice-President 1936–39 President 1939–49	Everton	Solicitor	1A
Morton Cadman	Committee 1927–39 Vice-President 1939–41	Tottenham Hotspur	Rate collector	2B
Phil Bach	Committee 1929–37	Middlesbrough	Ex-professional footballer and licensed victualler	2A
William Bassett	Committee 1930–37	West Bromwich Albion	Ex-professional footballer and cinema director	2A
Amos Brook Hirst	Committee 1931–39 Vice-President 1939–41	Huddersfield Town	Solicitor	1A
John Edwards	Committee 1936–40	Arsenal	Solicitor	1A
Walter Tempest	Committee 1939–41	Blackburn Rovers	Managing director	2B
Arthur Oakley	Committee 1937–41	Wolverhampton Wanderers	Coal merchant	2A
George Rutherford	Committee 1938–50	Newcastle United	Coalmine owner	2A
Bill Cearns	Committee 1939–50	West Ham United	Building contractor/ greyhound stadium owner	2A

Key to occupational classes:
1A = Higher professional
1B = Lower professional
2A = Employer or proprietor
2B = Manager or administrator
3 = Clerical worker
4 = Foreman, inspector or supervisor
5 = Skilled manual worker
6 = Semi-skilled manual worker
7 = Unskilled manual worker

Sources: Athletic News; All Sports Weekly; Birmingham Weekly Post; Birmingham Mail; Blackpool Gazette; Burnley Express; Huddersfield Weekly Examiner; The Lancashire Review; Liverpool Daily Post; Liverpool Echo; The Liverpolitan; Midland Chronicle and Free Press; Wolverhampton Express and Star; Kelly's Directory of Lancashire; Barrett's Directory of Preston and Flyde Districts; Barrett's Directory of Burnley and District; Gore's Liverpool Directory; Ward's Directory of Newcastle–on–Tyne; Wright's Directory of Nottingham; Kelly's Directory of Nottinghamshire; Post Office London Directory; Kelly's Directory of Staffordshire; Huddersfield County Borough Directory; FA, Register of Directors and Managers; Sutcliffe and Hargreaves, *Lancashire FA;* Gibson and Pickford (eds), *Association Football, vol. 3;* Inglis, *League Football*, pp. 387–95.

Bibliography

A. PRIMARY SOURCES

1. Archival Sources

Arsenal FC (AFC), London

Minutes of Board of Directors, 1930
James Catton Folders of newspaper cuttings, notes and letters, volumes A–Z
Minutes of Football League Management Committee, 1908, 1909, 1912–15
Minutes of Football League Annual General and Special General Meetings, 1912–15

Aston Villa FC (AVFC), Birmingham

Minutes of Board of Directors, 1899–1930
George Ramsay Correspondence Files, 47/82 (1907–08), 52/82 (1919–22)
Uncatalogued file, 1905

BBC Written Archives Centre (WAC), Caversham Park

Outside Broadcasts: Football League Ltd., File 1a: 1936–46, R30
Outside Broadcasts: Football, File 1: 1933–46
Outside Broadcasts – Sound: Aston Villa Ground, 1927–58, R30/53
Outside Broadcasts – Sound: Birmingham: St Andrew's Football Ground, 1927, R30/114
Outside Broadcasts – Sound: Manchester: Maine Road 1, 1928–46, R30
Outside Broadcasts – Sound: Huddersfield Football Ground 1, 1927–46, R30

Durham Record Office (DRO)

Minutes of Darlington FC (DFC) Board of Directors, 1934–39, D/XD 97/3

Football Association, London

Football Association Records

'Circular on Financial Arrangements Between Clubs and Players', 10 January 1909
Minutes of FA Council, 1899–1939
Minutes of Consultative Committee, 1899–1920
Minutes of Disciplinary Committee, 1936–39
Minutes of Emergency Committee, 1899–1939
Minutes of FA International Board, 1898–1939
Minutes of International Selection Committee, 1899–1939

Register of Directors and Managers
Reports of Commissions, Special Meetings, etc., 1899–1939

Football League Records

Football League Shareholders' Meeting Minutes
Minutes of Football League Management Committee, 1921–31
Minutes of Football League Annual General and Special General Meetings, 1921–31
Minutes of International Football League Board, 1921–31
Annual Financial Statements of Football League and Football League Mutual Insurance Federation (FLMIF), 1921–31
William Pickford newspaper cuttings, *Football Chat*, 1901–06

Football League, Lytham St Annes
Football League Handbooks, 1890/91–1938/39

Huddersfield Town FC (HTFC)
Minutes of Board of Directors, 1938–39

Oldham Athletic FC (OAFC)
Minutes of Board of Directors, April 1906–December 1907; December 1937–October 1939
Ledger, 1921/22–1938/39

Professional Footballers' Association (PFA), Manchester
Minutes of Association Football Players' Union (AFPU) Management Committee, 1907–15
Minutes of Association Football Players' Union (AFPU) Annual General and Special General Meetings, 1907–15
Minutes of Association Football Players' and Trainers' Union (AFPTU) Management Committee, 1919–39
Minutes of Association Football Players' and Trainers' Union (AFPTU) Annual General and Special General Meetings, 1919–35
Miscellaneous Files (PFA)
File 2, Copy of Small Heath FC Players' Agreement
File 6, Herbert Broomfield Correspondence, October–December 1908; February–April 1909
File 7, Herbert Broomfield Correspondence, May, June 1909
File 8, Herbert Broomfield Correspondence, July, August, September 1909
File 11, Rules of Association Football Players' Union, 1907
File 19, H. J. Newbould Correspondence, 1914
File 33, Correspondence between James Watson Hartley and James Fay, 1934; 1939
File 35, Correspondence between James Fay and Fred Howarth, 1938
Articles by James Fay and Charles Sutcliffe
Details of National Insurance and Inland Revenue cases, Millwall FC 1934; Manchester City FC, 1939

Public Record Office Northern Ireland, Belfast
Irish Football Association, Minutes of Finance Committee, 1924, D/4196

Sheffield United FC (SUFC)
Minutes of Football and Cricket Club, Football Committee, 1900–39
Club programmes, 1920–32
Revenue Accounts Book, 1900–39
Wages Book, 1899/1900–1904/05

Suffolk Record Office (SRO), Ipswich
Minutes of Ipswich Town FC (ITFC), Board of Directors, 1936–39
Minutes of Ipswich Town FC (ITFC), Finance Committee, 1936–39
Ipswich Town FC (ITFC), Wages Book, 1937/38–1938/39

Walsall Local History Centre (WLHC)
Minutes of Walsall FC (WFC) Board of Directors, October 1933–December 1935, 522/1/1
Walsall FC (WFC) Expenditure Analysis Book, 1921–46, 522/1/53
Walsall FC (WFC) Wage Book, 1920–30, 522/1/63
Walsall FC (WFC) Players' Registration Book, 1932–46, 522/1/66
Walsall FC (WFC) Letters File, 522/1/66

West Bromwich Albion FC (WBAFC), Staffordshire
Albion News (West Bromwich Albion club programme), 1920–23
Files of correspondence with creditors, 1905, 1907, 1908
Report of Liabilities and Assets, 1909

West Ham United FC (WHUFC), London
Minutes of Board of Directors, 1911, 1919, 1921–35

Wolverhampton Wanderers FC
Wolverhampton Wanderers FC club programmes, 1922–34

2. Contemporary Books, Articles and Pamphlets (pre-1938)

Allison, G. F., 'The Rise of Middlesbrough FC' in *Book of Football*, ed. Anon., London, The Amalgamated Press, 1906
Bassett, W., 'Big Transfers and the Transfer System' in *Book of Football*, ed. Anon., London, The Amalgamated Press, 1906
Book of Football, ed. Anon., London, The Amalgamated Press, 1906
Cameron, J., 'The Tottenham Hotspur: Its Story and Progress' in *Book of Football*, ed. Anon., London, The Amalgamated Press, 1906
Carter, F. W. and Capel-Kirby, W., *The Mighty Kick: The History, Romance and Humour of Football*, London, Jarrolds, 1933
Catton, J. A. H., *The Real Football: A Sketch of the Development of the Association Game*, London, Sands, 1900
Chapman, H., *Herbert Chapman on Football*, London, Garrick, 1934
Connell, R. M., 'The Scottish Football League and its History' in *Book of Football*, ed. Anon., London, The Amalgamated Press, 1906
Ensor, E., 'The Football Madness', *Contemporary Review*, Vol. 74, 1898
Football League Jubilee Souvenir Booklet, August 1938
Francis, C., *History of the Blackburn Rovers FC, 1875–1925*, Preston, Toulmin, 1925

Gibson, A. and Pickford, W. (eds), *Association Football and the Men Who Made It*, London, Caxton, 4 vols, 1906
Keates, T., *History of the Everton Football Club, 1878/9–1928/9*, Liverpool, Thomas Brakell, 1929
McDougall, *Fifty Years a Borough: The Story of West Ham*, London, West Ham County Borough Council, 1936
McGregor, W., 'The Origin and Future of the Football League' in *Association Football and the Men Who Made It*, ed. A. Gibson and W. Pickford, London, Caxton, vol. 2, 1906
McGregor, W., 'The League and the League System' in *Book of Football*, ed. Anon., London, The Amalgamated Press, 1906
McGregor, W., 'The £.s.d. of football', in *Book of Football*, ed. Anon., London, The Amalgamated Press, 1906
Pickford, W., 'How Soccer is Controlled', *The Listener*, 29 September 1937
Pickford, W., *A Glance Back at the FA Council, 1888–1938*, Bournemouth, Bournemouth Guardian, 1938
Rawcliffe, J., 'Blackpool Football Club: From Lancashire League to Second Division' in *Book of Football*, ed. Anon., London, The Amalgamated Press, 1906
Rous, S. F., 'Football as an International Sport', *The Listener*, 4 May 1938
Shearman, M. (ed.), *Football*, London, Longmans, 1899
Smith, G. O., 'Origin and Benefits of the League and the Effects of Professionalism on the Game' in *Football*, ed. M. Shearman, London, Longmans, 1899
Sutcliffe, C. E., Brierley, J. A. and Howarth, F., *The Story of the Football League, 1888–1939*, Preston, The Football League, 1938
Sutcliffe, C. E. and Hargreaves, F., *History of the Lancashire FA, 1878–1928*, Blackburn, Toulmin, 1928
Wall, F., *Fifty Years in Football*, London, Cassell, 1935

B. SECONDARY SOURCES

Abrams, N. D., 'Inhibited but not "Crowded Out": The Strange Fate of Soccer in the United States', *International Journal of the History of Sport*, Vol. 12, 1995
Ackers, P., 'On Paternalism: Seven Observations on the Uses and Abuses of the Concept in Industrial Relations, Past and Present', *Historical Studies in Industrial Relations*, Vol. 5, 1998
Adair, D., 'Psychic Income and the Administration of English County Cricket, 1870–1914', *The Sports Historian*, Vol. 14, 1994
Alford, B. W. E., 'New Industries for Old?: British Industry Between the Wars' in *The Economic History of Britain Since 1700, Volume 2: 1860 to the 1970s*, ed. R. Floud and D. McCloskey, Cambridge, Cambridge University Press, 1981
Allison, G., *Allison Calling*, London, Staples, 1948
Appleton, A., *Hotbed of Soccer: The Story of Football in the North East*, London, Rupert Hart-Davis, 1963
Archer, R. and Bouillon, A., *The South African Game: Sport and Racism*, London, Zed Books, 1982
Armstrong, G. and Giulianotti, R. (eds), *Football Cultures and Identities*, Basingstoke, Macmillan, 1999

Arnold, A. J., *A Game That Would Pay: A Business History of Professional Football in Bradford*, London, Duckworth, 1988

Arnold, A. J., 'The Belated Entry of Professional Soccer into the West Riding of Northern England', *International Journal of the History of Sport*, Vol. 6, 1989

Arnold, A. J., '"Not Playing the Game"?: Leeds City in the Great War', *International Journal of the History of Sport*, Vol. 7, 1990

Arnold, A. J., 'Rich Man, Poor Man: Economic Arrangements in the Football League' in *British Football and Social Change: Getting into Europe*, ed. J. Williams and S. Wagg, Leicester, Leicester University Press, 1991

Arnold, A. J. and Benveniste, I., 'Cross-Subsidisation and Competition Policy in English Professional Football', *Journal of Industrial Affairs*, Vol. 15, 1988

Bagwell, P. S., *Industrial Relations*, London, Irish University Press, 1974

Bailey, P., 'Custom, Capital and Culture in the Victorian Music-Hall' in *Popular Culture and Custom in Nineteenth-Century England*, ed. R. Storch, London, Croom Helm, 1982

Bailey, P. (ed.), *Music Hall: The Business of Pleasure*, Milton Keynes, Open University Press, 1986

Bailey, P., 'A Community of Friends: Business and Good Fellowship in London Music Hall Management, c. 1860–1885' in *Music Hall: The Business of Pleasure*, ed. P. Bailey, Milton Keynes, Open University Press, 1986

Bailey, P., *Leisure and Class in Victorian Britain: Rational Recreation and the Contest for Control, 1830–1885*, London, Methuen, 1987

Baker, N., *The Rise of the Victorian Actor*, London, Croom Helm, 1978

Bale, J., *Sport and Place: A Geography of Sport in England, Scotland and Wales*, London, C. Hurst, 1982

Bale, J. and Maguire, J. (eds), *The Global Sports Arena: Athletic Talent Migration in an Interdependent World*, London, Frank Cass, 1994

Bartrip, P., 'The Rise and Fall of Workmen's Compensation' in *The Social History of Occupational Health*, ed. P. Weindling, London, Croom Helm, 1985

Bartrip, P., *Workmen's Compensation in Twentieth Century Britain: Law, History and Social Policy*, Aldershot, Ashgate, 1987

Bartrip, P. and Burman, S. B., *The Wounded Soldiers of Industry: Industrial Compensation Policy, 1833–1897*, Oxford, Clarendon, 1983

Beck, P., *Scoring for Britain: International Football and International Politics, 1900–1939*, London, Frank Cass, 1999

Beck, P., 'Going to War, Peaceful Coexistence or Virtual Membership? British Football and FIFA, 1928–46', *International Journal of the History of Sport*, Vol. 17, 2000

Beckett, S. W., *Team From a Town of Chimneys – Revisited: The Official Chronicles of the Oldham Athletic AFC Ltd., 1897–1990*, Manchester, Comprehensive Art Services, 1990

Benson, J., *The Rise of Consumer Society in Britain, 1880–1980*, London, Longman, 1994

Benson, J. and Shaw, G. (eds), *The Evolution of Retail Systems, c. 1800–1914*, Leicester, Leicester University Press, 1992

Binns, G. S., *Huddersfield Town: 75 Years On*, Huddersfield, Huddersfield Town FC, 1984

Birley, D., *Land of Sport and Glory: Sport and British Society, 1887–1910*, Manchester, Manchester University Press, 1995

Bourne, J., Liddle, P. and Whitehead, I. (eds), *The Great World War 1914–45: Volume 2, The People's Experience*, London, Harper Collins, 2001

Boyle, R. and Haynes, R., *Power Play: Sport, the Media and Popular Culture*, London, Longman, 2000

Bradley, J., 'The MCC, Society and Empire: A Portrait of Cricket's Ruling Body, 1860–1914' in *The Cultural Bond: Sport, Empire, Society*, ed. J. A. Mangan, London, Frank Cass, 1992

Braverman, H., *Labor and Monopoly Capitalism: The Degradation of Work in the Twentieth Century*, New York, Monthly Review, 1974

Briggs, A., *The History of Broadcasting in the United Kingdom: Volume 2 – The Golden Age of Wireless*, London, Oxford University Press, 1965

Briggs, A., *Victorian Cities*, London, Penguin, 1968

Briggs, A., *The BBC: The First Fifty Years*, Oxford, Oxford University Press, 1985

Buchan, C., *A Lifetime in Football*, London, Phoenix, 1955

Burk, R., *Never Just a Game: Players, Owners and American Baseball to 1920*, Chapel Hill, University of North Carolina Press, 1994

Burk, R., *Much More Than a Game: Players, Owners and American Baseball since 1921*, Chapel Hill, University of North Carolina Press, 2001

Butler, B., *The Football League: The First 100 Years*, Guildford, Colour Library, 1988

Cain, P. J., 'Railways 1870–1914: The Maturity of the Private System' in *Transport in Victorian England*, ed. M. J. Freeman and D. H. Aldcroft, Manchester, Manchester University Press, 1988

Cairns, J., Jennett, N. and Sloane, P. J., 'The Economics of Professional Team Sports: A Survey of Theory and Evidence', *Journal of Economic Studies*, Vol. 13, 1986

Canes, M. E., 'The Social Benefits of Restrictions on Team Quality' in *Government and the Sports Business*, ed. R. G. Noll, Washington D.C., The Brookings Institute, 1974

Cannadine, D., 'The Context, Performance and Meaning of Ritual: The British Monarchy and the Invention of Tradition, c. 1820–1977' in *The Invention of Tradition*, ed. E. Hobsbawm and T. Ranger, Cambridge, Cambridge University Press, 1983

Carder, T. and Harris, R., *Seagulls! The Story of Brighton and Hove Albion FC*, Hove, Goldstone, 1993

Carter, R., *Footballer's Progress*, London, Sporting Handbooks, 1950

Cashman, R. and McKernan, M. (eds), *Sport in History*, St Lucia, University of Queensland Press, 1979

Cashman, R. and McKernan, M. (eds), *Sport: Money, Morality and the Media*, Brisbane, University of New South Wales Press, 1981

Cesarini, D., 'Anti-Alienism in England After the First World War', *Immigrants and Minorities*, Vol. 6, 1987

Chalk, G. and Holley, D., *The Saints: A Complete Record, 1885–1987*, Derby, Breedon, 1987

Churchill, R. C., *English League Football*, London, Nicholas Kaye, 1961

Clapson, M., *A Bit of a Flutter: Popular Gambling and English Society, c. 1823–1961*, Manchester, Manchester University Press, 1992

Clapson, M., 'Playing the System: The World of Organised Street Betting in Manchester, Salford and Bolton, c. 1880–1939' in *Workers' Worlds: Cultures and Communities in Manchester and Salford, 1880–1939*, ed. A. Davies and S. Fielding, Manchester, Manchester University Press, 1992

Clark, P., *British Clubs and Societies 1580–1800: The Origins of an Associational World*, Oxford, Oxford University Press, 2000

Clegg, H. A., *A History of British Trade Unions, Volume 2: 1911–1933*, Oxford, Oxford University Press, 1985

Clegg, H. A., Fox, A. and Thompson, A. F., *A History of British Trade Unions since 1889, Volume 1: 1889–1910*, Oxford, Oxford University Press, 1964

Collins, T., *Rugby's Great Split: Class, Culture and the Origins of Rugby League Football*, London, Frank Cass, 1998

Collins, T. and Vamplew, W. (eds), *Mud, Sweat and Beers: A Cultural History of Sport and Alcohol*, Oxford, Berg, 2002

Coyle, J., 'English sports leagues, franchising and the management of expansion: the Football League and the Northern Union up to 1923', unpublished MA dissertation, De Montfort University, 1997

Crampsey, B., *The Scottish Footballer*, Edinburgh, William Blackwood, 1978

Crampsey, B., *The Scottish Football League: The First 100 Years*, Glasgow, Scottish Football League, 1990

Cronin, M., *Sport and Nationalism in Ireland: Gaelic Games, Soccer and Irish Identity Since 1884*, Dublin, Four Courts, 1999

Cronin, M., 'Arthur Elvin and the Dogs of Wembley', *The Sports Historian*, Vol. 22, 2002

Crowhurst, A., 'London's "Music Hall War": Trade Unionism in an Edwardian Service Industry', *London Journal*, Vol. 21, 1996

Crowhurst, A., 'The "Portly Grabbers of 75 Per Cent": Capital Investment in the British Entertainment Industry, 1885–1914', *Leisure Studies*, Vol. 20, 2001

Cullis, S., *All For the Wolves*, London, Sportsman's Book Club, 1961

Cunningham, H., *Leisure in the Industrial Revolution*, London, Croom Helm, 1980

Cunningham, H., 'Leisure and Culture' in *The Cambridge Social History of Britain, 1750–1950, Volume 2 – People and their Environment*, ed. F. M. L. Thompson, Cambridge, Cambridge University Press, 1990

Dabscheck, B., '"Defensive Manchester": A History of the Professional Footballers' Association' in *Sport in History*, ed. R. Cashman and M. McKernan, St Lucia, University of Queensland Press, 1979

Dabscheck, B., '"A Man or a Puppet?": The Football Association's 1909 Attempt to Destroy the Association Football Players' Union', *International Journal of the History of Sport*, Vol. 8, 1991

Davies, A. and Fielding, S. (eds), *Workers' Worlds: Cultures and Communities in Manchester and Salford, 1880–1939*, Manchester, Manchester University Press, 1992

Devlin, R., 'Strike Patterns and Employers' Responses: Clydeside in Comparative Perspective' in *Roots of Red Clydeside, 1910–1914? Labour Unrest and Industrial Relations in West Scotland*, ed. W. Kenefick and A. McIvor, Edinburgh, John Donald, 1996

Dobbs, B., *Edwardians at Play: Sport, 1890–1914*, London, Pelham, 1973

Dobson, S. and Goddard, J., 'Performance, Revenue and Cross Subsidization in the Football League, 1927–1994', *Economic History Review*, Vol. 51, 1998

Dobson, S. and Goddard, J., *The Economics of Football*, Cambridge, Cambridge University Press, 2001

Drummond, D., *Crewe: Railway Town, Company and People, 1840–1914*, Aldershot, Scholar, 1995

Dummett, A. and Nichol, A., *Subjects, Citizens, Aliens and Others: Nationality and Immigration Law*, London, Weidenfeld & Nicolson, 1990

Dunning, E. and Sheard, K., *Barbarians, Gentlemen and Players: A Sociological Study of the Development of Rugby Football*, Oxford, Martin Robertson, 1979

Dykes, G., *Oldham Athletic: A Complete Record, 1899–1988*, Derby, Breedon, 1988

Dykes, G., *The United Alphabet: A Complete Who's Who of Manchester United FC*, Leicester, Polar, 1994

Euchner, C. C., *Playing the Field: Why Sports Teams Move and Cities Fight to Keep Them*, Baltimore, Johns Hopkins University Press, 1994

Evans, A., 'Football on the edge: the relationship between Welsh football policy-making and the British International Championship', unpublished MA dissertation, De Montfort University, 1996

Fabian, A. H. and Green, G. (eds), *Association Football*, 4 vols, London, Caxton, 1960

Finlayson, G., *Citizen, State and Social Welfare in Britain, 1830–1990*, Oxford, Clarendon, 1994

Finney, T., *Finney on Football*, London, Soccer Book Club, 1960

Fishwick, N., *English Football and Society, 1910–50*, Manchester, Manchester University Press, 1989

Fitzgerald, R., *British Labour Management and Industrial Welfare, 1846–1939*, London, Croom Helm, 1988

Floud, R. and McCloskey, D. (eds), *The Economic History of Britain Since 1700, Volume 2: 1860 to the 1970s*, Cambridge, Cambridge University Press, 1981

Francis, L., *Seventy Years of Southern League Football*, London, Pelham, 1969

Fraser, D., *The Evolution of the British Welfare State*, second edition, Basingstoke, Macmillan, 1984

Fraser, W. H., *The Coming of the Mass Market, 1850–1914*, London, Macmillan, 1981

Freeman, M. J. and Aldcroft, D. H. (eds), *Transport in Victorian England*, Manchester, Manchester University Press, 1988

Frost, T., *Huddersfield Town: A Complete Record, 1910–90*, Derby, Breedon, 1990

Garcia Castell, J., *Història del futbol catalá*, Barcelona, Aymà, 1968

Garnham, N. (ed.), *The Origins and Development of Football in Ireland*, Belfast, Ulster Historical Foundation, 1999

Garnham, N., 'Origins and Development of Irish Football' in *The Origins and Development of Football in Ireland*, ed. N. Garnham, Belfast, Ulster Historical Foundation, 1999

Giulianotti, R. and Williams, J. (eds), *Game Without Frontiers: Football, Identity and Modernity*, Aldershot, Arena, 1995

Glanville, B., *Soccer Round the Globe*, London, Sportsman's Book Club, 1961

Golesworthy, M., *The Encyclopaedia of Association Football*, London, Sportsman's Book Club, 1957

Golesworthy, M., *We Are the Champions: A History of the Football League Champions, 1888–1972*, London, Pelham, 1972

Goodwin, B., *Spurs: A Complete Record*, Derby, Breedon, 1993

Gore, V., 'Rank-and-File Dissent' in *A History of British Industrial Relations, Volume 2: 1914–1939*, ed. C. J. Wrigley, Brighton, Harvester, 1987

Gospel, H. F., 'Managerial Structure and Strategies: An Introduction' in *Managerial Strategies and Industrial Relations: An Historical and Comparative Study*, ed. H. F. Gospel and C. R. Littler, London, Heinemann, 1983

Gospel, H. F. and Littler, C. R. (eds), *Managerial Strategies and Industrial Relations: An Historical and Comparative Study*, London, Heinemann, 1983

Grant, A. and Stringer, K. (eds), *Uniting the Kingdom? The Making of British History*, London, Routledge, 1995

Green, G., *The History of the Football Association*, London, Naldrett, 1953

Green, G., 'The Football Association' in *Association Football, Volume 1*, ed. A. H. Fabian and G. Green, London, Caxton, 1960

Greenhalgh, P., '"The Work and Play Principle": The Professional Regulations of the Northern Rugby Football Union, 1898–1905', *International Journal of the History of Sport*, Vol. 9, 1992

Griffiths, J., '"Give My Regards to Uncle Billy…": The Rites and Rituals of Company Life at Lever Brothers, c.1900–c.1990', *Business History*, Vol. 37, 1995

Gunn, S., *The Public Culture of the Victorian Middle Class: Ritual and Authority and the English Industrial City, 1840–1914*, Manchester, Manchester University Press, 2000

Guthrie, J., *Soccer Rebel: The Evolution of the Professional Footballer*, London, Pentagon, 1976

Hannah, L., *The Rise of the Corporate Economy*, second edition, London, Methuen, 1983

Hannah, L., *Inventing Retirement: The Development of Occupational Pensions in Britain*, Cambridge, Cambridge University Press, 1986

Hapgood, E., *Football Ambassador*, London, Sporting Handbooks, 1944

Hardaker, A., *Hardaker of the League*, London, Pelham, 1977

Harding, J., *Football Wizard: The Story of Billy Meredith*, Derby, Breedon, 1985

Harding, J., *Alex James*, London, Robson, 1988

Harding, J., *For the Good of the Game: The Official History of the Professional Footballers' Association*, London, Robson, 1991

Hardy, S., 'Entrepreneurs, Organizations and the Sport Marketplace: Subjects in Search of Historians', *Journal of Sport History*, Vol. 13, 1986

Harris, J., *Private Lives, Public Spirit: A Social History of Britain, 1870–1914*, Oxford, Oxford University Press, 1993

Harrison, P., *Southern League Football: The First Fifty Years*, Gravesend, self-published, 1989

Hay, R., 'Employers and Social Policy in Britain: The Evolution of Welfare Legislation, 1905–14', *Social History*, Vol. 4, 1977

Hayes, D., *Bolton Wanderers: An A–Z*, Preston, Palatine, 1994

Haynes, R., '"There's Many a Slip 'Twixt the Eye and the Lip": An Exploratory History of Football Broadcasts and Running Commentaries on BBC Radio, 1927–1939', *International Review of the Sociology of Sport*, Vol. 34, 1999

Hill, J., 'Cricket and the Imperial Connection: Overseas Players in Lancashire in the Inter-War Years' in *The Global Sports Arena: Athletic Talent Migration in an Interdependent World*, ed. J. Bale and J. Maguire, London, Frank Cass, 1994

Hill, J., 'British Sports History: A Post-Modern Future?', *Journal of Sport History*, Vol. 23, 1996

Hill, J., *Sport, Leisure and Culture in Twentieth-Century Britain*, Basingstoke, Palgrave, 2002

Hill, J. and Williams, J. (eds), *Sport and Identity in the North of England*, Keele, Keele University Press, 1996

Hilton, M., *Smoking in British Popular Culture, 1800–2000*, Manchester, Manchester University Press, 2000

Hinton, J., *Labour and Socialism: A History of the British Labour Movement, 1867–1974*, Brighton, Harvester, 1983

Hobsbawm, E., 'Mass-Producing Traditions: Europe, 1870–1914' in *The Invention of Tradition*, ed. E. Hobsbawm and T. Ranger, Cambridge, Cambridge University Press, 1983

Hobsbawm, E. and Ranger, T. (eds), *The Invention of Tradition*, Cambridge, Cambridge University Press, 1983

Holland, J., *Spurs: A History of Tottenham Hotspur Football Club*, London, Sportsman's Book Club, 1957

Holmes, C., *John Bull's Island: Immigration and British Society, 1871–1971*, London, Macmillan, 1988

Holt, R., 'Football and the Urban Way of Life in Nineteenth-Century Britain' in *Pleasure, Profit and Proselytism: British Culture and Sport at Home and Abroad, 1700–1914*, ed. J. A. Mangan, London, Frank Cass, 1988

Holt, R., *Sport and the British: A Modern History*, Oxford, Clarendon, 1989

Holt, R. (ed.), *Sport and the Working Class in Modern Britain*, Manchester, Manchester University Press, 1991

Holt, R., 'Heroes of the North: Sport and the Shaping of Regional Identity' in *Sport and Identity in the North of England*, ed. J. Hill and J. Williams, Keele, Keele University Press, 1996

Holt, R., '"No Ideas But in Things": Tony Mason's *Association Football and English Society*', *The Sports Historian*, Vol. 22, 2002

Holt, R., Mangan, J. A. and Lanfranchi, P. (eds), *European Heroes: Myth, Identity, Sport*, London, Frank Cass, 1996

Holt, R. and Mason, T., *Sport in Britain, 1945–2000*, Oxford, Blackwell, 2000

Hopkins, E., *Working-Class Self Help in Nineteenth-Century England*, London, Macmillan, 1995

Horrall, A., *Popular Culture in London, c. 1890–1918: The Transformation of Entertainment*, Manchester, Manchester University Press, 2001

Hurseau, P., *L'histoire du Football Nordiste*, Lille, Ligue du Nord du Football, 1977

Hutchinson, J. A., 'The development of professional football 1870–1914, with special emphasis on Scotland', unpublished paper, University of Edinburgh, 1977

Hutchinson, J., *The Football Industry: The Early Years of the Professional Game*, Glasgow, R. Drew, 1982

Inglis, S., *Soccer in the Dock: A History of British Football Scandals*, London, Willow, 1985

Inglis, S., *The Football Grounds of Great Britain*, London, Collins Willow, 1987

Inglis, S., *League Football and the Men Who Made It*, London, Collins Willow, 1988

Jackman, M., *Blackburn Rovers: The Official Encyclopedia*, Derby, Breedon, 1994

Jarred, M. and MacDonald, M., *Leeds United: A Complete Record, 1919–1989*, Derby, Breedon, 1989

Jarvie, G. and Maguire, J., *Sport and Leisure in Social Thought*, London, Routledge, 1994

Jewell, H., *The North–South Divide: The Origins of Northern Consciousness in England*, Manchester, Manchester University Press, 1994

Joannou, P., *Wembley Wizards: The Story of a Legend*, Edinburgh, Mainstream, 1990

Johnes, M., *A History of Sport in Wales*, Cardiff, University of Wales Press, 2005

Johnes, M., *Soccer and Society: South Wales, 1900–1939*, Cardiff, University of Wales Press, 2002

Johnston, R., *Clydeside Capital, 1870–1920: A Social History of Employers*, East Linton, Tuckwell, 2000

Jones, S., 'The Economic Aspects of Association Football in England, 1918–39', *British Journal of Sports History*, Vol. 1, 1984

Jones, S., 'The Leisure Industry in Britain, 1918–39', *Service Industries Journal*, Vol. 5, 1985

Jones, S., *Sport, Politics and the Working Class*, Manchester, Manchester University Press, 1988

Jones, S., 'Cotton Employers and Industrial Welfare Between the Wars' in *Employers and Labour in the English Textile Industries, 1850–1939*, ed. J. A. Jowitt and A. J. McIvor, London, Routledge, 1988

Jordan, G., *Football européen*, Paris, Triolet, 1947

Jose, C., *American Soccer League, 1921–31: The Golden Years of American Soccer*, Maryland, Scarecrow, 1998

Jowitt, J. A. and McIvor, A. J. (eds), *Employers and Labour in the English Textile Industries, 1850–1939*, London, Routledge, 1988

Joyce, P., *Work, Society and Politics: The Culture of the Factory in Later Victorian Britain*, Brighton, Harvester, 1980

Kenefick, W. and McIvor, A (eds), *Roots of Red Clydeside, 1910–1914? Labour Unrest and Industrial Relations in West Scotland*, Edinburgh, John Donald, 1996

Kirk, N., *Labour and Society in Britain and the USA: Volume 2 – Challenge and Accommodation, 1850–1939*, Aldershot, Scholar, 1994

Kirk, N., *Change, Continuity and Class: Labour in British Society, 1850–1920*, Manchester, Manchester University Press, 1998

Kirkham, P. and Thoms, D. (eds), *War Culture: Social Change and Changing Experience in World War Two*, London, Lawrence and Wishart, 1995

Knox, W. W., *Industrial Nation: Work, Culture and Society in Scotland, 1800–Present*, Edinburgh, Edinburgh University Press, 1999

Korr, C., *West Ham United: The Making of a Football Club*, London, Duckworth, 1986

Lancaster, B., *The Department Store: A Social History*, London, Leicester University Press, 1995

Lanfranchi, P., 'Bologna: The Team that Shook the World', *International Journal of the History of Sport*, Vol. 8, 1991

Lanfranchi, P., 'Exporting Football: Notes on the Development of Football in Europe' in *Game Without Frontiers: Football, Identity and Modernity*, ed. R. Giulianotti and J. Williams, Aldershot, Arena, 1995

Lanfranchi, P., '"Mister" Garbutt: The First European Manager', *The Sports Historian*, Vol. 22, 2002

Lanfranchi, P. and Taylor, M., 'Professional Football in Second World War Britain' in *War Culture: Social Change and Changing Experience in World War Two*, ed. P. Kirkham and D. Thoms, London, Lawrence and Wishart, 1995

Lawton, T., *Football is my Business*, London, Sporting Handbooks, 1946

Laybourn, K. (ed.), *Social Conditions, Status and Community, 1860–c.1920*, Stroud, Sutton, 1997

Ledbrooke, A. and Turner, E., *Soccer from the Press Box*, London, Sportsman's Book Club, 1955

LeMahieu, D. L., *A Culture for Demoncracy: Mass Communication and the Cultivated Mind in Britain Between the Wars*, Oxford, Clarendon, 1988

Lewis, R. W., 'The development of professional football in Lancashire, 1870–1914', unpublished PhD thesis, University of Lancaster, 1993

Lewis, R. W., 'Football Hooliganism in England Before 1914: A Critique of the Dunning Thesis', *International Journal of the History of Sport*, Vol. 13, 1996

Licht, W., 'Fringe Benefits: A Review Essay of the American Workplace', *International Labor and Working-Class History*, No. 53, 1998

Lovell, J., *British Trade Unions, 1875–1933*, London, Macmillan, 1977

Lowenfish, L., *The Imperfect Diamond: A History of Baseball's Labor Wars*, New York, De Capo, 1991

Lowerson, J., *Sport and the English Middle Classes, 1870–1914*, Manchester, Manchester University Press, 1993

McIvor, A. J., *Organised Capital: Employers' Associations and Industrial Relations in Northern England, 1880–1939*, Cambridge, Cambridge University Press, 1996

McIvor, A. J., *A History of Work in Britain, 1880–1950*, London, Palgrave, 2001

McKernan, L., 'Sport and the First Films' in *Cinema: The Beginnings and the Future*, ed. C. Williams, London, University of Westminster Press, 1996

McKibbin, *Classes and Cultures: England, 1918–50*, Oxford, Oxford University Press, 1998

MacRaild, D. M. and Martin, D. E., *Labour in British Society, 1830–1914*, Basingstoke, Macmillan, 2000

Malcolmson, R. W., *Popular Recreations in English Society, 1700–1850*, Cambridge, Cambridge University Press, 1973

Mallory, J. (ed.), *Football League Tables: 1889 to the Present*, London, Collins, 1977

Mangan, J. A. (ed.), *Pleasure, Profit and Proselytism: British Culture and Sport at Home and Abroad, 1700–1914*, London, Frank Cass, 1988

Mangan, J. A. (ed.), *The Cultural Bond: Sport, Empire, Society*, London, Frank Cass, 1992

Mangan, J. A. (ed.), *Tribal Identities: Nationalism, Europe, Sport*, London, Frank Cass, 1996

Markham Lester, V., 'The Employers' Liability/Workmen's Compensation Debate of the 1890s Revisited', *The Historical Journal*, Vol. 44, 2001

Markovits, A. S. and Hellerman, S. L., *Offside: Soccer and American Exceptionalism*, Princeton, Princeton University Press, 2001

Marschik, M., 'Mitropa: Representations of "Central Europe" in Football', *International Review of the Sociology of Sport*, Vol. 36, 2001

Mason, T., *Association Football and English Society, 1863–1915*, Brighton, Harvester, 1980

Mason, T., *The Blues and the Reds: A History of the Liverpool and Everton Football Clubs*, Liverpool, Historic Society of Lancashire and Cheshire, 1985

Mason, T., 'Some Englishmen and Scotsmen Abroad: The Spread of World Football' in *Off the Ball: The Football World Cup*, ed. A. Tomlinson and G. Whannel, London, Pluto, 1986

Mason, T., 'Football and the Historians', *International Journal of the History of Sport*, Vol. 5, 1988

Mason, T. (ed.), *Sport in Britain: A Social History*, Cambridge, Cambridge University Press, 1989

Mason, T., 'Football' in *Sport in Britain: A Social History*, ed. T. Mason, Cambridge, Cambridge University Press, 1989

Mason, T., 'Stanley Matthews' in *Sport and the Working Class in Modern Britain*, ed. R. Holt, Manchester, Manchester University Press, 1991

Mason, T., 'All the Winners and the Half Times', *The Sports Historian*, Vol. 13, 1993

Mason, T., *Passion of the People? Football in South America*, London, Verso, 1995

Mason, T., 'Football, Sport of the North?', in *Sport and Identity in the North of England*, ed. J. Hill and J. Williams, Keele, Keele University Press, 1996

Mason, T., '"Our Stephen and Our Harold": Edwardian Footballers as Local Heroes' in *European Heroes: Myth, Identity, Sport*, ed. R. Holt, J. A. Mangan and P. Lanfranchi, London, Frank Cass, 1996

Mason, T., 'Defeat of the Soccer Exiles', *BBC History Magazine*, Vol. 1, 2000

Matthews, T. with Smith, L., *The Wolves: An Encyclopedia of Wolverhampton Wanderers Football Club, 1877–1989*, London, Paper Plane, 1989

Meisl, W., *Soccer Revolution*, London, Phoenix, 1955

Melling, J., 'Employers, Industrial Housing and the Evolution of Company Welfare Policies in Britain's Heavy Industry: West Scotland 1870–1920', *International Review of Social History*, Vol. 26, 1982

Melling, J., 'Employers, Industrial Welfare and the Struggle for Work-Place Control in British Industry, 1880–1920' in *Managerial Strategies and Industrial Relations: An Historical and Comparative Study*, ed. H. F. Gospel and C. R. Littler, London, Heinemann, 1983

Melling, J., 'Employers, Workplace Culture and Workers' Politics: British Industry and Workers' Welfare Programmes, 1870–1920' in *Culture in History: Production, Consumption and Values in Historical Perspective*, ed. J. Melling and J. Berry, Exeter, Exeter University Press, 1992

Melling, J. and Berry, J. (eds), *Culture in History: Production, Consumption and Values in Historical Perspective*, Exeter, Exeter University Press, 1992

Midwinter, E., *The Development of Social Welfare in Britain*, Buckingham, Open University Press, 1994

Miles, A. and Vincent, D. (eds), *Building European Society: Occupational Change and Social Mobility in Europe, 1840–1940*, Manchester, Manchester University Press, 1993

Miller, G. C., *Blackburn Worthies of Yesterday: A Biographical Galaxy*, Blackburn, Blackburn Society of Antiquaries, 1961

Moorhouse, G., *A People's Game: The Centenary History of Rugby League Football*, London, Hodder and Stoughton, 1995

Moorhouse, H. F., 'Scotland against England: Football and Popular Culture', *International Journal of the History of Sport*, Vol. 4, 1987

Moorhouse, H. F., 'Blue Bonnets over the Border: Scotland and the Migration of Footballers' in *The Global Sports Arena: Athletic Talent Migration in an Interdependent World*, ed. J. Bale and J. Maguire, London, Frank Cass, 1994

Moorhouse, H. F., 'One State, Several Countries: Soccer and Identies in a "United" Kingdom' in *Tribal Identities: Nationalism, Europe, Sport*, ed. J. A. Mangan, London, Frank Cass, 1996

Moorhouse, H. F., 'The Economic Effects of the Traditional Transfer System in European Professional Football', *Football Studies*, Vol. 2, 1999

Morris, B. and Smyth, J., 'Paternalism as an Employer Strategy, 1800–1960' in *Employer Strategy and the Labour Market*, ed. J. Rubery and F. Wilkinson, Oxford, Oxford University Press, 1994

Morris, R. J., 'Clubs, Societies and Associations' in *The Cambridge Social History of Britain, 1750–1950: Volume 3 – Social Agencies and Institutions*, ed. F. M. L. Thompson, Cambridge, Cambridge University Press, 1990

Munting, R., *Hedges and Hurdles: A Social and Economic History of National Hunt Racing*, London, Allen Lane, 1987

Murray, B., *Football: A History of the World Game*, Aldershot, Scholar, 1994

Nevett, T. R., *Advertising in Britain: A History*, London, Heinemann, 1982

Newby, H., 'The Deferential Dialect', *Comparative Studies in Society and History*, Vol. 13, 1975

Noll, R. G. (ed.), *Government and the Sports Business*, Washington D.C., The Brookings Institute, 1974

Noll, R. G., 'Professional Basketball: Economic and Business Perspectives' in *The Business of Professional Sports*, ed. P. D. Staudohar and J. A. Mangan, Urbana, University of Illinois Press, 1991

Panayi, P., *Immigration, Ethnicity and Racism in Britain, 1815–1945*, Manchester, Manchester University Press, 1994

Perkin, H., *The Rise of Professional Society: England Since 1880*, London, Routledge, 1989

Plumb, J. H., *The Commercialisation of Leisure in Eighteenth-Century England*, Reading, Reading University Press, 1974
Pocock, J. G. A., 'The Limits and Divisions of British History: In Search of the Unknown Subject', *American Historical Review*, Vol. 87, 1982
Political and Economic Planning, 'The Football Industry – 1', *Planning*, Vol. 17, 1951
Political and Economic Planning, 'English Professional Football', *Political and Economic Planning*, Vol. 32, 1966
Pozzo, V., *Campioni del Mondo: Quarant'anni di storio del calico italiano*, Rome, CEN, 1960
Quirk, J. and El Hodiri, M., 'The Economic Theory of a Professional Sports League' in *Government and the Sports Business*, ed. R. G. Noll, Washington D.C., The Brookings Institute, 1974
Quirk, J. and Fort, R. D., *Pay Dirt: The Business of Professional Team Sports*, Princeton, Princeton University Press, 1992
Read, D., *The English Provinces, c. 1760–1960: A Study in Influence*, London, Edward Arnold, 1964
Richards, J., *The Age of the Dream Palace: Cinema and Society in Britain, 1930–1939*, London, Routledge, 1984
Riegler, T., *Als Staulfauth noch im Tor Stand… Ein Buch vom deutschen Fussball*, Munich, Porta Varlag K. G. Schemm, 1953
Riess, S., 'Professional Baseball and Social Mobility', *Journal of Interdisciplinary History*, Vol. 11, 1980
Robbins, K., *Nineteenth-Century Britain: Integration and Diversity*, Oxford, Clarendon, 1988
Roberts, D., *Paternalism in Early Victorian England*, London, Croom Helm, 1979
Roberts, J. M., 'Freemasonry: Possibilities of a Neglected Subject', *English Historical Review*, Vol. 84, 1969
Rollin, J. (ed.), *Rothman's Football Yearbook, 1989–90*, London, Headline, 1989
Rous, S., *Football Worlds: A Lifetime in Sport*, London, Faber and Faber, 1978
Routh, G., *Occupation and Pay in Great Britain, 1906–79*, London, Macmillan, 1980
Rubery, J. and Wilkinson, F. (eds), *Employer Strategy and the Labour Market*, Oxford, Oxford University Press, 1994
Russell, A., 'Local Elites and Working-Class Response in the North-West, 1870–1895: Paternalism and Deference Reconsidered', *Northern History*, Vol. 23, 1987
Russell, A., *The Growth of Occupational Welfare in Britain*, Aldershot, Avebury, 1991
Russell, D., *Football and the English: A Social History of Association Football in England, 1863–1995*, Preston, Carnegie, 1997
Russell, D., 'Associating with Football: Social Identity in England, 1863–1998' in *Football Cultures and Identities*, ed. G. Armstrong and R. Giulianotti, Basingstoke, Macmillan, 1999
Russell, D., 'Football and Society in the North-West, 1919–1939', *North West Labour History*, Vol. 24, 1999/2000
Rutherford, L., '"Managers in a Small Way": The Professionalisation of Variety Artistes, 1860–1914' in *Music Hall: The Business of Pleasure*, ed. P. Bailey, Milton Keynes, Open University Press, 1986
Salt, J. and Kitching, R. T., 'Labour Migration and the Work Permit System in the United Kingdom', *International Migration*, Vol. 28, 1990
Samuel, R. (ed.), *Patriotism: The Making and Unmaking of British National Identity, Volume 1: History and Politics*, London, Routledge, 1989

Samuel, R., 'Introduction: Exciting to be English' in *Patriotism: The Making and Unmaking of British National Identity, Volume 1 – History and Politics*, ed. R. Samuel, London, Routledge, 1989

Samuel, R., 'British Dimensions: "Four Nations History"', *History Workshop Journal*, Vol. 40, 1995

Sanderson, M., *From Irving to Olivier: A Social History of the Acting Profession*, London, Athlone, 1984

Sandiford, K. A. P., 'The Birth of the Professional Cricketer's Benefit Match', *International Journal of the History of Sport*, Vol. 8, 1991

Sandiford, K. A. P., *Cricket and the Victorians*, Aldershot, Scholar, 1994

Sandiford, K. and Vamplew, W., 'The Peculiar Economics of English Cricket Before 1914', *British Journal of Sports History*, Vol. 3, 1986

Savage, M. and Miles, A., *The Remaking of the British Working Class, 1840–1940*, London, Routledge, 1994

Say, T., 'Herbert Chapman: Football Revolutionary?', *The Sports Historian*, Vol. 16, 1996

Scannell, P. and Cardiff, D., 'Serving the Nation: Public Service Broadcasting before the War' in *Popular Culture: Past and Present*, ed. B. Waites, T. Bennett and G. Martin, London, Croom Helm, 1982

Scannell, P. and Cardiff, D., *A Social History of British Broadcasting: Volume One – 1922–1939, Serving the Nation*, Oxford, Basil Blackwell, 1991

Schofield, J. A., 'The Development of First-Class Cricket in England: An Economic Analysis', *Journal of Industrial Economics*, Vol. 30, 1982

Seddon, P., *Steve Bloomer: The Story of Football's First Superstar*, Derby, Breedon, 1999

Sedgwick, J., *Popular Filmgoing in 1930s Britain: A Choice of Pleasures*, Exeter, Exeter University Press, 2000

Seed, J., *The Jimmy Seed Story*, London, Phoenix, 1957

Sharpe, I., *40 Years in Football*, London, Sportsman's Book Club, 1954

Sharpe, I., 'The Men who Made League Football' in *Association Football*, ed. A. H. Fabian and G. Green, London, Caxton, 1960

Shaw, G., 'The Evolution and Impact of Large-Scale Retailing in Britain' in *The Evolution of Retail Systems, c. 1800–1914*, ed. J. Benson and G. Shaw, Leicester, Leicester University Press, 1992

Shindler, C., *Fathers, Sons and Football*, London, Headline, 2002

Shipley, S., 'Tom Causer of Bermondsey: A Boxer Hero of the 1890s', *History Workshop Journal*, Vol. 15, 1983

Simmons, G. W., *Tottenham Hotspur Football Club: Its Birth and Progress, 1882–1946*, London, Tottenham Hotspur FC, 1947

Sissons, R., *The Players: A Social History of the Professional Cricketer*, Sydney, Pluto, 1988

Sloane, P. J., 'The Labour Market in Professional Football', *British Journal of Industrial Relations*, Vol. 7, 1969

Sloane, P. J., 'Restriction of Competition in Professional Team Sports', *Bulletin of Economic Research*, Vol. 18, 1976

Sloane, P. J., *Sport in the Market?*, London, Institute of Economic Affairs, 1980

Smith, D., 'Focal Heroes: A Welsh Fighting Class' in *Sport and the Working Class in Modern Britain*, ed. R. Holt, Manchester, Manchester University Press, 1991

Staudohar, P. D. and Mangan, J. A. (eds), *The Business of Professional Sports*, Urbana, University of Illinois Press, 1991

Storch, R. (ed.), *Popular Culture and Custom in Nineteenth-Century England*, London, Croom Helm, 1982

Studd, S., *Herbert Chapman, Football Emperor: A Study of the Origins of Modern Soccer*, London, Peter Owen, 1981
Sturdy, A., Knights, D. and Willmott, H. (eds), *Skill and Consent: Contemporary Studies in the Labour Process*, London, Routledge, 1992
Sugden, J. and Bairner, A., *Sport, Sectarianism and Society in a Divided Ireland*, Leicester, Leicester University Press, 1993
Sugden, J. and Tonmlinson, A., *FIFA and the Contest for World Football*, Cambridge, Polity Press, 1998
Summerfield, P., 'The Effingham Arms and Empire: Deliberate Selection in the Evolution of Music Hall in London' in *Popular Culture and Class Conflict, 1590–1914: Explorations in the History of Labour and Leisure*, ed. E. Yeo and S. Yeo, Brighton, Harvester, 1981
Szymanski, S. and Kuypers, T., *Winners and Losers: The Business Strategy of Football*, London, Penguin, 2000
Tabner, B., *Through the Turnstiles*, Harefield, Yore, 1992
Taylor, M., 'Leisure and Entertainment' in *The Great World War 1914–45: Volume 2 – The People's Experience*, ed. J. Bourne, P. Liddle and I. Whitehead, London, Harper Collins, 2001
Taylor, M., 'Work and Play: The Professional Footballer in England, c. 1900–1950', *The Sports Historian*, Vol. 22, 2002
Taylor, R., *Football and Its Fans: Supporters and their Relations with the Game, 1885–1985*, Leicester, Leicester University Press, 1992
Taylor, R. and Ward, A., *Kicking and Screaming: An Oral History of Football in England*, London, Robson, 1995
Thompson, E. P., *The Making of the English Working Class*, London, Penguin, 1968
Thompson, F. M. L. (ed.), *The Cambridge Social History of Britain, 1750–1950: Volume 2 – People and their Environment*, Cambridge, Cambridge University Press, 1990
Thompson, F. M. L. (ed.), *The Cambridge Social History of Britain, 1750–1950: Volume 3 – Social Agencies and Institutions*, Cambridge, Cambridge University Press, 1990
Tischler, S., *Footballers and Businessmen: The Origins of Professional Soccer in England*, New York, Holmes and Meier, 1981
Tolliday, S. and Zeitlin, J. (eds), *The Power to Manage? Employers and Industrial Relations in Comparative-Historical Perspective*, London, Routledge, 1991
Tolliday, S. and Zeitlin, J., 'Introduction: Employers and Industrial Relations Between Theory and History' in *The Power to Manage? Employers and Industrial Relations in Comparative-Historical Perspective*, ed. S. Tolliday and J. Zeitlin, London, Routledge, 1991
Tomlinson, A., 'Going Global: The FIFA Story' in *Off the Ball: The Football World Cup*, ed. A. Tomlinson and G. Whannel, London, Pluto, 1986
Tomlinson, A., 'North and South: The Rivalry of the Football League and the Football Association' in *British Football and Social Change: Getting into Europe*, ed. J. Williams and S. Wagg, Leicester, Leicester University Press, 1991
Tomlinson, A. and Whannel, G. (eds), *Off the Ball: The Football World Cup*, London, Pluto, 1986
Trainor, R. H., *Black Country Elites: The Exercise of Authority in an Industrialised Area, 1830–1900*, Oxford, Clarendon, 1993
Turner, D. and White, A., *Fulham: A Complete Record, 1879–1987*, Derby, Breedon, 1987
Turner, D. and White, A., *Football Managers*, Derby, Breedon, 1993
Turner, J., 'Man and Braverman: British Industrial Relations', *History*, Vol. 70, 1985

Twydell, D., *Rejected FC: Volume 3*, Harefield, Yore, 1992
Twydell, D., *Denied FC: The Football League Election Struggles*, Harefield, Yore, 2001
Tyler, M. and Soar, P., *Arsenal, 1886–1986: The Official Centenary History of Arsenal Football Club*, London, Hamlyn, 1986
Vamplew, W., 'Playing for Pay: The Earnings of Professional Sportsmen in England, 1860–1918' in *Sport: Money, Morality and the Media*, ed. R. Cashman and M. McKernan, Brisbane, University of New South Wales Press, 1981
Vamplew, W., *Pay Up and Play the Game: Professional Sport in Britain, 1875–1914*, Cambridge, Cambridge University Press, 1989
Vamplew, W., 'Riding for a Fall: The Health Hazards of Professional Jockeys in Nineteenth and Twentieth Century British Horse-Racing', paper presented at ISHPES Congress, Lyon, July 1997
Varrasi, F., 'Economic, politica e sport in Italia, 1925–35', unpublished Tesi di Laurea, Florence, 1996
Vasili, P., *The First Black Footballer: Arthur Wharton, 1865–1930*, London, Frank Cass, 1998
Vasili, P., *Colouring Over the White Line: The History of Black Footballers in Britain*, Edinburgh, Mainstream, 2000
Vincent, D., 'Mobility, Bureaucracy and Careers in Early-Twentieth-Century Britain' in *Building European Society: Occupational Change and Social Mobility in Europe, 1840–1940*, ed. A. Miles and D. Vincent, Manchester, Manchester University Press, 1993
Wagg, S., *The Football World: A Contemporary Social History*, Brighton, Harvester, 1984
Wahl, A. and Lanfranchi, P., *Les Footballeurs Professionnels*, Paris, Hachette, 1995
Waites, B., Bennett, T. and Martin, G. (eds), *Popular Culture: Past and Present*, London, Croom Helm, 1982
Walsh, N., *Dixie Dean: The Life of a Goalscoring Legend*, London, Soccer Book Club, 1977
Walvin, J., *The People's Game: The History of Football Revisited*, Edinburgh, Mainstream, 1994
Ward, S. V., *The Geography of Interwar Britain: The State and Uneven Development*, London, Routledge, 1988
Warde, A., 'Industrial Discipline: Factory Regime and Politics in Lancaster' in *Skill and Consent: Contemporary Studies in the Labour Process*, ed. A. Sturdy, D. Knights and H. Willmott, London, Routledge, 1992
Weindling, P. (ed.), *The Social History of Occupational Health*, London, Croom Helm, 1985
Whipp, R., *Patterns of Labour: Work and Social Change in the Pottery Industry*, London, Routledge, 1990
Whiteside, N., 'Social Welfare and Industrial Relations' in *A History of British Industrial Relations, Volume 2: 1914–1939*, ed. C. J. Wrigley, Brighton, Harvester, 1987
Wigglesworth, N., *The Evolution of English Sport*, London, Frank Cass, 1996
Williams, C. (ed.), *Cinema: The Beginnings and the Future*, London, University of Westminster, 1996
Williams, G., 'From Grand Slam to Great Slump: Economy, Society and Rugby Football in Wales During the Depression', *Welsh History Review*, Vol. 11, 1983
Williams, G., *The Code War: English Football Under the Historical Spotlight*, Harefield, Yore, 1994

Williams, J., '"One Could Literally Have Walked on the Heads of the People Congregated There": Sport, the Town and Identity' in *Social Conditions, Status and Community, 1860–c.1920*, ed. K. Laybourn, Stroud, Sutton, 1997
Williams, J., *Cricket and England: A Cultural and Social History of the Inter-war Years*, London, Frank Cass, 1999
Williams, J., '"A Wild Orgy of Speed": Responses to Speedway in Britain Before the Second World War', *The Sports Historian*, Vol. 19, 1999
Williams, J. and Wagg, S. (eds), *British Football and Social Change: Getting into Europe*, Leicester, Leicester University Press, 1991
Wray, D., 'Paternalism and its Discontents: A Case Study', *Work, Employment and Society*, Vol. 10, 1996
Wrigley, C. J. (ed.), *A History of British Industrial Relations, Volume 2: 1914–1939*, Brighton, Harvester, 1987
Wyman, M., *Round Trip to America: The Immigrants Return to Europe, 1880–1930*, London, Cornell University Press, 1993
Wyman, M., 'Return Migration – Old Story, New Story', *Immigrants and Minorities*, Vol. 20, 2001
Yeo, E. and Yeo, S. (eds), *Popular Culture and Class Conflict, 1590–1914: Explorations in the History of Labour and Leisure*, Brighton, Harvester, 1981
Young, P. M., *Bolton Wanderers*, London, Stanley Paul, 1961
Young, P. M., *Football on Merseyside*, London, Stanley Paul, 1963
Young, P. M., *Football in Sheffield*, London, Stanley Paul, 1964
Young, P. M., *A History of British Football*, London, Stanley Paul, 1968

Index